HISTORY OF THE GUIDES
1922-1947

**QUEEN'S OWN CORPS OF GUIDES (LUMSDEN'S)
CAVALRY AND INFANTRY**
(MacMunn and Lovat)

THE HISTORY OF THE GUIDES

PART II 1922-1947

10TH CAVALRY (Q.V.O. GUIDES)
5TH/12TH FRONTIER FORCE REGT. (Q.V.O. GUIDES INFANTRY)

WITH PAKISTAN POSTSCRIPT

By

LIEUT.-GENERAL SIR GEORGE MACMUNN, K.C.B., K.C.S.I., D.S.O.

The Naval & Military Press Ltd

Published by
The Naval & Military Press Ltd
Unit 10, Ridgewood Industrial Park,
Uckfield, East Sussex,
TN22 5QE England
Tel: +44 (0) 1825 749494
Fax: +44 (0) 1825 765701
www.naval-military-press.com
www.military-genealogy.com

© The Naval & Military Press Ltd 2010

The Naval & Military Press ...

...offer specialist books for the serious student of conflict. The range of titles stocked covers the whole spectrum of military history with titles on uniforms, battles, official histories, specialist works containing Medal Rolls and Casualties Lists, and numismatic titles for medal collectors and researchers.

The innovative approach they have to military bookselling and their commitment to publishing have made them Britain's leading independent military bookseller.

In reprinting in facsimile from the original, any imperfections are inevitably reproduced and the quality may fall short of modern type and cartographic standards.

FOREWORD

BY

BRIGADIER HECTOR CAMPBELL, C.B., D.S.O., M.V.O.

As the last Colonel of the Corps of Guides prior to its transfer to the Government of Pakistan, I have been pressed to write the Foreword to Sir George MacMunn's History of the Corps, Part II.

Raised in 1846 as the senior unit in the famous Punjab Frontier Force (The Piffers), The Guides—Cavalry and Infantry—served as a Corps under one Commandant till the 1914-18 War, when the inevitable happened and the two branches of the Corps were separated under their own Commanding Officers.

The Centenary was celebrated in 1946—the Infantry at Gardai, Waziristan, and the Cavalry at Ahmednagar—and with this momentous event in our minds it is appropriate to mention here some of our distinguished Commandants. For instance, Lieutenant-General Sir Harry Lumsden, who invented khaki and raised the Corps; Lieutenant-General Sir A. T. Wilde, General Sir Samuel Browne, V.C. (inventor of the Sam Browne belt), General Sir C. Keyes (father of Admiral Lord Keyes), Colonel Sir F. Jenkins, Major-General R. B. Campbell, Colonel Sir A. Hammond, V.C., Field-Marshal Sir C. Egerton, Major-General Sir R. Adams, V.C., Major-General Sir G. J. Younghusband and Lieutenant-General Sir R. Egerton.

In 1876 Her Majesty Queen Victoria was graciously pleased to confer on the Corps the distinction of being styled "Queen's Own" and to appoint His Royal Highness The Prince of Wales (later King Edward VII) to be Honorary Colonel. It was after the latter's demise that the title was altered to "Queen Victoria's Own."

I feel that in no unit has *esprit de corps* played a greater part in fostering comradeship amongst individuals of all creeds and classes, such as Ghilzais, Usbegs, Turkos, Trans-Border and other Pathans, Gurkhas, Dogras, Sikhs, Punjabi Mussulmans and others, than in the Guides.

The story of the Corps up to the end of the First World War has been told in Part I of this History, but I must mention a few of the old heroes among the Indian ranks. It is impossible to mention all, such as the trooper who, when Major Wigram Battye had been mortally wounded in Afghanistan and was beset by enemy swordsmen, threw himself on his body and was himself cut to pieces; but the following selected at random might be singled out for special notice as conspicuous for their gallantry and devotion to duty and to the Sirkar: Risaldar Fatteh Khan Khattak, Risaldar Mahomed Khan, Subedar Samundar, Subedar-Major Jai Singh, Risaldar-Major Duni Chand, Subedar Ali Gul, Risaldar Mogul Baz, Subedar-Major Sarfaraz Khan, Risaldar-Major Bahadur Singh and Naik Sohbat.

FOREWORD

In this second volume the services of the Cavalry and Infantry since 1922 in the Mohmand country, in the Peshawar and Eusafzai troubles and in Waziristan are recorded. In the Second World War it was the fate of both the Cavalry and Infantry to form part of PAI Force and the forces in Syria, and enormously important though PAI Force was, they were thus prohibited from taking an active share in the Second War. As may be imagined their disappointment was acute; but as all soldiers know, one just has to go to where one is ordered.

There were, however, two brief exceptions, "A" Squadron, which had been pushed into Iraq after the rebellion, took part in the brief hostilities in the invasion of Persia. In 1942 the Regiment was hurried down from Syria to join the force in North Africa and took some part in covering the final stages of the withdrawal of the British before Rommel, while "B" Squadron had joined the French in the distant oasis of Jarabub, carrying out some astounding reconnaissances in the desert. Once again there was disappointment, for as the Regiment was hoping to take part in the famous victorious operations of the Eighth Army it was recalled to PAI Force. How that force and the Russians safeguarded Persia and expelled German and Japanese agents, and then prepared to withstand the German advance from the Caucasus, which at that time seemed imminent, is told at some length. The consolation of the Guides Cavalry and Infantry, as well as of all that often changing force, must lie in Milton's line, "They also serve who only stand and wait."

The Corps of Guides is but one example of the power of that personality, born of the British spirit, which has imbued soldiers of the Indian Empire to such an extent that all religious prejudices were overridden in their loyalty to the Crown, and now a new era has begun.

I share with all ranks who have been sundered the grief inseparable to all partings, but am confident with them that the soul of the Corps will endure.

Hector Campbell,

Brigadier.

AUTHOR'S PREFACE

WHILE Volume I, the main History of the Guides, covered over seventy-five years of the making of a peaceful, prosperous and secure India, this volume but covers the story of the next twenty-five years to the end of the Second World War, and the disastrous passing of the British Raj. During the period the Cavalry were employed in the ludicrous and vexatious invasion of Peshawar by the Afridis, and in the trouble of the Red Shirt disturbances in Yuzafzai in the early thirties. The Infantry had more to do in the Mohmand and adjacent disturbances of between 1923 and 1925, with the ever-memorable story of Hill 4080, west of the Nahakki Pass. In 1936-37 they were constantly engaged in the severe campaign in Waziristan.

When the Second World War fell on an astonished world, the Guides, both Cavalry and Infantry, found themselves in Iraq and Persia from 1941 onward—a very important but, as it happened, dreary period with PAI Force. This was relieved for the Cavalry by the short but important capture of Khurramabad (late Mohammerah) and Ahwaz on the Karun river, near the mouth of the Shatt-el-Arab, by "A" Squadron, and the brief but distinguished service in North Africa covering the withdrawal of the Eighth Army to El Alamein–Ruweisat.

I have mingled the Cavalry and Infantry story through the years, which I understand is their wish, as if the two corps were still one, and I have mentioned regimental happenings that will be fresh in the minds of the present generation, and have dwelt at some length on the happy days together at Mardan.

The ending of the Raj in India had delayed the volume somewhat.

I have brought the Polo chapter into the middle of the book where it belongs in chronology and where it may be read. Appendices are overlooked. I have also brought into the text certain details for the same reason, and through it all I have tried to remember that, whereas Volume I dealt with a glorious past, this volume is written largely of men who are with us.

I have added a chapter on Sacrifices and Services to record the glory of those Guides or ex-Guides who fell, and the military record of those officers who attained General or Brigadier's rank. I have been much privileged in having this work entrusted to me.

GEORGE MacMUNN.

SACKVILLE COLLEGE,
    EAST GRINSTEAD,
25th December, 1949.

CONTENTS

Chapter		Page
	Foreword	v
	Author's Preface	vii
I.	A Review of the Years of the Guides 1922-1946	1

Part I of the History—The Last Years of John Company—The Mutiny—Umbeyla—The Second Afghan War, 1878-1880—The Chitral Campaign, 1895—The Pathan Revolt, 1897-98—The First World War—Onward from 1922.

| II. | The Old Brown Battlefields | 12 |

After World War I—The Guides Infantry in Aden, 1924-26—Regimental Happenings (Infantry), 1924-31—The Corps Together Again—Regimental Happenings (Cavalry), 1922-31—The North-West Frontier from 1930—The Troubles of the Muslim World—The Red Shirt Movement—The Trouble in Peshawar—The Decay of the "Hukm."

| III. | The Explosions in Peshawar and Yuzafzai | 23 |

The Guides Infantry in the Khaiber—The Guides Cavalry in the Red Shirt Trouble, 1930—The Afridi Invasion of Peshawar—The Cavalry in the First Afridi Inroad—Quieting the Mardan Area—The Second Afridi Inroad—The Disturbed Yuzufzai Border during 1931—The Occupation of the Khajuri Plain—The Cavalry at Bannu.

| IV. | Operations North of the Khaiber, 1933-35 | 38 |

The Frontier North of the Khaiber—The Chitral Reliefs of 1932—The Mohmand Story—Mohmand Operations, 1933—Bajaur Operations, 1933—The Loe Agra Trouble, 1934—The Second Expedition, 1934—The Third Expedition, 1935—The Mohmand Rising of 1935—Across the Nahakki Pass—The Famous Fight of the Guides Infantry—Detail of the Guides' Fight—The Overwhelming of Nos. 3 and 4 Platoons—The Withdrawal of the Guides—The Losses and Rewards of the Guides—The End of the Campaign.

| V. | The Waziristan Campaigns, 1936-1937 | 57 |

The Story of Waziristan—Waziristan since 1920—Tribal Economics—The Faqir of Ipi and the Islam Bibi—Operations in the Lower Khaisora, 25, 26, 27 November 1936—The Guides at Zerpezai—The Adventures of Tocol—Operations against the Tori Khel (28 November-24 December 1936 — February-April 1937): Numerous Outrages—The Attack in Force on the Razmak Convoy, April 1937.

| VI. | The Waziristan Campaigns (*continued*) | 69 |

The Tragedy of the Shahur Tangi—The Aftermath—Renewed Operations in the Khaisora, 23 April-3 May—The Decision to Beat Up Arsal Kot and the Sham Plain—The Seizure of the Plain—The Situation on the Derajat Border—The Destruction of Arsal Kot—Algad-whacking in Sham and Shaktu—The Guides Lose their Colonel—The Return to Razmak and the "Crag" Affair—Affair of Ridgeway Hill—"Pat" Grant, an Appreciation.

| VII. | Waziristan to the Second World War | 83 |

The Cavalry at Mardan, 1935-37—Joyous Return of the Paltan—Honours for the Khaisora—Reorganization of Indian Cavalry—Class Composition of the Guides Cavalry—Pipe Band of the Paltan—Honours for Waziristan—The New Infantry Organization—The Transfer of the Khattaks from the Infantry, 1938—The Happy Last Years in Mardan—Reunion, the Mardan Week, 1938—The Autumn of 1938 and Early 1939—Regimental Happenings, 1937-39.

CONTENTS

Chapter	Page
VIII. THE EARLY DAYS OF THE SECOND WORLD WAR	99

The Second World War and the Last Days in Mardan—Regimental Happenings—The Tragedy of Major-General C. I. B. Hay—The Cavalry go to Quetta and are Mechanized—The Infantry march out to the Peshawar Border—The Early Days of the War—The Golden Square Coup and the Rebellion of the Iraqi Army—Brief Outline of the Persian Story, 1914-39—The Allies enter Persia in 1941—Major Duncan.

IX. THE GUIDES IN IRAQ AND PERSIA ... 109

The Outline Story of PAI Force—The Guides Cavalry ("A" Squadron) in Iraq and Persia—The British Invasion of Persia on the Karun River—The Share of "A" Squadron—The Guides Infantry in Persia and North Kurdistan—The Guides Cavalry in Iraq and Syria—Brigade Training at Khanaqin and the March to Sultanabad.

X. THE GUIDES CAVALRY IN NORTH AFRICA ... 121

The Strange Sequence of Events in Libya and the Levant—The Guides Cavalry Arrive and Move up—The Withdrawal to the El Alamein Position—"B" Squadron in the Desert—War Patrols in the Desert (*Chicago Tribune*)—Behind the Line—The Changed Scene—The Great Offensive and the Disappointment of the Guides Cavalry.

XI. THE LONG YEARS WITH PAI FORCE (INFANTRY) ... 135

Bagdad and Musayib (1942)—Back to Persia and 27th Brigade, 1942—Colonel Rich leaves the Battalion—The Length and Breadth of Iraq—The Story of the Poles in Iraq—The Disappointment of the Lebanon—On the Trans-Persian Railway—Some Regimental Happenings (Infantry)—The Infantry Return to Iraq and thence Home.

XII. THE LAST YEARS OF THE RAJ ... 145

The Cavalry in India Again (1943-1946)—The Victory Celebrations at Delhi, 1946,—The Infantry Return to India (1945)—The Centenary of the Corps of Guides, 1946, in Ahmednagar and Waziristan—Gardai to Razmak (Infantry), 1947—Regimental Happenings (Cavalry), 1944-46—A Note on the Organization and Equipment of the Guides Cavalry, 1922-46—The Ringing to Evensong—Farewell, the Raj—The Special Service in the Garrison Church at Razmak—The Farewell Order of the Day from the Colonel—Officers with the Guides Cavalry on 15 August 1947—Officers serving with the Battalion with appointments in Waziristan, 1946.

XIII. THE GUIDES POLO CHAPTER ... 159

The Guides Polo, 1922-1939—Account of the Semi-Finals and Final of the Last Indian Cavalry Polo Tournament, 1939—The Record of Matches Played, 1922-1939.

XIV. SACRIFICES AND SERVICES ... 167

I. THE STORY OF GLORY: Flight Commander H. Dane, D.S.O. (late the Guides)—Lieutenant David Monteith, the Guides Cavalry—Lieutenant-Colonel A. K. Murcott, the Guides Infantry—Major M. H. Hodson, the Guides Infantry—Lieutenant-Colonel C. H. H. Eales, M.C., the Guides Cavalry.

II. SERVICES OF DISTINGUISHED OFFICERS: Brigadier Hector Campbell, C.B., D.S.O., M.V.O.—Lieutenant-General Sir Kenneth McLeod, K.C.I.E., C.B., D.S.O.—Major-General A. V. Hammond, C.B., D.S.O.—Brigadier J. H. Gradidge, C.B.E.—Brigadier R. Macnamara, D.S.O.—Brigadier K. A. Garrett, M.C.—Brigadier C. P. J. Prioleau—Brigadier G. V. L. Coleman—Lieutenant-Colonel (T./Brigadier) M. H. H. Baily, D.S.O.

XV. PAKISTAN POSTSCRIPT ... 176

The Division of the King Emperor's Empire and Army—The Army of Pakistan—The Frontier Force Regimental Centres—The Guides Infantry at Razmak—The March Out from Razmak—The two Guides Corps, Cavalry and Infantry, at Kohat.

INDEX ... 205

APPENDICES

		PAGE
I.	THE VICTORIA CROSS	185
II.	(A) COLONELS OF THE GUIDES	187
	(B) COMMANDANTS AND RISALDAR-MAJORS (CAVALRY)	187
	(C) COMMANDANTS AND SUBADAR-MAJORS (INFANTRY)	188
III.	VARIOUS LISTS (CAVALRY)	189
IV.	VARIOUS LISTS (INFANTRY)	195
V.	HONOURS AND REWARDS	200

IN COLOUR

Queen's Own Corps of Guides (Lumsden's), Cavalry and Infantry (MacMunn and Lovat)	*Frontispiece*
Risaldar Mahmud Khan	FACING PAGE 4
The Scene in Swat. Adams and MacLean (Hobday) ... ... ,,	9

IN MONOCHROME

Letter from Sir Dighton Probyn ... ... ,,	6
The Chapel and Mess ... ... ,,	15
Interior of the Chapel .. .. ,,	16
The Last Parade of the Corps Together ... ... ,,	23
Brigadier Hector Campbell (the last Colonel of the Guides) ... ,,	36
Lieut.-General Sir Kenneth McLeod, K.C.I.E., C.B., D.S.O. ... ,,	39
The Attack of The Guides on Hill 4080 ... ... ,,	54
Captain Godfrey Meynell, V.C., M.C. ... ... ,,	55
Laddha and the Khaisora Valley ... ... ,,	75
Major-General A. V. Hammond ... ... ,,	85
Types of the Guides ... ... ,,	87
Interior of the Guides' Mess ... ... ,,	92
The Mess Garden ... ... ,,	94
British Officers of Cavalry and Infantry in 1939 ... ... ,,	96
March Past of the Corps, 1 January 1939 ... ... ,,	98
Quetta Hounds and the Cavalry's Farewell to its Horses ... ,,	101
Officers and V.C.Os. of Infantry, Secunderabad, 1941 ... ... ,,	115
David Monteith, and Desert Reconnaissance ... ... ,,	126
The Guides Cavalry in the Desert ... ... ,,	127
Colonel Gradidge and General Alexander ... ... ,,	132
Guides Infantry Athletic Team, Iraq ... ... ,,	140
Victory Parade at Delhi—Cavalry. I ... ... ,,	146
Victory Parade at Delhi—Cavalry. II ... ... ,,	147
Officers and V.C.Os., Infantry, 1947 ... ... ,,	151
Officers, Guides Cavalry, 1941, and Tournament Polo Team, 1938 ,,	158

MAPS AND PLANS

ACTION AT SHEKH MUHAMMADI	FACING PAGE 29
SKETCH MAP OF YUZAFZAI, LOE AGRA AND THE MOHMAND COUNTRY	,, 33
SKETCH OF NAHAKKI AND WUCHA JAWAR	,, 52
SKETCH MAP OF WAZIRISTAN	,, 61
SKETCH MAP OF PERSIA, IRAQ AND SYRIA	,, 119
SKETCH MAP OF NORTH AFRICA	,, 131
YUSAFZAI	at end
WAZIRISTAN	at end

CHAPTER I

A REVIEW OF THE YEARS OF THE GUIDES 1922–1946

PART I OF THE HISTORY—THE LAST YEARS OF JOHN COMPANY—THE MUTINY—UMBEYLA—THE SECOND AFGHAN WAR, 1878-1880—THE CHITRAL CAMPAIGN, 1895—THE PATHAN REVOLT, 1897-98 —THE FIRST WORLD WAR—ONWARD FROM 1922.

IN 1938 appeared the regimental history of the Guides—viz., Queen Victoria's Own Corps of Guides Frontier Force, from 1846–1922; perhaps the most famous of all the famous Indian regiments. The history was the work of love of several officers of the Corps and is a most vivid story of three-quarters of a century of distinguished service on the North-West Frontier of India, added to the wandering far afield in the First World War of its original and war-time cadres.

Then in 1946 came the centenary of the Corps first raised under the ægis of the great Henry Lawrence, the British Resident at the Court of the reformed Sikh State after the First Sikh War, by the equally famous Lieutenant Harry Lumsden.[1] In this centenary year, with many campaigns and the Second World War in their last quarter-century, the Corps decided to celebrate the event with a second volume.

To do this to the understanding of those readers who may not be familiar with the great Volume I, a brief outline of the formation of the Corps is now repeated, with a few words on the history of Northern India which gave rise to it. To this also is added a very brief outline of the great campaigns that so vividly filled the original volume, so that this Part II may be properly escorted on to the stage.

THE LAST YEARS OF JOHN COMPANY

The last twenty years of the famous rule of the Honourable East India Company, which passed to the Crown's direct administration in 1858, after the Mutiny—not of the Indian Armies, but of that portion known as the "Bengal" Army—were years of severe campaigns. The Company in the last hundred years of its rule was never a private company, but was but the "Crown in commission," with a British Cabinet Minister eventually responsible through the "Board of Control." The large body of European officers of Hon. E. I. C.'s service in the Company's three armies, held the Royal as well as the Company's commission. These last twenty years were notable for five important campaigns—viz., the First Afghan War, the War with Gwalior, the Conquest of Sind and the two Sikh Wars. There has been much false history written of them. The First Afghan War was due to a statesmanlike, but not fully considered, attempt, urged from England, to put an end to the rivalries and civil wars there which were destroying all trade, in and through Afghanistan, by replacing on the throne the lawful Royal dynasty of Ahmed Shah Duranni in the person of the exiled Shah Shujah. This was done in alliance with that refugee prince and the Maharajah of the Punjab.

---

[1] The late Sir Harry Lumsden, K.C.S.I., C.B.

How it was all brilliantly successful for two years, and then miscarried, is not part of this story, save to say that most of the earlier officers connected with the Guides had earned their spurs in that campaign. But because historians copy each other, and repeat, or of their ignorance mis-state, one or two points may be referred to here. The Kabul Brigade was destroyed by its own folly, not 16,000 men as the feebler historians love to repeat, but 4,500 soldiers with 12,000 unarmed, unmartial, frost-bitten "followers." The force at Kandahar was never defeated, but eventually marched to Kabul to meet General Pollock's "avenging army."[2] The Jellalabad Brigade beat the Afghans handsomely before being relieved by Pollock. The Kelat-i-Ghilzai force made a famous defence, but Ghuzni fell. That is the military story; policy is another matter.

But the occasion for the formation of the Guides was the First Sikh War, known militarily as the Sutlej Campaign because it was largely fought out on that river. The great Maharajah Ranjhit Singh, originally Governor of the Lahore Province under the Afghans, had formed and raised the one-man kingdom of the Punjab. Shortly after signing, with ourselves and the exiled Duranni Emperor, the Tripartite Treaty referred to, he died—and was not alive to implement that treaty. He had raised a very large army, partly Muslim, drilled and equipped on the Company's model. It had many foreign adventurers among its officers: American, French, Italian and here and there an Englishman, most of whom the Sikhs murdered after Ranjhit's death. With Ranjhit gone, the army grew more and more out of hand, being run on early Bolshevist lines by regimental committees. Probably to save itself from them, the Sikh Government launched it on an invasion of British India in the autumn of 1845. The Governor-General (Lieutenant-General Sir Henry Harding) and the Commander-in-Chief (Sir Hugh Gough) had been bringing up troops to meet the threat of which they had some inkling. The invasion came and was defeated in four desperate battles, the Eastern Sikh Army being finally destroyed at the battle of Sobraon on the Sutlej in January 1846.

The victorious British moved on to Lahore and a new Sikh Government was inaugurated on behalf of Dhulip Singh, the child son of Ranjhit Singh. Sir Henry Lawrence was appointed Resident at the Lahore Durbar (Government) with very definite powers to help reorganize the disordered Punjab.

The Jullundhur Doab was ceded to the British, and a frontier force to watch the hill frontier was raised from the defeated Sikh Army. The Guide Corps, a special design of Henry Lawrence's, was included in this force, which was under the latter's orders as "Agent" to the Governor-General. The force consisted of four battalions (1st to 4th Sikh Infantry) with some light field batteries, who occupied the Jullundhur Doab, and the Guides, a small corps mounted and dismounted, the senior of them all, who carried out special and difficult missions for the British Agent and the remodelled Government of the Punjab. It should be mentioned perhaps here that the governing Sikhs were a small though outstanding body, for even in 1946 their numbers of both sexes and all ages were but six millions. The rest of the Punjab population is largely Muslim with some Hindus.

---

[1] See the inscription "Victoria Vindex" on the Kabul medal.

In 1848 the peace of the new régime collapsed, Lawrence being sick at home at the time. The Diwan or Governor of Mooltan broke into rebellion against his own Government. The Sikh armies sent against him eventually joined him, as did the Sikh troops on the Afghan frontier. The British garrison from Lahore plus a Bombay Brigade from Sind took Mooltan after a prolonged siege and daring storm, while a large army under the Commander-in-Chief assembled at Lahore. The Punjab Campaign—Second Sikh War—followed, with severe battles, the great victory of Goojerat and the pursuit of the fugitive Afghan contingent who had foolishly come down from the Khaiber, through which they were "kicked back like dogs." The Sikh army laid down its arms, each man receiving a rupee, the mushroom edifice of Ranjhit Singh disappeared, and the Punjab was annexed to British India. So brilliantly was it administered that in 1857 tens of thousands of Punjabis—including many of Ranjhit's old soldiers—flocked to the new regiments for the Siege of Delhi, the Relief of Lucknow, and the suppression of the Mutiny—not again of the three great Indian armies, but of the Bengal army, which alone was responsible.

The small, versatile and intrepid Guides unit under Harry Lumsden took an active share in the Second Sikh War, and with the irregular force in the Jullundhur Doab moved up to the new frontier of India, as a nucleus of the new Punjab Irregular Force. The Guides were expanded into a composite corps of a regiment of horse and a battalion —not a new feature in turbulent parts of India—and Lumsden enlisted the most daring, adventurous men of the frontier tribes, both trans- and cis-frontier, to add to the many wild races already in the ranks, and he was responsible for carrying out many adventurous missions which appealed to lawless young men of the turbulent countryside. The headquarters of the corps was properly established at Mardan, near the border in the Yuzafzai country, not far from the scenes of Alexander the Great's storming of Aornos and passage of the Indus.[3]

This was what the army sang at their camp fires after the hard-fought fight at Chillianwallah in 1849, fought where Alexander had defeated King Poros and the elephants that were his "tanks":

> "Sabres drawn and bayonets fixed
> Where fought Alexander,
> Paddy Gough's a cross betwixt
> Hero and Salamander."

THE MUTINY

The Guides became world famous for the march in 1857 in the hottest season of the year from Mardan to the siege of Delhi, now becoming a concentration centre for the mutinous Bengal army. Their actions there, long talked of with bated breath, and their triumphant return to watch and ward on the frontier with the bullock carts with red silk curtains behind them, were long a saga among the wild frontier men.

All this story of "derring-do" is fully told, of course, in Part I. Suffice it here to say that they marched out of Mardan at 6 p.m. on 13 May, three days after the outbreak at Meerut and Delhi, believing they were only going to Jhelum, but actually to march

---

[3] Not at Mahaban as once thought, but at Pir Sar, some miles farther up the Indus.

hot-foot to the recapture of Delhi. Under the renowned Daly, they marched out, 153 sabres and 349 rifles with five British officers (including the surgeon), in the hottest season of the year—during, too, the Ramazan, when most of their men would not avail themselves of the Qoranic licence to forgo the fast in time of travel. After seizing Attock Fort from its garrison of Bengal Infantry, till replaced by a detachment from Kohat, halting two days, they marched on the 16th on the first stage to Delhi, thirty-two miles in a dust-storm, and on 9 June reached the camp on the Ridge, having come the 586 miles from Mardan in twenty-six days, to be welcomed tumultuously by the European troops before the city. Furlough men had rejoined *en route*, and the arrival strength had grown to 646 in the ranks.

From that day to the capture of the city on 13 September hardly a day's rest was given them, and on the afternoon of their arrival they were both engaged. Their gallant Adjutant, Quentin Battye,[4] fell mortally wounded.

When Delhi fell the Guides went home to the frontier, which was badly in need of them, in that memorable return of which the frontiersmen so long spoke, with no doubt loot, and the long string of little bullock carts aforesaid, with crimson curtains, in which sat women of Delhi who had elected to share a new life with the victors.

Among the officers who joined after Battye's death was Lieutenant R. H. Shebbeare, officiating second-in-command and also for a while officiating commandant, who was wounded six times and won the Victoria Cross. Owing to some misunderstanding, his name was not entered in Part I among the winners of the Cross, so his name now stands at the head of the V.C. Roll in the Appendices to this volume, with explanatory note. He was, alas! killed when serving with another unit in the China War of 1860.

Umbeyla

From 1849 to the Mutiny there had been many frontier expeditions to reduce the frontier to some sort of order, the principal being perhaps against Mohmands in 1852. Thirteen of these were rewarded by the grant of the India Medal of 1854 with clasp "North-West Frontier." The grant, however, was not made till 1869—twenty years after the first expedition to be thus commemorated. But the big frontier campaign was yet to come, that known as "Umbeyla" (to use the spelling on the clasp of the 1854 medal) against an immense gathering within the hills a few miles north-east of Mardan.

The situation began with a small expedition to expel a nest of "Hindustan Fanatics," largely from the Pindaris of Central India, established in the days of the Sikh kingdom and constantly reinforced by irreconcilables since. During the Mutiny they had been very tiresome, and in 1858 had been driven from Sitana and had settled at Malka deeper in the same hills. The repressive measures finally necessary in 1863 against them and the tribes who had let them through to raid, developed into practically a religious war to which clans came from far and near, and the situation continually called for a large

---

[4] The author joined the famous old Kensington School in Kensington Square nearly seventy years ago—the School, like Haileybury, founded by the East India Company. There in the schoolroom was a tablet to Quentin Battye, an old boy. (Kensington faded when St. Paul's came west.)

RISALDAR MAHMUD KHAN
Guides Cavalry
Killed in the "Kamnari" War (Cavagnari), Afghanistan, 1879

force. Reverses and checks at first received created considerable sensation in post-Mutiny India, and our prestige had to be restored.

Much severe fighting occurred while reinforcements were arriving, and the Guides, both Cavalry and Infantry, were frequently involved, always with great distinction (*vide* Part I, p. 65). The fighting for a point known as "Crag" Picquet was especially famous, the point being taken and retaken by each side. Those were the days when many troops had smooth-bore muskets and only the British units had the rifled muzzle-loader—the Enfield—and it was from these days the old story comes that when someone had ordered dismounted volley-firing, an old Risaldar[5] had shouted: "*Kaun b - ch - te volley-fire bolta ; yih drah sword and holler ki-waqt hai.*" ["What (opprobrious name) orders volley-fire ? This is the time for draw swords and holler."]

The severe type of fighting and the unflinching zeal of the Pathan swordsmen showed that many of the Indian regiments needed better leading. The post-Mutiny reconstruction had gone from the old Regular system, with many British officers, to the irregular one of very few British officers and reliance on good Indian leaders. This had proved a success in the suppression of the Mutiny against the disgruntled mutineers and the swordsmen of Oudh, but, except in the very best regiments, failed both in Umbeyla and in the Second Afghan War, and the British officer cadres were slowly increased.

The long years of Imperial Russia's absorption of Turkestan and the threat to India, especially after the Panjdeh incident of 1885, still further accentuated the need.

It was to take many years of education and training before the "Brindian," a slang word for the Indian officer holding the King's Commission—such a feature of the Second World War—was to be possible. The slang term soon passed and we have the admirable story of the Indian officer with a King's commission of the Second World War.

THE SECOND AFGHAN WAR, 1878-80

Part I, p. 77, tells of the share taken by the Guides in the war forced on us by the constant attempts of Russia to gain influence in Afghanistan. A Russian Mission had been received in Kabul and a British Mission, led by the famous General Sir Neville Chamberlain, was refused admission at the mouth of the Khaiber by the Afghan commander. His escort was found by the Guides, under Lieutenant-Colonel Jenkins, with 100 sabres of the Cavalry and 50 bayonets of the Infantry.

This was too much for the British Government, who invaded Afghanistan via Quetta, the Kurram valley, and the Khaiber, as the finale of a long, unsatisfactory story. General Roberts gained a brilliant victory at the Peiwar Kotal at the head of the Kurram valley. General Sam Browne[6] took Ali Musjid and advanced on Kabul and General Donald Stewart occupied Kandahar.

The Guides Cavalry formed part of the cavalry brigade of Sam Browne's force, and the Guides Infantry were in his 2nd Infantry Brigade.

These advances were enough for the Amir Sher Ali, who fled and soon after died, and

---
[5] Said to have been Risaldar Tura Baz, Guides Corps. His son Maghul Baz, also a Risaldar of the Guides, rose high in the Political service and rescued Miss Ellis, kidnapped by the Afridis.
[6] Later General Sir Sam Browne, V.C., G.C.B., K.C.S.I., a former commandant of the Guides.

the British acknowledged his son, Yacub Khan, as Amir, making with him the treaty of Gandamuk, which rectified our frontier so far as the protection of India against Russia and the support of Afghanistan were concerned. An important but, as it proved, unhappy point was the admission of a British Agent to the court of the Amir.

In the advance up the Khaiber towards Jallalabad, the Guides earned great distinction. Lieutenant W. R. P. Hamilton of the Cavalry gained the V.C. and the gallant Wigram Battye was killed.

Thus ended what is known as the First Phase of the Second Afghan War. The Second Phase was really a separate war and would have been so known had a longer interval intervened between the "phases."

And now comes this Second Phase—and a Guide tragedy and glorious episode. The new Amir ascended his throne and sent to meet the new Agent, Major Sir Louis Cavagnari, and his secretary, Mr. Jenkyns, and medical officer Dr. Kelly, escorted by a detachment of 25 cavalry and 52 bayonets of the Guides, under command of Lieutenant Hamilton, V.C. Met at the head of the Kurram by high Afghan officials, the Mission arrived at Kabul on 24 July 1879 and was lodged in a spacious building in the Bala Hissar, 250 yards from the Amir's palace.

A few days later, six Afghan regiments arrived in Kabul from Herat, loudly abusing the Mission. The Agent was thoroughly warned that there was danger, but said "our loss will not upset the British Empire"! On 3 September the Mission was attacked by Afghan regiments and after a desperate defence was wiped out (*vide* Chapter VII of Part I).

That was that, and the Second Phase of the war began. Sir Frederick Roberts now led a force on Kabul via the Peiwar Kotal, defeating an enemy force at Charasiab, and he reached Kabul on 8 October. The Amir came to meet him and surrender.

In the meantime another force was moving up the Khaiber, led by the Guides Cavalry and Infantry. Eventually the two units marched through to join Roberts, who was faced with a national and Islamic rising round Kabul. This, after some fierce fighting round the city, drove him into the entrenched camp of Sherpur outside Kabul, on which the Kohistani tribesmen made fierce attacks. To relieve him, General Sir Donald Stewart marched up from Kandahar, fighting the battle of Ahmed Khel *en route*; another force was also pressing up from the Khaiber, and this put an end to the struggle round Kabul.

In these operations the Guides took an ample share, and another V.C. to the Corps tally was earned by Captain A. G. Hammond.

The search for an Amir who could rule the country, which had been long in uproar, and who could keep the Russians out, ended in arrangements being made with Sirdar Abdur-rahman Khan, who ruled for twenty-one years, and whose son Habibullah was our staunch friend during the First World War, being murdered for his pains, after which his successor, Amanullah, launched his extraordinary and treacherous invasion on demobilizing India in 1919.

While negotiations with Abdur-rahman were in progress, a disaster had overtaken what we should now call a brigade group at Maiwand in the Helmund Valley, at the

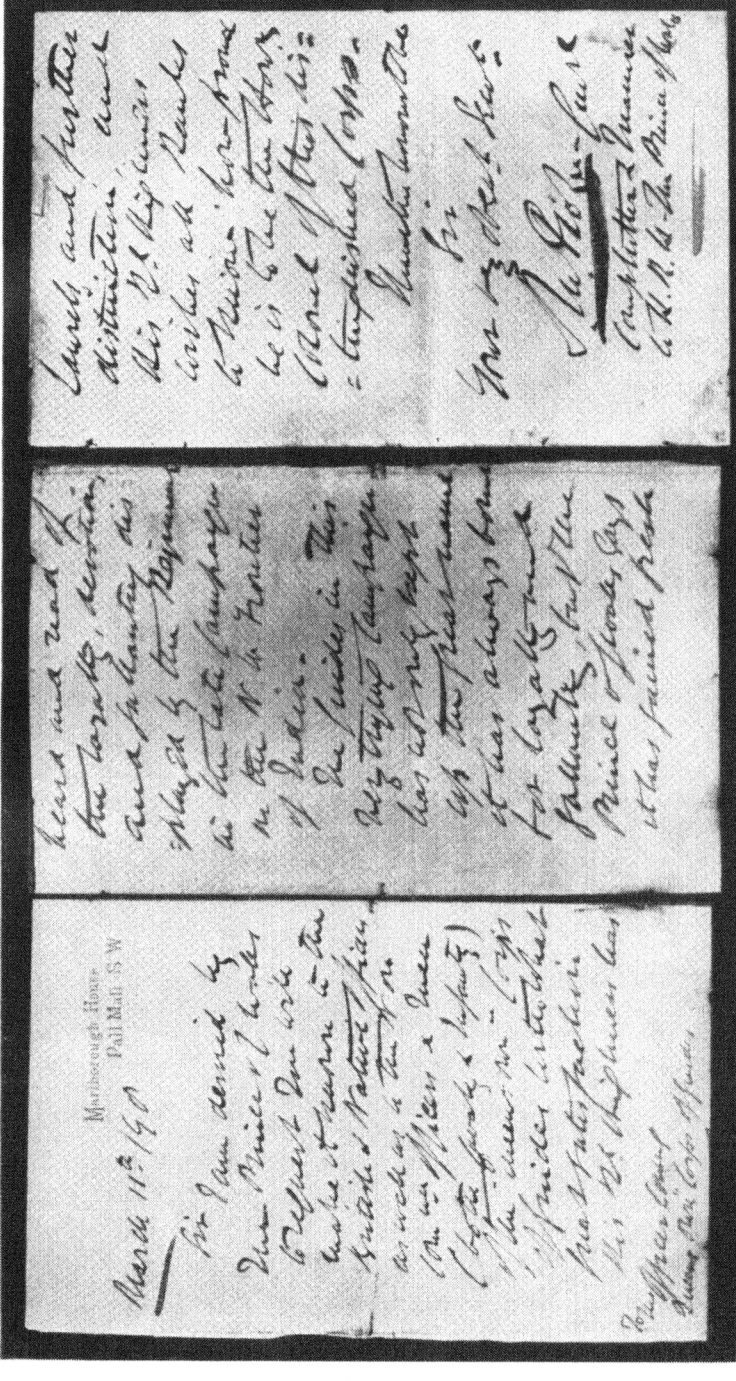

Letter of appreciation written by General Sir Dighton Probyn on behalf of H.R.H. The Prince of Wales (later King Edward VII), Colonel-in-Chief of Q.V.O. Corps of Guides F.F., after the Malakand Campaign.

This letter, framed in ebony and silver, was presented to the Guides Mess by F. K. Hensley. After the partition of India in 1947 it was sent by the Officers of the Infantry to Brigadier Hector Campbell who, on behalf of the Officers of the Corps, presented it to the Indian Army Room at Sandhurst.

hands of another son of Shere Ali, and the garrison of Kandahar was surrounded. To meet this, Sir Donald Stewart, then commanding at Kabul, sent Sir Frederick Roberts with the pick of his troops to Kandahar. There he defeated Ayub Khan at the battle of Kandahar. That practically ended the Second Afghan War.

The Chitral Relief Expedition, 1895

In this brief retrospect of the story of the war-bred Guides that is so fully dealt with in Part I, the main history, there now occurs a campaign that once more brought the Guides an opportunity of remarkable service and gained them the admiration of the whole army. That was the Chitral Relief Expedition of 1895.

The occasion that called for it was the dramatic result of the necessary policy of closing the passes from the Pamirs into British India—viz., the Baroghil and the Dorah—through which adventurous Russian officers had been penetrating into the Khanates between this portion of the Hindu Kush and the State of Kashmir. To this State these Khanates owed some allegiance, and it was decided that the Kashmir army, somewhat decadent for all its good material, should be strengthened and trained by British officers with a slight leavening of Indian Army troops, and that the Kashmir Government should assert its position. The brief Hunza-Nagar campaign in the mountains beyond Gilgit followed in 1891 with its super-gallant happenings, and in due course a Kashmir force with a few Indian troops asserted its control over the little State of Chitral. This Khanate is largely outside the Pathan zone, its peoples being of ancient hill stock. Some of the chiefs claimed descent from the Greeks who held Afghanistan and Northern India for so many generations, longer indeed than the British have ruled India. The ruler of Nagar, indeed, would invite visitors to admire his Greek profile. The folk were Muslims, but chiefly of the Shiah or the Ismaili persuasion. Pathan neighbours, however, inspired and led an attempt to destroy the troops in Chitral, who were besieged in Chitral fort. To rescue them, a couple of hundred miles of continuous frontier hills or as much by almost non-existent precipitous roads from Gilgit, was a very great problem. While Gilgit was cut off by vast snowbound passes, an attempt from Nowshera-Mardan was possible and the Guides, Cavalry and Infantry, joined the Relief Force now assembling. After the successful actions of the Malakand Pass and ridge and various subsequent operations, the Guides Infantry had been ordered to cross the Panjkora river and visit certain Utman Khel villages on the far side. Crossing at dusk by a raft bridge and entrenching on the opposite bank, they had advanced at dawn to carry out their task. About noon, forces estimated at several thousands were reported to be advancing on them. Floods, in the meantime, had carried away the bridge. They could not be reinforced and their orderly withdrawal, supported by fire from the hither bank, was the most astounding piece of disciplined valour. The enemy were swarming on all sides—even to within twenty yards of their bayonets and rifles—while a large party coming down the river bank endeavoured to cut them off from their entrenchments at the broken bridgehead. Alas! as they reached the plain to safety, their Colonel, Fred Battye, was mortally wounded, that the saying might be fulfilled "a Battye lost in every campaign." Delhi, Fattehabad and now the Panjkora—small wonder that this 13th day of April 1895 remains famous, while all the troops on the other bank watched anxiously and spoke for a generation of the exhibition of courage and discipline.

The story of the relief of Chitral Fort by Colonel Kelly's little force from Gilgit, helped by the rumour of the force advancing from India, is not to be told here, nor that of the march, over the Lowarai Pass, of General Gatacre's 3rd Brigade to Chitral—for this short review is but to remind readers of the glorious past as told in the original history.

The Pathan Revolt, 1897–98

One more story remains to complete the review before the new story begins, and that is an outline of the events of the Pathan Revolt of 1897–98, when Islam was much stirred by the Graeco-Turkish War and all the Mirs, Mullahs and Faqirs banged the drum ecclesiastic, so that even down as far as Rawalpindi the roll of the drum reverberated.

At the bottom of it all, too, as Vol. I tells us, the demarcation of the frontier between Afghanistan and India—the Pathan areas to be in the British sphere, thus bringing order to the trade routes—gave much occasion for irritation due to false propaganda and general misrepresentation.

The conflagration began in Waziristan and then burst out sporadically, now here, now there, the whole length of the frontier from the Gomal up to the hills near Mardan. It flew from one spot to another so unexpectedly that the orderly mobilization in progress to meet the occasion was thrown to the winds, and units had to be snatched at railheads and thrown anywhere regardless of the brigade and division to which they belonged. The operations eventually crystallized into three phases, north, central and south—viz., those of the Malakand, Swat and Bajour, following on the immense tribal gatherings that threw themselves on the former, the Afridi and Orakzai Tirah in the centre, and Waziristan. How the Guides took a leading part in the northern sphere and their famous cavalry charge in which Adams and Hector MacLean[7] won the V.C., are they not fully told in Part I ? The actions in which the Guides took part gained them renown as great as the Panjkora incident two years before.

Minor frontier troubles, including Sir James Willcocks's short campaign beyond the Khaiber in 1908, brought the Corps to the days of the First World War.

The First World War

The Regimental History now Part I tells the story of the Guides in the First World War at some length. As in the Second War, it was some little time before the Cavalry and Infantry could be loosed from the Frontier, where the troubles were considerable, especially in the repelling of the great incursion of the Bunerwals. In September, however, the Cavalry went to Mesopotamia, where they took part in the destruction of the large Turkish Force at Khan Bagdadi on the Euphrates, in March 1918,

---

[7] Posthumous—gazetted some years after, when the posthumous grant was introduced.

THE SCENE IN SWAT. ADAMS AND MacLEAN (Hobday)

and later in General Cobbe's destruction of the last Turkish force on the Tigris and the seizure of Mosul.

In this War the Guides Infantry raised two War battalions, but in the Second World War such were raised for the 12th F.F. Regiment, in which the Infantry by the post-war reorganization had become the 5th Battalion.

The Infantry (1st Battalion) proceeded to Mesopotamia early in 1917, joining the 7th Division, and taking part in the capture of Tekrit on the Tigris above Bagdad, and in December proceeded to Palestine with that Division, taking part in Allenby's victorious campaign. The 2nd Battalion also went to Palestine in 1917 and served with the 60th Division in that same campaign. The 3rd Battalion, raised in October 1917, served with credit in the defeat of the Afghan invasion of India in the Kurram, and in the punitive operations against the Mahsuds. Thus, in the absence of the 1st and 2nd Battalions, the 3rd well sustained the record on the Indian Frontier till disbanded in 1921.

And that in very brief is the outline of the story of the Guides till this centenary volume, Part II, begins in 1922.

Among the many famous names of the Corps there are two specially to be remembered by the whole army: that of the founder, Harry Lumsden, who invented "khaki," the "dust like" dress, from the dye known as Multani *mati* (Earth of Multan); and Sam Browne, V.C., who designed the famous service belt and, like the Duke of Wellington, thus perpetuated his name. After losing his arm, this famous old swordsman, who was also a rifle shot, lay on his back to fire, his rifle muzzle between his toes. He was also a famous revolver shot, once killing a snake in the mess-room roof from his chair.

Onward from 1922

At the close of the First World War, a general policy of reorganizing the Indian Army was in progress which took the very proper form of grouping the old and often famous individual single-battalion regiments into regimental groups, based on tradition and racial constitution as far as possible. This also involved new numbering, an essential of the new organization, but involving unavoidably the drowning of the old numbers under which the various Corps had won great renown in the war just over. It was the retired British officer, with his heart deeply involved in love for and pride in his regiment, and the pensioned Indian ranks, who felt this change most.

The reorganization also involved changes in the classes enlisted, and this needs some explanation.

In studying the question of Indian Army recruitment it is well to realize the complete difference between conditions of recruiting in British and Indian Regiments. The problems have little resemblance to each other. The British recruiter is only concerned with getting a lad of likely appearance and adequate health. In times of conscription he has only to deal with the men sent him by the conscripting machinery. Ninety-nine out of every hundred, if properly trained and led, will fight.

In India the matter is entirely different. Out of close on 400 million, not forty million have the "guts" to fight or make a soldier. Between the first-class fighting man and the many millions of quite useless folk there were a number of folk who had been part of the older Anglo-Indian armies, but had lost their fighting proclivities. They were quite prepared to draw pay and stand on parade like rocks, but with little or no desire to face the enemy, and these, as the years passed, were all got rid of. In the two World Wars some reappeared with credit.

There is another great difference between your first-class Indian soldier and his British comrades. The latter—when voluntary enlistment, the usual peace-time practice, is in vogue—does not join for the honour and glory, as a rule ; *Res angusta domi*, love troubles, employment difficulties, send him to take the shilling. That does not make him any the less a good soldier, however. But in India, among the fighting classes, the very reverse is the case. The young man of the good tribes joins because it is the finest thing he can do ; pride of race and caste and hereditary calling him, and serving the British Crown, these are his motives.

Now when the new regiments, in the Punjab especially, were being formed, just before and after the Mutiny, the Indian Army from the north was small. Commanding officers were able to pick and choose and soon found that they got men who were first-class from certain clans and tribes, and did not go farther afield. For generations they drew their men from the same villages, men who made superb soldiers, father to son, and the famous regiments had the pick of the villages. Thus many useful tribes were stood aside. Why should the Commanding Officer bother to go farther afield ? But as the years rolled on and many of the older corps in Madras and Bombay were recruited from Northern men, the demand greatly increased and new and good sources were tapped. The First World War, and indeed the Afghan War of 1878–80, showed that in larger campaigns the finding of drafts to replace casualties was a very big business and gradually the Adjutant-General aimed at a more level recruitment. This meant that many of the famous old units had to extend their intake and lose some of their most treasured classes; and we shall see this affecting the Guides, to their sorrow. Whether it was really necessary to break regiments' hearts is another matter. These famous old regiments, with their almost religious *esprit*, were the finest storm troops, and their views were worth considering. To pull down for the sake of improving the general level is not necessarily wisdom. The Guides were, and are, pre-eminently among the first of this class. There are a dozen or so more, such as the "Cokis," the old *Bis Lumber* (20th) and several more, on the tip of the tongue of the older officers.

But authority has thought otherwise and so the loyal corps have accepted painful, if necessary, decisions, and have lost their Khattaks, their Yuzafzais, their Dogras or whoever it might be, with good grace. How the rank and file felt will be told in this narrative. Another and sadder change for the Guides was yet to come. In days gone by various corps engaged in watch and ward in some disturbed country were localized, chiefly in Central India, and as the times changed they were abolished and joined the general line of the army. The Guides Cavalry and Infantry, however, while part of the general line, had been located in Yuzafzai, to preserve order in that troublesome area, to watch the raider tribes trans-frontier, and above all keep an eye on those embittered Hindustani fanatics of the Wahabi persuasion, refugees from India, who had installed themselves in the tribal mountains beyond the Indus.

So the Guides, Horse and Foot, lived in a cantonment of their own at Mardan near the border, just as Gurkha and Garhwali corps lived in the hills, and there they had resided for the best part of a century. From there, apart from their constant watch and ward, they departed to take part in some campaign, or to do a tour of the frontier outposts of Waziristan, returning to their home after a couple of years, while as far as possible either the Cavalry or the Infantry were present at headquarters when the other was away. There they built many regimental institutions, gardens and avenues. In the Officers' Mess, collections of trophies of war and shikar, portrait groups, medals and all that makes an Army Home were shared by the two component corps.

But at last the spirit of uniformity—with or without reason—the bug, perhaps, that gets into an Adjutant-General's head, decreed that this old Home must go and the Guides be made just as any other homeless unit of the Army. Alas and alack! But it should be said that all the old training lands around Mardan had been converted to highly irrigated agricultural land by the coming of the Swat canal, and it was necessary to go far afield to train. The Guides, of course, could take it, and prepared for the blow. Treasures were divided between the two corps, and the Guides, sad but undismayed, took up their new burden. Fortunately, the Second World War came as a deadener of the blow. *Sic transit gloria mundi*, but not the glory of the Guides, which will long survive the ringing to evensong with which this story ends.

CHAPTER II

THE OLD BROWN BATTLEFIELDS

AFTER WORLD WAR I—THE GUIDES INFANTRY IN ADEN, 1924-26—REGIMENTAL HAPPENINGS (INFANTRY), 1924-31—THE CORPS TOGETHER AGAIN—REGIMENTAL HAPPENINGS (CAVALRY), 1922-31—THE NORTH-WEST FRONTIER FROM 1930—THE TROUBLES OF THE MUSLIM WORLD—THE RED SHIRT MOVEMENT—THE TROUBLE IN PESHAWAR—THE DECAY OF THE "HUKM."

AFTER WORLD WAR I

THE foregoing outline retells the old saga, and the story of the Guides from 1922 begins with the Cavalry and the Infantry returning for a short while to their own cantonment, and taking up the old fraternal and intimate life of the Corps at Mardan.

The Infantry arrived in Mardan in December 1920 from Syria, while the Cavalry did not get back from Mesopotamia till July of 1921, and the whole Corps was now together till the Infantry went to Aden in 1924. But after such a war, reorganization of an army not hitherto geared for world war was unavoidable. The Corps was to be split, the components to join the Line of cavalry and infantry units of the Army. The Cavalry became the 10th (Q.V.O. Corps of Guides) Cavalry and the Infantry the 5th Battalion (Q.V.O. Corps of Guides) 12th Frontier Force Regiment.[8] As the oldest unit in the Frontier Force the Infantry had the right to be the 1st Battalion, but for the reasons given in the footnote they accepted the fifth place. The passion for levelling, which was perhaps intelligible under war conditions, deprived the battalion of their Gurkhas, whom they had had since 1846, drawn originally from the disbanded Gurkha units of the Sikh Army. Most of them were averse to transfer and took their discharge. With the change the Commandant of the joint Corps, as distinct from the honorary "Colonel of the Guides," was out of place, and Lieutenant-Colonel A. H. Buist, M.V.O., retired, with the sad distinction of being the last.

The years 1922 and 1923 were busy in so far as giving effect to the changes; 1923 was a bad cholera year, and as the native city of Hoti abutted on the cantonment of Mardan, rigid precautions had to be taken to prevent the disease spreading to the cantonment.

The old life went on till the Infantry left for Aden in 1924. The Cavalry stayed in their old haunt till they left for Bannu in 1931, the Infantry coming back home in 1926 for a few years of quiet. Throughout the years that followed between the two wars,

---
[8] The Guides were the senior of the five battalions of the new regiment, but offered to take the number "5" so as to allow the 1st, 2nd, 3rd and 4th Sikhs to retain their own numbers. It might be mentioned here that in Lord Kitchener's reorganization these regiments had become the 51st, 52nd, 53rd and 54th "Sikhs." They were never "Sikh" class regiments, like the old 14th, 15th and 45th Sikhs, being Punjabi class regiments, and until Lord Kitchener's days were the 1st, etc., Sikh Infantry, so named because in 1846 they were raised from the old Sikh Army for the Irregular Force occupying the newly annexed Jullundhur Doab. The 2nd Sikhs were known as the 2nd or (Hill) Sikh Infantry, because they were largely Dogras, generally called in these days "Hill" Sikhs. This force was made part of the Punjab Irregular Force in 1849 and went to the Pathan frontier.

the Cavalry spent their leisure hours, as will be seen, building up their polo, till they achieved the culminating success by winning the Indian Cavalry Polo Tournament, in the last two years of that famous contest, in 1938 and 1939.

The constant absence of the Infantry in trans-frontier service kept them to a great extent out of the picture. The story of the Guides' polo glories, not always confined to the Risala, are given in Chapter XIII.

THE GUIDES INFANTRY IN ADEN, 1924–26

The year 1924 opened with preparations for the move of the Infantry to Aden, and the battalion left Karachi in H.M.T. *City of Marseilles* on 2 February, receiving many farewell messages, including one from Field-Marshal Sir William Birdwood. Many of the men had enlisted since the return from Egypt after the World War, and the sea was a great mystery. How was the way found? They could see, they said, the track behind, but not that in front!

The officers on board were:

> Lieutenant-Colonel Battye
> Major Sandeman (Second-in-Command)
> Major Hensley
> Captain Redding (Adjutant)
> Captain Knight
> Captain Duncan
> Captain Rich
> Captain Taylor (Quartermaster)
> Captain Coleman
> Lieutenant Macnamara

"Pat" Grant, who had gone on with the advance party, was already in Aden, where Barlow, who had been home to recover from a wound received in Waziristan with the Tochi Scouts, had also proceeded.

There were many friends of the Guides in Aden: first and foremost, the Resident and G.O.C., Lieutenant-General "Tommy" Scott (3rd Sikhs), a Piffer and an old friend. The Aden Troop (two horse and one camel troops), the Border Regiment, with which were Major Ellis and his daughter Molly, whose abduction a year or so before from Kohat by Ajab, the outlaw, after he had murdered her mother, had caused such a sensation in India. Heavy and field artillery were there too, and an R.A.F. unit commanded by B. E. Baker (in the Second World War to become famous as Air Marshal Sir Bernard Baker).

At Lahej, capital of a small Arab state, twelve miles away, was an Arab levy known as the 1st Yemen Infantry, with British officers. In Aden itself were several hundred European civilians, so that there was plenty doing in this often very hot seaport and fuelling station.

But to men of northern India and the frontier hills, however—used to great heat in summer, but a dry heat—Aden was a trial. Here are some normal temperatures recorded in 1924, and the wet bulb as high as the dry one is the feature that tries most, meaning, as it does, great moisture.

	SUMMER		WINTER
	1st *July*	14th *July*	1st *January*
Max. … …	104°	90°	86°
Min. … …	91°	90°	85°
Dry … …	91°	91°	73°
Wet … …	90°	90°	75°

To the men, Aden was not too pleasant, for fish and vegetables were scarce and had to be imported, while the water supply piped from Lahej was somewhat brackish for Indians, to whom good water is an important consideration. However, they enjoyed sea-bathing and all learned to swim.

Polo, games of all kinds, and shooting in the Aden hinterland or on the African coast made the time pass happily enough for the officers, while the hospitality of the port, the Navy, the P. & O., and many others, was long remembered. The officers like to remember their own entertainment of the officers of the British cruiser *Effingham* and the U.S.A. cruiser *Trentham*, and all with whom they forgathered so heartily— Pop Riley, who later became Resident and C.-in-C., greatly wedded to the Rocks; Phipson of the I.M.S., the Port Health Officer; Peiniger, the Gunner; Hurst, the Political; Davey, head of the Perim Coal Company; Robert Black, doyen of the bank managers; and many another, "jolly good fellows every one."

During 1924 the Yemen was considerably disturbed, and in September occurred the only "incident" that affected the Guides Infantry during their tour on the Barren Rock. The island of Perim at the entrance to the Red Sea, 100 miles west of Aden itself, was occupied by a detachment of the Yemen Infantry, under Lieutenant Lawrence of that Corps; on 3 September Lieutenant Lawrence was stabbed to death at night by the guard of the unit in his bungalow. The N.C.O., bugler and six men of the guard fled to the mainland with several thousands of Government rupees that had been in the island commandant's safe.

Perim was always an important point with some European residents, and in the morning a political officer and the commandant of Yemen Infantry, with an escort of twenty men of the Guides under Subadar Jaimal Singh, were sent off to the scene. Orders came shortly afterwards for a British officer and suitable party to occupy Perim and disarm the Yemen Infantry detachment and another to go to the island of Kamaran, a British possession near the coast of the Yemen some 150 miles north of Perim. Lieutenant Coleman and R.D. company left on the 4th in the R.I.M.S. *Elphinstone* for Kamaran, and on the 6th Lieutenant Barlow took the balance of "D" to Perim and the Yemen detachment laid down their arms.

The Yemen battalion was shortly after disbanded, and during the next two years five of the eight criminals were brought to justice. The British officer's detachments on both islands were maintained by the battalion during the whole of its tour at Aden.

[Photo: R. B. Holmes, Peshawar

THE CHAPEL

[Photo: R. B. Holmes, Peshawar

THE MESS

Perim was not unpleasant for the rank and file. Bathing was good and fishing plentiful and the companies spent a pleasant enough time there. The O.C. the detachment flew the Union Jack, held second-class magisterial powers and had a naval cutter at his disposal, while Government eventually gave him an entertainment allowance to cope with the hospitality necessary to his position.

In October the policy of controlling recalcitrant Arab tribes in the Aden Protectorate from the air was being developed, and a temporary air base for operations was opened at Shukri, forty miles up the coast. Subadar Shadi Khan and eighteen Guides were sent to guard the aerodrome. Their ship had to lie two miles off the shore, which entailed a very unpleasant surf landing in dhows, and at the final stage in dug-outs.

Early in September the King and Queen of the Belgians landed at Aden, on their way to visit India.

In 1925 the Battalion distinguished itself by winning the King Emperor's Cup for polo with Lieutenant-Colonel Abbott, Major Hensley, Lieutenant Bailey and Captain Grant. That year Major Hensley succeeded to the command, and in February 1926 the pleasant two years of exile came to an end with their embarkation for India in the same ship that brought them to Aden—the *City of Marseilles*. Some twelve days later a train with the Guides Infantry on board steamed into Mardan amid great rejoicings.

REGIMENTAL HAPPENINGS (INFANTRY), 1924–31

Service at Aden gave no great opportunities for distinction, but elsewhere Guides officers and men serving away from the Corps had won distinction and commendation to the great satisfaction of the Corps.

In June 1924, after the operations in Waziristan in 1922–23, the following were mentioned in despatches:

    Major D. G. Sandeman,
    Major C. E. T. Erskine, M.C.,
    Jemadar Abdul Ghani (attached to the Intelligence),

and the D.S.O. was awarded to **Major Erskine** and the Military Cross to **L. M. Barlow**, for services in Waziristan.

In July, Major M. H. Prendergast, D.S.O., who had been in charge of the King's orderly officers that summer, received the Membership of the Royal Victorian Order (M.V.O.).

In November, to the supreme satisfaction of the Frontier Force Regiment, the Prince of Wales was appointed their Colonel-in-Chief.

On the first January parade, 1928, General Sir Thomas Scott presented Lieutenant L. M. Barlow, who had now recovered from his wound in Waziristan, with the Military Cross awarded him for his distinguished conduct.

This year the Royal Scots came to Aden and the opportunity was taken of sending the Drum-Major and the best two pipers to a course with that corps. The story of the pipe band that eventually took the place of the brass band is told in Chapter VII; but it may be said here that in 1923, after consideration of the tartans worn by the pipers of various Indian regiments, an order was issued that no units were to use Royal Stuart tartan, hitherto used by the Guides for pipe bag and strings—in view of their title of Queen Victoria's Own Corps of Guides—without the special permission of the King. This was not given till some years later.[9] It was with great satisfaction, however, that in April 1925 sanction was given that the Guides Infantry should continue to wear their own buttons and distinctions, though a battalion of the Frontier Force Regiment.[10]

In May 1925 Lieutenant-Colonel Battye took over command of Aden while the G.O.C., now Major-General J. H. K. Stewart, was on leave, Major Sandeman commanding the Battalion.

On 27 May the Lieutenant-Colonel was gazetted to a brevet Colonelcy.

It should be recorded here that Lieutenant G. Meynell, later Captain Meynell, V.C., M.C., whose death in the Mohmand Campaign of 1935 is so famous, joined the Guides on 8 September 1926 from the King's Shropshire Light Infantry.

On the return of the Infantry from Aden they found Mardan a truly "Guide" Station, for, in addition to the Cavalry, the Training Battalion (late the 10th Guides) were in the fort. The next three and a half years were quiet and the Frontier more settled than it had been for many a long year. In the autumn the Infantry, commanded by Battye, took part in the biennial Chitral Reliefs, under Colonel-Commandant[11] Muspratt.

3rd/8th Punjab Regiment (Burma). Guides Infantry. Section 117 Pack Battery.

The Chitral garrison reliefs, maintained since the murder of the Prince and siege of the British garrison in 1895, lest Pathan adventurers and disturbing Cossack colonels should again distract the roost, were usually uneventful. The route was some eighty miles, and the Khan of Dir, now among the ruling princes of India, kept the road clear; his sentries, being properly alert and fairly swift to strike, usually prevented anything more than sniping for the Glory of God. But wherever Islam obtains in backward parts, fanatical, unreasoned outbreaks must be guarded against. The Battalion diary record shows that the reliefs of 1913 were very well received. In 1922 the looks were of the blackest, owing to Turkish troubles and Bolshevik intrigue. By 1924 and again in 1926 the atmosphere was favourable. Before starting, the Battalion which had the two years at Aden, and all the young soldiers of the post-war period, with little frontier training—which applied equally to the young British officer—were taken to Takht-i-Bhai for short training in picqueting hills, valleys or passes. The force actually marched from Dargai for Chitral on 10 September in two regimental échelons and was back at Dargai on 12 October, bringing down the Kumaon Battalion and leaving the 3rd/8th.

In April 1927 the Guides and the Nowshera Brigade were out for thirty-six hours, holding the road from Akara to Mardan while the Police beat for a raiding gang of

---

[9] *Vide* Chapter VII.
[10] G.I. Instruction 584 of 24 April 1925.
[11] The short-lived post-war title that took the place of Brigadier-General and eventually resolved into the pre-Mutiny one of Brigadier. The fact that in the French Army *brigadier* meant "corporal" had written it off for some time, while our small-war title of Brigadier-General—an appointment, not an army rank—had been found in France to be too inconvenient in the matter of honours to be paid by guards, etc.

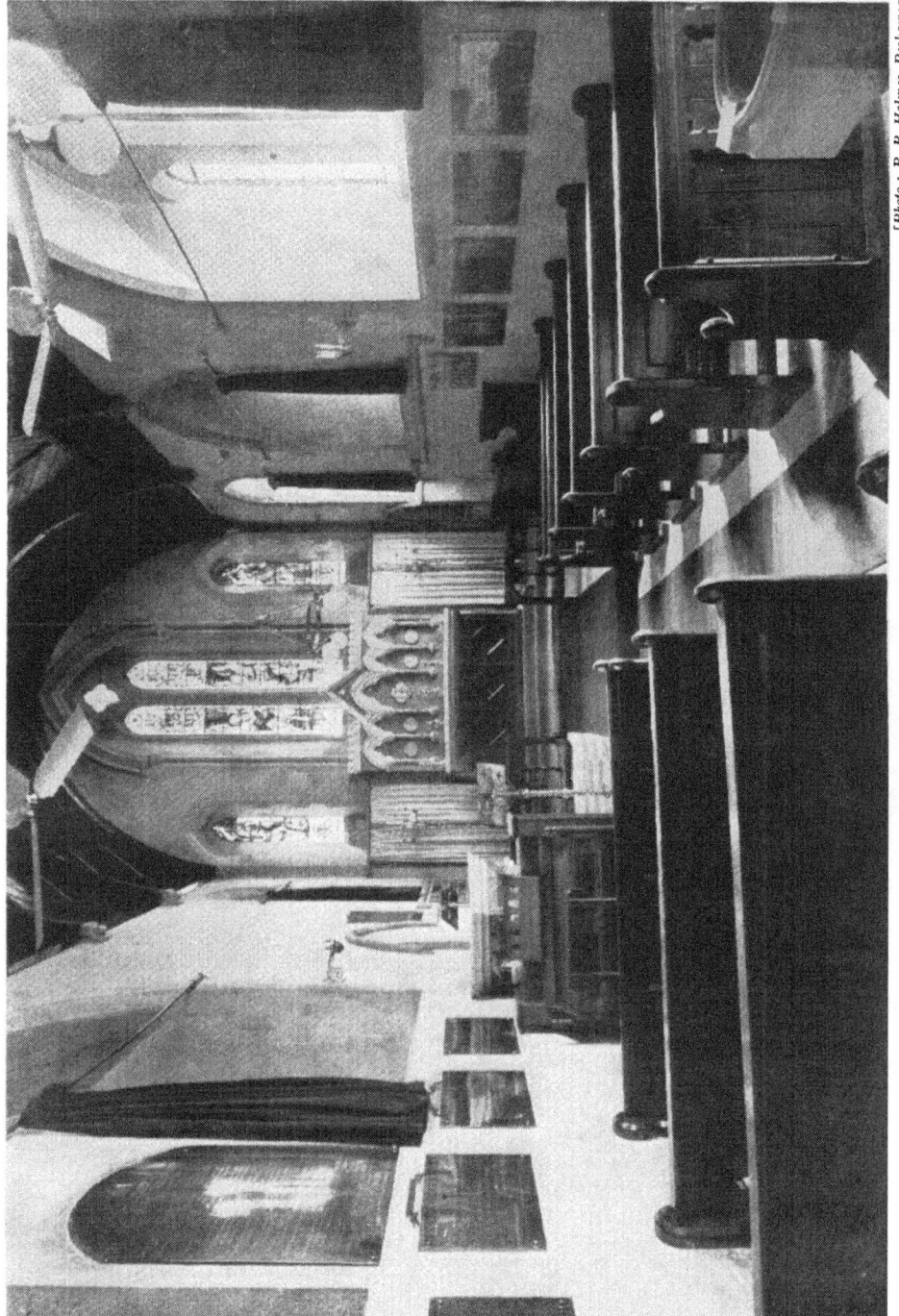

INTERIOR OF THE GUIDES CHAPEL

[Photo: R. B. Holmes, Peshawar

Shinwaris under an outlaw who was an ex-sepoy of the Guides. As two of his gang were killed and he and ten others were captured, he had not put his Guide training to the best advantage.

In the hot weather of 1927 there was a Mohmand scare and the Battalion stood-to for three weeks, although the brigade column was not called out.

In April 1928 the Infantry won the Frontier Force Polo Tournament, which they had not done since 1899. But this time it was won from the Cavalry, if you please, at 4½ goals to 4.

In 1929 the Battalion, in common with the rest of the Indian Army, was reorganized into three rifle companies, a machine gun company and a headquarters wing. This year, too, their famous full Colonel of the two Corps (Cavalry and Infantry) Major-General Sir George Younghusband, vacated the Colonelcy on attaining the age of seventy and was succeeded by an equally famous Guide—Lieutenant-General Sir Raleigh Egerton. Younghusband's tour had been very short, owing to the introduction of an age limit into what had been a life tenure.

The Training Battalion, which had now become the 10th Battalion of the 12th F.F. Regiment, moved to Sialkot from Mardan in 1929.

As this year passed to its comparatively peaceful close, the Muslim troubles that had followed the break-up of Turkey, the fourteen points of President Wilson, and the prospects of rule by the Montague-Hindu ballot-box were to bring a long period of unrest to the Frontier and the old brown battlefields of the past.

Regimental Happenings (Cavalry), 1922–31

In 1924 Lieutenant-Colonel H. Dening was appointed commandant *vice* C. W. Carey, and Major G. G. E. Wylly, V.C., D.S.O., second-in-command. In May 1925 Major F. A. Hamilton, O.B.E., succeeded Wylly in the latter appointment. Honorary Captain Rur Naryan, Sirdar Bahadur, returned from duty in England as the King's orderly officer.

In September 1928 Brevet Lieutenant-Colonel D. K. McLeod, D.S.O., was appointed commandant *vice* H. Dening, and Major W. H. Blood, M.V.O., Second-in-Command.

An extract from the diary of the Corps shows an interesting juxtaposition—doubtless unintentional! :

April 1925. "His Excellency the C.-in-C. inspected the Regiment at 1015 hours on Monday 8 April. The Dental Surgeon inspected the teeth of the men of this unit at 1100 hours on 24th."

In May 1930 the first active moves in connection with the Red Shirt and Afridi troubles took place. These began with a hurried move out to Charsadda and thence on the 30th over to Peshawar for the first Afridi inroad, twice during June, and again for the second inroad at the beginning of August, details of which are given below. In 1930 Field-Marshal Sir William Birdwood, the C.-in-C., came to Mardan to say farewell to the Risala, the Paltan being in the Khaiber. In the first half of 1931 squadrons were constantly out in support of the police in the Red Shirt disturbances—also described below.

Between 1922 and 1931 the following honours and rewards were bestowed on the Guides Cavalry.

British Officers

The 4th Class of the Royal Victorian Order (on the occasion of the Prince of Wales's visit to India) :
  Major W. H. Holcraft Blood.

Indian Ranks

Order of British India. Raised to 1st Class (Sirdar Bahadur), 1930 :
  Risaldar-major and Honorary Lieutenant Zardad Khan, I.D.S.M.

Order of British India, 2nd Class, 1922 :
  Risaldar-major Nur Khan (Bahadur).

Indian Distinguished Service Medal :
  Risaldar-major Zardad Khan (Bahadur).

Meritorious Service Medal (with annuity) :

1922	No. 1728	Daffadar Nanak Singh.
1924	No. 1889	S./Daffadar-major Shah Passand.
1925	No. 1804	S./Daffadar-major Ahmed Shah.
1926	No. 1410	Daffadar Ghambo Ram.
1928	No. 2086	S./Daffadar-major Kehar Singh.
1930	No. 2142	Regt./Daffadar-major Bawa Singh.
1931	No. 2245	R.Q.M. Daffadar Sham Singh.

Long Service and Good Conduct Medal (with gratuity) :

1922	No. 1853	A./Lance-Daffadar Narain Singh.
1924	No. 2167½	Lance-Daffadar Kartar Singh.
1925	No. 2025	Lance-Daffadar Nand Singh.

Land Grants :
  1922 Risaldar-major (Pen.) and Honorary Lieutenant Abnashi Ram Bahadur : Land value 400 rupees in the Gujarat District, Punjab.

The North-West Frontier from 1930

We are now come to a period that was to see several years of severe fighting on the Frontier from the Gomal Pass to the Mohmand country north-east of the Khaiber—fighting that brought home to many thoughtful people, not that the British policy had been wrong, but that the problem was almost insoluble. The British had great experience of the question. Our young politicals first came in touch with it in 1846 when they represented the Sikh Durbar, after the boy Dhulip Singh had been placed on the Sikh throne and the Sikh forces that invaded India had been crushed. With Sikh troops they had secured the Sikh frontier on the far side of the Indus and obtained for the Sikhs the revenue which formerly had only been procurable by force of arms. When in 1849 the Punjab had been annexed after the Sikh rising, the same officers were carrying out the same duties, on behalf of the British Government itself. But during the Afghan War of 1838–42 our troops had traversed much of the hills of Roh. The Khaiber and its tribes had very much to be dealt with and one force had returned to India from Kabul via the Gomal. Acquaintance with and a liking for the frontier men were always a feature of our connections with them.

From the date of our annexation of the Punjab till long after the Mutiny, we kept the border closed and did not if possible take troops into the hills, save in the area south of the Gomal. But after the Mutiny the long tale of outrages at the hands of the tribes of Waziristan had to be considered, and gradually the needs of trade and trade protection and the approach of Russia compelled us to take the hills and especially the routes through them under our control; and with the Afghan Boundary Commission of the early nineties, our spheres of control between India and Afghanistan were quite definitely fixed. But we have always avoided the impossible task of administration which, as the hills cannot pay revenue, could only be at the expense of the Indian taxpayer. Further, the Afghan writ does not freely run in their own hills—outlaws skip across freely and disarmament is impossible. The other side of the insoluble problem is perhaps contained in the saying of a distinguished Frontier General, who summed up the matter thus: "I can understand the advantages of a 'Buffer State' between you and a powerful neighbour, but I cannot see the point of having Buffer B-hnch-ts between you and the Buffer State." But that obvious truth does not show the solution.

The Troubles of the Muslim World

The above brings us to the disturbed state of the Frontier which involved the Guides, and especially the Guides Infantry, in a long series of campaigns between 1930 and 1937, while the tribal areas were growing out of the memory of the heavy losses in 1920 and Afghanistan of her defeat in India; but it was not till 1930 that the pot began to boil.

The boiling was due to many causes, but among them the natural feelings of Muslims at Turkey taking the wrong side in the First World War, and at the disruption of the Ottoman Empire as they knew it. Then came the régime of Mustapha Kemal and the disappearance of the Caliphate. Many religious movements of sympathy and sorrow arose in India, a unique opportunity for the disturbance propagandist to fish in muddy waters.

The trouble began with the "Khilafat" movement, a movement at first in sympathy with the troubles of Turkey, concerning which many deputations waited on the Viceroy. The Greek occupation of Asia Minor, when Mr. Lloyd George had been nobbled, and which continually wrought such disaster for them, was a leading grievance. The worldwide status of Islam, indeed, should always be in our minds, and how a stone thrown into a pond in Morocco will send ripples into every Muslim pond across to China. In this Muslim upset in India every underground propagandist, especially the Congress, lent a hand. The first fruits were in the nature of a boomerang when the fanatical, ignorant Muslim Moplahs of Western India broke into rebellion and the Government of India would not listen to Lord Willingdon in Bombay. It meant large numbers of

Hindus murdered, and many more circumcised with brutality, and, further, a large-scale campaign—so large that a medal was given to the troops. The next Muslim trouble burst out on the Frontier, but especially in Sind. It was not very formidable as a disorder, but was responsible for much misery. Many, known as the Muhajarin (Pilgrims), decided that India was *dharab al haram*, "unholy and unsafe for Islam," and they sold their lands and migrated to Afghanistan, where no one wanted them. After enduring much hardship and exhaustion of resources, often selling their wives and children to the Afghans, they struggled back. A benevolent Government was often able to restore them to the land they had alienated.

All these disturbing factors were to produce more ill-winded phenomena, many attributable to Bapoo Gandhi's civil disobedience in which so many Indian lives were lost. As an instance of the evil mischief of the propagandists may be mentioned the Sirda Act—a bill introduced by a body of westernized Indians to control the marriage customs, whose evils had been so forcibly brought before the world by Miss Katherine Mayo in "Mother India." It was a harmless, well-meant bill, neither popular nor very effective. It was immediately represented all along the Frontier that it involved the examination of both Hindu and Muslim girls by British doctors! A furore followed.

The Red Shirt Movement

Amid such scenes arose early in 1930 a semi-rebellious body, the *"Khuda-i-Khidmatgaran"* (the servants of God), known as the Red Shirts because of the garment they adopted. A civil officer was disgracefully murdered by vast crowds in semi-military guise and the Indian Government funked the issue; and from this arose the series of troubles which were to involve the Frontier troops, including of course the Guides, in seven years of trouble and war.

This movement, though partly the outcome of the various Islamic perturbations, was still more the result of Congress intrigue spreading every sort of malicious rumour regarding the British Government—an intrigue which would have justified a strong and realistic government wiping out Congress by fire and sword.

During the year 1929, Congress were busy organizing throughout India a Civil Disobedience campaign. This had not met with much support in the Frontier Province, where, outside the Hindu traders in the towns, the Hindu is always anathema, until it succeeded in nobbling one Abdul Ghafar, Khan of Utmanzai, a considerable landowner and a man of good family. His brother, who was in the I.M.S. and at one time medical officer of the Guides, had married a Yorkshire girl while training at an English University and subsequently became Prime Minister of the Frontier Province.

Abdul Ghafar[12] was not a well-educated man and therefore the easier inoculated with Islamic zeal. He had been imprisoned from 1920 to 1923 for his share in the Khilafat agitation. On release he organized youth movements, the Azad School (School of Leaders) among the lads in his own and neighbouring villages, and towards the end of 1929 this blossomed into a Frontier Youth League within the Frontier Province. The Congress

---

[12] In 1948 given three years' imprisonment by the Pakistan Government for sedition!

germ had penetrated and its programme was announced to be complete independence. In the winter of 1929-30 he toured all the Frontier provinces, and matters came to a climax when he summoned a meeting at his village, which was largely attended, many contingents arriving with band, banners and red uniform, at which sedition was openly preached. The Government now took action and Abdul Ghafar and a number of leaders were arrested. Then followed the Peshawar riots, described in the next section. Many young men all along the Frontier now joined the movement, with their clothes dyed red, and the excitement extended as far as Kohat. The Risalpur Flying Column, which included the Guides Cavalry, was sent along the border, rounding up excited gatherings. Charsadda, Abdul Ghafar's home, was surrounded and blockaded. Very shortly the Flying Column had to go to Peshawar to deal with the situation there and the 6th Lancers took its place. Disturbances, threats of trans-border lashkars, the Afridi attack on Peshawar, all added to the trouble along the border north of Peshawar, and it was not till the end of 1931 that the whole Red Shirt movement was scotched and eventually faded out of the public interest.

During all this time considerable use was made of the Guides to counter hostile propaganda, and the share taken by the two Corps and many individuals was successful and highly appreciated by the civil authorities, and is referred to later on. Before doing so it may be remarked that, while the actions of Abdul Ghafar and company were nothing but Congress-instituted sedition and rebellion, the support that came from so many young men was due to the increased population and the difficulty of finding careers and subsistence.

But popular views can be volatile, and it is interesting to learn that when Pundit Jowahir Lal Nehru was attacked in 1946 by frontier men as he was returning from the Malakand and was slightly injured, Abdul Ghafar, who was with him, had his skull fractured by a stone.

The Trouble in Peshawar

The leaders who had been working hard in the Peshawar bazaars, and who had been fomenting two fanatical youth movements, now thought the time had come to stage a large-scale demonstration. Outside the city was a cantonment full of the best regiments in India, long seething with anger at the futility of local and supreme government—on the very ground where in 1857 the situation had been saved by blowing away mutineers from the guns, on which the tribes had flocked to our service. It was now April 1930, and no John Lawrence or Herbert Edwards was there to give the troops clear-cut directions.

Peshawar, always a city full of difficult characters and Border desperadoes, now broke into rebellion. Authority was flouted. The City Disturbance Column was marched into the city, but the Civil Authorities had lost their nerve and the troops were not strong enough to defend themselves and were disgracefully entreated. An armoured car was burnt, a British despatch rider was killed and the troops endured. But you cannot have troops with arms in their hands badgered by rioters, as the Government have found in Palestine, with impunity. A natural and disconcerting thing occurred. A battalion of a famous regiment, cruelly badgered about, had gone sour in the night and the next day refused to obey orders. They were disarmed and escorted away to another cantonment. There, happily, a Court of Inquiry vindicated them and they were restored to their position of disciplined honour.

The Civil Authorities, disgracefully many thought, now decided to withdraw from the city. The British had funked the issue, or so the Border imagined, and the results were soon to be seen, though Peshawar was eventually pacified.

The Afridis opened the ball, for the first time in the British record, by invading the valley and attacking Peshawar.

The Decay of the "Hukm"

There is one point which must be thoroughly grasped to understand the reason for all these disturbances with indeed the pitiful loss of life to Indians and frontiersmen alike. That reason is the destruction of the *Hukm*, which politicians, white and brown, had been working for so long. India had been ruled as one peaceful whole for close on two centuries by the British *Hukm*—namely, the "Order," as it was in the days of the Mogul Empire. A good government through its agents gave the *Hukm*, and the people happily and cheerfully obeyed; but whereas in Mogul times the *Hukm* was sometimes tyrannical and cruel, in British times it ran for peace and good-will and as much prosperity as the difficult economics of India would allow for. The word *Hukm* contains in its makeup the prestige of the British Raj—the *Ikbal* (prestige) of the Sirkar. Anything tending to diminish that through bad administration or the permitting of disorder has always brought about some form of catastrophe. The political aspirations of the lawyers and educationalists, drawn almost entirely from a clever if unmartial stratum, have still little to coincide with the needs and aspirations of the vast agricultural community of which India is made up. With the decay of the *Hukm*, the Red Shirt Movement, the Moplah Rebellion, trouble in Peshawar and all along the Border is inextricably mixed up, and incidentally was the reason for much hard fighting for the British and Indian troops and much upset and loss to the Frontier people themselves.

THE LAST PARADE OF THE CORPS TOGETHER
1 January 1939

[Photo: R. B. Holmes, Peshawar]

CHAPTER III

THE EXPLOSIONS IN PESHAWAR AND YUZAFZAI

THE GUIDES INFANTRY IN THE KHAIBER—THE GUIDES CAVALRY IN THE RED SHIRT TROUBLE, 1930—
THE AFRIDI INVASION OF PESHAWAR—THE CAVALRY IN THE FIRST AFRIDI INROAD—QUIETING THE
MARDAN AREA—THE SECOND AFRIDI INROAD—THE DISTURBED YUZAFZAI BORDER DURING 1931—
THE OCCUPATION OF THE KHAJURI PLAIN—THE CAVALRY AT BANNU.

THE GUIDES INFANTRY IN THE KHAIBER IN 1930

BEFORE the Red Shirt outbreak and the Afridi invasion of the Peshawar plain in 1930 it must be recorded how, late in 1929, soon after the return from Chitral, the Guides Infantry had been informed that for unforeseen reasons they would shortly go to the Peshawar frontier, probably the Khaiber. Accordingly, on 26 January 1930, they moved by train to Shagai in that pass and took over from the 3rd/4th Bombay Grenadiers the various posts. This month had come news that Lieutenant Meynell, serving with the Tochi Scouts, had been wounded in the back, but not seriously.

The Brigadier, Milward, visited the Corps as it arrived; and the Battalion settled in happily enough. But there were incidents of unrest, picquets now and again being sniped, and during the night of 25 February Lieutenant Hawke, R.E., the Assistant Garrison Engineer, was murdered at Landi Kotal. On 9 April the Guides Infantry moved to Landi Kotal, and another serious incident occurred on 20 April when the new manager of the Imperial Bank of India at Peshawar, and another bank official visiting the Khaiber, were both shot dead near Michni Kandao by a Khassadar havildar (a Mohmand). The man himself was shot dead at ninety yards by Shinwari Khassadars. The outrage had perhaps no serious political motive as a post-mortem examination showed that the murderer was suffering from acute cerebral-meningitis.

On 23 April the civil disturbance began in Peshawar, and next day Major-General B. R. Moberly arrived at Landi Kotal to take over from Brigadier Milward. The aftermath of the Red Shirt and Peshawar city disturbances and of the whole Red Shirt movement was now showing in the Khaiber. The Afridis attacked some of the Khassadar posts and reports of a lashkar about to attack the Khaiber military posts were received.

However, the Khaiber stayed quiet, but on 25 May Captain Murphy of the police was murdered by the inhabitants of Takkar[13] while bringing in some arrested men. This was a peculiarly outrageous incident.

The days were employed by the Guides Infantry and other units in the brigade in improving defences and familiarizing all with the terrain, and on 5 and 6 June came the news of the first Afridi invasion of the Peshawar Valley. On 11 June Lieutenant-Colonel Sandeman, Subadar Barkat Shah and several rank and file of the Guides were sent by

---

[13] Ten miles north-west of Mardan on the Abazai road.

lorry into Yuzafzai to collect all possible evidence of the Red Shirt movement and, when suitable, to use their influence to appease it. No more suitable envoys could have been found and they returned in eight days, having collected much information and made many suggestions, most of which were at once adopted.

On the 18 July they went out again and matters were found to be much better, largely owing to these suggestions and the prompt taking of stronger measures.

On 9 and 10 August came the second Afridi inroad on Peshawar, but in neither of these inroads did the Guides Infantry take any share other than against minor local moves. The Cavalry, however, were more actively engaged, as will be related. In October the battalion was ordered down to Jamrud, at the mouth of the Pass, arriving on 6–8 October.

In Corps matters, on 25 September it was announced that Brigadier-General G. M. Baldwin, D.S.O., had been appointed Colonel of the Corps *vice* General Sir Raleigh Egerton, whose tenure, like that of General Younghusband, had been cut short by the new age rule.

At the end of September, Brigadier-General I. U. Battye came to say good-bye, on retirement, *en route* to take up the appointment of game warden in Tanganyika. On 3 November Field-Marshal Lord Birdwood came to visit the battalion he had known so long and take farewell as he closed his long and famous service in India.

The Guides Cavalry in the Red Shirt Trouble, 1930

The unprofitable story of the Red Shirt trouble has just been told, and we should now read of the share of the Guides Cavalry in helping the civil authority on the Mohmand and Utmanzai border. Of all the disorderly and criminal pockets alongside that border, Charsadda and its neighbourhood were the worst, and it was along this portion of the border that the insidious propaganda of the Red Shirts and the Youth League had been most effective. The situation the Cavalry were to help in was unpleasant, as Government had shirked the obvious duty of declaring martial law—a *sine qua non* if troops are to support the police. As it was, small bodies of troops often found themselves surrounded by yelling crowds with no room for action. The police, naturally inadequate to cope with mass hysteria, were then often placed in positions of extreme danger.

In April 1930 the situation was boiling up, and on the 24th the Guides Cavalry were ordered to Charsadda to assist in the evacuation of political prisoners. It is well here to remind readers how peculiarly suited the whole Guides organization was to help quiet a country thus disturbed, for every village had some of their ex-Guides, usually a stronghold of common sense and loyalty.

It has already been told how Colonel Sandeman and several members of the Guides were sent from the Khaiber into the district in June, and were able to make valuable contacts and make intimate suggestions as to the course to be taken. Some reference has already been made to the grievances of the countryside, and it might be well that these should be outlined at a little greater length as evident to the civil administration and the officers of the Guides as they went among the people.

The Khilafat movement, that mourned the disappearance of Turkish lands of the Caliph of Islam, the Successor to the Prophet, upset Islamic feeling completely—but was, of course, no act of the British. The assumption of the Caliphate by Sheikh Hussain, of the clan of the Prophet—a far better claim than ever that of the Turkish Sultan was— cut no ice in Islam.

The situation was thus prepared for the movement of the Red Shirts and *Khuda-i-Khidmatgaran* (servants of God), as well as the Youth League. These were, however, fostered by political revolutionaries for their own ends. It might be worth while to remark that ever since the Muslim conquest, Brahmin intrigue travelled underground in a manner unknown to British ways of thought—and has been the Congress basis. The Turks who ruled India had short ways with it.

The basis of the discontent in the countryside was, however, non-religious. The causes of unrest were mainly twofold—the first, the Sirda Marriage Act, already referred to, while the second cause was economic and may to some extent have been attributable to the steady deterioration of administration that the reforms had inaugurated.

The third main trouble was that owners of land considered that land and water taxes were too high. The latter were presumably based on the capital and working costs of the irrigation system, points not easily understood. The former was due to the periodic review of the "Settlement"—viz., the taxation of the land on the basis of production, the age-old Indian system. A revision had been due after the First World War, and the people said it was based on war-time values and prices not now obtaining.

Another grievance seems to have been that the proposals for extending Indian self-government were being withheld from the Frontier Province for a while, a proceeding for which there were excellent governmental reasons. However, what with religious and economic tub-thumping, matters had become very dangerous and beyond the power of the civil authorities to control. Military assistance was now called for, and on 24 April 1930 the Cavalry under Major Blood were ordered out to the plague spot of Charsadda, to help evacuate political prisoners.

This was carried out satisfactorily and the Regiment was back in Mardan next day. This, however, was but the commencement of perpetual sallies from Mardan to various troubled areas to arrest offenders or disperse gatherings and was to continue well into 1931—duties trying and vexatious, but thoroughly carried out, to the prevention of much bloodshed.

On 11 May a large portion of the Risalpur Brigade was to be engaged in enveloping and preventive action, the Guides marching about twenty-eight miles to the Nagoman boat bridges on the Kabul river, where they found the 15th/19th Hussars and a section of E/R.H.A. To allow of duties in Mardan, the Regiment was organized on a two-squadron basis from "A," "B" and "C" Squadrons. Reports of local gatherings were now coming in from all sides, and on the 12th the Brigade marched to Shabkadr at 2100 hours, where 200 police joined the force, the object being to surround the turbulent village of Kattozai before daylight.

The Guides were detailed to cut off the escape of villagers to the north, while the 15th/19th Hussars surrounded Kattozai by 0500 hours, when the village was entered by the police. Eight people were arrested and cases of arms and revolutionary banners captured. The D.C. appeared satisfied with the result and the column moved up the Shabkadr–Abazai road, as some 300 Mohmands were reported to have come down to join in the fun. They were handsomely bombed for their pains. The column returned to Nagoman by the afternoon of the 14th. The Brigade marched at 0001 hours on a similar mission to Utmanzai (thirteen miles), the Guides being detailed to block the village from the south. The 15th/19th Hussars broke into the Khilafat headquarters, arresting twenty-one of the *mafruz* and seizing a quantity of arms. The prisoners were then taken to the police thana at Charsadda. The Brigade remained that night at Kula Dheri, and next day moved to Charsadda, which was still considered to be the main centre of the trouble. Next day the Guides, accompanied by a Shiah detachment from the Kurram Militia—some way from their home—were to surround the village of Dargai. All was quiet, however, and the D.C.[14] found all the arms on the register present and addressed the villagers. Coming away, however, a crowd of Red Shirts were shouting a few hundred yards off and these were forcibly dispersed by the police and Kurram Militia. The Regiment was back in Charsadda at noon and on 22 May returned to Mardan.

On the 25th trouble blew up towards Mardan itself, the Cavalry being deployed to block the approaches from the Charsadda direction, and the 2nd/13th F.F. Rifles were to do the same in the direction of Takht-i-Bhai. Later in the day the Cavalry were hurried back to Charsadda, of which spot they were heartily sick—the time of year being especially unpleasant. Here too came part of the 15th/19th Hussars and the 20th Lancers. On the 27th the Guides were ordered back to Mardan to support the 2nd/13th, so kaleidoscopic were the disturbances and so distracted the civil authorities. On the 28th they supported the police and 2nd/13th towards Takht-i-Bhai in seizing disturbers at Kacha Garhi, confiscating arms and burning *hujras*.

It was also reported that bodies of the Ranizai, a Yuzafzai tribe around Dargai, were filtering down towards Takkar to interfere with operations. Some firing took place but the Cavalry were not engaged and by the afternoon of the 28 May they were back in Mardan, though with no prospect of any rest, for next day they marched to Charsadda once more. In the meantime—a measure of the apprehension of the Frontier Government —three battalions and the 6th Cavalry arrived in Mardan.

The next two or three days at Charsadda were spent in surrounding certain villages, making arrests and seizing arms, and the inevitable result of fooling with the *Hukm* occurred, which was to change the venue—the Afridi lashkars were over the border.

The various moves, however, just recorded, dreary and monotonous though they sound, did just keep the situation in hand.

The Afridi Invasion of Peshawar

We must now hark back to the Afridi invasion, of which the Guides Infantry in the Khaiber posts had seen very little, and the Afridi story is briefly outlined to explain the happenings.

---

[14] Deputy Commissioner.

Some twenty miles to the south-west of Peshawar lie the hills of the Afridi Tirah beyond the sloping plateau of the Khajuri plain. Across the border, up the valley of the Bara river which runs into the Kabul river, lie our friends and enemies the Afridis : friends because so many of them have served in the Indian Army, enemies because they compelled us to invade the Tirah and because of their occasional outbreaks of raiding. Unfortunately, there was a good deal of unrest and want among them, because in the First World War their desertions to the enemy and their unreliability had caused them to be largely eliminated from the Army. In this there is one point worth remembering, however, which to some extent accounts for their desertion. Tribal politics in the Tirah are very involved and acrimonious, and should by any chance one clan in an Indian regiment lose heavily and other clans very little, the balance of power politics and power of self-defence in their own lands is much affected. To preserve this balance, desertion seemed the simplest way ; but the result of it all is that pay and pensions which used to form such a large part of the economic life of the Afridis have disappeared. Just as some relaxation in the enlistment rules had been introduced, our friends must needs, seeing our incapacity in the Peshawar and Red Shirt riots, invade British territory in large numbers. That was an insult which the British had never seen before, never since Sir John Gilbert's force, after the battle of Googerat, pursued the Afghan Horse to the Frontier and, to use the Sikh expression, kicked them "like dogs" through the Khaiber. This invasion turned the Peshawar plain into a fairly large-scale battlefield into which troops had to be poured. With the general discontent and unrest came, of course, the usual accessories—the propaganda of the agitator, the banging of the drum of Islam and the screaming of the mullahs. The manner of it was as follows :

A peculiar feature of politics in the Peshawar area was this matter of the Khajuri or Afridi plain just referred to. Whereas along the Frontier the administrative border runs along the foot-hills, in the case of Peshawar it ran across the country and left the flat Afridi plain outside the administration. In this Afridi plain the tribes and their women and families would come down to camp every winter to avoid the climate of their own hills, camping, or inhabiting caves in the cliffs that had been cut by various streams through the conglomerate of the plain. It was perhaps not illegal therefore for Afridis to assemble in and about the plain, but as a lashkar only assembles for mischief, it was equally legal for British Administration to order them to disperse or take the consequences, and on this occasion it was known that Afridi lashkars had assembled for some days. However, authority funked the issue and a few weeks after the Red Shirt scandal some five thousand tribesmen had assembled on the western side of the plain between 31 May and 3 June, and some two thousand of the choicest spirits had reached the outskirts of Peshawar. They were too late. Bombed and attacked by troops they found it not so amusing as they imagined, but the authorities were naturally alarmed that a large force had succeeded in getting into close touch with the rebels of the city. The actual bombing produced little effect since, at this season of the year, high crops—over six-foot sugar-cane and millet—afford plenty of concealment. Huge quantities of bombs were now expended where, a little earlier, a tenth of the number would have broken up the lashkars, as the Army and Air Commanders had recommended. In a few days the

Afridis had oozed back to the hills for the moment, but the news of this invasion, unparalleled in its presumption, had spread to the neighbouring country and everywhere raids were prevalent. But a far larger inroad was now to occur. On 1 August the Afridi jirgas decided to launch another attack on Peshawar. Within a week 5,000 men assembled and, advancing by a dry watercourse, they succeeded in evading a military force watching the border. Another lashkar joined them and at least two thousand Afridis were in the gardens around Peshawar engaged in attacking the military posts. The country was deep in the hot weather haze of dust, and neither troops nor planes could be very effectively used against well-armed marksmen lurking in the high crops, behind walls and irrigation ditches, and in a country intersected by the covered ways which dry nullahs furnish.

It can be well imagined how cavalry, trying to operate against the tribesmen, and armoured cars were constantly ditched and held up. A remarkable incident of this attack on Peshawar was the raid on the afternoon of 9 August on "K" Supply Depot lying three and a half miles north of the centre of the cantonment and north-east of the city. Its garrison consisted of fifty other ranks of the 4th/11th Sikh Regiment, under Jemadar Alla Ditta. The depot was a large one surrounded by a fairly high wall in bad repair. The enemy got into the depot, but were stiffly opposed by the guard; the Jemadar, with a Lewis gun and seven sepoys, joined the guard on the roof. The Jemadar had been able to telephone to the Brigade and prompt assistance arrived; but the scenes in the area had been desperate and a great credit to the garrison.

In the meantime the Afridis were attacking trains on the railway line, which had to be protected, and various troops began to arrive. Martial law was now declared in the district, the G.O.C.-in-C. of the Northern Command took charge and the Chief Commissioner was appointed to administer the martial law. An extended campaign was inaugurated to clear up the invasion and generally advance on to the Khajuri plain, and by the end of September the situation was well in hand. Among the troops hurried up was the Nowshera Brigade and the Risalpur Cavalry Brigade, which included the Guides Cavalry. Some account of the share of the Guides therein will be given a little later.

The general failure, however, of the Afridi invasion produced a good bazaar yarn. It was said that the Congress had only paid for a certain amount of ammunition, and that when this had been expended the lashkars packed up. At any rate, a *bien trovato* yarn.

The Cavalry in the First Afridi Inroad

We must now glance at the share taken by the Guides Cavalry in the repulsion of the Afridi inroads, when the scene for them was to change from the activities against the Red Shirts and their dupes.

On 3 June the Risalpur Brigade was reconcentrated at Charsadda after various minor operations—viz.:

>   Two guns E/R.H.A.
>   The 15th/19th Hussars
>   Guides Cavalry (on a squadron basis, "A" and "C," with
>   two Vickers guns) with the usual services.

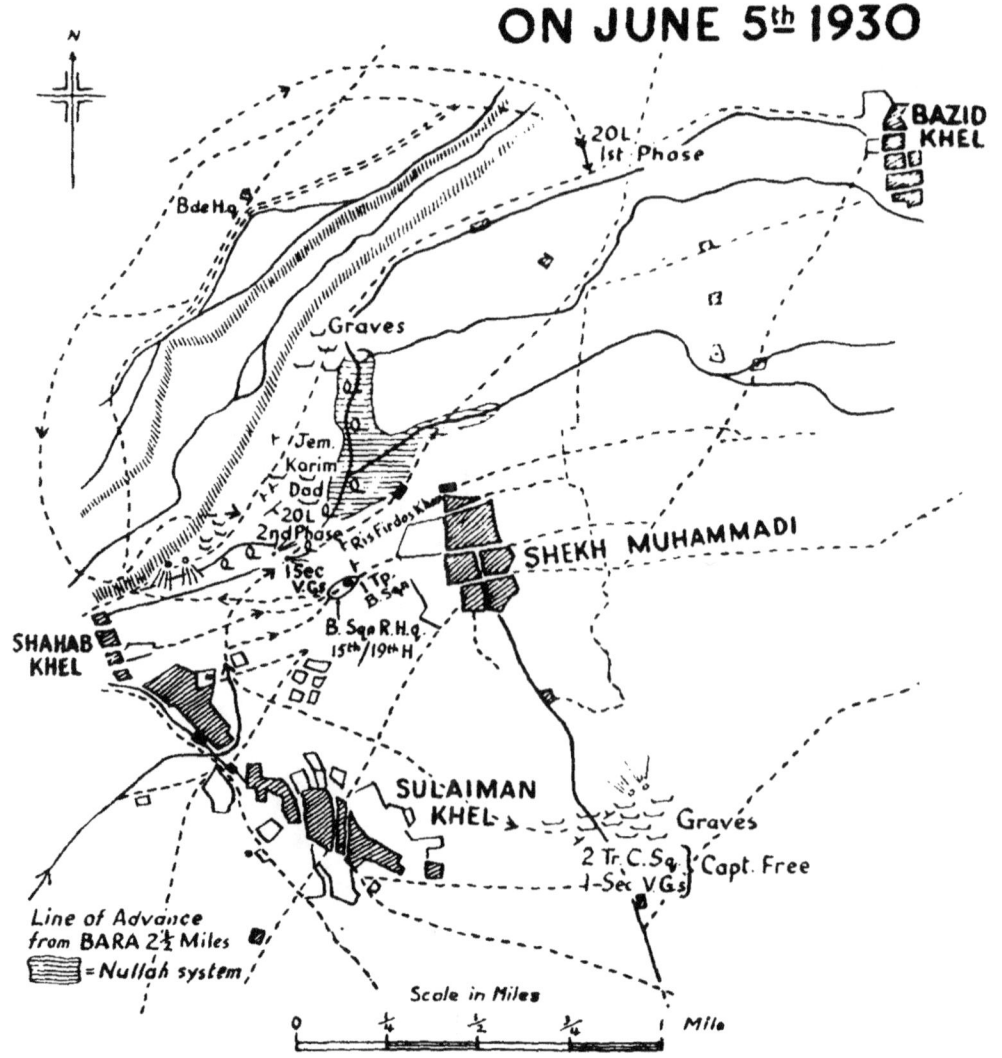

On the evening of that day the Brigade was ordered to march next morning for Peshawar and encamped on the Saddar Bazaar Polo Ground, being joined by the rest of E/R.H.A., the 20th Lancers, and Lieutenant Egerton and sixty Guides. During the day many reports came in of the Afridis swarming over the Khajuri plain. Early on 5 June a reconnaissance under Lieutenant-Colonel Bromilow of the 20th Lancers was ordered, with a squadron of his regiment, in which Major Hankin, Captain Free and Captain Walton of the Guides Cavalry took part. Shortly after the start of the reconnaissance, the Guides Cavalry (with Major Blood and Lieutenants Gimson and Plunkett) were ordered out along the Bara road, and then to turn south towards Landi, where Afridi infiltration was reported. But it was soon found that the enemy were in considerable numbers at Shekhan, immediately east of Bara, and the Guides, with whom was Mr. Metcalf, the D.C., were recalled to take part in a sweep eastward from Bara by the whole Brigade. This was to take place on both sides of the Bara river, towards the cantonment of Peshawar, with the Nowshera Brigade co-operating. So many trees, however, had been felled across the Bara road by the Afridis that E/R.H.A. was left behind.

The operation was to commence at noon (5 June), the Guides on the right bank of the river, the 15th/19th Hussars and the 20th Lancers on the left, the Hussars being in the centre. The Nowshera Brigade was to be disposed along the Peshawar road, having a 4.5 howitzer battery with it, as a stop to prevent the enemy making south.

The Cavalry column left Peshawar at 1000 hours and was at Bara by 1100 hours, where it watered and fed, and moved off at noon; the Guides Cavalry, which their reconnoitring officers had now joined, crossing the Bara by the ford half a mile below the fort. The nearer villages were clear of the enemy, but on approaching Shekh Muhammadi, a considerable fire was opened on the leading troops from its walls and the complicated nullah system between it and the Bara river.

It is well here to remind readers of the extremely complicated nature of the terrain which made all operations extremely difficult—viz., old water-courses, with steep banks, irrigation cuts and feeders innumerable, overhung with willows, and avenues of shisham, plus high crops of mealies and jowar and the like. A low-flying aeroplane, shot at for its pains, had been able to see little of the well-placed marksmen.

The enemy were cleared out of a wooded nullah running into the Bara, and the Guides Cavalry advanced to a sunken road between Shahab Khel and Shekh Muhammadi to support the advanced troops, but it was obviously not a cavalry country. A squadron under Captain Free was disposed to block any infiltration on the south or south-west while the situation was reported to Brigade Headquarters, whence came orders to hold the line while arrangements were made for the Nowshera Brigade to attack Shekh Muhammadi. This attack, by a Gurkha battalion, had actually commenced when severe trouble arose elsewhere.

Across the Bara river there had been little to record, but a squadron of the 20th ordered to attack Shekh Muhammadi could make no progress. The trouble just alluded to put a stop to the Nowshera Brigade attack on Shekh Muhammadi, two of its battalions having become engaged with Afridis at Spina Warai, north of the Bara road. It was still hoped, however, that the remaining battalion, with which were a couple of howitzers, would be able to give assistance, but atmospherics were so bad that the battalion on the Kohat road did not get orders till it was too late to give effect to them.

The position was now one of stalemate, the enemy were infiltrating round flanks and getting at the horses, and it was decided to withdraw the Cavalry Brigade from an operation for which they were not suited, since a cavalry sweep, however suitable it might look on the map, was, in this case, impracticable. The various regiments, under mutual support and assisted by two howitzers, withdrew without loss, after a harassing and disappointing day. Losses happily were trivial, the Guides having but one I.O.R. wounded with two horses killed and two wounded, and the Hussars one O.R. killed and two wounded, with three horses killed and three wounded.

By 2100 hours the brigade was back in camp near Peshawar. Reports indicated that the Afridis, after the bombing which, if carried out earlier, would have prevented the inroad, had withdrawn across the Border. Next day, the 6th, the Guides Cavalry with a squadron of the Poona Horse and E/R.H.A. surrounded various villages south-west of Peshawar that had harboured Afridis while the D.C., with the Border Regiment, actually entered them. The next few days passed uneventfully, the regiment visiting various villages, and on 12 June they were ordered to return to Mardan via Pabbhi—this, however, was changed for Charsadda, to relieve the 6th Lancers—and the rest of the Brigade marched to Pabbhi.

Quieting the Mardan Area

On 13 June the Regiment was ordered to Mardan, where it arrived next day, but now received orders to go with two companies of the 2nd/13th F.F. Rifles to Swabi, to deal with disturbances. The Afridi inroads had naturally added fuel to the Red Shirt movement, and lowered all respect for law and order, and the country needed quieting.

It arrived at Swabi with the Infantry in lorries on the 18th, and left next day to round up the village of Marghuz. This was successful, for the "General," President, Vice-President and Secretary of the very seditious Youth League Movement and eleven others were secured. The actual inhabitants appeared in a very repentant mood. This raid was to be followed by several others equally successful. On the 20th the column marched ten miles to Topi. From Topi the column marched before dawn on the 21st to round up the village of Maini—a difficult operation owing to hilly terrain which it was not possible to reconnoitre; however, thirty-five persons wanted for questioning were secured, of whom five were arrested, while eight hostages for the good behaviour of the village were taken. The attitude of the village, however, was inclined to be truculent.

The column returned to Topi the same day and remained there till the 23rd, when it marched back to Swabi, the Infantry by the main road, the Cavalry by Kotah and Marghuz.

Next day, the 24th, it was necessary to raid Kotah, which had felt secure after the troops had passed by it the day before, where thirty-one out of thirty-five wanted persons were secured, of whom ten were arrested. The house of Lambadar Sarwar, a recalcitrant leader, was destroyed by men of his village under police supervision. On the 26th the village of Yar Hussain was surrounded and a very successful bag made. Eight wanted people were arrested, including the President, Secretary, General, a captain and two subadars of a local revolutionary body, and valuable papers were secured.

Another successful raid was made on the 27th, when the village of Tordher was taken by complete surprise and more *opéra-bouffe* revolutionaries secured in the persons of a general, a colonel, two subadar-majors, two havildar-majors, eleven in all being arrested. The "General's" flag was flying from "Flag-shot House"!

The trouble was now over, and on 28 June the Cavalry returned to Mardan. It is not a very exciting or interesting story, but it meant trying work, carried out with energy, resolution, good temper and judgment, which averted what might well have been nasty scenes of bloodshed. It definitely pricked the absurd and evil Red Shirt bubble in the Mardan district.

The Second Afridi Inroad

As already related, the Afridi incursions into the Peshawar valley were not over. The loot acquired and the banging of the drum ecclesiastic were to produce accession of strength and a larger inroad.

This time the authorities were prepared and this meant no rest for the Guides. They had arrived in Mardan on the 28th and on the 29th were ordered to march next day via Charsadda to Peshawar to rejoin their Cavalry Brigade. Arriving on 1 July, they went into camp on the south face of the polo ground.

With the Regiment were:

    Major W. H. Blood, M.V.O., Commanding.
    Major H. M. Hankin.
    Captain Gradige, O.B.E., "A" Squadron.
    Captain F. Walton, Adjutant.
    Captain I. W. Beatty, "C" Squadron.
    Captain E. K. Wood, Officer S.C. of Risalpur Brigade.
    Lieutenant W. A. Gimson, "B" Squadron.
    Lieutenant B. G. Egerton, Quartermaster.
    Lieutenant the Hon. R. A. H. Plunkett.

On 20 July the Regiment marched back to Mardan via Charsadda, doing the whole thirty-five miles in seventeen hours.

The unit now remained quietly at Mardan till 3 August, when orders were received to march to Peshawar, arriving on the 5th in very hot weather. On the 6th the Risalpur Cavalry Brigade was moved out to Bara Fort; on the 7th the Brigade moved about in the vicinity of Bara, exchanging a few shots, and on the 8th returned to their old camp site at Peshawar.

On the 9th the Brigade was ordered to clear the villages east of Bara, but save for a little sniping there were no incidents as reports now came of the Afridi attack on "K" Supply Depot and of the Poona Horse heavily engaged elsewhere (already described). The 20th Lancers and 15th/19th Hussars moved towards the scene, but the enemy had been beaten off, and the Brigade was back in camp by dark.

On the 11th the ubiquitous Afridis were reported to be in the vicinity of the Cherat Hills and the Brigade marched thither without result, returning to camp in the afternoon. On the 13th and 14th various villages were visited, but no contact made. For the next ten days, except for an odd reconnaissance or so, the Brigade remained in camp at short notice.

The same sort of life and odd operations to clear the countryside went on till 4 September, when orders were received to return to Mardan.

During this long and trying period the movement of the Cavalry Brigade undoubtedly kept the countryside clear of the enemy, but the main operations to clear that district fell on the infantry formations, who were able to tackle the terrain, and in these movements the cavalry at times had been able to take part.

The end of it was that in long, trying days the Guides Cavalry had not been able to get on terms with the intruders or do more than exchange a few shots with them.

The Disturbed Yuzafzai Border during 1931

From September till the end of January 1931 the border districts remained manageable, during which time the troops in Peshawar were busy occupying the Khajuri plain and putting the cordon of forts already described, beyond the Afridi winter camping grounds.

On 28 January, however, the old trouble began, and "C" squadron under Captain Prioleau was hurried out to Charsadda to support the civil power, moving on to Utmanzai, where trouble was brewing. There were some eight hundred Red Shirts with eleven banners and three to four thousand spectators. After the assembly was declared illegal, the crowd, with some hesitation, dispersed—save for a body of some four hundred just north of Utmanzai. Then the police and other squadrons dispersed them. In the meantime, a company of the 4th/11th Sikhs had arrived, and next day the squadron returned to Mardan.

Matters now remained quiet till 2 February when again a mixed squadron under Captain Prioleau was moved up the familiar road. The report on the operations submitted by Captain Prioleau is very informing and shows the folly of sending a few police and a handful of troops to meet what was very near rebellion, without at least making the military commander responsible.

The events were as follows: a company of the 4th/11th Sikhs arrived the same afternoon as the cavalry. The civil government had forbidden a Red Shirt assembly. On the 20th the squadron "showed the flag" by marching out to Turangzai and back, and at eight that evening the C.C. informed the O.C. troops that the Red Shirts intended to defy the order next day at Utmanzai; and at 0630 hours next morning (21st) the squadron of the Guides, with the company of the 4th/11th Sikhs and 250 police, marched out to a point on the road eight hundred yards south of Utmanzai, and at 1055 hours a message dropped from a plane by Colonel Sandeman reported large gatherings, especially north of Utmanzai, in all directions, and the force moved towards Utmanzai, the infantry and police through the village—the cavalry round the east end. Considerable

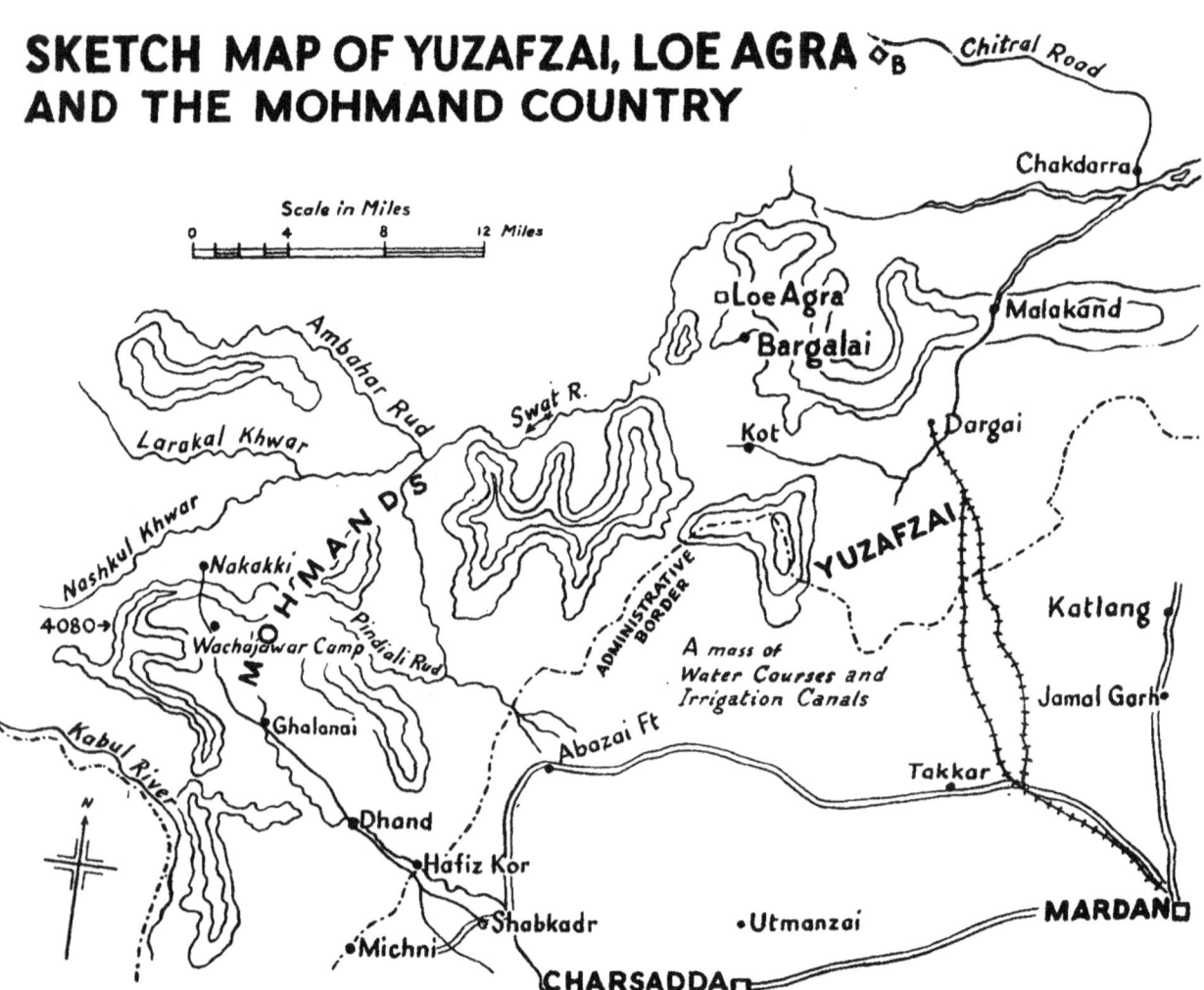

gatherings were in evidence on various mounds north of the village and large bodies of Red Shirts and *tamashabins* (spectators) approaching from several directions.

At 1130 hours the police proceeded to break up the nearest meeting and a fracas took place, but *lathis* of the police and stones from the Red Shirts were the only weapons at first; then shots were fired and the police opened on the crowd, which retired with two dead and several injured.

By now a dangerous and truculent crowd of several thousands was approaching from Utmanzai, against whom the infantry had to use their rifle butts.

The A.C. of Police now decided to break up the other two bodies with his men, and asked the O.C. troops to support them and extricate them if need be. The Cavalry Squadron accordingly closed in. The A.C. Police eventually succeeded and the day was over. The casualties were—Police, 3 seriously and 37 slightly injured, and the Red Shirts, 2 killed and 57 admitted later to Peshawar hospital !

Captain Prioleau reported that the angry mob numbered twenty thousand, and that the troops marched out through them with fixed bayonets and swords drawn. He very properly reported that, though the operation had been successful, it had been highly dangerous, and the A.C. Police—Mr. McCrea—might easily have lost his life, as poor Murphy had a few weeks earlier. In fact, the force had been in danger—should have been a military operation—and that the situation pretty well called for the Napoleonic remedy of "a whiff of grape." Firing from the middle of a brawl as occurred on this occasion could only be dangerous to the small body of troops involved. At any rate, the police had operated with courage and the troops with steady judgment. However, a few days later Colonel Sandeman wrote to Lieutenant-Colonel Hankin, commanding the Cavalry, that the Military authorities had made it clear that it was intended that operations of this sort were to be in the hands of the troops, and that orders to the effect would be issued at once.

On the 22nd the police reported that more processions were likely, so the force marched through Utmanzai again and arrested two ringleaders. Things now remained fairly quiet for a month when the excitement moved across to Mardan itself, where on 3 April a meeting was advertised, and the Guides Cavalry and the 2nd/13th were disposed to keep the cantonments clear. This and assemblies to meet Abdul Ghafar lasted on and off till the 23rd, to the scandal of the countryside. From 21 to 26 April "C" Squadron, under Captain Free, toured the villages in the Katlang area, the reception varying remarkably from place to place. Captain Free's report was most informing, showing how the poison had worked very irregularly, and it may be inferred that the good leaven of the ex-Guides was often at work.

At some villages the reception was chilling and unwilling, Red Shirts dodging about among the houses. At Khui-Barmol it was exactly the contrary, the old enthusiasms and hospitality being to the fore and sports being organized.

Katlang and neighbouring villages showed a disagreeable spirit, and ex-Guide officers reported matters had gone quite mad under the influence of one Khausta Khan, who declared himself *Sipah-Salar*—viz., Commander-in-Chief. The results of the tour on the whole were beneficial, restoring confidence among the friendly and warning the disloyal.

At Jumalgarhi, however, a procession showed the greatest insolence and defiance in endeavouring to bring the squadron and Government into contempt. The officer commanding the Guides Cavalry, in reporting this, observed very properly that action should be taken and military officers empowered to arrest the leaders. Indeed, a generation earlier the latter would have been brought in in tow of sowars.

On 12 June a Red Shirt meeting was held at Ghalladhar to mourn the execution of Hari Kishan, the Congress murderer and would-be assassinator of the Governor.

The emergency squadron under Captain Prioleau rode to the scene, but matters passed off peacefully.

And so, in mid-June 1931, the disturbances began to fade out, and the face of the countryside to return to normal. The *Hukm* had been partly restored.

1931: THE OCCUPATION OF THE KHAJURI PLAIN

The big Afridi assembly of all the jirgas to hear the orders of the Government of India, after their astounding and heinous escapade, assembled at Jamrud on 16 November in no very amicable mood. The actual terms of Government had been very carefully considered and a strong, yet simple and paternal, decision had been come to.

It was that the Khajuri and Akka Khel plains north and south of the Bara river and only some seven miles south-west of Peshawar, just over our administrative borders —but of course part of our tribal areas—should be brought under control by a line of military posts at the foot of the main hills. There would not seem to be much in this to those who know not the Frontier, but it was a commanding, yet avuncular decision. The point involved is simple enough. The Afridi Tirah, a mass of tumbled mountains where even the habitable valleys are of considerable height above the sea, however pleasant in summer, is very disagreeable in winter. Most of the clans migrate for the winter to these two adjoining plains, living in tents, or where possible in caves dug from the sides of gorges cut in the plain by water-courses as aforesaid.

With the clans come old and young, sheep and goats, the ox and the ass, and everything that is theirs. In spring they trek home again. That is an eastern feature; for centuries the Ghilzai from Afghanistan have come into the Indus plains. The Bakhtiaris from North Persia come down to the plains between the Tigris and the mountains. The return of the Ghilzai and of the Bakhtiaris is a great spectacle of organization and order—that of the Afridis, who have only to climb upstairs, is a simpler matter; but to the Afridis in the Khajuri and Akka plains a line of posts and a circular road from Jamrud to the Bara river and beyond was a serious matter. Their families and flocks to be hostages to fortune! No longer were they to rest unwatched a few miles from a great Indian city.

The jirgas objected, but found themselves up against a Government of India this time who meant business, and they had to acquiesce or be kept out of their winter camping grounds to sojourn in the snow.

THE EXPLOSIONS IN PESHAWAR AND YUZAFZAI

The Guides Infantry, whose business it was to see that there was no "rough stuff" at Jamrud, were rather like Mr. Wackford Squeers' practical class, "This is a bucket, spell it and fill it." They were to have the privilege of forming the first permanent garrison of the Khajuri plain posts, already being selected and constructed by the force in the plain. So they marched there on 15 April for three months.

While occupying the posts there was a certain amount of sniping by malcontents and at times the post guns had to come into action, while mobile columns were constantly out.

At the end of three months the battalion returned to Shagai on 16 July, relieving the 2nd/6th Rajputana Rifles and handing over Fort Salop and Jhansi posts to the 4th/7th Rajputs. The Red Shirt movement was still giving trouble in Yuzafzai, and in August Lieutenant Meynell, with Subadar Barkat Ali and Sepoy Muhamad Yunus, was sent to tour that district and reassure loyalists. The Subadar was later rewarded for his services by the grant of the Indian Distinguished Service Medal. In December there was a round-up of still-recalcitrant Red Shirts in Yuzafzai.

1932 In January the Battalion left the Shagai posts for Landi Kotal, their last sojourn in the Khaiber. Hearts were somewhat cast down when rumour said that the return to Mardan was postponed, but on 16 February came definite orders to leave in March, and by the 18th the Battalion was back in its old home. The two years away had been years of hard work with few of the excitements at the hands of their Afridi friends which had so electrified Peshawar.

THE CAVALRY AT BANNU

The Regiment left Mardan on 24 October 1931, being relieved by the 8th K.G.O. Light Cavalry from Secunderabad, and arrived at Bannu on 3 November, relieving the P.A.V.O. Cavalry, a tiring march on a modern tarmac road.

The Cavalry lines were of mud (cooler than brick), but built on the old jhori-dar system (two sowars with their kit in each hut) converted into barracks. A bad parade and training ground was five miles away. New lines were being slowly built. A squadron was detached to Wana in South Waziristan. The Regiment now formed part of a mixed movable column and soon became adept at scrambling up hills; all horses, even walers, are like cats on the hillside if trained. Major-General S. R. Pope—an old Piffer (58th)—commanded the district and Brigadier Scott the Bannu Brigade. Since Bannu—the official name being Edwardesabad, after the famous Herbert Edwards—has been a cantonment since 1849, its amenities, subject to restriction of irrigation, were long established, its winter glorious, its summer damnable.

There was plenty to do in the service line. The Tochi column (Tocol) exercised once a month, and in the end of January it moved out to support the scouts against Ghilzais from Afghanistan. These gentlemen had contracted the habit of intruding into the Kabul Khel country to graze their flocks, well this side of the Durand Line, and on more than one occasion had fired on the Scouts. So it was now decided that the Scouts should round up the Ghilzai flocks. The plan was to picquet the valley through which captured stock would be driven, with a force to round them up at the head. In support, Tocol, including of course the Guides Cavalry, concentrated at Mir Ali, and was to move forward to where the main nullahs left the high hills and the ground became more open. This was some twenty-four miles beyond Mir Ali, and it was expected that the Scouts and their booty would pass through the column, which would then cover them from the nest of hornets which a raid would naturally bring down on them as they withdrew. The Ghilzais, however, having heard of the column awaiting them, thought better of it, and the firing which had been going on all day died away. The Cavalry camped that night at Spinwam in bitter cold, but surprisingly were not molested.

The column was back in Bannu by the end of January, but not to peace, for severe trouble was brewing in South Afghanistan. It will be remembered how King Amanullah had been ousted by the strange rising of the Bacha Saqao—the water-carrier's son—and had fled to India and Italy. The province of Khost was always pro-Amanullah, and now the Faqir of Lawanai—a relation, it was said, of the ex-King—flooded the country on both sides of the Durand Line with statements that Amanullah was about to return to retake the throne. He would come by plane, and hundreds of planes would shower gold on all lashkars who came to his assistance. This was strong meat for the young men of the tribes on our side of the border, and at the worst it meant loot. Something had to be done, and that quickly, for hundreds and thousands of Wazirs were flocking into Afghan territory, which it was obviously our business to stop, especially as the excitement was spreading to the Afridi hills across the Kurram.

The British Government decided to put a military cordon across country from Arawali in the Kurram to Degan in the Tochi and to proclaim formidable penalties to those who did not return forthwith, while the cordon was to stop more men and food from crossing the Durand Line. In front of the troops would be scouts and in front of them again Khassadars.

So Tocol moved up to Mir Ali to hold the line from Spinwam to Miran-shah, and the Razmak column (Razcol) from Miran-shah to Degan where the Cavalry were posted. The total of troops engaged was considerable, consisting of the Guides Cavalry, two mountain batteries and eight and a half battalions. But the front covered was not enough, and tribesmen were slipping northwards beyond our left, so that the force had to passage leftwards, which had a steadying effect.

On 9 March the Governor of the N.W.F. Province flew from Peshawar to Wana and Sararogha, with two R.A.F. squadrons, and summoned the tribal jirgas. What he had to say was brief and forceful. The lashkars were given four days in which to return. If not, they must take the consequences. That evening two hundred Maliks left to bring their lads back. The lashkars had taken two small Afghan forts and a few arms, but were beaten back from Matun, the capital of Khost. The local tribes had not risen for Amanullah as was expected, but had remained loyal to King Nadir. The Maliks with the Government's message came to a hungry, cold and disappointed throng. During 13 and 14 March some eight thousand draggle-tails came back.

The now-discredited Faqir of Lawanai had taken refuge in the Madda Khel country and that could not be permitted. Three squadrons of R.A.F. flying over made the Maliks

BRIGADIER HECTOR CAMPBELL
Last Colonel of the Guides

agree to expel him. As a punishment, the tribe who had sent lashkars were fined two lakhs and Rs.20,000, to be paid in rifles.

That was the end of what was expected to be a very nasty business, and it had passed off without the hostilities with our own tribes which had seemed probable. In fact, the Maliks and tribal Khassadars had behaved admirably, and the troops returned without any molestation, a satisfactory conclusion for all concerned—and a credit to the political officers.

In November 1933 the Regiment carried out a training march along the border, from Bannu to Dera Ismail Khan, an area in which large numbers of the Ghilzai tribes (Powindahs) spend the winter. The Regiment gave tea parties for the Maliks and games and sports for all who cared to come, and much good feeling was engendered.

On the way an interesting incident occurred. Farrier-major Feroze Khan, in charge of sick horses, with six sowars, came across a traveller who had just been robbed of all his money (Rs.105). The robbers had bound their victim with his own puggaree and filled his eyes with dust. The man had managed to free himself and met the Guide party. The robbers could be seen making for the hills. Feroze Khan gave chase and, after a sharp gallop, captured them and recovered the loot. The robbers got three years each; the two Guides who caught them received commendatory certificates and a money grant.

The new lines at Bannu were now ready and the Regiment moved in for the hot season (1934). At this time the unit received Vickers-Berthiers to replace the ordinary Vickers, and very satisfactory they seemed. A sad incident was the death at Bannu on 31 March 1934 of Lieutenant L. M. Tweedie as the result of a riding accident.

But now came the joyful order to return to Mardan in October, on relief by the 20th Lancers, and for the first time since 1930 to be together with the "paltan" in the ancestral cantonment.

The march, which took eleven days, was a series of compliments and entertainment by Magistrates, Chiefs and Regiments. At Kohat, Probyn's Horse entertained them and their old comrades of the 56th. At Peshawar they were met and feasted by the 10th Cavalry. At Risalpur the troops were away, but there was a reception by the Municipal Committee. At Mardan itself, unfortunately, the "paltan" was away, but everyone left in the station, the police and the boy scouts, were there to welcome them home.

CHAPTER IV

OPERATIONS NORTH OF THE KHAIBER, 1933-1935

THE FRONTIER NORTH OF THE KHAIBER—THE CHITRAL RELIEFS OF 1932—THE MOHMAND STORY—
MOHMAND OPERATIONS, 1933—BAJAUR OPERATIONS, 1933—THE LOE AGRA TROUBLE, 1934—
THE SECOND EXPEDITION, 1934—THE THIRD EXPEDITION, 1935—THE MOHMAND RISING OF 1935—
ACROSS THE NAHAKKI PASS—THE FAMOUS FIGHT OF THE GUIDES INFANTRY—DETAIL OF THE
GUIDES' FIGHT—THE OVERWHELMING OF NOS. 3 AND 4 PLATOONS—THE WITHDRAWAL OF THE
GUIDES—THE LOSSES AND REWARDS OF THE GUIDES—THE END OF THE CAMPAIGN.

THE FRONTIER NORTH OF THE KHAIBER

THE astounding invasion of the Afridis was now over, and over fairly successfully with a display of governmental "guts" which, if exercised earlier, would have prevented all the trouble. But the folly, and the premeditated destruction of the *Hukm* in which politicians had so large a share, was not to be pardoned so easily, for first the Mohmand border, north of the Khaiber, was to blow up, and then for two years Northern and Southern Waziristan, the latter a pretty show-up, for all our crowing over the success of our road policy and our new garrison system. It was indeed a sad disappointment to those who worked for the good of the clans to whom they were deputed.

Both the Mohmand and the Waziristan troubles were to keep the Guides Infantry extremely busy for some five years. Indeed, in the Mohmand country they were to be involved in perhaps the most desperate fighting of all their long career and were to add the brightest of spots to their tally of brilliant service, surpassing even the Panjkora in 1895. Before, however, coming to these, the story of the Nowshera Brigade forming a column to cover the Chitral Relief column of the autumn of 1932, in which the Guides Infantry took a prominent part, must be told; it is only another illustration of the Islamic unrest which was sweeping the Frontier in the thirties.

THE CHITRAL RELIEFS OF 1932

The Battalion soon settled down to what were to be somewhat strenuous conditions and on 5 April received orders to find the Guard of Honour for the Viceroy at the investiture of all those to be rewarded for their services in the late disturbances. Before the time arrived, Yuzafzai was to indulge in the excitement of the new-fangled election. "Donnybrook" was just the thing that the countryside really fancied, better even than such films as Duck Tarpin (Dick Turpin). The occasion of 11 April was a very rowdy one in Mardan and the police had to fire twice on the crowds. Fifty men of the Guides stood by in reserve and the regimental quarter-guards of the Corps had to turn out more than once. On the 12th Captain Baily and Lieutenant Still were called out to Shawhi and Shahbaz-garhi.

On 17 April Captains Duncan and Barlow, Lieutenant Still, and Subadars Siraj ud Din and Barkat Ali, with fifty rank and file, proceeded to Peshawar as the special Guard

[Photo: Andrew Paterson, Inverness
LIEUT.-GENERAL SIR KENNETH McLEOD, K.C.I.E., C.B., D.S.O.

of Honour at the investiture. Their turn-out and appearance were much admired. By 21 May the aftermath of the election had died away, and Captain Barlow with Lieutenants Still and Rendall and fifty rank and file made a goodwill march through Yuzafzai, to be enthusiastically received, especially by the pensioners of their own corps, and others, and were lavishly entertained.

Guides Infantry. 2nd/9th Gurkhas. 1st/11th Sikhs. The season for the biennial Chitral reliefs was now at hand and rumours of the unrest in Bajour called for a protective force to cover their advance through the first portion of the route between Serai and Sado, to take posts at Bandagai and watch events. This was to be the Nowshera Brigade, which of course included the Guides Infantry. In addition to the three battalions enumerated, 5th/10th Baluchis and 3rd/14th Punjabis joined for a short time when this force moved up to Jalala and Dargai on 7 and 8 September and halted at Dargai, when the actual Chitral Relief Column joined them.

The Brigade was to proceed to Bandagai, and from that as their main centre cover the Chitral road where it passed near the Bajour territory. Bandagai was reached on the 13th, and Bajouris across the Panjkora river maintained a considerable fire, which was replied to while the camp was made secure and strong picquets established. The Guides and Gurkhas established picquets, and that night the picquet held by the 1st/11th Sikhs was heavily attacked.

On the night of the 14th Lieutenant Meynell took out a *chapao*[15] up the Bandagai nullah, a mile and a half from camp, and was run into by five Bajouris intent on sniping into camp. Three were killed and the other two knocked over but got away, and Meynell was back in camp by 1 a.m. On the 15th a very tired Brigade, who had been fortifying camps and picquets, rested, and the tribesmen sniped the latter.

On the 16th the Brigade moved out to cover the march of the Chitral Column (Chit-col) to Sado, the Guides Infantry holding the long ridge, on one end of which the Guides picquet had been constructed, while a small column of two companies of 2nd/9th Gurkhas and the machine-gun platoon of "A" Company of the Guides moved ahead of Chit-col, finally turning west to Shiga Kach as Chit-col moved on. During the morning a bombing attack was made on Shamozai across the Panjkora due west of Bandagai camp. As the Chitral column was now fairly launched it was possible by 1330 to order the withdrawal of the Brigade. Across the Panjkora were a good many of the Bajouris and firing went on all the morning, Nos. 13 and 14 Machine Gun platoons firing frequently on both flanks. The Guides were back in camp by 1615 hours, all except "A" Company which was to remain out on the Kamanai feature west of the Chitral road, so as to cover the relief-column camp at Khong (Sado) and also for the ambushing of any riverside movement of the enemy. It was this that caused the main dramatic business of the covering operation. Nos. 2 and 3 Platoons were distributed about the Kamanai hill feature on the east. No. 4 Platoon was established in a lightly built sangar on top of 3495, with a rifle section in a small sangar protecting the eastern end of the ridge. No. 1

---

[15] A surprise party.

Platoon was established twenty-five yards west of the main sangar, behind lying-down cover protected and camouflaged after dark. Lieutenant Meynell was in command of "A" Company.

At 2250 hours there was a sudden fierce attack by a force of some 120 tribesmen; a party of twenty-five rushed No. 1 Platoon in the low cover, from the sanatha bush near by. After killing seven men at point-blank range and another with the bayonet, the platoon then withdrew to the main sangar twenty-five yards away, having two of their number killed outside the entrance. Constant enemy rushes now followed from the scrub, which was so close, and on more than one occasion the attackers got within five yards of the sangar wall. No. 4 Platoon was also attacked and all of them fought practically hand to hand with rifle, bayonet and grenade. It was 0425 hours before the frustrated enemy withdrew. At dawn a strong patrol discovered in front of the position a standard, six enemy corpses, a tulwar and several rounds of ammunition, and a prisoner was also taken. While all this was going on in "A" Company's post, the Brigade camp was heavily fired into and "Guides' Picquet" attacked several times. The next day was a day of rest and cleaning up. Subadar Kaka took over "Guides' Picquet" with No. 7 Platoon (Manjhas) and was attacked several times on the night of the 17th. Subadar Ram Labhya and No. 2 Platoon now took over and were attacked on the night of the 18th.

The Brigade Commander had, in view of the night firing, selected a site for a new camp, in which nullahs would give some cover to the animals, and the Brigade moved to this on the 19th. The Battalion now took over Sado post and also Warai.

The tribesmen had had their *élan* considerably damped, and in the new camp things were much quieter. The Brigade made various exploratory tours, returning to camp at night. On 11 October Chit-col returned, with the relieved battalion, and were duly picqueted and protected as they marched through the edge of the disturbed area. There was some firing, but there were women and children to be seen in the villages, which meant that no large-scale attack was on the *tapis*.

Everything was now closed down and the troops back by 16 October.

The Mohmand Story

The Mohmand story and the periodical bursting into flames sometimes of only the tribes farther away, sometimes of all of them, need some explanation.

Many tribes under this generic name inhabit the mountains between the administrative and the Afghan borders, north of the Khaiber and south-west of the Malakand–Chitral road. In relation to the British Government, they are, as all the other tribes between the two borders, uncontrolled save as to their relations with their neighbours. But two factors somewhat complicate the situation: first, the fact that several clans have resided *within* British India since the British took over the Sikh frontier in 1849. Normally their behaviour is good and they have in the past furnished good soldiers, especially to the Guides, and the cis-frontier men have helped in relations with the trans-border Mohmands. But the connection could also work in reverse, in the sheltering within the borders of tribal disturbers.

Some Mohmand clans, too, dwell actually in Afghan territory, and when from time to time it pleased Kabul to poke fun at the British Lion, this condition made it easy. When the Durand frontier between Afghanistan and the British tribal areas was delimited in 1892, the bit between the Mohmands and Bajouris and Afghanistan had for various reasons to be left unfinished. A "presumptive line," however, was accepted by both parties for normal requirements. The northern and southern Mohmand tribes, however, were often at variance, the chief trouble being the acquiescence usually shown by the southern clans in the absurd British leaning towards peaceful behaviour. We need not go back to the past save to say that in the great upheaval of the border in 1897—partly due to Islamic propaganda during the Graeco-Turkish War—the Mohmands had invaded British India and fought a severe action in the open with a column of the Peshawar Brigade, an action distinguished by a spectacular charge of the 13th Bengal Lancers. A punitive expedition had resulted in 1898, and some twelve years later Sir James Willcocks had to take a force into the lower regions of the long Gandab valley, which formed the principal part of the country.

In 1933 the northern and southern tribes were again in actual disagreement, the direct outcome of Congress intrigues and Khilafat and Red Shirt troubles. The Nahakki range far up the Gandab valley was the general dividing line between the two factions. A firebrand of long standing, the Haji of Turangzai, and his sons, were the principal disturbers of the peace, again the grievance being mainly that the "lower" Mohmands furnished Khassadars to keep the peace that the people and their traders so wanted. To support the Red Shirts, the Haji and his supporters, after threatening to attack the Halimzai in March 1932, actually raided the latter's territory.

The difficulties of the "presumptive border" hampered any Air Force reprisal, but in July 1932, the Halimzai appealed for protection, and the Indian Government issued, with some effect, a proclamation that they would support the Halimzai against any invasion of their territory. But in July 1933 an "upper" Mohmand was murdered by a "lower" Mohmand. This was an excellent excuse for the invasion of Halimzai and to try and detach the "lower" Mohmands from the British. The Halimzai eventually expelled the invaders, but had several villages burnt. The "upper" Mohmands now collected considerable lashkars. The British Government decided to send a force and to make a motor road to the Halimzai territory, but stated that they had no intention of permanently occupying any trans-border territory.

The Mohmand Operations of 1933

A force under Brigadier C. Auchinleck, temporarily in command of the Peshawar Division, marched from Peshawar with the Peshawar Brigade on 30 July 1933, reaching Ghalanai two days later, and was followed by the Nowshera Brigade, who reached Dand on the 3rd to protect the communications.

The 2nd Brigade from Rawalpindi moved up to Peshawar. Large enemy lashkars were reported north of the Nahakki range and reconnaissances to the Khapak and Nahakki passes resulted in skirmishes. At a jirga, attended only by the "lower" Mohmand tribes, it was announced that the motor road would be brought up to Yusaf Khel, at the foot of the Nahakki Pass, and that if the "upper" Mohmands attempted any hostility, the road would be made into their territory over the pass. The "lower" Mohmands were described henceforth as "assured" and "protected" tribes. Further, the Afghan Government had now intimated to the Viceroy that they would not object to air or army action against Mohmands on their side of the frontier who had taken part in the "upper" Mohmand outrages and the burning of Halimzai hamlets. The "upper" Mohmands now sent their jirga in, and accepted the British terms, so that when the road to Yusaf Khel was completed the force withdrew and peace and quiet obtained.

Though the actual fighting was not very serious there was of course plenty of sniping. On 27 July the Guides Infantry were ordered to march and join Brigadier Auchinleck's force at Pir Qila, marching by night in view of the great heat in the irrigated plains. The principal operation so far as the Guides were concerned was the occupation of the Khazana Sar Ridge. Lashkars were reported to be thereon and behind it. This operation involved a climb of 2,300 feet, but only a few shots were fired and the tribesmen had evidently thought better of it. But the road up from Ghalanai was crowded with Halimzai women and children, refugees from the invader's threat. Auchinleck was then able to reconnoitre over the Nahakki Pass.

During the autumn the Guides with other units were very busy road-making and there was a good deal of sniping and long-range attacks, but when the settlement referred to above came the troops were withdrawn, the Guides being back in Mardan by 5 October. The Battalion had three men wounded in this expedition of whom one died. The above outline prepares the way for the severe Mohmand Campaign of 1935.

The Bajaur Operations of 1933

This part of the Frontier was not, however, to enjoy peace till the severe trouble of 1935, though it was fortunate that the areas that were disturbed did not all explode together as they did in the historic 1897, when 70,000 troops were involved. Up till 1933 the Government of India had never attempted to control the tribes in Bajaur— that is to say the hills between the Swat river and the "assumed" frontier with Afghanistan. If orders had to be given to the Bajauris, they had to be given with troops as the messengers. Because this remote country was uncontrolled it was a favourite refuge of outlaws and disturbers.

In May 1933 an individual calling himself a relation of ex-King Amanullah of Kabul, and assuming the style of a pretender to the Afghan throne, appeared in Bajaur and was given shelter by the Khan of Kotkai in the Charmang valley. He and another were trying to raise the local tribes against King Nadir Shah, and the Afghan Government very properly called on the British to suppress these activities. First, political pressure was brought on the Khans of Kotkai and Khar, but without effect, and then air action. This was increased and, though the Khan of Khar promised to comply with orders, intensive bombing of Kotkai had to be continued. A brigade from Abbottabad was detailed to go to the Panjkora river to protect the reconstruction of a bridge that had been swept away. The extended bombing and this threatened move had the necessary results; the pretender was publicly expelled from Kotkai and the agitator from Khar handed over to the Afghan authorities. The Afghan Government expressed its satisfaction.

But this satisfactory conclusion was not to end the trouble in this part of the Frontier, which was now to break out quite close to the actual border within, by agreement for many years, the protective area of the Malakand garrison. The hills about Loe Agra rise to well over 4,000 feet. It is from this area that the Upper Swat Canal derives and maintenance of good order is essential to the prosperity of the beneficiaries of the canal water. This was perfectly well understood by the local tribal chiefs, the Khans of Khanori and Bura Tutai, of the Sinazai subsection of the Utman Khel. But an old stormy petrel now put in appearance in the shape of Faqir Shah, the Faqir of Alingar in Bajaur, a product of Khilafat and Congress, a mullah always hostile to Government who had been giving trouble on and off for several years. In 1934 the Faqir, though forbidden by the Political authorities, crossed the Swat river with his following. Ostensibly he claimed that he was concerned with *Amir-bi-Maruff*—i.e., trying cases against religious law—but actually his object was to stir up feeling against the Government. The tribes in the protected area, that is to say those cis-Swat, did not oppose his entry, and a party of Swat levies sent to do so were forced to withdraw after suffering casualties. The Faqir now persuaded the Loe Agra jirga to promise to accept his orders and disregard those of Government.

The Loe Agra Trouble

Loe Agra was only a very few miles from the administrative border and the railway station at Dargai, and the impertinence involved was considerable. The first step taken by Government was to send a company of infantry to strengthen the Levy Post at Kot, seven miles east of Dargai, and some three miles south of Loe Agra. By February 1934 Government had decided to take strong steps, and reasserted the tribal agreement of 1907, which stated that a motor road to Kot would be made and also a Levy Post at Loe Agra, and promulgated fines on the Khanori and Bura Tutai jirgas. (This, of course, meant cutting off the allowances for preserving order.) A column would be moved up into the area, which was a difficult one to manœuvre in. A road from the Malakand ran to Kalangai on the Swat river, eight miles east of Loe Agra, and a motorable track ran from Dargai eastwards to Kot. Otherwise there are no routes for vehicles. Brigadier the Hon. H. R. L. G. Alexander (now Field-Marshal Viscount Alexander) was ordered to take his Nowshera Brigade and clear up the situation at Agra. At Dargai, at the foot of the Malakand range, he changed from wheel to pack transport, and struck across the hills for Khar on the Swat river, intending to reach Kalangai next day, whence he hoped to march straight away to Loe Agra over several passes. The troops consisted of the Duke of Wellington's, 5th/12th (Guides), and the 3rd/2nd Punjabis—the fourth battalion, the 2nd/15th Punjabis, having been diverted to Kot from Dargai to get the road up to Loe Agra, or rather Bargholai, improved. With the Brigade was the 4th Mountain Battery. There was a detachment of the 1st/4th Gurkhas at Kalangai, and there the Brigadier went, taking with him the Os.C. Guides and 1st/4th Gurkhas. He had planned to start from Kalangai the next morning, the 23rd, and march through to Loe Agra.

To do this it was essential to secure a high point north of the Hurmalo pass, and the detachment of the Gurkhas at Kalangai were to do this on the morning of the 23 February and establish a strong picquet. It was believed that no enemy were about. While the Gurkhas were carrying out this, the Nowshera Brigade were advancing to Kalangai, but as it happened the enemy had occupied point 4020, the high feature, and the small party of Gurkhas were held up. A company of the Guides was the advanced guard of the Brigade. As it came up it was ordered to work its way round the enemy's left, taking with it a section of the 4th Battery. Despite this support, the company was unable to make much progress, and the enemy were visible in considerable numbers. The rest of the Guides were now ordered forward with two companies of the Duke of Wellington's to cover their right, while aircraft were to support them. The Guides were now able to carry their objective, with the loss of one man killed and two wounded. The picquet was completed and occupied by dusk and the rest of the force returned to Kalangai. The Brigadier now realized that his advance must be deliberate and next day, the 24th, was spent in building more picquets on the road to Agra and improving the track as much as possible. This was done in two columns, the Guides advancing on the Hurmalo pass, a company of the 3rd/2nd Punjabis moving on the left, while the Brigade moved up the valley. Two picquets of that corps were established on the Yariliali pass, there being no opposition, the troops returning to camp, where they were fired upon.

On the 25th the Brigade was able to march straight to Loe Agra, finding the road atrocious but having no other difficulties. Loe Agra, a large, scattered village, was found to be deserted; but the inhabitants soon began to return. Next day was spent in making the road down to the Jindai Khwar, on the way to Bargholai, while Mr. Best, the political agent, a very distinguished officer, interviewed the tribal jirga. He said that a levy post must be established at once at Agra with forty local men with a nucleus of twenty Swat levies. A strong stone-built house was at once arranged for this purpose till a regular post could be built. The Brigade now marched back to British India; *en route* a battalion surrounded Kanoli in daylight, there finding seven men whom the Political Agent wanted. A night of sniping was followed by a continuation of the return march to Nowshera. The Faqir had been driven north of the Swat, and it was not advisable to disturb the hornet's nest of Bajaur. Yet little punishment had been inflicted, as the sequel shows. Among raiding tribes and especially among fanatics Essex's dictum "Stone dead hath no fellow" was the only cure, and there had been few tribal dead.

THE SECOND EXPEDITION TO LOE AGRA

A small portion of the Brigade on its return to cantonments was at once told off as a flying column to act if need be at the shortest notice. But the peace was to be a very short one, for the Faqir, not having lost enough men, began at once collecting new lashkars and the very day that the Brigade got back came a report of their doings. By the 5th came the news that the Faqir of Alangir had again crossed the Swat with the intention of burning Loe Agra. His deputy, Faghfur, on the night of the 5/6 March had seized the Agra Levy Post, the jirga having sent off the Swat levies to Kalangai as they could not oppose the strong lashkar. The flying column, the 3rd/2nd Punjabis with two mountain guns and two medium howitzers, moved off at once (6 March), reaching Kot at dawn on the 7th, reconnoitring towards Bargholai. By the 8th the whole Brigade was at Kot, and to put a stop to the sniping of the night of the 7th, the Punjabis organized a very good ambush. One killed and four wounded, of whom two died, was the bag, with no casualties among the troops—a useful little lesson to snipers. On the early morning of the 10th the column moved off to Agra once more, leaving the Duke of Wellington's at Bargholai to simplify the rationing. The Guides seized Naranji Banda on the left of the Agra pass and the high point 4870, and this enabled the Brigade to enter Agra unmolested, the Faqir clearing out.

It was not a very satisfactory result, for only dead men could wipe out the impertinent insult of his return, but the levy post was re-established and strengthened and the jirga's morale stimulated. On the 16th the Brigade withdrew to Kot and thence to Nowshera, but this time leaving a whole battalion, the 3rd/2nd Punjabis, at Bargholai with four mountain guns and the two 6-inch howitzers. The 2nd Duke's were now at Kot on their way to Nowshera from Bargholai, which they had held for a few days.

The Third Episode

So much for the restored British prestige, which did not amount to anything very great, for five days later another stormy petrel, Badshah Gul I, eldest son of our old friend the Haji of Turangzai, the Mohmand, with a small following, arrived in the Utmanzai country just across the Swat river, with inflammatory posters—"La Illa Ha ! the Faith is in danger." "Join the sacred lashkars !" "Don't listen to the Elders." "Fie, Fie, Grey beards must die," and the little drums rolled once more up all the valleys and the Upper Bajauris promised men.

In the camp at Bargholai the 3rd/2nd Punjabis had only just taken over from the Duke of Wellington's, who were back at Kot and had not yet left for Nowshera. The Brigade Commander at Nowshera ordered that Agra must be denied to the Faqir by artillery fire, news having come that he had recrossed the Swat on 21 April. The 2nd Duke of Wellington's therefore moved forward again to Bargholai, leaving only a rifle company and the machine guns in Kot. On this, the 3rd/2nd Punjabis moved forward, accompanied by two mountain guns, and took up a position on the high ridge about two miles north of Bargholai and proceeded to put the ridge in a state of defence, returning the next day to Bargholai, leaving a rifle company in a strong post—Qila Hari—at point 4768. On 26 March the Bargholai column again occupied the ridge, trailing their coats in the hope of being attacked. By 23 April more of the enemy had crossed the Swat and were trying to hem in Loe Agra. On the 26th the ridge was again occupied in force and the Qila Hari picquet relieved. The force, however, was not yet strong enough to advance on Loe Agra, and it withdrew in the afternoon after shelling enemy bodies. By 1400 hours next day came news that the levies who had been opposing the lashkars' advance at the Ghund pass had withdrawn and the enemy were close to Agra. Next day the ridge, a good post of observation, was again occupied in force till the afternoon.

That night a fierce and determined attack was made on the Qila Hari picquet. At about 1700 hours bugle calls were sounded from several points round Agra and considerable hostile bodies were seen on the move.

At 1915 hours *dhols* could be heard beating below the Qila Hari and shortly after a rush of yelling swordsmen attacked the picquet, even crouching under the sangars and seizing the rifle barrels of the Punjabis inside. Fighting was now intensely close and fierce with stones, revolvers, and sabres on locking ring. The attack was largely defeated by the initiative of the stout-hearted subadar commanding the picquet, who was unfortunately mortally wounded. Fire from the guns in Bargholai helped the garrison and eventually the assailants were beaten off, with the loss of some 28 killed and many wounded. The picquet's losses were less than might have been expected, amounting to a V.C.O. who died of his wounds and 11 O.R. killed and 7 wounded. The Bargholai troops came up next morning, relieved the picquet and, as wire had arrived, proceeded to wire the posts. One I.O.R. of the Punjabis was wounded, but the enemy were fairly quiet, licking their wounds after their repulse. The rest of the Nowshera Brigade was now called up, the Guides arriving at Kot on the 8th, one company proceeding at once to Bargholai. By the 9th the Brigade was concentrated at Bargholai, the 1st/4th Bombay Grenadiers from the Peshawar Brigade taking over Kot.

On 8 April a company of the Guides took over the Qila Hari picquet and next day the force advanced on Agra, the Guides attacking the Agra pass. By 1500 hours the village of Agra was in our hands, but a serious tragedy occurred when Mr. Best, who was leading the levies on the right rear of the Guides, was killed and several of the levies wounded, by tribesmen hidden in some crops. There had been considerable firing from all sides, but by dusk the enemy had disappeared. Political controls were now fully established and Agra was in future to be held by a disciplined force of eight platoons of Frontier Constabulary. Our total casualties were 3 killed, including Mr. Best, and 16 wounded, of whom 7 were men of the levies. The tribal losses were ascertained to have been 160 killed and probably as many wounded. This was enough to ensure quiet for a few years, and allow normal life to go on.

In a few days the Brigade for the third time returned to their cantonments. The whole episode is illustrative of the difficulties that Frontier problems present, especially with the Congress inflaming feeling and financing disturbances.

The Mohmand Rising of 1935

It was May 1935 when the third phase of the Loe Agra operation came to an end and it seemed that this part of the Frontier might expect some period of good behaviour among our tribes. But such was not to be for long, and the autumn was to see the widespread Mohmand rising for no sort of reason save the machinations of Congress and the old cry of the Muslim zealots. It was in these operations that was to occur that heavy fighting already alluded to, which was to gain the Guides Infantry great glory, but to cause them heavy loss.

This is the story in outline. During the Loe Agra operations the "upper" Mohmands were showing signs of unrest, the Haji of Turangzai and his three sons, Badshah Gul I,

II, and III, being the principal originators. We have just seen indeed that Badshah Gul I had come over to contribute to the Loe Agra trouble. The trouble began by their persuading the tribes not to surrender certain outlaws agreed on. Their defeat in 1933 had not been severe enough to produce a long effect on them and, basing themselves on Safi country in the north-east of the watershed of the Gandab valley, specially linked with outlawed Chimnai, they raided constantly into the Peshawar valley. As the attitude of the other tribes was reasonable, Government took the old-fashioned and effective step of launching a *barampta* against the Safis, Kandaharis, and some of the Utman Khel of Ambahar—that is to say, any men of these clans found in British territory were rounded up and held as hostages. As this did not produce any great effect, it was enforced again and some thirty-five Safis were now in the "jug." The Safis now demanded that the Haji of Turangzai should procure their release. On 11 May a full jirga of the "upper" Mohmands assembled to discuss the matter. The Haji declared that he would not turn out Chimnai and the other outlaws even if all the Safis died in jail. The situation, however, became awkward for the Haji. In July two of the "lower" Mohmand clans, the Burhan and Isa Khel, fell out over the matter of the distribution of the money for work on the road, and a small hostile gathering assembled near the road. Frontier Constabulary and Mohmand Khassadars were fired on and each day it was necessary to send a considerable party to the Karappa pass to support working parties. Military aid was now asked for, and each day a battalion from Peshawar, two guns and a section of armoured cars went out from the cantonment. By the beginning of August the hostile gathering had dispersed. Badshah Gul, however, now appeared in the Pindialli country east of the road within the "assured" area, apparently to satisfy the Safis, who were furious at the prolonged detention of their relatives. There were still a few hostile parties along the road, destroying telephone lines and the like, and eventually Badshah Gul I persuaded the Burhan Khel to destroy the road itself. But many of the clan wanted to get rid of Badshah Gul's intruders, knowing the trouble that would follow more folly. Badshah Gul, however, over-persuaded the younger men and brought some 1,400 men to destroy the road—young men of the Burhan Khel, the Isa Khel and the Safis—on the night of 14/15 August, a total which rose to close on 2,000 by the next day. The actual damage was carried out far down the road close to the frontier between Dand and the actual border, the work being covered by a strong tribal body against troops coming from Peshawar. The Peshawar Column at once moved out, being at Michni on the 15th. The next day it moved to Pir Qila half-way between Michni and Shabkadr, in case an incursion into British India was intended. In the meantime, many lashkars were joining the intruders basing themselves on the Pindialli country. The various lashkars were now heavily bombed and warning notices dropped on all concerned. This continued for four days while the military arrangements were being developed, the Nowshera Brigade being called up and arriving at Suban Khwa, north-east of Pir Qila, on the 21st.

2nd Mountain Battery. Squadron 18th Lancers. 2nd H.L.I. 5th/1st Punjabis. 1st/4th Grenadiers. 5th/10th Baluchis. Section of Armoured Cars. Section of Bengal Sappers.

66th Field Battery. 4th Mountain Battery. 2nd Duke of Wellington's. The Guides Infantry. 2nd/15th Punjabis. 3rd/2nd Punjabis (left in Nowshera till relieved).

The weather had been so bad after the Peshawar Brigade had reached Pir Qila that for the moment activity was impossible. It was now known that not only the "upper" and "lower" Mohmands were in the lashkars, but also numbers of Afghan Mohmands.

On the 18th and 20th the camp at Pir Qila was fired into. As the operations now promised to be considerable, the force was styled "Mohforce" and Brigadier C. Auchinleck, temporarily commanding the Peshawar Division in place of Major-General Muspratt, on leave in England, assumed command.

On the 23rd the force advanced to Kilagai, just over the border, surprising the enemy in the foothills and inflicting some loss, and at 0730 hours the Nowshera Brigade, which remained holding Kilagai hill, advanced through the Peshawar Brigade, who had been leading, and now headed the advance, with the Guides in front. Near Nelmena, on the Gandab river, a mile short of Dand, the resistance stiffened, especially on the flanks, and the country was most intricate and difficult and used up many troops to protect the route. The resistance from well-prepared ridges was considerable, but eventually, with the reserve and the 1st/4th Grenadiers lent from the Peshawar Brigade, supported by the 2nd and 4th Mountain Batteries, Dand and the hills around were carried. The troops had no time to form a perimeter camp, but were ordered to hold on to the ground they had gained. Camp picquets were attacked, especially one of the Guides. The rearguard of the Brigade did not get in till 2230 hours. Considering the amount of firing, the casualties were not heavy, Lieutenant A. C. S. Moore of the Guides being wounded, 5 I.O.Rs. killed and 2 V.C.Os. wounded with 4 B.O.R. and 14 I.O.Rs.[16] Sniping went on all night, and early in the morning 1 I.O.R. was killed and another wounded. The Peshawar Brigade had camped at Kilagai, a few miles back, and had had a quiet night. Tribal casualties were later computed at 40 killed and 54 seriously wounded. So far the difficulties had been more in the broken country, high hills and thick scrub rather than in the seriousness of the tribal resistance, but ahead the country grew more mountainous and there was the Karappa pass to be attained and permanently picqueted. A pleasing incident is related of a company of the Duke of Wellington's who were holding a picquet above Dand on 23 August and who could not get two of their sections in. A company of Guides under Lieutenant Rendall was sent to their aid, and when leaving gave up all their ammunition save five rounds per man, carried the British wounded down and then came up again with more ammunition, an act of camaraderie handsomely acclaimed in a letter from the O.C. the Duke's. The 24 August had to be devoted to getting square, repairing the road and establishing the L. of C. defences. Reconnaissances brought contact with the enemy, but the action was principally of artillery. Next day the force advanced on Ghalanai, the well-known camp on the Gandab, across the Karappa. The Nowshera Brigade was to make the advance to within a mile of the pass, after which the Peshawar Brigade would go through to secure the pass itself. The enemy, severely handled on the 23rd, were not much *en evidence*,

---

[16] The Guides' loss being 1 O.R. killed and 7 wounded.

OPERATIONS NORTH OF THE KHAIBER, 1933-1935

but a considerable accession of fresh lashkars was reported in the Saligo Khwar to the north-west, where they were bombed and presented fresh artillery targets. Soon after noon the Karappa Kandao was occupied and the cavalry and light tanks galloped to Ghalanai, without incident, and by 1400 hours the Brigade had arrived too.

For some days now the defence of the life-line of the communications was the chief concern. The road had been damaged right up to the pass, but this was easily repaired. It is to be remembered that once a graded road is made, its destruction, save only such as troops can put right in a few hours, is hardly possible, except where it has been galleried or built up in a gorge. A road once made remains and an example is the old Buddhist road over the Malakand, which was discovered and reopened during the storming of that ridge in 1895. All this time, too, there were some dealings with the "lower" Mohmand jirgas, who did not like what they had been let in for, and the houses of recalcitrant maliks were bombed. Even the "upper" Mohmands were uncertain and dreaded the extension of the road beyond the Yusaf Khel of the 1933 expedition. The Faqir of Alingar had gone to Afghanistan for more ammunition, only to find that Afghan commissioners were talking very straight to the Afghan Mohmands who had come over the "assumed line." Chimnai, the notorious outlaw, already mentioned among the stormy petrels, had met his end in a quarrel with an "upper" Mohmand, to everyone's relief. Outlaws really are no asset or support to tribes even when belligerent. While work was going on, the brigades made various reconnaissances, with minor collisions.

On 3 September, however, a large operation was staged towards the Khappak Kandao, four or five miles east of the Nahakki, up the Toratigga valley, which led over the hills to the valleys on the west. This brought on a good deal of firing from villages, but while much information needed was gained, the force had only eight casualties to some sixty of the enemy. But the troops were followed up fairly viciously as they marched to camp. After the rearguard had got in, the enemy attacked at Sangar hill and another, and the 5th/1st Punjabis, who had been in camp, were ordered to turn out and drive them away, but not to get involved. They succeeded in inflicting several casualties with no loss to themselves; but the Ghalanai camp was fired into all night. Next day the troops again moved out before dawn to clear and if possible surprise the sniping knots round the camp, and the Guides were moved up from Dand to Ghalanai in case help was needed. Nothing particular occurred except the finding of a few of the tribal casualties of the day before, who belonged to Badshah Gul's following.

The following immediate awards were made to the Guides for their hard day's fighting on the 23rd—one I.O.M. and three I.D.S.Ms.

Subadar Rur Singh—the I.O.M. for conspicuous gallantry and leadership right through the day.

No. 9378 Sepoy Dheru—the I.D.S.M. for outstanding courage and disregard of danger, and bringing in a wounded N.C.O. left lying in an exposed position.

Havildar Major Lal Mast—the I.D.S.M. for conspicuous gallantry in bringing up ammunition, whom a wound did not deter.

Havildar Daya Ram—the I.D.S.M. for gallantry and devotion to duty in charge of an independent section of machine guns.

Across the Nahakki Pass

The proclamation, that how far the troops would proceed beyond Ghalanai depended on the behaviour of the tribes, having produced no effect, the plans for proceeding over the Nahakki pass and extending the road now went ahead. The Air Force and the Political control were now put under the Military Authorities and what might be a major campaign catered for, and Mohforce was separated from the Peshawar divisional command.

The Nowshera Brigade advanced to Katsai, some four miles beyond Ghalanai, and the Gandab valley on 11 September without any special incident save that the camp at Katsai was heavily fired into that night. The 2nd Brigade from Rawalpindi and the 3rd from Jhelum were on their way up now to provide defence for the daily lengthening line of communications. From the 12th to the 14th the troops carried out reconnaissances and beat up the sniping lashkars, with no particular incidents.

Water supply was now to be the difficulty, for the column had two thousand mules in the leading brigade alone, and it was necessary to bring a pipe line for several miles, a very great feat in such a country.

On the 17th at 2330 hours the advance on the Nahakki pass commenced by the Peshawar Brigade, followed one and a half hours later by the Nowshera Brigade ; and by 0445 hours the high ground both right and left being secured with little opposition by the Guides and the 3rd/2nd Punjabis, by 0700 hours the H.L.I. had secured the actual pass and Force Headquarters moved up to the summit. That ended it, and by dusk the Peshawar Brigade were comfortably in camp east of Nahakki itself, the Nowshera Brigade at Wucha Jawar camp on the south side of the pass, where, *mirabile dictu*, the pipe line arrived at 1400 hours, while the 3rd Brigade had moved up the line to Ghalanai. A few parties of the enemy were engaged north of the Nahakki during the day.

The next ten days passed in making the road, erecting the road picquet posts and in reconnaissances, with no important events.

The Famous Fight of the Guides Infantry, 29 September 1935

The weeks had now rolled on to the end of September. The road over the Nahakki pass was nearly finished, to the great chagrin of the tribes to the north, whose *purdah* (veil) was now permanently lifted, and it was time to try and "take tea" properly with the "upper" Mohmands and their supporters from Bajour and Afghanistan. It was necessary to so harry the lashkars that all the tribes would pray for peace and conditions. The striking part of the force, now numbering three brigades, was either camped at Nahakki itself in the open beyond the ridge of mountains that ran east and west or in the neighbourhood. Some were at Nahakki and some camped at Wucha Jawar camp half a mile on the south side of the Nahakki pass and the same distance north of the village of the former name.

The bulk of the lashkars seemed to be either about Muzi Kor, some three miles west-north-west of Nahakki, or else in and beyond the hills some four miles west of the Nahakki pass. It was believed that the bulk of them were about Muzi Kor.

It was proposed that the Peshawar Brigade from Nahakki with the 18th Cavalry should tackle the Muzi Kor lot on the 29th, while the Nowshera Brigade from Wucha Jawar should move up the valley of that name and secure the Nahakki range and also seize a high point, 4080, some four miles west of the camp, at the head of the Wucha Jawar valley. From this point they could look down to the more open country on the far side of the range by Zanawar China.

It should perhaps be explained here that three miles west of the Nahakki pass this lofty, rocky range culminates at point 4080 and turns sharp to the south, while three-quarters of a mile north of 4080 a big spur runs north in the direction of Muzi Khor. South of the Wucha Jawar Khor another range breaks off east from point 4080. That is to say that the hills north, west and south of the Wucha Jawar form a long U, lying west and east, with the bottom curve about 4080.

The southern arm of the U was to be guarded by the 3rd Brigade. Now the Wucha Jawar camp had been steadily fired into for several nights, and to add to the effect of the morrow's battle, and stop this nuisance, a very successful ambush was laid by the 1st/14th Punjabis to the south of the southern leg of the U, which resulted in the snipers losing 8 killed and 14 wounded without any cost to the five platoons of the unit taking part (which belonged to the 3rd Brigade). The brigades were to start early on the 29th and to be in position by daylight, the main operation being the prospective but problematical tea-taking with the lashkars by the Peshawar Brigade and 18th Cavalry, supported by the 3rd Light Battery.

The Nowshera Brigade marched at 0200 hours to be in their position by 0600 hours; their right battalion, the 2nd/15th Punjabis, were to hold point 3838, a mile and a half west of the Nahakki pass, and to work along the spur already referred to that ran north towards Muzi Kor, and the Guides were to move up the valley and climb on to the ridge west of 3838 and thence seize 4080.

The 3rd/2nd Punjabis were to hold a line across the Wucha Jawar, a mile and a half west of the camp, thus forming a strong support in rear of the Guides and 2nd/15th. The 3rd Brigade was to form a line across the valley leading to the Khappak Kandao and secure the hills south of the Wucha Jawar so far as a point some 1,200 yards due south of 4080. This brigade was in position according to programme, but its infantry were not engaged, though considerable numbers of tribesmen were seen moving up the valley towards 4203, close on a mile south of 4080. These were shelled. The force had a very strong body of artillery at its disposal; the Peshawar Brigade being accompanied by the 22nd Mountain Brigade (less one battery), and the 3rd Brigade by the 7th Field and 13th Mountain Batteries, while the Artillery Commander had a force artillery of the 4th and 66th Field and 15th Medium Batteries, primarily for the support of the Nowshera Brigade.

Nowshera Brigade Headquarters and also Mohforce Headquarters were both established a little west of point 3838 on the Nahakki ridge a mile and a half west of the pass. The command of Mohforce had been assumed five days before by Major-General Muspratt of the Peshawar Division, on his return from leave, and Brigadier Auchinleck had resumed that of the Peshawar Brigade.

THE DETAIL OF THE GUIDES' FIGHT

It is now time to trace in detail the story of the Guides this day,[17] on whom by mere chance fell the principal action of this expedition and the opportunity to inflict heavy loss on the enemy, despite their own serious casualties. By 0400 hours the battalion (only 370 strong), with no other support, were at the foot of the spur leading up to point 138367, hereafter known as the "Teeth," where their share of the protection of the Peshawar Brigade's left was taken up from the 2nd/15th Punjabis. The ascent was a very steep one and everything had to be handled by men in a climb, unexpectedly unopposed, of several hundred feet. This was made by "B" Company under Lieutenant Hamilton, who occupied "Teeth," some 1,000 yards from 4080. In the meantime Major Good, temporarily in command, had led the rest of the battalion along the base of the hills and sent "C" Company up the next spur to secure a bump known as "Nipple." This was attained, one shot only being fired in the dusk and the man taken prisoner.[18] Major Good, coming up to "Nipple," now ordered a halt to allow of "C" and "A" behind them to close up, after the long, difficult climb. Nos. 9 and 10 Platoons with a machine-gun section were to stay at "Nipple" and support the advance; the balance of "C" under Hon. Lieutenant Shadi Khan, closely followed by Lieutenant Rendall and "A" Company, moved on 4080 at 0550 hours. "Nipple" was about 700 yards' range from 4080, but a good deal longer by the spur. It was realized as the day began to dawn that the ridge leading from "Teeth" to 4080 was a knife edge along which men could only go in single file. "C" Company, less the party left at "Nipple," advanced another 300 yards to take up a position at another bump, "Pimple," and cover the advance of "A" to secure 4080. There was now fire from that hill, but not exceptional, though it gradually increased. It should be noted that up to now the operation had been carried out with some skill but no opposition. Lieutenant Rendall now led forward with considerable difficulty and intrepidity Nos. 3 and 4 Platoons to secure 4080, only some 400 yards ahead. By 0615 hours, under what was now considerable fire, the east side of 4080 was gained by Rendall. Major Good was with the balance of "A" Company (Nos. 1 and 2 Platoons), and by 0645 was established to the left of Lieutenant Rendall's Nos. 3 and 4 Platoons, on the slope trending south-west, and trying hard to keep down the heavy fire now coming from point 4198, some 800 yards south of 4080. As it got lighter the enemy fire came from all directions. The faces of 4080 were fairly precipitous and contained many caves in which the enemy had been sleeping, who had now hurried into action. Good, seeing he could not advance farther with but two platoons, ordered up the two platoons of "C" at the "Nipple" (Nos. 11 and 12), who came into position on the left of Nos. 1 and 2 Platoons. Captain Meynell, the Adjutant, had now joined the two forward platoons (Nos. 3 and 4) to find Lieutenant Rendall had been killed and a terrific struggle was in progress, and he assumed command. These two platoons were now practically surrounded, tribesmen hurrying up and fire very heavy from surrounding spurs. The din was considerable, for besides the crack of the rifles there was the far

---

[17] 29 September, 1935.
[18] This fact entirely contradicts the scandalous newspaper charge of "surprise."

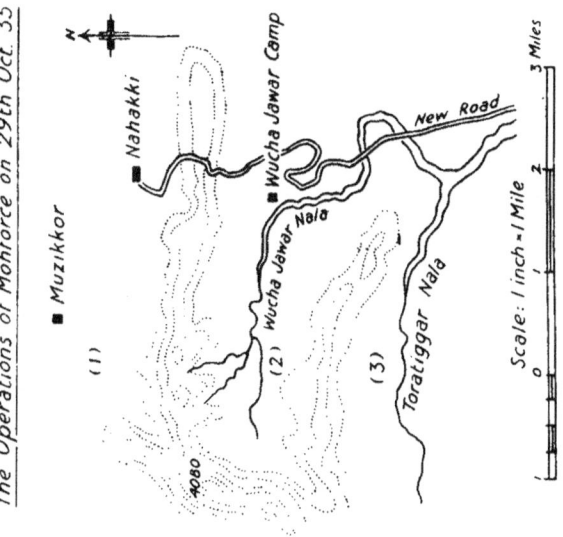

The Operations of Mohforce on 29th Oct. 35

(1) Area of Peshawar Brigade
(2) Area of Nowshera Brigade
    Duke of Wellington's Regt.
    3/2nd Punjab Regt.
    5/12th FF Regt (Guides Infantry)
    2/15th Punjab Regt
(3) Area held by the 3rd Infantry Brigade

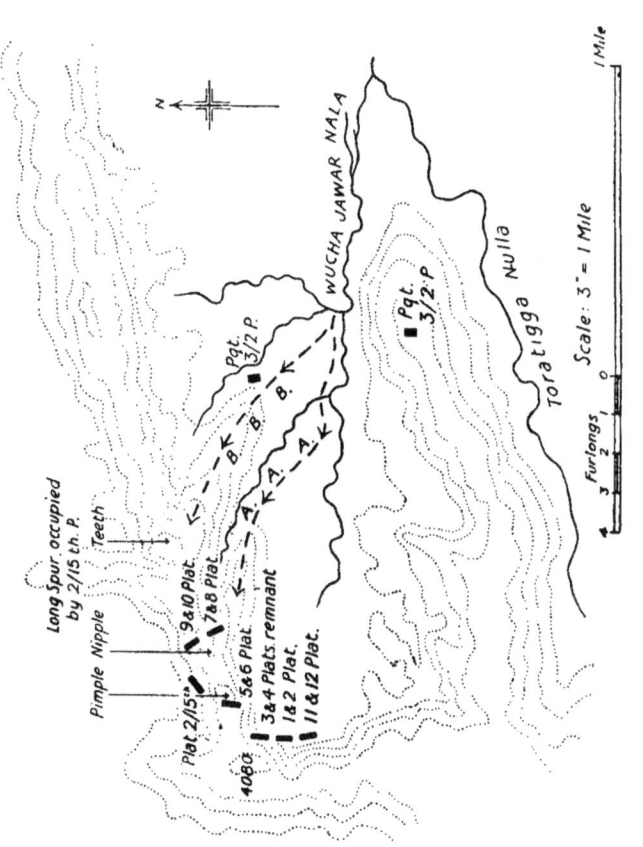

Hand Sketch showing the attack of The Guides Infantry on Hill 4080 Sept 29th 1935 reached by Platoons 3 & 4 but subsequently driven off.

B.B.B.   Original advance of B Coy.
A.A.A.   Advance of A & C. Coys (C. leading)

louder noise of enemy bullets and our own striking the rocks, and the position was a fair inferno.

Now, if ever, was the occasion for artillery support and there were several batteries waiting. Unfortunately, Lieutenant N. P. Tyler, of the 3rd Light Battery, and Second-Lieutenant R. E. T. Keeling, the F.O.Os. of the Field and Medium Artillery, with many of their party, were also hit, and word to the artillery headquarters could not be sent. As the sun rose, a helio without a stand was set up, but rocks and ridge prevented connection. However, a signaller with a shutter got through to Hamilton at "Teeth" with "B" Company, and he brought up (0730 hours) two platoons (Nos. 5 and 6) to "Nipple," he and five of his men being wounded. There he met Captain Doherty, the regimental Medical Officer at the R.A.P., from whom he learnt something of the situation and at once went towards "Pimple." The signaller with Good who had contacted him was killed just as he had started a message to the 2nd/15th for help, but this battalion had got one platoon over, who were able to join Nos. 7 and 8 Platoons at the "Nipple."

Hamilton was now able to join Nos. 5 and 6 Platoons at "Pimple" and hold on despite his wound (till 1100 hours). The work being done by Captain Doherty at "Nipple" in collecting not only the wounded but the large number injured in crossing the spur, and getting up to 4080, was at a very high level of devotion.

The Overwhelming of Nos. 3 and 4 Platoons

The above, then, was the general situation at 0800 hours. Now, however, the enemy, increasing every minute, after prolonged, bitter and often hand-to-hand fighting with Nos. 3 and 4 Platoons on the edge of the top of 4080 that they had so brilliantly gained, surrounded and overwhelmed them. Meynell, too, had been killed after performing prodigies of valour and command, and the two platoons were wiped out save a few who got through to Major Good's position, which was now entirely overlooked by the enemy at close range.

At Brigade Headquarters[19] there was no information of what was going on, and signal communications when the sun rose could not be opened, chiefly because of intervening features. The Artillery Commander having no request, from the sad circumstances narrated, and having heard that the Guides had got to 4080, dared not open fire on it without some details from the Brigade or Good, but was only too anxious to give support.

Hamilton, at "Pimple," had consolidated his position with Nos. 5 and 6 Platoons and the platoons of the 2nd/15th, and the two platoons of "B" Company (Nos. 7 and 8) now at "Nipple" also were in a position to assist Major Good's remnants. Good himself had now been wounded and realized that there was nothing to do but to withdraw the platoons, as this would not now affect the security of the left of the Peshawar Brigade.

A pathetic yet glorious account of the destruction of the wounded was given by the Artillery F.O.O. attached to the 3rd/2nd Punjabis. He saw, after the firing on 4080 had ceased, ten of the enemy go down to where the dead and wounded Guides lay. They started picking up the rifles, when five Guides attempted to get to their feet;

---

[19] Brigadier The Hon. H. R. L. G. Alexander (Field-Marshal and Viscount) was away in hospital, and the O.C. The Duke of Wellington's was temporarily in command.

one a British officer. A signaller, propped against a rock, started to flash a lamp. The wounded men put up a good fight and at least one of the tribesmen went down. The British officer got on a rock and defended himself with a clubbed rifle, but was bayoneted with three of the others. A fifth was led away. No more pathetic tale has ever been told.

The Withdrawal of the Guides

Hamilton, at "Nipple," had been trying to get the Brigade, sending signal messages and a runner, but neither got through. At 0915 another F.O.O. arrived at "Nipple" from the artillery, and an hour later the long-needed but now too late bombardment of 4080 began and lasted an hour, no doubt causing losses till the tribes went to earth in the caves. At 1100 hours Hamilton had to be evacuated, but on the way he met Lieutenant Campbell, who had arrived at Wucha Jawar camp to join the Battalion a couple of hours earlier. Having heard of the situation, he then took command of the part of the Battalion at "Pimple" and "Nipple" and carried out the withdrawal, which was unmolested owing to artillery fire and the very severe losses the Guides had inflicted. Light tanks in the valley now supported them also, and so the Guides, exultant but sad —for never before had they left British officers' bodies in enemy hands, let alone a large number of their rank and file—returned to camp.

At Brigade Headquarters[20] it was not till 0800 hours that any firing even was heard from the direction of 4080. As some broken bits of news trickled through regarding what was an entirely unlooked-for situation, the Brigade Commander went to the 2nd/15th to see if they had any news, but it only amounted to the report that the Guides had taken 4080 and had been driven off. At 0945 hours he asked Force Headquarters to place the whole of the 2nd/15th at his disposal to extricate the Guides, though that was now hardly necessary, and he brought up a company of the Duke of Wellington's with machine-gun companies to help cover the withdrawal.

In the meantime the Peshawar Brigade had finished their operations early, without, however, any successful major *five-o-cloqer* with the tribes, the principal events being action by the cavalry in the open ground east of Muzi Kor and shelling of enemy parties in the distance. The Brigade had commenced its return at 1000 hours and, hearing of the difficulties of the Guides, detached the 1st/4th Grenadiers to assist them. Hamilton's and Campbell's extrications of the platoons on "Pimple" and "Nipple," however, had made this unnecessary. The Brigade had neither been able to inflict major casualties nor had to endure them, but the fact that the British troops went where they liked among the tribal ground was not without good effect.

It was some little time before the exact facts were known at Army Headquarters,[21]

---

[20] They do not seem to have been able to ensure touch with the 370-strong Guides.

[21] Another point is worthy of record. A military journal published an entirely inaccurate account of the happening which missed all the main facts and the determination displayed. It, however, when better informed, published a handsome expression of regret, with a brief but forceful account showing what did happen. Unfortunately, the English Press had also published this suggestion that the Guides were "surprised." If anyone was surprised it would appear to have been the Brigade and the Force Intelligence. *The Times*, however, soon published the correct story. The official account has some criticisms as to the want of cohesion in the handling and disposal of the Peshawar Brigade. Sir James Grigg, in *Prejudices and Judgements*, repeats the original canard.

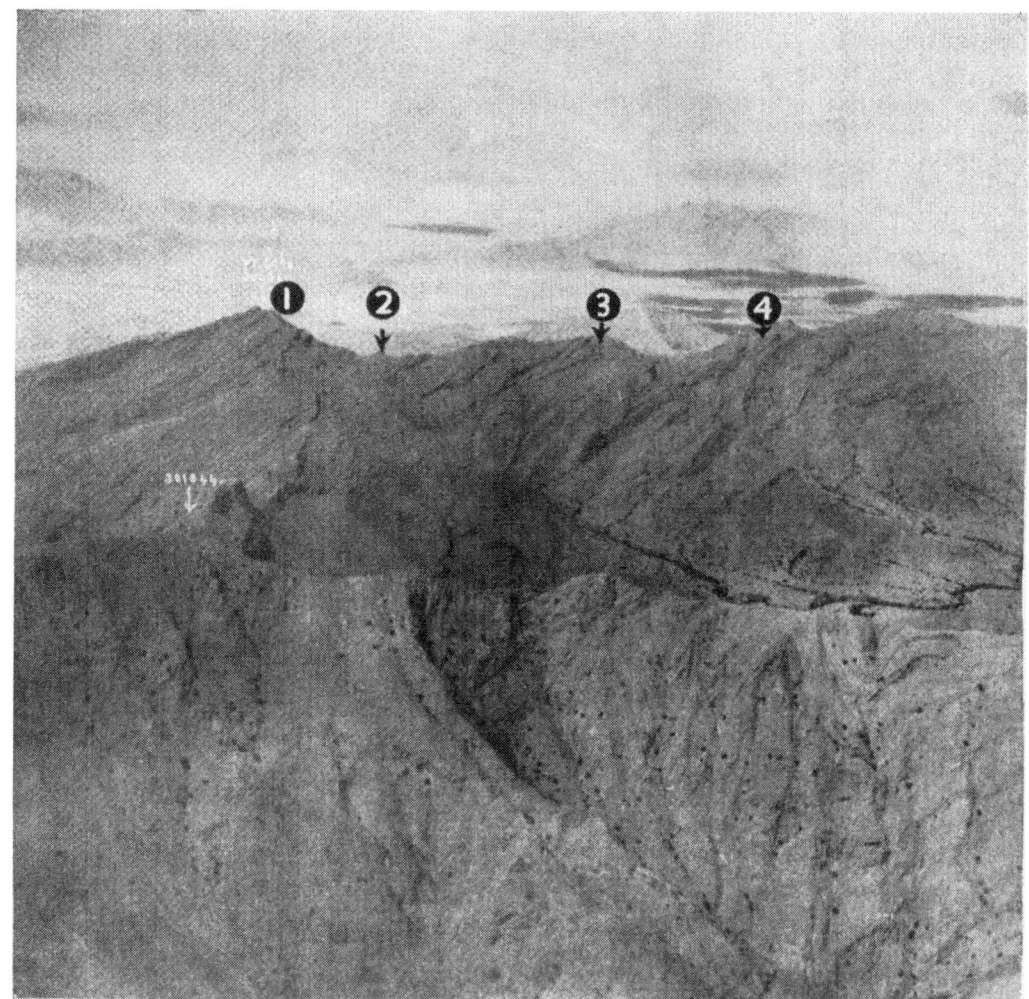

[Photo: R.A.F. Official, Crown Copyright Reserved

HILL 4080 FROM THE AIR

1 = Hill 4080
2 = "Pimple"
3 = "Nipple"
4 = "Teeth"

The Attack of the Guides on Hill 4080, 29 September 1935

CAPTAIN GODFREY MEYNELL, V.C., M.C.

but when they were, General Sir Philip Chetwode, the Commander-in-Chief, at once sent the following wire to General Wigram, commanding the Northern Army:

> *"From Chief, 4 October. Please deliver following personal message from me to Comdg. 5/12 F.F. Regt. (Guides). It took me some days to get reliable account of action in which your distinguished regiment unfortunately lost so many gallant soldiers. I have now heard particulars and as I fully expected conduct of your regiment confronted by overwhelming odds has added great honour to your already fine war record. I congratulate the Regiment while sympathising with them on the losses they have sustained."*

This was soon followed by the issue of immediate rewards by the Chief to survivors. A posthumous Victoria Cross was awarded to the glorious memory of Captain Meynell.

Major Good received also a very cordial and congratulatory letter from H.E. the Governor of the Frontier Province, Sir R. Griffith, who specially dwelt on the devastating loss suffered by the enemy on 4080—far greater, he opined, than admitted. The eagerness of the jirgas to throw in their hand he attributed to this.

The Battalion was soon brought up to strength: Captain A. N. Marshall from the 10th F.F.R. and Lieutenants V. W. Tregar and A. B. E. Wall from the 3/R.F.F.R., with men from the training Battalion and from other F.F. Regiments, while Major Knight took over the command.

The Losses and Rewards of the Guides

We must now look at the casualties sustained by the Guides Infantry and mourn their grievous loss as well as rejoice at the honours bestowed on them. Their attempt and fight had indeed done more to bring the tribes to their senses than any other feature of this arduous expedition.

First we have the two British officers killed—Captain Meynell and Lieutenant A. P. S. Rendall—with 2 V.C.Os. and 19 O.Rs., and 8 missing; then, wounded, Major S. B. Good, Lieutenant G. J. Hamilton, 2 V.C.Os. and 39 O.Rs.; a total of 21 killed, 8 missing and 43 wounded—72 casualties in all besides 37 injured from falls (5 prisoners, 3 Muslims and 2 Sikhs, were recovered later).

Careful collection of evidence eventually elicited that the tribes lost 144 certain, of whom half were killed, and on this day most of these losses were in those opposing the Guides.

So the Force's intention of inflicting severe casualties was attained, if not quite in the tactical manner planned. To quote the great Napoleon's diagnosis of the course of a fight, "On s'engage, et on voit."

The other losses to the force were as related: the two gunner officers, Lieutenant J. N. D. Tyler and Second-Lieutenant R. E. T. Keelan, wounded; and of the 3rd Light Battery, 1 B.O.R. killed and 1 wounded and 1 I.O.R. killed and 1 wounded; 1 I.O.R. of the 2nd/15th was wounded, and with the Peshawar Brigade 1 man of the 18th Cavalry wounded. The platoons engaged on 4080 numbered 4 B.Os., 5 V.C Os. and 130 O.Rs. Only 1 V.C.O. and 32 O.Rs. came out unharmed.

THE GUIDES

The End of the Campaign

The first thing to be done after the 29th was to recover those wounded believed to be prisoners.

The jirgas had been uncertain for some little time and after the 29th were ready to chuck their hands in, only bargaining for such easements as they could get. The Political Officers were in touch with the Halimzai jirgas, and on 1 October a full jirga of all the tribes had assembled and an urgent message was sent that they and the Musa Khel maliks should go at once to the Khwaezai country and arrange to bring in any dead and all wounded prisoners. The very next day, 30 September, brought word that the now anxious lashkar agreed. During the next three days six prisoners and the bodies of Captain Meynell, Lieutenant Rendall and 1 B.O.R. and 21 I.O.Rs. were brought in.

In the meantime, on 1 October, a fully representative jirga of all the tribes came in and on the 2nd were interviewed by the G.O.C. and his Political Agent.

The terms announced were not severe. In brief they ran :

(1) All lashkars to disperse immediately and tribal hostilities to cease.
(2) The Military road on to Kamali over the Nahakki pass to be completed without interference.
(3) The tribes must enter into friendly negotiations and be responsible for the misdeeds of all outlaws and bad characters against Government or its friends.
(4) Government would be free from any previous conditions they had accepted and would come and go when they liked, but no fines or hostages would be exacted.

On 5 November 1935 the Guides Infantry marched into Mardan, to be greeted by all the officers of the Cavalry, the ladies of the Corps and the Viceroy's commissioned officers, the roads being lined by the Boy Scouts and local school children. On 22 November the G.O.C.-in-Chief, Northern Army, arrived to distribute the decorations for the fight at 4080. The Corps formed a hollow square, the Cavalry on one flank and the Infantry in the centre and on the opposite flank. Those present to receive their decorations were :

The Distinguished Service Order.
    Captain J. H. Doherty, I.M.S. (attached).
    Lieutenant G. H. Hamilton.

Indian Order of Merit.
    Subadar Rur Singh.
    Havildar Yusaf Khan.

Indian Distinguished Service Medal.
    Havildar Lal Mast.
    Havildar Fateh Khan.
    L./Naik Munshi Ram.
    Sig. Gurdial Singh.
    Sig. Guncha Gul.

The posthumous award of the Victoria Cross to Captain G. Meynell has already been mentioned.

CHAPTER V

THE WAZIRISTAN CAMPAIGNS, 1936–1937

THE STORY OF WAZIRISTAN—WAZIRISTAN SINCE 1920—TRIBAL ECONOMICS—THE FAQIR OF IPI AND THE ISLAM BIBI—OPERATIONS IN THE LOWER KHAISORA—25, 26 AND 27 NOVEMBER 1936—THE GUIDES AT ZERPEZAI—THE ADVENTURES OF TOCOL—OPERATIONS AGAINST THE TORI KHEL (28 NOVEMBER TO 24 DECEMBER 1936—FEBRUARY TO APRIL 1937): NUMEROUS OUTRAGES—THE ATTACK IN FORCE ON THE RAZMAK CONVOY (APRIL 1937).

THE STORY OF WAZIRISTAN

THE Guides as a corps, whether cavalry or infantry, had had little to do with Waziristan in the earlier days. Yuzafzai and its frontiers had been their pigeon, and for those who have only served with the Corps of late years, some outline of the early story may be of interest, for it was not till 1935 that it came into their purview, save that some of their officers had served in the Militia, who were now called Scouts. In 1917, however, their 3rd Infantry Battalion had taken part in the very hard campaign that continued misbehaviour during the First World War had called for.

In Mogul days, when their Empire ran to the Oxus, the frontier hills were never controlled; the Gomal, the Tochi and Kurram routes were held, as was the Khaiber, militarily, to allow of safe passage by troops and traders. The enmity between tribesmen and troops was as ever, but with this difference, however much India disliked the Rohilla—viz., the tribesmen of the Frontier hills—it did not matter. The Raj was Muslim and the overcrowding in those hills which breed many and feed few, was eased by service in the Mogul forces, as with the British, and by the constant colonization of Indian lands. How deep is the memory of their origin in the minds of their descendants was realized by the writer when visiting the fortress of Doulatabad, in the Nizam's dominions, that hill fortress to which the sole access is by a rising tunnel of which the only defence is a charcoal furnace. It was garrisoned by a unit of the Nizam's Artillery, all of them were wearing shoulder-belts and Royal Artillery pouches! They were all Muslims and styled themselves Pathan—this one an Afridi, that one a Jowaki, another a Bhitanni, a fourth a Wazir and so forth—and they looked it too, though perhaps two hundred years and more had passed over their heads in India.

When the Sikhs expelled the Afghans from Mooltan, the Indus valley, Peshawar and Kashmir, their troops kept raiders at bay and they counter-raided. When the British came in 1849 they took over the same line and the same posts, organized their Frontier Force and their Border Military Police, but endeavoured to get on human terms with these very inhuman gentlemen of the hills—the most, perhaps, that they could do was to prevent the rape of Hindu traders' girls.

During the Mutiny the Frontier troops had gone to Delhi and the Bailey Guard (Lucknow), and the tribesmen's raids had exceeded the permissible number, so in 1863

Brigadier-General Sir Neville Chamberlain, the famous Indian soldier and Field-Marshal, led the first Mahsood-Wuzeerie (to use the old spelling) Expedition of punishment. Now the Mahsuds were and are swordsmen—not as the Afridi, who always (the Frontier will tell you) "shot at the strong and slashed at the weak"—and they fell on Sir Neville's camp at Palosin Ziarat, near Jandola, on the Takhi Zam, just before dawn, so that those who were to die might see the sunrise. There was a desperate struggle—perimeter camps were then unknown; the attackers were beaten off, but both sides lost heavily. Then Chamberlain marched up through the Barari Tangi into the heart of their country. After this, for nearly twenty years the Waziris behaved, but the Afghan wars and the call of Islam were too much for them, and in 1881 another expedition entered the country and extracted some fines and short-lived contrition.

By now things were moving, and in 1892 the frontier between Afghanistan and the British sphere was agreed on. A Boundary Delimitation Commission was at work in 1894, escorted by a brigade. Encamped in open camp in Wazir territory at Wana, the scene of Palosin Ziarat was repeated. Hundreds of swordsmen rushed the picquets and camp, a desperate mêlée inside the camp followed, and it was perhaps the superb behaviour of the 20th Punjabis, who cleared the camp at the point of the bayonet, and the star shell of the Peshawar Mountain Battery, that restored the situation.

The attack on the Boundary Commission stimulated perhaps that fanatical unrest which was to culminate in the great Frontier rebellion of 1897, that broke out from Waziristan to the Malakand, in which all the tribes were involved, Wazirs, Orakzais, Afridis, Mohmands, Swatis, Bajauris. It began in the upper Tochi when a small column with a couple of guns were visiting Maizar in the Madar Khel territory in a friendly manner. Resting in Maizar with some undue carelessness, they were suddenly attacked on all sides by friendly visitors and only escaped after heavy loss and disorganization. A punitive expedition was necessary, and hardly had this got to its destination when the great storm broke which involved 70,000 troops.

It was after this, when a costly occupation of tribal territory caused some concern, that Lord Curzon devised his "Militia" system, already in existence in some parts of the border. The principle was to employ the young men of the tribes in disciplined and organized units under British officers, to maintain order in their own lands and incidentally earn a pleasant livelihood. This system, successful elsewhere, failed in Waziristan owing to the congenital unreliability of the Waziris, especially the Mahsuds, who had to be replaced by other frontier clans. This, of course, vitiated the principle of honourable employment inherent in the scheme.

Matters progressed fairly happily till the great disturbance of the First World War which, despite the loyal friendliness of the Amir Habibulla Khan, did not prevent Turkey's proclamation of *Jehad* from disturbing the clans.

By 1917 the outrages were so glaring that troops, mostly young troops, had to be sent beyond Tank. This was the occasion when the Viceroy gave a message to the Amir to say that he could no longer hold his hand, and the latter had replied to this effect, "I agree they are swine, but for my sake don't send too cruel a general."

The results were not very successful and in 1919 a large expedition under Sir

Andrew Skeen was necessary. Again the troops were young and the Mahsuds traded on this with fierce attacks. It was their undoing, for better troops had come up and they lost, for the first time in their history, very severely, and were in a very chastened state when the settlement came. The good effect lasted many years, while schemes for their human betterment went forward. It was after this that the Wana and Razmak brigade cantonments were established and the roads were made, which afforded profitable employment. Indeed, it was not till the drum ecclesiastic was rolling so fiercely on the Frontier, as just related, that the great Waziristan outbreak, in which the Guides Infantry were to be employed, took place in 1936-37.

Waziristan since 1920

The heavy fighting of the post-Afghan War period and the severe tribal losses throughout the whole of Waziristan have been referred to. The country was now pierced with motor roads, and considerable forces were stationed far up into the mountains. It is, of course, common knowledge that the main tribal division is into Mahsud clans and Wazir clans, the former the more implacable and the latter easier to control and handle. The Wazir clans are located north and west of the Mahsuds, and the general policy has been to make cantonments overlooking, but not in, Mahsud territory with the consent and good will of the Wazirs. Thus the central road from Bannu on the north-east runs to the Razmak plateau, headquarters of a brigade group, and then on to Wana on the west of the Mahsud territory. From Wana the motor road runs down to the frontier of the Derajat, making practically a large circle. But these roads must needs run through narrow gorges and difficult valleys and have to be protected by military and militia posts (the militia now called Scouts, which is not a very suitable designation for well-organized corps) and by the Khassadars or tribal levies under the control of the tribal head-men. So long as the tribes as a whole are quiet, protection against outlaws and bandits is fairly well maintained. *But*, and it is a large but, any failure in military alertness or soldierly habit usually finds its Nemesis.

Tribal Economics

To understand the recurring troubles which have existed through the ages, only palliated by the fact that the Muslim invader would usually enrol young tribesmen to eventually become colonists in India, some outline of the economic set-up is desirable. First and foremost is the disastrous fact that these frontier hills breed many and feed few, and that at basis is the whole story—breed many and feed few. Falstaff sums up the result effectively enough—"Young men must live and gor-bellied knaves with fat purses are fair game." The tribesman must raid or starve, unless employment can be found for him, so he raids into India. Lord Curzon started the theory that if employed in an honourable career in a Militia to guard the trade routes and suppress the *mauvais sujets*, the object would be to some extent attained. But, alas! the faithlessness of the Mahsud and Wazir, especially the former, brought this experiment to an end. These charming lads, like some of the Irish, will take you shooting with enthusiasm one day and shoot you the next—so the Militia were reorganized from more reliable people.

Then to employ the young men in India is not very feasible, for India hates them. In the Army the same unreliability has, save for war-time enlistments, had the same results. The growing oblivion of the lessons of 1920, the desire of the young men for something exciting, the decline of employment on the roads, and the short commons of the mountain-side, all contributed to a *milieu* in which the fanaticism of a new firebrand, the Faqir of Ipi, could thrive. When to other troubles you can add the ferment of fanatical Islam there is occasion for a flare-up that only the machine gun can cope with. The cries of "La Illah ha, il Allah ho" (There is no God but Allah), and "Allah! Allah! Allah ho Akhbar," and the rub-a-dub of the drum, can set a whole countryside in a blaze. The Faqir's chief activities as yet were in the Lower Khaisora among the Tori Khel Wazirs. The headmen found life and allowances good enough, but their young men were defiant. To strengthen the hands of the Maliks it was arranged that the Razmak Brigade and a force from Bannu should march up and down the Khaisora, and meet at Bichkekashkai, and there announce to the Maliks that in return for extra allowances our patrols must be free to move in the Lower Khaisora and be protected. This was at first happily arranged and the column returned. But the settlement was by no means acceptable to the Faqir and the group of malcontents he influenced.

Except for a little sniping with hostile tribesmen, the above operations were entirely peaceful and there was at that time no sign of the chief anxiety, namely, Mahsud activity in the districts west of the Khaisora.

The Faqir of Ipi, and the Islam Bibi

One cannot talk of the disturbing factors in Waziristan without knowing of the life story of Mirza Ali Khan, the Faqir of Ipi, successor in some sense to the headache of the earlier generation of Politicals and Frontier soldiers—the Mullah-Powinda of Kaniguram and Makin. The Faqir was born of the Banga Khel clan of the Maddi Khel section of the Tori Khel Wazirs, that tribe of the Wazirs who live in and about the Lower Khaisora, near indeed, the Bannu border. He is said to have been born about 1897 at Khajuri, a village in the western edge of the Shinki Defile through which the Tochi river runs down to the Kurram and up which winds the main road to the Tochi posts and to Razmak. The Faqir's father owned property in the neighbourhood, but in 1922 he and his brother sold it and bought instead land near Spalga, and in the Sham plain, the latter some five miles south of Dosali Post on the Razmak Road. At Spalga they built a house and mosque. While living at Spalga, Mirza Ali frequented the village of Ipi to study his religion with the mullah there, Ipi lying just south of the Bannu–Razmak road not far from Mir Ali. In 1926 he went to live at Ipi and in 1928 performed the *Hajj* to Mecca, living on his return a purely religious life, visiting shrines and religious leaders.

It was not indeed till what is now known as the *Islam Bibi* case in 1936 had occurred that he appeared to take any part in Border politics, or aspire to be a leader. Faqirs and mullahs of influence come by chance as well as character, and an odour of sanctity must be acquired and cultivated.

The *Islam Bibi* case which so agitated the Bannu frontier was in this wise: A

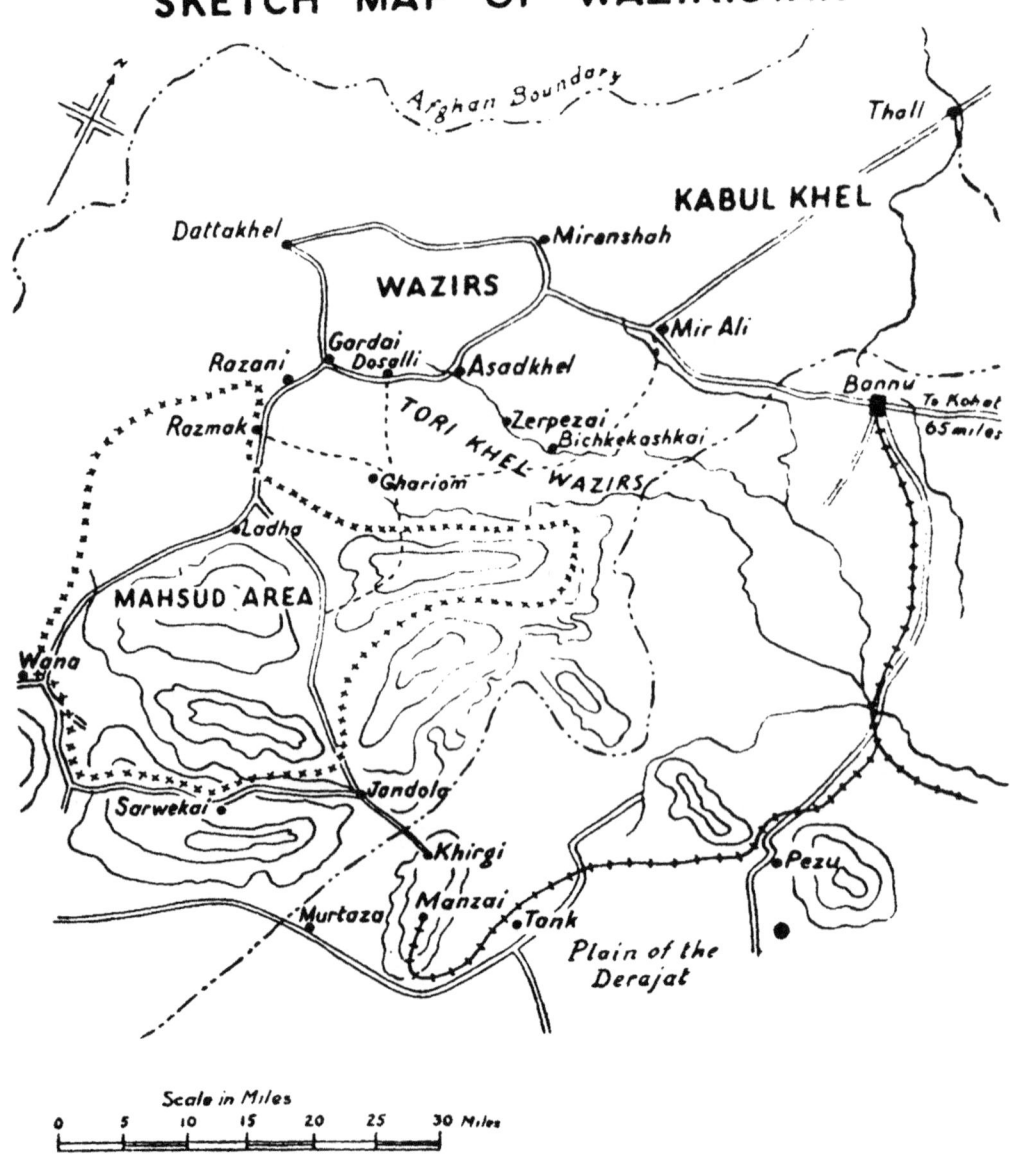

Hindu girl had eloped with a young Muslim student. Her relations brought a charge of abduction and the girl was recovered. But the Muslims asserted that she had adopted their faith and had taken the name of *Islam Bibi*, when the question of which community had the right to her, arose. On 7 April, the trial of the student on the charge of abduction was to take place, both parties and their locations being within administered British India. Some 2,000 Muslims assembled near the court to overawe the magistrate and the case could not be tried.

In the meantime, the Daurs, a fanatically minded tribe who lived in the Tochi valley just across the frontier, now threatened to march on Bannu, where the case was to come up again on 16 April. The Faqir of Ipi had found his occasion and was leading, the quiet mullah turned fanatic—"La Illah ha, il Allah ho !" Action was taken against the tribe, their lashkar dispersed, and their leaders arrested, all save the Faqir, who had escaped to the Sham area, among the Mahsuds. The girl had become a shuttle-cock among the antagonistic religions. The trial on the 16th had declared that she belonged to the Muslim community, but this was reversed on appeal and the Hindu community were made her custodians. What a heaven-sent occasion for stirring the tribes !—whose business, incidentally, it was not.

When the Faqir left the Daurs and the Tori Khel of the Lower Khaisora, he cursed them for not hurling themselves against the bayonets of the makers of law and the profession of order. Sir Alfred Lyall may be quoted here :

> "When ye kneel to God in penitence
> And cringe no more to men,
> Ye shall smite the stiff-necked infidel
> And rule, but not till then."

OPERATIONS IN THE LOWER KHAISORA, 25, 26 AND 27 NOVEMBER 1936

As it was essential to support the Maliks and to nip in the bud attempts to raise the Tori Khel, the two columns were again to march to the Lower Khaisora, but this time opposition seemed more likely and Tocol and the Razmak column (entitled Razcol) would start from Damdil and Mir Ali on the 25th, meeting that night again at Bichkekashkai and both return as before by the same route.

1st Northampton. Guides Infantry (5th/12th).
6th/13th F.F. Rifles.   1st/9th Gurkhas.

Razcol was to move along the Khaisora and Tocol over the hills to the Katira river and the Jaler Algad. This was still an operation directed by the G.O.C. Waziristan, who with the Resident accompanied Razcol. The Guides Infantry were of course with the Razmak Brigade. Their route was to be a very rough one along the river-bed, with the stream to be constantly crossed, while Tocol's line was much easier. Eight platoons of the Tochi Scouts were to picquet the flanks of Razcol, while six platoons of the Scouts were to go as far as the camp. The Regular troops were to close-picquet the route. The column got as far as Zerpezai without opposition, but now they heard that the narrow defile in front was occupied by considerable numbers of the Tori Khel, who could be seen on the ridges in front. The advance troops came under fire almost immediately and more fire was opened from a high feature east of the village of Zerpezai.

The Guides at Zerpezai

The following officers of the Guides were present :

Major S. B. Good	Major G. F. Taylor
Lieutenant C. G. Campbell	Lieutenant C. J. Hamilton
Second-Lieutenant W. G. Watt	Lieutenant R. M. Crowe, Royal Canadian Regt.

The strength of the battalion was 6 British, 16 I.Os. and 461 O.Rs.

The advance guard was found by the 6th/13th F.F. Rifles, the Guides forming its second echelon. Progress was now slower, for the hills in front were held in strength ; to rush ahead meant possibly heavy losses, and a methodical attack was developed. A mountain battery was told off to cover each sector in front and flank. The ridges running north from Zerpezai, on the left bank of the Khaisora—which now made a sharp turn to the south—were strongly held, and it was necessary to clear them. Information was also brought that the *tangi* leading to Dakai Kalai was held. A number of the enemy soon opened from a hill on the left, but were driven off by the Scouts, supported by the artillery, and the hills were secured with a few casualties by 1015 hours.

While the Tochi Scouts and "C" Company were fighting on the right, the Scouts on the left were also finding it hard going on the ground north of Zerpezai. Nos. 9 and 10 Platoons were sent up to secure the high ground on the nearer end of the ridge, and soon after Nos. 11 and 12 Platoons were sent to the ground farther along the crest. Nos. 9 and 10 Platoons found their objective firmly held, but eventually carried it, not, however, without the loss of a naik killed and three men wounded. The other two platoons could not get to the far end of their objective, but, holding their own half-way, sufficiently protected the column.

By now the 6th/13th were expended in various picquets and the Guides (5th/12th) took up the job. On the right the six companies of Scouts were about to make their way up the heights from the river-bed that ran south-east from Zerpezai, supported by the 7th Mountain Battery and a rifle company ("B") of the Guides under Lieutenant G. J. Hamilton, with a machine-gun section. Another rifle company, supported by the 3rd Light (*i.e.*, British Mountain) Battery, attacked the high ground east of Zerpezai with the object of establishing a picquet thereon. This was attained fairly easily, while on the right the Scouts, supported by the Guides' "C" Company, pushed on to a height overlooking Sheikh Muhammad Ziarat. This was a satisfactory point to protect the march along the river-bed, but it was not gained till nearly 1500 hours on a short afternoon. Farther back the Tochi Scouts had secured the heights on both sides of the Khaisora and west of the *tangi*. Shortly after noon, as the Guides were now "used up" in picquets, the 1st Northamptonshire Regiment took up the duties of the moving advanced guard. Half a mile west of the Sheikh Muhammad Ziarat, a considerable number of the enemy showed on the ridge overlooking the river-bed and then had to be dealt with before the march to Bichkekashkai could proceed. At about 1500 hours the Northamptonshires had cleared the ridge overlooking Dakai Kalai, while the column moved along to the junction of the Khaisora and the Dakai Algad, and the head reached Bichkekashkai by 1800 hours.

With the rearguard it was, as always, another matter and they were not at Dakai Kalai till 1830 hours with three miles more to go. There had been little news of Tocol, coming down from the north, so the Brigadier had determined to push for Bichkekashkai rather than elect the simpler course of bivouacking about Dakai Kalai, which would have got his rearguard—always the anxious spot—into safety earlier. But a march in the dark along a boulder-strewn road must always be a difficult business. The train got into some confusion and was a good deal shot up. It was here that Major J. Seccombe of the 6th/13th, an experienced frontier officer, trying apparently to inform the rearguard of the whereabouts of one of his picquets, with two of his men, met in the dark a party of the enemy and the three, alas! lost their lives.

At Dakai Kalai "B" Company rejoined the main body about 1700 hours, and as Brigade Headquarters had wirelessed for a company, "C" went forward and the Battalion reached the bivouac soon after 1900 hours without more casualties, but Razcol had lost 9 killed and 25 wounded during the day. The train and rearguard, helped by the good picqueting of "C" Company under Subadar Dost Mohammad,[22] whose personal exertions in getting his picquets in in the dark, were responsible for the successful withdrawal, bivouacked soon after 2000 hours. It was now known that Tocol had been heavily opposed and was bivouacking some four miles away on the Jaler Algad.

The Adventures of Tocol

Tocol, it will be remembered, was to start off from Mir Ali at the same time as Razcol left Damdil, also to Bichkekashkai. This distance was some twelve miles, also due south and for the most part over less hilly country, with wider valleys and gentler slopes. But opposition was considerable and after marching eight miles west of the Katira river to the Jaler Algad it was desirable to halt there, four miles short of their objective. Fighting had been heavy and the troops had had 10 killed and 44 wounded, of whom the Tochi Scouts with them had most of the 10 killed. Tocol was considerably weaker than Razcol, having only two battalions—the 1st/17th Dogras and 3rd/7th Rajputs—and no artillery, but a squadron (horsed) of Probyn's Horse and a machine-gun section. Tori Khel Maliks accompanied the column and reported that there were hostile tribesmen in the hills ahead. These were soon in evidence on the right front. In attacking, the 3rd/7th Rajputs lost considerably, Major Tyndall and Captain Boyd being wounded—the former fatally—with several I.O.Rs. A second company of this regiment now moved to the support, as the resistance was still quite strong, but the country was rideable, so the squadron of Probyn's Horse were ordered to gallop the crest. This they did very successfully, only suffering two casualties, and by 1435 hours the hills were cleared and the 3rd/7th Rajputs able to push on to the Jaler Algad, but another British officer was wounded and all its companies were commanded by V.C.Os.

On the left flank, the Tochi Scouts, who had two of their own mounted infantry platoons, were heavily engaged, and it was not till the 1st/17th Dogras moved in support that the advance could continue. There was nothing definite from Razcol, but it was

---

[22] Received I.D.S.M., *vide* Appendix V, Honours and Awards, p. 200.

believed that it was held up about Sheikh Muhammad Ziarat. Tocol commander, considering that some troops should get to Bichkekashkai, decided that he would push on after dark if need be, and as dusk was falling the column was ordered to close up to the Jaler Algad and at 1930 hours started to move forward ; but as it did so it was attacked from the left and rear, the train thrown into confusion, and loads lost, as cavalry horses and mules stampeded. By 2030 hours, however, order was restored and the force ready to advance, when the news came that Razcol had reached Bichkekashkai. Tocol commander therefore ordered the advance to continue, but being heavily attacked from the front and the animals again thrown into confusion, he decided to bivouac where he was. The bivouac was fired into all night and at 0400 hours the rearguard picquet was attacked unsuccessfully. At dawn troops went back to recover loads lost, and it was therefore 1100 hours before they could advance. By this time Razcol, which had had a quiet night, had sent forward at 0800 hours the 1st/9th Gurkhas, the Guides and a mountain battery to help them in, and the forces joined Tocol, the two eventually concentrating at Bichkekashkai. The R.A.F., who had been supporting Tocol, had dropped them ammunition, which they had to expend freely ; but as the two columns had only come out for a two days' operation and with a two days' ration, it was necessary to return. It was therefore decided that both columns should march back to Mir Ali next morning.

The picquets were withdrawn at 0900 hours and the march commenced, Tocol leading ; but firing soon broke out on flanks and rear, and the Guides Infantry were detailed for rearguard. On passing the Katira, Tocol took up the rear as Razcol passed through there, and though the enemy kept up fire, the two columns reached Mir Ali without special incident.

That ended the first attempts to support the Tori Khel maliks. The extent to which the tribesmen had broken away from the malik's control and all their agreements came as a considerable surprise to the Army, to the Politicals, and to the Government of India. Two British officers and 19 rank and file had been killed, with 4 British officers and 87 rank and file wounded. Further, the Tochi Scouts had had 7 killed and 16 wounded.

It was a lot to pay for finding out what should have been known before, and proved the malign effect of the Faqir of Ipi's propaganda, and Government had now to make up their mind what they were going to do about it. The tribesmen, it is true, had burnt their fingers and suffered more casualties than they liked, but the Faqir's prestige had if anything been enhanced—while he had succeeded in getting some 200 Mahsuds to join him.

Happily, the decisions of the Government of India were prompt and it was decided that the Tori Khel and any other participants must be properly called to account and the Faqir be expelled. General Sir John Coleridge, commanding the Northern Army, was to take military and political control, and the troops at his disposal were reinforced by two mountain batteries, the 2nd (Rawalpindi) Infantry Brigade and two companies of Sappers. No. 3 Indian Wing, R.A.F., under Wing Commander J. Slessor, M.C., was placed at Sir John's disposal, and the O.C. joined the latter's Headquarters at Mir Ali.

THE WAZIRISTAN CAMPAIGNS, 1936-1937

Operations against the Tori Khel
28 November 1936—24 December 1936

The operations to give effect to Government's decisions were to be prolonged, however. Those decisions included the making of a motor road from Mir Ali to the Lower Khaisora and called for definite action to prevent the trouble spreading to other tribes, for it was feared that the Faqir might be able to bring out the Mahsuds.

Sir John, as soon as the extra troops arrived, formed a striking force under Major-General Robertson, consisting of the Razmak Brigade plus two battalions (Khaicol), with the 2nd Brigade in reserve at Mir Ali. The remainder of the troops in Sir John's command were to garrison the frontier itself, the Bannu Brigade watching the mouth of the Khaisora and garrisoning the lines of communication. The first thing the striking force was to do was to make the road from Mir Ali to the Khaisora. The unrest as yet seemed to be confined to the Lower Khaisora and a few Mahsuds; but the Faqir, concealing his losses, was describing the recent operation as a great success, and was calling on all and sundry, including the Afghans, to come and share in the spoil. Razcol now started from Mir Ali on 5 December to make the new road, and on this date the new organization came into being. The work on the road went on apace, though the Faqir was reported to be with several hundred tribesmen on the Jaler Algad. Razcol, now known as "the Striking Force" and Khaicol, reached Jaler camp on the 9th without the hoped-for main attack of tribesmen which alone could give severe casualties. Heavy rain impeded and damaged the road work, but many of the Faqir's followers had come without arms, hoping to be equipped from the Faqir's loot. Thus no one felt inclined to face the British troops, who were on the Khaisora by the 18th, busily destroying the towers of the hostile section, and who were joined by the 2nd Brigade on the 21st. For the moment the Faqir's influence waned, and his lashkars, hungry and wet, dispersed, while the 2nd Brigade operated to destroy towers beyond Dakai Kalai, where considerable resistance was experienced. The 2nd/2nd Punjabis had to be extricated by the artillery and 2nd/11th Sikhs from a nasty position, in which assistance from the air had to be called in; and the Brigade had to stay the night at Bichkekashkai. A smart attack, however, on pursuing tribesmen enabled the force to regain the bivouac in comfort. Khaicol itself had now broken up, Razcol marching on to Damdil after seeing that the 2nd Brigade had attained its objective. All this time the Guides Infantry, save for taking their share in protecting the road-making, experienced no particular incidents.

Sir John Coleridge, having sent Razcol back to Razmak, kept Tocol and the 2nd Brigade in the Mir Ali–Khaisora area and made another road from the Jaler Algad down the Seni valley north-west of the long Kharaghora range which bordered the Bannu plain. This road was to join the central road to Razmak near Dregandhi post, and would much simplify movement of troops and supplies from Bannu to the Khaisora.

During these operations Major Williams of the 2nd/2nd Punjabis and 4 I.O.Rs. were killed, and 1 B.O. and 12 O.Rs. wounded, these casualties being a good indication of the amount of ammunition in tribal hands. They lost fairly severely, having at least twenty killed.

As it now seemed that the Tori tribes had had enough and would accept Government terms, some of the forces were dispersed. In the meantime, the Faqir had fled to Arsal Kot on the Shaktu river in Mahsud territory with the Tori Khel irreconcilables, and continued to pour forth his stories of all that he and his supporters from many areas would do. His disappointed Afghan followers had had enough and went home. To support the Mahsud maliks in their endeavours to ensure peace, Arsal Kot, where the Faqir had his mosque and residence, was now subject to constant air bombing. This too helped the Tori Khel maliks, who said they were powerless without constant support.

On 8 January the Razmak Brigade again entered the Khaisora as a preliminary to a carefully prepared night bombardment of villages harbouring recalcitrants. That night they were at Zerpezai, and the Bannu Brigade at Dakai Kalai. The two 6-inch howitzers at Razmak were brought to Damdil for this party. A picquet of the 2nd/13th F.F. Rifles was heavily attacked, but thrice were the enemy beaten off, the picquet, however, losing 4 killed and 8 wounded. The artillery bombardment was successful, causing considerable loss and sending some 250 Afghan sympathizers scampering back to their own country. By the 14th both columns were back in their stations, having for the time completely broken up the Faqir's supporters, and the Tori Khel accepted Government terms. By 2 February Sir John was able to return political control to the Frontier Government and it was hoped that normal conditions would prevail.

February to April 1937: Numerous Outrages

The trouble for the moment had been scotched, but you cannot destroy the *Hukm* or indulge in kiss-mammydom with Red Shirts with impunity. The Faqir of Ipi was still banging the drum ecclesiastic and British prestige, whenever on the verge of restoration, would receive a slap in the face from some London-born, Viceroy-delivered, *bêtise*—and the good British lives thus sacrificed to formula-finding secretariats are always to be remembered with bitter hatred. However, it was to the good that the Tori Khel had had their *paquet* before the Mahsuds joined in. The Mahsud troubles were now to ensue, opened by a bitter, unsought tragedy. Before this, however, the so-called peace was to be disturbed by needless murders. The Faqir called on the tribes to kidnap British officials and all who served them. Early in February two British officers were murdered, one in Mahsud and one in Wazir territory, to mark the Faqir's holiday. On 6 February Captain J. C. Keogh, 1st/12th F.F.R., serving with the South Waziristan Scouts, travelling by motor from Laddha to Jandola with his orderly, was shot by one man, dying next day, the orderly being killed. Next day Lieutenant R. N. Beatty of Hodson's Horse, attached to the Tochi Scouts and acting as a political officer, *en route* from Miranshah to Razmak, taking the pay of the Khassadars with the pay clerk and three orderlies, was attacked by a number of men in ambush. Beatty was mortally wounded and two of his party killed; Rs.32,000 were then stolen. The robbed Khassadars soon took up the pursuit and recovered some of the money, but not the murderers. A blockade was immediately imposed on the sections responsible, and a heavy fine, Keogh's assailants being Mahsuds, Beatty's being Maddi Khel in Daur

THE WAZIRISTAN CAMPAIGNS, 1936–1937

territory. All jirgas, now called up, condemned the murders and offered to find the murderers—offers which came to nothing. The Maddi Khel wrote open defiance.

On 17 February a party of Ghilzais from Birmal in Afghanistan attacked troops from Wana—the Ghilzais being a people who migrated each winter to India and thus gave many hostages to fortune. The Wana force, though giving as good as they got, had 4 killed and 5 wounded.

General Sir John Coleridge now moved the 1st (Abbottabad) Brigade and another mountain battery into the area, foreseeing that the matter might blow up again. In the meantime the Faqir, calling down High Heaven to his aid, gathered together many desperadoes from both sides of the border and called on all Khassadars to desert the Service. Now that two of Sir John's Brigades had gone up, the H.Q., 1st Division, from Rawalpindi moved up too and were given charge of a sector of the Tochi road, the G.O.C. Waziristan commanding the rest. But as yet only the Air Force action was to be aggressive; that of the Army defensive.

Attacks and hostilities of all kinds, however, were general; roads, telegraphs and bridges were interfered with, and most posts were fired into at night. On the night of 20 March a picquet of the 2nd/5th R.G.R. at Damdil was heavily attacked, but after desperate fighting, was held. When rescued, only 4 of the 8 men could stand, though 31 of the enemy lay dead in the post.

The Faqir was now moving about with many followers and Government had to face even more extended hostilities—very shortly the 1st Brigade was to be engaged in a pitched battle to get a convoy into Razmak.

THE ATTACK IN FORCE ON THE RAZMAK CONVOY

Towards the end of March the Utman Khel Wazirs jirga came in and agreed to put pressure on the recalcitrant Tori Khels and the Faqir, and the latter announced that his followers would commit no acts of aggression. How little this was of avail was soon apparent. On 29 March 1937 a largish convoy was due to run by the central Waziristan road from Mir Ali to Damdil *en route* for Razmak. This move in the ordinary course of routine was to be protected by the 1st (Abbottabad) Brigade for six miles either side of Damdil.

There was a more or less routine distribution of the Brigade on such occasions—viz., a battalion and two guns to the Nariwala Narai six miles from Damdil towards Mir Ali, another with two guns on the "Ring Contour" near Asad Khel, and the third, also with two guns, forward towards mile 52 and Dosali Post; the fourth battalion stayed in Damdil to help in handling convoy stores. On this day the 1st South Wales Borderers were on the Nariwala Narai sector, the 1st/6th Gurkhas and two guns round about the Ring Contour, while the 2nd/6th Gurkhas, in lorries, moved through the 1st/6th to a ridge near milestone $50\frac{1}{2}$. Both battalions of the 6th were working in extremely difficult country. The routes used by various battalions in taking up positions were rarely the same, to avoid surprise.

At 0805 hours the two platoons and machine-gun section of the 1st/6th Gurkhas near mile $51\frac{3}{4}$ were heavily attacked both by rifle fire and by swordsmen from heavy scrub. Machine-gunners were shot down, the British officer in command, with two Gurkha officers, was wounded, and the remnant of the party rallied as best they could in a small water-course. Armoured cars from Dosali at once came out down the road and prevented the enemy carrying off ammunition and mules. It was now realized that the advanced guard had got too far ahead and had lost touch with the main body, which was now gripping the situation. The Brigadier had actually gone with the South Wales Borderers to the Nariwala Narai, as he had rather expected trouble in that direction, and as soon as he heard he proceeded to the Ring Contour, ordered the 2nd/6th Gurkhas at Damdil to go to the Contour and the Borderers to make for the same point. By now, large numbers of tribesmen were to be seen in the nullahs and scrub north of the road. It was noon before Brigadier Inskip got to the Ring Contour. We need not go into detail, but suffice it to say that the companies of the 1st/6th Gurkhas had moved up to support and extricate the advance guard. The 2nd/6th Gurkhas at hill 4621, some 600 yards west of the Ring Contour, were threatened with an attempt to seize this commanding height. It was not till 1330 hours that the Brigadier's counter-moves were ready, for distances were great, and with enemy swarming on all sides there were grave dangers to guard against. His scheme was straightforward and effective. The 2nd/6th Gurkhas would attack from point 4641, supported by the Borderers over the hilltop 4792, some 2,000 yards north of the convoy road, and thus drive the main body down on to the road and into the ravines and broken ground close by. The attack of the 2nd/6th Gurkhas was entirely successful, despite strong resistance on the high point. A large number of the enemy were surrounded in the nullahs by three battalions and came under heavy shell fire. But the afternoons were very short and by 1630 hours dusk was coming on with eastern swiftness, so that a withdrawal was necessary, or the enemy would have had a devastating defeat. As it was they were known to have lost 94 killed and 64 severely wounded—a very big loss for them. British losses had been heavy too—Captain O. R. Bethune of the 2nd/6th Gurkhas and Lieutenant R. A. L. Marks of the 1st/6th Gurkhas, with 2 Gurkha officers and 30 O.Rs., killed, and Lieutenant P. F. C. Nicholson, 1st/6th Gurkhas, a Gurkha officer and 42 O.Rs. wounded.

All bodies and wounded of the Gurkhas were recovered before the troops withdrew, and so ended a very difficult day. It gave some indication of the extent to which the tribesmen were disturbed. Twelve miles is a long stretch for a brigade to cover if anything more than raiding parties is to be met with. The next chapter will show how the Mahsuds could not resist the excitement.

CHAPTER VI

THE WAZIRISTAN CAMPAIGNS (*continued*)

THE TRAGEDY OF THE SHAHUR TANGI—THE AFTERMATH—RENEWED OPERATIONS IN THE KHAISORA (23 APRIL–3 MAY)—THE DECISION TO BEAT UP ARSAL KOT AND THE SHAM PLAIN—THE SEIZURE OF THE PLAIN—THE SITUATION ON THE DERAJAT BORDER—THE DESTRUCTION OF ARSAL KOT—ALGAD-WHACKING IN SHAM AND SHAKTU—THE GUIDES LOSE THEIR COLONEL—THE RETURN TO RAZMAK AND THE "CRAG" AFFAIR—AFFAIR OF RIDGEWAY HILL—"PAT" GRANT, AN APPRECIATION.

THE TRAGEDY OF THE SHAHUR TANGI
(9 April 1937)

THE anxiety of the authorities during the operation against the Tori Khel, lest the Mahsud clans of South Waziristan should be upset, has been referred to. To get the Mahsuds to either expel or control the Faqir of Ipi was, of course, their object, but so pressed as not to upset the tribal feelings.

But on 9 April occurred one of those unforeseen and perhaps inexplicable incidents to be found from time to time in all the story of the spreading of the *Pax Britannica*. It is also perhaps illustrative of the seemingly ineradicable British habit of forgetting the danger that surrounds them if not constantly or forcibly reminded of it.

The scene must be transferred from North Waziristan, the Tochi and the Khaisora, to the famous area of Jandola post in the Bhittani country. The Bhittanis are the small tribe that inhabit the outer layer of hills between the Tank plain and the Bannu plain and they are a people often described as the "jackals of the Mahsuds," long known as sneak raiders, some of whom have done good service in the Border Military Police and their successors. Now they were under the influence of the Din Faqir, a myrmidon of him of Ipi. The post at Jandola had long ago been constructed to protect the considerable town of Tank from Mahsud and Bhittani raids, on the far side of the difficult gorge of the Takki (Tank) Zam, as it cut its way through the outer range of the Bhittani Hills.

Later years had brought the Frontier railway to Manzai in a wide valley which the dying end of these hills formed with the next range on the farther side of the Administrative Border. Since the establishment of a Brigade at Wana, a motor road from Manzai had been driven to that place through the Shahur Tangi of evil memory, and then up to the mountain post of Sarwekai and on to Wana. This road was guarded by posts of the South Waziristan Scouts, while Khassadars patrolled the actual routes when convoys were moving, and on the day in question patrols of Scouts were also out.

The convoy to leave Manzai on 9 April was a normal one—save that it happened to have an abnormally large number of officers and men returning from leave—and consisted of forty-nine army or hired civilian lorries and two private cars. The escort consisted of 51 O.Rs. of the 4th/16th Punjabis under a V.C.O., and four armoured cars. Two senior officers awaiting passage were placed in command and on duty, while Major

T. Z. Waters, M.C., R.I.A.S.C., who had often taken convoys through, commanded the vehicles. Everybody was in lorries and it was a question of getting through a protected route. The officers returning from leave rode in the leading lorries, preceded by an armoured car, and the convoy was in four "blocks" with a space in between, two armoured cars in the intervals and one bringing up the rear.

The infantry escort was in three parties—one close to the head. The 72 leave details were mostly armed.

The convoy, marching from Manzai at 0600 hours was at Jandola an hour later. Early morning air reconnaissance had seen no tribesmen and at 0735 hours the leading armoured car entered the Shahur Tangi, all seeming quiet. At 0745 hours the tail was well within the defile and the convoy occupied one and a half miles of road.

Suddenly a murderous fire was opened all along the convoy, heaviest on the front half. Drivers were killed, lorries splayed all over the road, which was blocked, and as officers and men jumped out they were shot down. In vain parties tried to attack, in vain the armoured cars moved and fired—any attempt to move meant men were shot down, along almost the whole length of the convoy, by men on the heights above. In the front lorry all the men of the escort were shot before they were out of the lorry. The actual number of killed was 6 British officers, and Captain Durrani, I.M.S., and 45 O.Rs. and civilian drivers; the wounded were 5 British officers, 2 V.C.Os., 43 O.Rs. and civilian drivers—a tragedy of tragedies. Major Waters, commanding the lorries, was hit three times.

Gallant help came soon, from Lieutenant Wetheral of the 8th Light Tank Company from Sarwekai, but they could do little save extricate a few leading lorries. Wetheral forced his way into the unoccupied post of Spitoi and was able to telephone to the Wana Brigade. The enemy were still *in situ*, firing at all and sundry. By noon three platoons of Scouts arrived and, with some Khassadars, established picquets at the western exit from the Tangi.

In the meantime news had got down the road and more armoured cars came up from the Jandola direction towards the tail of the convoy and some scouts and platoons of the 4th/16th Punjabis. They began to clear the north side, but the troops had to withdraw as dusk came. Some twenty lorries at the head of the convoy were got away, with all dead and wounded, to Sarwekai—troops remaining to protect the others. At dawn many reinforcements came up, including 2nd/11th Sikhs from Bannu in lorries, and by noon on the 10th the whole business was cleared up and the convoy extricated, save one burnt-out lorry.

The Aftermath

Who had done it, in face of peacefully inclined maliks? It soon transpired that one Khonia Khel, to be known to the troops as "Bloody Bill," a Mahsud murderer and outlaw and follower of the Faqir of Ipi, and another, were responsible, but there was no doubt that their presence in the area was known and should have been reported. His party, at first about 60, had soon swollen to 300, and their losses were 10 killed and 26 badly wounded.

THE WAZIRISTAN CAMPAIGNS—contd.

It took some little time for the situation to be fully assessed, but the 2nd Brigade from Rawalpindi was concentrated at Mir Ali. All the Mahsuds were very excited and several attacks on posts were made. The Jalal Khel jirgas, however, came in and were ordered to hand over Khonia Khel and his coadjutor, one Dilbogh. If they did not do this, thirty hostages were demanded. If not, they would be regarded as hostile. Excitement now spread to the Tori Khel and clans round the Razmak road; lashkars from many sections and from Afghanistan were reported in all directions, and the maliks had little control.

As soon as the situation had cleared, the Government of India took a strong line. General Sir John Coleridge was put in charge again and also took over political affairs. Perhaps this arrangement should be explained; it meant that the Resident (or in other cases whoever was in political charge) became head of the political department in military headquarters in closest touch with the General Staff. Orders from Government came to the G.O.C. and communications went out in his name. It means that all clash of action is obviated and that only such dealings with the enemy go on as the Chief approves of. Many difficulties and absurdities of earlier days are thus avoided. War can only be conducted by one King in Brentford.

The combined military and political policy in Waziristan was now to penetrate every doubtful valley, with no reservations, and above all to chase the Faqir from every valley—easier to prescribe than to do—and to make roads where necessary. The new series of operations was to bring the Guides Infantry back into the scene, with a tragic loss. Razcol had returned to its cantonment at Razmak, after the second expedition into the Khaisora and, until the Shahur Tangi aftermath, had been concerned chiefly with keeping the vicinity of the station clear of intruders and taking its share in lower reconnaissance and the occupation of the Alexandra Ridge post on the high hill overlooking the main road some five miles towards Damdil.

Renewed Operations in the Khaisora
(23 April to 3 May 1937)

Before undertaking operations to chase the Faqir and punish the Mahsuds, however, there was work to be done in the Khaisora, where his constant exhortations had assembled considerable lashkars again. Further, the bulk of the Tori Khel had not complied with the terms recently imposed. The 1st Indian Division was detailed for this duty, which lasted from 23 April to 3 May. It is not proposed to give the details of these operations, as the Guides were not concerned. Suffice it is to say that while the enemy in the Khaisora were not brought to a definite battle, yet bombing and shelling of lashkars as well as fire from picquets were known to have inflicted 20 dead and 57 seriously wounded. Again Afghan lashkars were present. These short operations had been very arduous, as had the previous ones—constant climbing up and down steep and lofty hills, with constant vigilance necessary.

In preparation for the operations, the 9th Jhansi Brigade was brought up and various useful units and batteries, as well as Air Force squadrons.

The Decision to Beat up Arsal Kot and the Sham Plain

Sir John Coleridge now decided to beat up the Faqir in his home at Arsal Kot in Mahsud country, high up in the Shaktu valley. The Faqir's sanctum, which he boasted could not be reached, some eight mountainous miles due south, was to be Sir John's first objective, coupled with the Sham plain, four miles south of Dosali post and about five miles west of Arsal Kot. These crow-fly distances, of course, bear no reference to the tortuous and difficult methods of approach. Surprise and capture of the Faqir, owing to conditions, was not a possible course and the lifting of his *purdah* with a direct road was the obvious procedure. This would put an end to any idea of immunity and enable visitation. There were several possible routes and the one from Dosali via the Sham plain seemed best. It was necessary to wait to begin till the Khaisora troops were back, and the actual Scout garrison in the Khaisora was withdrawn for a while to lessen liabilities. This measure, however, gave the Faqir occasion to proclaim a victory and shout that the British were evacuating Waziristan.

All this while the Political officers and the tribal jirgas were holding communications, but the latter were quite powerless to restrain their young men and the situation had grown worse; while the Jalal Khel Mahsuds, from whose valley "Bloody Bill" had made his Shahur Tangi raid, repudiated the Government terms. So the days of possible amelioration and contrition had passed away.

The Seizure of the Sham Plain

The first move, kept a very close secret—so close that Sir John hardly told it to his pillow—was to secure the Sham Plain and there establish bases from which to attack and at any rate flatten the Faqir's stronghold.

It was to be made by the 1st Brigade via the Sremela Algad and the Bannu Brigade along the Iblanki spur which flanked the Algad, both moving on the night of 11/12 May to camps known as "Kach" and "A" (later "Coronation") respectively. The moves by night over rock-strewn knife-edges were extremely difficult. The enemy could be heard reassuring each other by shouting that it was "only the Militia" and that no one would ever get up the Sremela Algad. Unexpectedly slow, however, as that advance had to be, through it went. At 0630 hours the Iblanki Narai was carried for the slight loss of 3 killed and 9 wounded in the Bannu Brigade. This operation was suggested by Major Gimson of the Guides Cavalry, attached to the Tochi Scouts, and was carried out, he and the Scouts leading, with great éclat. By 1000 hours the edge of the Sham Plain was in our hands, and by noon the ground of Camp "A," the "Coronation" Camp, was fully occupied. The 1st Brigade, struggling up the rock-strewn Algad, was practically unopposed. Communications and water being the problem, and the ground supremely difficult, no thought of a farther bound could be entertained till camps and road were improved and protected, and, in fact, on the 13th supplies came by air. Reconnaissance now showed that at Ghariom a few miles south-west there would be enough water for both brigades.

On the 18th the Bannu Brigade advanced to Ghariom, being heavily opposed, losing

THE WAZIRISTAN CAMPAIGNS—contd.

27 killed and 23 wounded among troops, and the tribesmen's loss was 37 killed and 3 severely wounded. On 17 May in a temporary brigade known as Grant-col,[23] the Guides Infantry, with the 2nd/1st and 1st/4th Punjabis and the 13th Mountain Battery, arrived at Kach and Coronation camps for camp and road duties.

Several days were now necessary to get the motor road through from Dosali to Ghariom and collect supplies for the final bound, and some heavy engineering on the road onward was also necessary. Convoys and the camps were constantly attacked and back at Dosali a picquet of the Argyll and Sutherland Highlanders was heavily attacked, losing 2 killed and 9 wounded and inflicting much the same. But all these engagements showed that the temper of the lashkars, despite defections, was still implacable.

Some of the 3rd Brigade now came up to protect the communications ahead of Coronation camp, and by the 24th the 1st Brigade also moved up to the roomy camp at Ghariom. The enemy had now withdrawn to the hills between Ghariom and Arsal Kot, whither the Faqir was said to have removed himself. The Tori Khel had now practically left him, his lashkars being Mahsuds, Bhittanis and Afghans. Nevertheless the wildest yarns were still being spread by him.

The Situation on the Derajat Border

As was to be expected, after the Shahur Tangi tragedy disorder flew round the borders of the Derajat plain, always part of British India, along the Sheranni border below the Takht-i-Suleiman—that Tahkt whence Solomon, flying home with an Indian bride, bade her look back from her magic carpet on the country she was leaving. The armed constabulary posts were attacked, Hindu girls carried off and shared among the raiders, and the village of Paharpur, perhaps fifty miles within British territory, was most insolently raided. The gang who did this, however, were to some extent scored off in their favourite get-away in one of the deep, dry, mud-cliffed nullahs of the plain by a troop of cavalry. A gang of close on 400 Bhittanis, the Mahsud jackals, raided the frontier railway at the Pezu pass where it runs through a small isolated range of hills, several miles within the border. Troops were on the train and the raiders were fired on, to their surprise, but the engine driver lost his head and stopped the train instead of "stamping on the juice" and then the troops, before they could detrain, suffered some casualties. The raiders, however, broke up and tried to get home, despite many attempts to cut them off. After this Sir John Coleridge took over the command of the Border Constabulary for the time being also.

The Destruction of Arsal Kot

While this Derajat trouble had been boiling up, the arrangements at Ghariom for the march on the Faqir's "Home Town" were being completed. Very heavy storms put the start back a day or so, but on 27 May the move started, which was to be done and all troops back in three days. The Guides, however, were not included in the raiding force, which would consist of the Bannu and 1st Brigades, moving to Pasal camp on the Shaktu above and south-west of Arsal Kot, while the 2nd Brigade from Mir Ali would

---

[23] Lieut.-Colonel Grant had Captain Pollard assigned as his brigade major.

move by the Khaisora, reaching Bichkekashkai on the 27th. All moves were kept very secret. On the 28th both forces were expected to meet at Arsal Kot and return on the 29th, but the 2nd Brigade, after climbing 4,000 feet, could not get farther than Mazia Ragza, a mile north of the Shaktu Algad and some three miles from Arsal Kot. The force from Ghariom of two Brigades met a considerable resistance *en route* to Pasal, and a picquet of the Argyll and Sutherlands had a bad time and several casualties. On the 28th the Ghariom force had occupied Arsal Kot, already ruined from the air, without any opposition; demolition was completed and the Faqir's emergency living caves, thirty feet below the ground, blown up with 1,900 lb. of dynamite, to "larn" him. Nothing was found in them save some documents. On the 30th all three Brigades went back to Ghariom, or its vicinity, enduring the loss of 2 killed, including a British officer, and some 13 wounded. During these operations from the 23rd to the 30th the lashkars had lost 59 killed and 45 severely wounded, of whom 24 and 17 respectively were Mahsuds. For the six months their losses were 715 killed and 657 severely wounded. The British losses for the same period, including the Shahur Tangi, were 164 killed, of whom 15 were British officers, and 431 wounded, of whom 14 were B.Os. From these figures one might deduce once more the old lesson, not only of the Frontier but of the world, from Napoleon to Hitler, that it does not pay to poke fun at John Bull.

During this period the air support was very complete and exceedingly good, both in strategic bombing and in tactical bombing and close support, though hampered often enough by Government's delay in lifting foolish restrictions and refusal to allow Sir John to do what he considered necessary from the air without referring to Headquarters in India.

Algad-whacking in Sham and Shaktu

There was a good deal of algad-whacking to be done yet, and the Bannu Brigade marched south from Ghariom via Madamir Kalai, south of Arsal Kot on the Shaktu, and thence on to Janata to join the main military road from the Derajat frontier to Razmak at Sararogha and thence up to Razmak cantonment. The Razmak Brigade, now rejoined by the Guides, was to march down the main road eight miles to Piazha Raghza, to assist them. *En route* Mahsud valleys were to be looked up. The march of the Bannu Brigade started on 6 June and the route was very bad with very high hills, but except for sniping there was no great incident and they joined the Razmak Brigade at Piazha Raghza on the 9th. While this was in progress various other moves were undertaken to settle the Bhittani goose, rescue the Hindu girls if that were now desirable, and generally exact retribution. We need not follow these in detail; but Sir John Coleridge had proposed more roads, one from the lower Khaisora to Razmak and the other from Dosali on the Bannu–Razmak road to Ahmedwam, near where the Bannu Brigade had joined the western military road at Sararogha. To carry this out was the duty of various brigades in the force.

On the 9th the Razmak and Bannu Brigades marched to Tauda China, a mile north-west of Makin, and the Mahsuds of that important centre picqueted the camp for them. When the Mahsud jirga was informed that it was intended to destroy the house

LADDHA, 1937
Group of officers (Infantry) taken shortly before Lieut.-Colonel P. Grant was killed
L. to R.: R. R. Griffith.   C. G. Campbell.   R. V. E. Hodson.   W. G. Watt.   W. J. Cumming.   P. Grant.

KHAISORA VALLEY, DECEMBER 1936
Major G. F. Taylor gives out orders for the burning of the Zarinai villages (including Ipi's house)

THE WAZIRISTAN CAMPAIGNS—contd.

and tower of one Bahram, a notorious offender, the jirga said they would do it for themselves, and not only did so but handed over the ruffian, a quite unprecedented act, showing at any rate that they were very apprehensive of what might be in store if authority were not placated.

But despite this and despite the fact that the Tori Khel had thrown their hand in and that the Mahsud jirgas were apprehensive for their own position and allowances, the whole country was still out of hand. The Faqir continued to call on all and sundry, and our friend the Shewa Faqir was almost the only one of the religious fraternity who would not listen to him. Operations were now undertaken against lashkars in the Shawali Algad, a couple of miles or so over the hills east of Razmak itself. There was a good deal of desultory fighting, in which the enemy lost 15 killed and seriously wounded. In one of the skirmishes a well-known mullah was surprised and killed as he lay down to shoot, and on 20 June eleven prisoners were taken in a raid from our camp at Ghariom, including one Arsal Khan, the Faqir's host. In one village the Scouts rescued two Hindus who had been kept captive, their feet in stocks, for nearly four months. These last series of operations round the Sham plain, the Shaktu and Ghariom, had been in fact pretty effective for our purpose.

THE GUIDES LOSE THEIR COLONEL

We have now come to the series of operations in which the Guides Infantry were to lose their Colonel—"Pat" Grant of famous family—and this was the manner of it.

After the march of the Razmak Brigade (Razcol) to Tauda China, the two Brigades were to advance down the main road to Wana, usually held by Scouts and Khassadars till the Shahur Tangi happening, as far as Torwam on the Western Khaisora (not connected with the Tori Khel valley of the same name), some five miles from Wana, and were then to explore the Badar Algad and beat up the mulla Sher Ali, a principal leader of local lashkars.

On 20 June the Bannu Brigade (Tocol as before) was to join Razcol at Ladha, and next day Razcol marched to Chalwesti, where it was joined on the 22nd by Tocol. The two Brigades were sniped pretty freely and that camp was close to very thick woods. On the 23rd, Tocal was to advance to the Sherwangi Narai and there establish a Scout post of eight platoons, while Razcol, leaving Chalwesti at 0730 hours, was to pass through Tocol's picquets up to the Narai and then march on to Torwam. Occupying the Narai took some time and the Scouts had some ten casualties, but were supported by Tocol. After passing the Narai, Razcol took over the picqueting, leaving Tocol, who would return to Chalwesti as soon as the Scouts' picquet was safely established and defended.

"A" Company under Hodson was the advance guard and had seized a low feature from whence Colonel Grant wished to reconnoitre the route ahead, and from that spur he ordered "C" Company (Campbell) and "B" (Jagat Singh) to take a big spur some three hundred yards ahead. While "B" and "C" were forging ahead, Grant moved to the forward edge of the ridge to watch them cross a deep nullah, and as he did so a small party of snipers began firing from the ridge ahead. One bullet caught the colonel in the chest and another slightly wounded Jemadar Arjan Singh. Major Redding assumed command,[24] and it was soon realized that their Colonel was mortally wounded, and he died in fifteen minutes. The advance, however, continued without much incident save for a very severe hailstorm, and Torwam on the Khaisora was reached. Next day (24 June) Razcol picqueted back to let Tocol march in to Torwam camp.

The next few days were spent in road opening and reconnaissance, and on the 28th the Wana Brigade, which had been working down to Sarwekai and up the Shahur, arrived, assisted by Tocol, at a camp on the opposite bank of the Khaisora to Torwam. The Divisional Commander thus had his three Brigades together, where the Guides were able to forgather with another famous Piffer battalion—the 3rd Sikhs.

On the 29th the three Brigades started up various nullahs to the north-east of Torwam to rout out the mullah Sher Ali and destroy his caves. The bulk of the fighting fell to Tocol, who had 2 killed and 6 wounded but succeeded in killing and wounding 50 of the enemy, largely Birmal Wazirs from over the Afghan border.

On the 30th the Wana Brigade returned to Wana, and on 1 July Tocol and Razcol returned towards Razmak, Razcol being left at Asman Manza just north of Kaniguram. This was a magnificent high camp which was not snipable, only two picquets being needed for its protection. Tocol went back to Razmak and this phase of the operations was now over.

The Return to Razmak and the "Crag" Affair

On 8 August, soon after dawn, Razcol left its pleasant camp at Asman Manza (which presumably means the "Heavenly Plain") for garrison work in Razmak, halting at Laddha. Covering the withdrawal on the 9th, the Guides joined the main body at Tauda and were then ordered to act as right flank picqueting troops; this included looking after "Crag," a high feature that overlooked Tauda, not far from Razmak.

"B" Company took the advance guard, and "A" and "C" under Captain Eliott-Lockhart[25] were to approach "Crag" by way of a spur that led to it, passing through the picquets of the Northamptons. At 1300 hours "B" Company had reached the farther outskirts of Tauda China, and at this moment a heavy fire was opened from "Crag" on "A" and "C," who were half-way to their objective. Lieutenant Kreyer,[26] commanding "B," was called to Battalion Headquarters and there was shown the position and ordered to attack "Crag," in which "A" and "C" would support him. As this was a pattern piece of mountain tactics it is worth following in detail. Subadar Jagat Singh with No. 7 Platoon, occupied a low feature for covering fire, and Subadar Brig Lal, with No. 8 Platoon, worked his way slowly up "Crag" spur, hard going with close scrub. On reaching an intermediate position, No. 8 Platoon was left and Nos. 5 and 6 Platoons pushed on. After a short halt immediately below "Crag," these platoons went up an almost precipitous face with rifles slung. On arriving on top the enemy were seen to have gone back

---

[24] An account of the tragedy and an appreciation of Colonel Grant and his services, written by Colonel Redding, are included at the end of this chapter.

[25] Eliott-Lockhart was the last Guides Cavalry officer to serve with the Infantry on active service, having been attached at his own request, and spending several months with the Paltan.

[26] Attached to Guides Infantry from 1st Sikhs.

THE WAZIRISTAN CAMPAIGNS—contd.

a hundred yards and now opened hot fire. A brisk exchange took place, though up to this point "B" had only endured a few shots.

As the only object of this well-handled little action was to protect the passing of the Brigade, the three companies now arranged for their withdrawal as soon as the column was clear. However, the enemy realized that they were dealing with past-masters at their game and the follow-up was not close, while a battalion with machine guns and battery of artillery were warned in case of closer fighting. Owing to good handling, the casualties were slight, "A" and "C" having Lance-Naik Shingara Singh killed and a naik wounded in their original advance, the precipitous nature of the terrain giving perhaps good cover. The force then marched on to Razmak.

Life in Razmak now seems to have had two periods, the first of some peace and leisure, varied during August by making and protecting the road from Razmak to Engamal towards Sham, and covering the construction of a Scout post at Olai. In this a Guide was wounded and a sapper with them mortally so. At the end of August "A" Company under Eliott-Lockhart marched out to Alexandra picquet, some five miles on the Dosali road.

On 28 August General Marshall, who had commanded the Razmak Brigade during the Khaisora and subsequent operations, left for England and wrote the Officer Commanding the Guides a farewell letter:

"Before leaving the Razmak Brigade, I must send you this line to say how very proud and pleased I am to have the privilege of having your battalion in my command. You have throughout all these operations fully lived up to your great reputation, and I need hardly tell you that I had nothing but the fullest confidence that whatever you were called upon to do would be well and truly done and in the most efficient manner.

"In saying 'Goodbye' to you I feel I am doing so to personal friends, whose friendship I value most highly. I would like you to let your British and Indian officers and all ranks know how very grateful I am to them and how much I appreciate the very fine work they have done whilst with me here.

"The very best of luck to you all and may you soon have a rest from many years of war.

"J. S. MARSHALL."

The General's wishes for some rest were followed by news that they would probably return to Mardan in November.

The Affair of Ridgeway Hill

The Guides were not to leave Wazir Force, however, without another scrap, and a very satisfactory one, with the tribes, on very much the same lines as that of "Crag," but somewhat larger. Before, however, describing this and the recrudescence of tribal activity that preceded it, we should glance at what was going on in Sir John Coleridge's area in the east and south. Down the Khaisora and in the Shaktu the implacable and irrepressible Ipi was still carrying on his activities. The Faqir had now taken up his abode in the range known as the Prekari Sar, about five miles from the Bannu border where the Shaktu emerges from the formidable Shaktu Tangi, and where the Karresti Algad joins the Shaktu. There, on the western slopes of the Sar, he occupied five natural caves, one as his own dwelling and stronghold, the other four being used as mosques and meeting places. There he was in close touch with the Tori Khel, some of the Mahsuds and the Bhittanis.

Operations had also been necessary in the Spinwam area on the motor road from Mir Ali to Thal, where the Faqir had endeavoured to rouse those old irreconcilables—the Kabul Khel Wazirs. Now it was the 9th Brigade who were to proceed against the caves on the Prekari Sar, in support of Scouts and Border Constabulary, while the caves themselves were subject to an air raid which was naturally not very effective. But the Faqir thought planes and troops together too much for his holiness and he disappeared, to be reported at Mandeck, west of Razmak, a move which no doubt started the activities in which the Guides were now to take part.

Towards the end of September a considerable gathering of various lashkars was known to be in the Sirdar Algad, which ran down towards Razmak from the north-east in the general direction of Spinkamar and below the famous peak Shuidar and the Razmak water supply.

It was decided that the Bannu Brigade, reinforced by the Guides and the 1st/3rd Gurkhas, should take this force on. The enemy were not more than 5,000 yards from Razmak and the Brigadier thought that a move by night might result in a surprise, especially as the hill-tops, on which the enemy were to be seen, were likely to be abandoned at night for the shelter of the valleys. This tendency to night moves by our troops, in very rough country, so often carried out during these operations in Waziristan is striking evidence of the high state of individual training of the troops.

The features ahead, backed by the peaks of Babusar and Mamu Sar, were given, as usual, names by which they could be recognized in orders and messages. There were a series of ridges facing the line of advance and the most important was termed "Ridgeway," on the far side of which would be the main valley. On the way to this Ridgeway was a small hill, dubbed from its recognizable appearance "Black Rocks."

The Bannu Brigade was to make the main advance, the Guides protecting the left and the 1st/3rd Gurkhas their right. Both battalions moved out of the cantonment gates at 0100 hours on 27 September. As a company of the Guides was away at Alexandra, a company of the 2nd/14th Punjabis was attached to them, old frontier friends, long famous under their original name of the 20th Punjabis (Brownlow's). The Guides moved off in the following order: "C" Company leading, then "B" and the company of the 2nd/14th. No machine guns and no mules were taken, save a mule with one wireless set.

By 0300 hours Black Rocks was reached without incident, and a halt was called while the 2nd/14th Company was settled in. It was known that Ridgeway was connected with Black Rocks by a spur so that the former was the head of a "T" and the spur the long leg. Major Redding, commanding, now planned to move along the "T" leg with "B" and "C" Companies and carry Ridgeway. At 0340 hours the two companies moved forward along the leg when three shots were fired at close range. Battalion Headquarters were close up and halted the two companies some 400 yards from Ridgeway, from which

THE WAZIRISTAN CAMPAIGNS—contd.

shouting broke out all along its length and firing grew heavy. It was at first thought that the Guides were visible in the moonlight, but if so the opposite was not the case and it was hard to tell where the enemy were. Redding now decided that to advance before daylight in the face of the heavy fire would mean too heavy casualties and no hope of surprise, so at 0600 hours he moved back himself to Black Rocks to prepare his attack and inform Brigade Headquarters that he would attack at dawn, but asked for another company and his machine guns to come up. At 0550 hours firing in front increased and also broke out to the left from Mamu Sar.

At this stage "C" Company had two men wounded. It was dawn by 0630 hours and the enemy fire from the Ridgeway slackened as artillery fire was opened. At 0700 hours the machine guns and first-line mules arrived, followed also, a little later, by a company of the 1st/17th Dogras. Major Cumming, the Second-in-Command, at this stage had a narrow escape as a bullet struck the rock over which he was peering and pieces of rock hit his face.

Redding now gave out his orders for the attack, "C" Company to advance along the spur towards Ridgeway and protect the left of "B," which would attack the right of Ridgeway and then spread along to the left, while the company of the Dogras was to climb a spur which led to the enemy's left flank.

The definite support of the artillery was arranged and also the battalion's own machine guns, the latter to plaster the Ridgeway from Zero to 15 secs. Major Cumming now moved up to direct "B" and "C," and as soon as the artillery finally ceased and switched to Mamu Sar, the attack went forward.

The judicious arrangements and good support did the trick and in twenty minutes the whole ridge had been captured ; the Guides' casualties being only the two wounded while waiting, but the Dogras lost a man killed and five wounded.

But the enemy had another prepared position sixty yards to the rear. Heavy fire, however, drove them from this, and in retiring they were caught by the machine guns of both Guides and Gurkhas, and as party after party were flushed the enemy could be seen to be suffering heavily. Four dead were brought into our lines and some more seen could not be collected.

The work having been done, withdrawal was ordered, but as the Guides abandoned Black Rocks they were ordered to reoccupy the point, as a light tank in the Algad was in trouble and there were Gurkha casualties to get in. However, the enemy had suffered too heavily to follow up (casualties later ascertained to be 25 killed and 30 or so seriously wounded) and the force withdrew comfortably ; the Guides' total casualties being but five wounded and none very seriously. The 1st/17th Dogras unfortunately had an officer—Second-Lieutenant O. C. W. Bellamy—killed. It was an enjoyable day out and a little operation carried out in a masterly way. It certainly "larned" the lashkars to let the Razmak water supply alone.

Next day the following letter was received from Major-General Hartley, commanding the Waziristan Division :

"I have just received a letter from the Army Commander to say how pleased he was over yesterday's operation. He particularly mentions the first-rate work by your battalion. I very heartily endorse everything he says."

A very pleasant ending to a day in the country.

This ended the Faqir's activity in this direction, but there were five days' work to be done in repairing the water-works.

The officers with the Guides Infantry in these days were:

Major Redding	Commanding.
Major Cumming	Second-in-Command and Machine Guns.
Captain MacMunn ...	Adjutant (lately rejoined from leave in England).

"A" Company
Captain Eliott-Lockhart	Absent during Ridgeway at Alexandra Picquet.

"B" Company
Lieutenant Kreyer ...	1st Sikhs (attached).
Second-Lieutenant Watt.	

"C" Company
Lieutenant Campbell.
Lieutenant Griffith.

With them at Ridgeway were also:

Captain Tighe	2nd/14th Punjab Company.
Major Rogers	1st/17th Dogra Company.
Subadar Sher Muhammad	3rd Mtn. Batty. F.O.O.

That was the last that the Guides Infantry were to see of Waziristan and they shortly moved to Damdil on their way home.[27] It was December, however, before Sir John Coleridge could report that all was over. The Southern Bhittanis had yet to be given their lesson and learn that it did not pay to be the Mahsud "Jackal," while there were several sections of the Mahsuds who had not yet had enough. Eventually, however, all jirgas accepted the British terms, the pleasing fiction being adopted that the young men had got out of the hands of their elders. An unsatisfactory feature of the trouble was that of lashkars from the Ghilzai clans, who for centuries have come down the Gomal to winter and to trade in India, lodging their arms at frontier posts. For them to join in this entirely unnecessary rising was a clear proof how much Islam was disturbed by the drum ecclesiastic, trading on the folly of the British Cabinet and the weakness of the Government of India in 1930. And so, after much loss of life, December 1937 saw the end of it, and our attempts to help the tribes restarted.

"Pat" Grant

Since Lieutenant-Colonel Grant was the second Commanding Officer to be killed at the head of a Guides unit in the field, an appreciation by his Second-in-Command is not out of place in the Corps History. Only once before had this tragedy occurred—when

---

[27] Honours for members of the Guides for these operations are given in the next chapter.

Fred Battye fell on the Panjkora (1895). Lieutenant-Colonel Redding has communicated this appreciation :—

"Lieutenant-Colonel Patrick Grant, affectionately known to all his brother officers as 'Pat,' was a man beloved by all who came in contact with him.

"His integrity and forceful character, coupled with his gentleness and sympathy at all times for others, endeared him to his fellow-officers and other ranks. He was a first-rate soldier and a true friend, ready at all times to give sound advice, and thought much more about others than he did about himself. He was a great loss to the Guides Infantry not only as a soldier but as a friend."

On 23 June, he continued, the Battalion was ordered to march with other units in Tocol and Razcol from a camp at Chalwesti to Torwam, a distance of nine miles. Tocol led the advance as far as the Sherwangi pass and there Razcol took the lead, the Guides being the leading Battalion in Razcol.

The enemy held the pass and by 0900 hours little progress had been made to secure the dominating features of the pass. "Pat" received his orders from the Razcol Commander (Major-General Marshall). There had been a good deal of firing in the area and the visibility was not good on account of the trees which covered the features on the pass. Major J. E. Redding was Second-in-Command and in charge of Battalion Headquarters. He arranged for its position while "Pat" Grant went off a short distance with the Company Commander who was detailed to advance to the top of the pass, and the officers commanding supporting arms—*i.e.*, machine guns and artillery. Having given out his orders, Grant, together with Jemadar Arjan Singh, O.C. M.Gs., and their runners, stood on the slope of a tree-covered spur to watch the progress of the company he had detailed to take a parallel spur. A good deal of enemy fire was concentrated on the spur Battalion Headquarters were occupying. About 1000 hours an orderly came running up to Major Redding to say that the Colonel had been hit. Redding and his orderly ran down the slope about fifty yards and found Jemadar Arjan Singh and his orderly carrying "Pat" to the reverse side of the slope. The M.O. was sent for and "Pat," still conscious, was made as comfortable as possible till the M.O. came, asking only for a drink of water. Redding stayed with him till the M.O. and a stretcher arrived and it was obvious by then that "Pat" was dying. He was taken down the road to an ambulance, but passed away shortly afterwards.

It was arranged with the R.A.F. that his body should be flown to Mardan for burial, the place where he had spent so much of his soldiering, and which he loved so dearly. He rests with many other Guides in the little cemetery of the Guides' Chapel. Here is an outline of his service :

Eldest son of Colonel H. G. Grant, C.B., of the Seaforth Highlanders, grandson of Field-Marshal Sir Patrick Grant, G.C.B., G.C.M.G., and great-grandson of Field-Marshal Viscount Gough, he was educated at Wellington College, gaining an entrance scholarship. He passed into Sandhurst second, was commissioned on 20 January 1912 and attached to the 1st Battalion The Seaforth Highlanders in India.

He took part in the attack on the Malandri in Buner, February 1914, and in the campaign against the Mohmands in 1915, and he also took part in the action at Rustum.

When the Battalion went to Mesopotamia, he commanded the depot at Mardan afterwards rejoining them in Mesopotamia, and was with them in Palestine throughout the campaign. He reinforced the attack on the "Sisters" when the Battalion was hard pressed. He was with the Battalion against the Mohmands in 1933—Loe Agra in 1934. During 1935–36 he was an instructor at Sandhurst, returning to the Battalion for the operations against Mahsuds and Waziris in 1937, when he was killed at the Sherwangi pass on 23 June 1937, as just related.

CHAPTER VII

WAZIRISTAN TO THE SECOND WORLD WAR

THE CAVALRY AT MARDAN, 1935–1937—JOYOUS RETURN OF THE PALTAN—HONOURS FOR THE KHAISORA—REORGANIZATION OF INDIAN CAVALRY—CLASS COMPOSITION OF THE GUIDES CAVALRY—PIPE BAND OF THE PALTAN—HONOURS FOR WAZIRISTAN—THE NEW INFANTRY ORGANIZATION—THE TRANSFER OF THE KHATTAKS FROM THE INFANTRY, 1938—THE HAPPY LAST YEARS IN MARDAN—REUNION, THE MARDAN WEEK, 1938—THE AUTUMN OF 1938 AND EARLY 1939—REGIMENTAL HAPPENINGS, 1937–1939.

THE CAVALRY AT MARDAN, 1935–37

THE period with the Paltan at Mardan, hoped for in 1933, was not to be very extended, for the latter were now to be engaged in the first Mohmand operations of 1933–34, the Loe Agra operations and the campaign of 1935, again against the Mohmands, which was to bring them the tragedy and glory of the Nahakki fight—all caused by the ill-winded machinations of various faqirs, stirred up by the Red Shirt troubles of the early thirties.

Outside the routine of military training and Brigade camp, life sped easily, and spare days were spent in much training of polo ponies and polo teams. The Mardan week, planned for 1935, had to be abandoned, with the Paltan chasing their faqirs; but a Mess dance, this time the garden lit by electric light, was a great success, and, after all, the ladies of the Paltan were there.

In 1936, Mrs. Macpherson, sister of Major-General R. Adams, who won the V.C. in the Swat valley in 1897, put in two beautiful stained-glass windows in the south side of the chapel to his memory. It will be remembered how Lieutenant H. L. S. MacLean of the Guides was killed on the same desperate occasion, and it was noted in orders that he would have been awarded the Cross had he survived. Ten years later, when the principle of "Posthumous Award" was accepted, the dead lieutenant was gazetted. It will interest readers of today to learn that, of course, Winston Churchill was thereabouts in this campaign of the Pathan Revolt of 1897.

Mrs. Eliott-Lockhart also presented two silver cups to the cavalry in memory of Colonel P. C. Eliott-Lockhart.

This year, 1936, the Risala were in the final of the Indian Cavalry polo tournament once more, which they were to win in 1938 and 1939, as the effect of the sojourn at Bannu in making serious polo impossible passed off.

But this year the ponies were not good enough, and serious measures to produce the winning mounts had to be taken, with the triumphant results referred to.[28] In September 1936 Colonel Blood left the Regiment to take over the post of Secretary of the Horse Breeding Society of India and Majors Prioleau and Gradidge to jobs with the State Forces. At home, Captains the Hon. W. Edwardes and the Hon. R. A. H. Plunkett both took official part in the Coronation. Risaldar-major Ratan Chand was with the

---
[28] *Vide* Polo, Chapter XIII.

Coronation contingent, and Major Duncan and Subadar Sapuran Singh from the Paltan. Lieutenant-Colonel A. V. Hammond succeeded Lieutenant-Colonel Blood in command of the Cavalry (14 October 1936).

The Joyous Return Home of the Paltan

October 1937 passed quietly in Razmak, though Sepoy Kartar Singh, a Sikh signaller, was seriously wounded at one of the camp picquets at Damdil. On the 5th of the month, Major K. A. Garrett arrived as the new Commandant in succession to "Pat" Grant. On the 24th, before the departure from Razmak, Sir John Coleridge pinned the ribbon of the I.D.S.M. on Lance-Havildar Azram, an Orakzai, for his gallant leading of his platoon under heavy and accurate fire on the Ridgeway. At the end of the month the battalion was ordered to take over the Damdil section of the lines of communication, and an ominous rumour arose that their return was to be delayed, not to be lifted till definite orders for Mardan arrived at the end of November.

Before they left, however, they took part in a very pleasing ceremony, giving effect to a wish of Lieutenant-Colonel Grant and indeed of all the officers, carried out by Major Redding—viz., to present to the 4th (Hazara) Mountain Battery, one of the earliest in the army, a silver trumpet.

This battery had been in practically the same brigade group with the Guides Infantry in a long series of expeditions and the "liaison" was very complete and enduring. These operations were Mohmand, 1932, 1933-34; Loe Agra and Mohmand, 1935; Waziristan, 1936 and 1937. By a piece of good fortune, on the day that the Guides arrived at Damdil, the battery was marching to join the 9th Brigade. That evening the battalion formed two sides of a square, the battery on the third side, the British and Indian officers of both corps occupying the fourth side. Lieutenant-Colonel Garrett addressed the parade, alluding to the marked admiration and affection felt by the Guides Infantry for the Hazara Mountain Battery, and then Major Redding handed the trumpet to Captain G. R. L. Hawkes, M.C., temporarily in command in the unavoidable absence of Major H. G. de Burgh, O.B.E., M.C. The Subadar-major of the Guides then called for three hearty cheers.

The trumpet was inscribed with the badge of the Hazara Mountain Battery and these words:

> "Presented by Lieutenant-Colonel Grant and the British and Indian Officers of the Guides Infantry F.F. to the 4th Hazara Mountain Battery, R.A. (F.F.)
> In memory of many happy days spent together on the Frontier in 1932, 1933, 1935-36-37.
> (Mohmand and Waziristan)"

On 21 November their old Frontier friends the "Cokis" (Coke's Rifles) swung in to relieve them.

On the 23rd they embussed for Bannu, and after handing in stores at Bannu on the 25th they entrained on the 2-foot 6-in. little Frontier railway for Mari Indus, the

MAJOR-GENERAL A. V. HAMMOND

ferry on that river that connects with the broad gauge. Then up the Indus to Chabb and Jhand, through much of the country from which their Khattaks and Awans came, of whom there was a cheering collection at Chabb junction of friends and relatives, mothers, wives and sons in great enthusiasm, and a dozen future recruits were presented. In happy mood the returning train moved on, reaching Mardan at an early hour on 27 November. By seven the stores had been unloaded, and at eight the battalion marched for their century-old home amid showers of flowers, arches of welcome, and bazaar bombs. That night in the Mess was a ladies' guest night, a scene of much happiness.

The Battalion soon settled down to its old routine. Officers were rejoining—Baily from the Training Battalion, Hamilton from the Small Arms School at Pachmari; while Campbell had left them at Damdil on eight months' leave and Pollard had gone to the Territorial Battalion. That left, with the Battalion :

Lieut.-Colonel Garrett	Commanding.
Major Redding	Second-in-Command.
Major Cumming	"C" Company.
Lieutenant Hodson	"A" Company.
Major Barlow	"B" Company.
Captain Baily	"B" Company.
Lieutenant Watt	"C" Company.
Captain MacMunn	Adjutant.
Lieutenant Hamilton	Quartermaster.

On 4 December Major-General Dashwood Strettell, commanding the Peshawar Division, inspected the Battalion and made very complimentary comments on its appearance.

Honours for the Khaisora Operations, 1936–37

The following rewards and encomiums were issued for the various operations in the Khaisora in which the Guides took part.

The Indian Distinguished Service Medal.
    Subadar Dost Muhammad, for his able leading of "C" Company, and his gallantry in calling in his picquets in the dark on 25th November, 1936.

Mentioned in the despatches of H.E. the C.-in-C.
    Major G. F. Taylor.
    Subadar Jaggat Singh (Sikh).
    Naik Wilayat Khan (P.M.).
    Naik Murid Khan (P.M.) (transferred to 2nd/15th Punjabis).

Army Commander's Certificates for devotion to duty.
    Subadar Khial Din.
    Jemadar Arjan Singh.
    Jemadar Misri Khan.
    Jemadar Sirdar Khan (then Regimental Quartermaster-Havildar).
    2439 Havildar-Major Sukh Ram.
    2437 Havildar Sohan Singh.
    3686 Havildar Sahu Singh (then Naik) (Mess Havildar).
    7416 Lance-Naik Sadara Singh.
    13254 Sepoy Rais Khan (runner).

THE GUIDES

About this time appeared General Sir John Coleridge's farewell order on the break up of the force soon after the departure of the Guides. This is how it began:

"On the break up of Wazir Force, I wish to express to all ranks my high appreciation of the fine work done by all throughout this arduous campaign. In battle the enemy have been so successfully dealt with that only a few hostile bands remain. . . . I am honoured by having commanded so fine a force and thank you all, while wishing you farewell and all good fortune in the future."

It was well-earned praise, for never has a force on the Frontier had more unremitting arduous work or more difficult fighting.

REORGANIZATION OF THE INDIAN CAVALRY, 1937

In 1937 orders were issued for the reorganization of the Indian cavalry into three groups, with a training regiment for each group. The grouping was as follows:

1st Group	*2nd Group*	*3rd Group*
Training Regiments		
15th Lancers	Sam Browne's	20th Lancers
(Jhansi)	(Ferozepore)	(Lucknow)
Service Regiments		
Skinner's Horse	Hodson's Horse	6th Lancers
2nd Lancers	Probyn's Horse	7th Cavalry
3rd Cavalry	Guides Cavalry	Deccan Horse
Poona Horse	P.A.V.O. Cavalry	19th Lancers
18th Cavalry	13th Lancers	C.I. Horse
	Scinde Horse	

The class composition of the units was to be levelled up, a process dear to the Adjutant-General's department but a source of heart-break to many men. Under this, the Guides had to lose all their staunch Punjabi Mohammedans and take in more Pathans, and also lost many Dogras. The Training Regiments were to have three training squadrons each, a squadron supporting two service regiments. They were to have an essential new feature, a British quartermaster of the trained quartermaster class.

To give effect to the new order meant much work in the regimental office for several months. It also meant much rearrangement of classes. It is not out of place to remark here again on the difference between the British and Indian service. In the one, the soldier is a soldier, and transfers to carry out a new organization are a simple matter; but in the class company system we see prevailing throughout the Indian Army it is a very different matter, so often attended with grave heart-breaking. In the new system, for instance, the 6th Lancers would lose all their Dogras and the Guides Cavalry their P.Ms. A conference of all Commanding Officers at Army Headquarters was necessary and took ten days, being rather like a game of pit. To the Guides, the net result was that they took in from other corps 2 British officers, 7 V.C.Os. and 150 O.Rs., and sent to the new Training Regiment 1 British officer, 2 V.C.Os., 23 I.O.Rs. and all the recruits.

All this meant immense efforts to blend the new-comers into the fine steel of the Corps, while to the oriental mind it meant a terrible lot of new personalities to take the measure of! In the final baking of the pot, however, the new was as good as the old.

TYPES OF THE GUIDES

CLASS COMPOSITION OF GUIDES CAVALRY F.F., 1921–46

The following note on the above may be suitably included here:

In 1921, when all Indian Cavalry was reorganized and formed into groups, the Regiment was reconstituted as follows:

"A" Sqn. Dogras
"B" „   Sikhs
"C" „   Punjabi Musalmans
H.Q. „   A proportion of all above classes.

Sanction was obtained to include half a squadron of Pathans in place of P.Ms. The actual constitution of "C" Squadron was therefore two troops of P.Ms., one troop of Yuzafzai Pathans, and one troop half Akora Khattaks and half Saghri Khattaks from the Punjab. A proportion of Pathans was included in H.Q. Squadron. This organization was maintained until 1937.

In that year three Indian Cavalry regiments were, as just recorded, converted into recruit training centres. These were Sam Browne's Cavalry, 15th Lancers and 20th Lancers. The 15th Lancers were one of the three Indian Cavalry regiments officially to enlist a squadron of Pathans, the other two being 13th D.C.O. Lancers and 14th P.W.O. Sind Horse. It was the policy at G.H.Q. to continue to maintain three squadrons of Pathans in the Indian Cavalry. The Regiment was therefore asked if they would accept a complete Pathan squadron from 15th Lancers in place of their P.M. squadron. They answered that they were prepared to have a complete Pathan squadron and get rid of the P.Ms., but that they already had half a squadron of Pathans. It was therefore decided that half a squadron of Pathans plus a proportion for H.Q. Squadron should be transferred to the Regiment from 15th Lancers. This was done in April 1937. The P.Ms. were either mustered out or transferred to other units. Some went to Probyn's Horse, some to Hodson's Horse, and at the last minute a further batch were transferred to 4th/15th Punjab Regiment, who were raising a new P.M. Company. Many of these P.Ms. became V.C.Os. Two became Risaldar-majors and one Subadar-major.

There was considerable argument with the Adjutant-General regarding what sub-classes of Pathans the regiment should take. Owing to over-recruitment of that class, the A.G. wished the Regiment to stop taking Cis-Indus Sagari Khattaks, one of their old classes. As they were one of the best classes and fine horsemen, the Commanding Officer was not prepared to give them up. It was finally decided that they should continue in the Regiment as long as a large proportion of other classes was also taken. In addition to the three original old sub-classes of Pathans, therefore, men from the following tribes were also taken: Adam Khel and Hassan Khel Afridis from the Kohat Pass and Kui, Khalils Seni and Barak Khattaks, and one or two Bangash. It was obviously impossible to keep all these tribes in separate sub-units; they were therefore all mixed up in one Pathan squadron.

In addition to the substitution of Pathans for P.Ms., during the reorganization a number of Sikhs and Dogras were brought in from 15th Lancers, Sam Browne's Cavalry, and 6th Lancers. Altogether about 25 per cent. of the Regiment was changed, including many V.C.Os. and N.C.Os.

88 THE GUIDES

The organization of Dogras, Sikhs and Pathans was maintained up to August 1947. During the war of 1939–45, the Sikh and Dogra strength fell owing chiefly to the low priority of the Regiment for reinforcements while on the Frontier in 1943–47. Regiments in the field who were similarly placed were forced to accept other classes, such as Jats or Hindu Rajputs, to make up for the shortage of Sikhs and Dogras, which was widespread throughout the Army. However, Pathan recruiting did not fall and by increasing slightly the numbers of that class it was possible to avoid having to take a new class.

THE PIPE BAND OF THE PALTAN

In 1936, as in many other Indian corps, the decision had been taken to give up the brass band. The Guides had also some pipers and it was now agreed that the Infantry should have an enlarged Pipe Band, which would include drummers who would also be buglers. Brass bands in India were always a difficulty, and it was not every one of the bandmasters usually obtained from the bands of British corps who could get the best out of the undoubted musical talent inherent in the Indian. Pipes, however, were in some form or other the instrument of the tribes on both sides of the Frontier and also of the Dogra hills. Sometimes there was a bag, though never drones, but the usual form of the instrument was only the chanter, known on the Frontier as the sarnai, and many of the Frontier corps have a small secondary band of dole and sarnai—the dole being the inciting little drum hung from the neck and played with the hands, played with a wild incitement to love or to war as the case might be. All officers who have been on the Frontier know that exciting and *na manassib* (improper) love air "Zakhmi Dil" ("The Bleeding Heart"), first heard, it is said, in Kabul by a British bandmaster of the Army of Occupation in Kabul in the 1840's and set to western music. It is perhaps the most typical of the airs played on the sarnai, and its lure and lilt are amazing. So the bands of the northern regiments took readily to the pipe bands, and regiments with Royal distinctions took to wearing pipe strings and even shoulder plaids of Royal Stuart tartan. In the Guides this was confined to the pipe strings and bag. But, as related in Chapter II, in 1923 this wearing of tartan was reviewed at Army Headquarters, and an order issued that the Royal tartan was not to be used without special permission from the King. It was several years before this permission was accorded to the Guides, who were the only corps of the Indian Army thus distinguished.

The new Pipe Band of the Corps was to consist of a Pipe-major and 17 pipers and a Drum-Major and 13 buglers, who were also the drummers; but all the pipers could not be trained for some while.

Incidentally, it was not always the Saxon side of the British officers who were thrilled, but in the Guides all were enthusiastic.

Here is a story of what actually took place between the author and an ex-piper of the 17th Bengal Lancers, playing for a living in Mianmir. The 17th Bengal Lancers, when commanded by "Charlie" Muir—it was largely a Pathan regiment—started a pipe band, though whether or not it played a-horse I cannot remember. What became of it may be told in the words of the ex-piper. "Us waqt Charlie Muir Sahib Colonel tha, and main us ke niche bharti tha. Phir usne pinsin ko gya, aur nauwa colonel aya. Wuh to [note the *to*] Englishman tha, usne ekdam [note the *ekdam*, in a moment] nikala," and that was the tragedy of the Pipe band of the 17th Bengal Lancers. For the uninitiated let us translate: "At that time Charlie Muir was our Colonel and under him I enlisted as a piper. Then he went to pension and a new colonel came; he, however, was an Englishman. He at one breath rooted out the pipes."

The dress of the new Pipe Band was, of course, a matter of careful consideration, for "many have fancy and few have taste." As the pipes were the only band, it was obvious that they must make a brave show on occasion. The Corps, as all the world knows, has worn since its birth a khaki drab cloth, so the pipers were to wear:

(a) A long kurta to the knees, of cavalry pattern.
(b) Blue lungis and red kullas, as for the old brass band, the pipe- and bugle-majors to have the gold thread in the ends as did the former band-havildar.
(c) The understandings to be plus-fours of the same material as the kurta, with a narrow red stripe on the sides. They were to have the continuations like the old 20th, so that they could be worn with chaplis, though black puttees and boots were to be the full-dress order.
(d) The scarlet kammarband of the cavalry was also to be worn with the brown belt over it, while pipe and drum-majors were to have the extra dignity of cross straps to the belts rather than slings.
(e) But the most important point almost was the facings and buttons to be adopted as the witness of the history of the dress of the Corps—viz., the historic red pipings on the collar, red cuffs, red shoulder straps and badges in red. Buttons and titles were to be of white metal.

In addition to this picturesque outfit, the drum-major was to have a sash designed by Lieutenant Hamilton, having a scarlet ground, with two gold stripes down the edges, and on the top the regimental crest, worked in scarlet, gold and silver, the Garter in blue. Below were the battle honours of the Corps worked in gold on scarlet, with a pattern of green leaves around. It was made by Henry Potter of London. New panther skins mounted on scarlet for the big and tenor drummers were also to be provided.

Honours for Waziristan, 1937

A postscript to the Khaisora honours came with a mention in the Commander-in-Chief's despatches of Lieutenant R. M. Crowe of the Royal Canadian Regiment, who had been attached to the Guides in Waziristan and who had endeared himself to all ranks.

The Commander-in-Chief's Waziristan Despatches mentioned:
Major J. E. Redding,
W. J. Cumming,
Lieut. A. C. S. Moore (with the Tochi Scouts),
Jemadar Arian Singh,

while Army Commander's certificates were issued to:
Jemadar Dad Muhammad,
5604 Havildar Sadhu Singh (C.S.M., "C" Company),
9870 Lance-Naik Bishan Singh,
6993 Havildar Amil Hamza (Akora Khattak).

The New Infantry Organization

The Battalion in the hot season of 1938 had another new problem to keep it busy—viz., the rearrangement of the companies to follow that of British rifle battalions, which had very properly now been introduced for the Indian Army—very properly, for as the British and Indian Army always fought side by side in large and small wars, similarity was essential both for matters of tactics and of munitions supply. There was only one drawback, that the General Staff at the War Office made changes too often, not realizing how everyone had to trail after them; this applied not only in the actual formation, but in the equally important matter of regulations. Even the smallest change would upset stores and equipment tables, and mobilization store tables, the remaking of which was a long and costly job, and very often till they were rewritten and issued the change could not be given effect to.

The important change now introduced was a considerable one. The Battalion had to be arranged into a headquarters and five companies instead of four—viz., a headquarters company and four rifle companies of three platoons of 38 each. The H.Q. Company would eventually have six specialist platoons, but at present, in India, only Nos. 1, 4 and 6 Platoons would be arranged for—viz., Signals (No. 1), Machine Guns (No. 4), four sections of two guns each, and No. 6 Administrative Personnel.

It should be noted that the three vacant platoons with the H.Q. company were for specialists not yet ready in the Indian Army.

With a unit made up of various classes who had to be kept separate, there was a good deal of thinking to be done and for a while the class distribution was as follows:

"A" Company	No. 7 Platoon	Two sections Cis-Indus and Trans-Indus Khattaks and one section Yuzafzais.
	No. 8 Platoon	Three sections Malwa Sikhs.
	No. 9 Platoon	Three sections Punjabi Muslims.
"B" Company	No. 10 Platoon	Two sections Yuzafzis, one section Punjabis Muslims.
	No. 11 Platoon	Three sections Manja Sikhs.
	No. 12 Platoon	Three sections Dogras.
"C" Company	No. 13 Platoon	Three sections Yuzafzais.
	No. 14 Platoon	Three sections Manja and Malwa Sikhs mixed.
	No. 15 Platoon	Three sections Dogras.
"D" Company	No. 16 Platoon	Three sections Punjabi Muslims.
	No. 17 Platoon	Three sections Orakzais and Akora Khattaks (mixed).
	No. 18 Platoon	Three sections Dogras.

In each rifle platoon one of the sections was light machine gun (Vickers-Berthier). It should be noted that the new fourth company was formed by taking a platoon from each of the original three rifle companies and the total battalion strength was not altered.

The Transfer of Khattaks from the Infantry

We now come to a minor tragedy—viz., the transfer of the Khattaks just alluded to. To understand what an important matter this was one must needs understand the original recruiting of the famous old regiments. For a century the Guides had more or less continued recruiting from the castes and clans chosen by their original founders.

For a hundred years the Guides and others so formed had a wonderful connection with certain clans and certain villages—an intimate family connection from generation to generation. We have seen that, for instance, as the Guides passed through Chabb junction on their way home from Waziristan, a dozen likely *umedwars* or would-be recruits, sons and nephews of pensioned or serving men, were produced to be looked at. This had resulted in the old regiments having a wonderful rank and file of intense respectability, reliability and martial inheritance, a condition which later-raised corps could not hope to emulate for many a long year. The men clung very affectionately to this grouping and it is an excellent illustration, so often forgotten, of how intensely life in an Indian regiment differs from, say, that in the British Service. The whole fighting spirit and record of a corps is largely produced by it.

Now the Guides, among others, from the old time before, had a large number of an extensive group of a Pathan clan living within the British border—viz., the Khattaks. They chiefly are recognized in three groups: the Akora Khattaks, who lived in the hills near Nowshera and the Kabul river; the Nareb Sagris, who lived along the left bank of the Indus above Mari Indus; and the Trans-Indus group. They are a peculiarly fine martial race, and their record in the Guides is a famous one.

It had been hoped that this change would be held over; but in 1937 had come orders to transfer a number of the Khattaks to the 4th Sikhs and to receive an equal number of the Yuzafzais instead. Yuzafzais they had several of and they were well enough, but the Khattaks were after their own heart and the flower of the regiment ever since the days of the Khattak outlaw and wolf's head who died a Subadar of the Guides and a Christian, Dilawar Khan.

But there was a reason for the change, apart from the overweening desire of the Adjutant-General's office to make all corps alike, and that is that the Khattaks, though a large clan, were still a limited field of recruitment. The Militia policy (the Scouts were the same as Militia though under another name, since the Afghan invasion had so tarnished the original name of honour) had failed in so far as it aimed at giving suitable and honourable employment to young local tribesmen and thus weaning them from the desire to raid their neighbours. This applied more to Waziristan than to other tracts. The young Mahsuds and Wazirs made fine young soldiers, but were very liable to fits of misrule and desertion and at times murdered their officers for the glory of God and the exaltation of their own sub-clan, and when the Afghans came in 1919 they deserted almost *en masse*.

Therefore, though the Militia or their successors, the Scouts, had to be filled with Pathans, they were to be Pathans of a more trustworthy calibre—Afridis, Yuzafzais and especially the always reliable Khattak. Therefore the army recruiting field became over drained and the fiat had gone forth to reduce the intake for the army. It was all very understandable, but to a corps like the Guides very distressful, and the men found it more so even than the officers. Thus when fifty Khattaks marched out under Jemadar Spin Gul, one havildar and two naiks, it was a great loss. It left, however, some fifty Khattaks in the Battalion, enough to keep touch with these staunchest of His Majesty's subjects, but enabled it to retain the Yuzafzais.

The marching away of Spin Gul's party was a remarkable occasion, for all the Corps and all the Corps' friends lined the road to the station and the departure was such a scene of grief and enthusiasm as almost to amount to mass hysteria, and one of those reminders to authority of how strange a psychological entity was that which we call the Indian Army. Some further orders on the class composition of the companies were expected by the Battalion, but did not arrive for some months.

The departing detachment, however, was very well received and entreated in their new corps—a "Piffer" one, of course (the 4th Sikhs)—and the men soon settled down happily enough.

The Happy Last Years in Mardan

There now supervened after all the strain of Waziristan a period of nearly three years in their old home and the Risala and the Paltan were together. A good Indian corps is always a home of camaraderie, but for the Guides in the station they had developed for so long it was especially so. The families came together again and many were the dance-dinners and garden parties at which the regimental ladies and other residents were entertained. Many important visitors came their way; Viceroys, Commanders-in-Chief and provincial Governors found the hospitality of the Corps a charming finale to a tour in the Swat valley on the far side of the Malakand. Noticeable in the regimental diaries are the domestic touches, while even the affairs of the regimental dogs are freely recorded. We read of Hannah Hodson, a bull terrier pup, and how Jeanie MacMunn had five pups to Kim Murcot, a cocker, of whom one was a cocker, and how Bill Griffith died of heart failure in the Kashmir Hills.

The relations with the rank and file and the Indian officers, always cordial, became even more so as modern amenities for the men developed, and the British officers and the Indians entertained each other. This camaraderie between the British officers and their men was one of the great attractions of service in the Indian Army, and many a man asked nothing better than to spend his life with his corps. For the Guides, more perhaps than for any, their corps was "an Abiding City," but with it all the mutual discipline remained as tight beneath the velvet glove of sympathy and camaraderie as any martinet could wish for. If you went to look for sport or recruits among the villages, your reception by the pensioners and the wives of the serving men would be truly regal, a condition anathema to the spirit of the Indian Congress, who have so long tried to break it.

The years 1937 and 1938 and early 1939 had their usual Brigade and Divisional Commanders' inspections which, since always satisfactory, need not be further recorded; but the Pipe Band were in all the glory of their new kit, and which added to the éclat of these occasions. The constant training, camps and exercises of all kinds, often in the hills across the Kabul river, rigorous and instructive, have not been described. There were plenty of them. *Horas non numero nisi serenas*, and this chapter deals largely with the lighter side of a happy life; and since it is the last period in the old life of the Corps it is dwelt on at some length, so that the dead past may live.

A charming addition to the Regimental trophies now came from the 4th Hazara Battery (to whom, it will be remembered, the Infantry had presented a silver trumpet)

INTERIOR OF THE GUIDES' MESS

[Photo: R. B. Holmes, Peshawar

To face page 92

in the form of a plaque with the crests of the two corps and the engraved signatures of officers of the Battery. It bore the inscription "1947, presented to the Guides Infantry by the 4th (Hazara) Mountain Battery, in memory of many years' service together."

The Mess had also received a gift, preparatory to the separation of Cavalry and Infantry, from Colonels Prendergast and Blood, an extremely good copy of the portrait of their first commander, Sir Harry Lumsden, of which the Mess had already the original. It was made by the Mayo Art School of Lahore. Alec Moore also presented the Mess with a silver calendar for the writing table.

On Sunday 27 February 1938, the Reverend G. Laurence, Chaplain of Risalpur, came over to dedicate Regimental Memorials. There were brass tablets to Lieutenant-Colonel Patrick Grant, Lieutenant Norman, Lieutenant Tweedie, and a memorial window to the memory of Captain Godfrey Meynell, V.C.

The tablet in brass to Colonel Grant read as follows :

"In proud and loving memory of Lieutenant-Colonel Patrick Grant, commanding Q.V.O. Guides Infantry, Eldest son of Colonel Hugh Gough Grant of the Seaforth Highlanders and A.A. Punjab Command. Killed in action during the advance to Torwam, 23 June, 1937.

"And all the Trumpets sounded for him on the other side."

But it did not say that his father was the son of the famous Indian Army Officer—Field-Marshal Sir Patrick Grant, for many years Governor of the Royal Hospital, Chelsea, and that his grandmother was a daughter of Field-Marshal Viscount Gough. It was a very famous army strain of which that sniper's bullet took toll.

For the Cavalry, 1938 was a year of successes. At the great North of India Horse Show the Regiment took the first prize for Indian troop horses, and the second in the open jumping. But far greater than this was the winning by the Cavalry of the Indian Cavalry Polo Tournament, thus bringing the cup back to the Mess after a lapse of thirty-two years of annual endeavour.[29]

In the semi-finals the Guides had beaten the 6th Lancers by 11 goals to 3, and in the final, Skinner's Horse by 10 to 1.

The team was : Birnie, No. 1 ; Roffey, No. 2 ; Plunkett, No. 3 ; Gradidge, Back.

But this was not all their polo triumphs, for in April a team composed of Eales, Walton, Birnie and Mainwaring won the cup presented by the 15th Hussars, beating the runners-up, Skinner's Horse, by 4½ goals to nil.

On 27/28 January 1938 occurred in Kohat—the Headquarters and the long-established home of the Frontier Force—a sad disaster. The Garrison Church was burnt to the ground. To the Guides, with their own church, the loss was not so intimate, but to the rest of that Abiding City it was an unimaginable and irreplaceable loss. There were the monuments to the Glory of God and to the evergreen memory of officers who had died for their country and the peace of the Frontier peoples. There, reverently deposited not only by the British officers but by the Muslim and Sikh and Hindu rank and file, were the battle-worn Regimental Colours that had become too frail to serve

---

[29] *Vide* Polo, Chapter XIII.

longer. There were the carved pews, the memorial chapels, the reredos and the chancel arches to the memory of the brave, gone in a whirl of flame like Wren's churches in the City of London at the hands of the Hun. And all the Punjab Frontier Force that once was the original "Piffers," the Punjab Irregular Force, bowed their heads in sorrow. To the Guides and their memorial Church was to come, at the hands of man, a tragedy almost as sad.

REUNION: THE MARDAN WEEK OF 1938

In the intervals between the various types of training, which were pretty strenuous, there was plenty of fun. A large contingent of officers and men went to Kohat for the first "Piffer" week since Waziristan. Kohat in April, when the young shisham trees (*Dalbergia Sissu*) are in their first leaf, is a very charming place to forgather, as indeed is Mardan for the same reason. The shisham is indeed something like the lime trees of Europe, and hardly had the merrymakers returned when the Viceroy, Lord Linlithgow, with the Vicereine came to Mardan. He was visiting the new Canal Works and the Malakand, and on his way down the party stopped for tea in the Guides' Mess, passing through a long lane of the Indian ranks and then through a line of the British officers and their ladies; and of course the Pipe Band was there, and stirred the Viceroy's Scottish blood and indeed performed very creditably for so young a formation.

In April came Mardan Week, with the return of the Infantry like, no doubt, many that had gone before; but as "weeks" are so typical of happy station life, and as the Guides had long been so happily endowed with their own cantonment, some account of the happenings in this balmy month of the shisham leaf is worth preserving. To the "week" would come every Guide within hail, and many pensioners from the villages round, largely Yuzafzais, would turn up; the civil residents would of course be there. Polo, hockey, cricket, sports for the rank and file, tea parties on the polo ground or in the mess garden, and this time there was something quite new, most suitable for a balmy April evening, in the shape of an open-air dance. Never in the annals of Mardan, since 1846, had there been such a thing before. The whole garden was floodlit. Coloured lights were among the trees on the south end, by the swimming bath; floodlights, too, were hidden among the flower-beds and under the great cotton trees and the *longifolia*. Opposite the Mess, on the tennis courts, were two shamianas, lit by Chinese lanterns, and beyond again the refreshment and supper tents. Under the shamianas were stretched druggets so taut as to be like ice. The lovelies, bints and the frippets, had come in their numbers from far and near, from Kohat, from Peshawar, from Nowshera and from Risalpur, so close on 300 were assembled to sing the Mardan swan song, and no one saw ahead the Hitler bomb that was to fall on their happy world. The Persian couplet from the Diwan i Khas at Delhi might well describe the scene of fair women and brave men in their happy revelry that spoke only of the end of the operations in Waziristan: "Agar ba ru i dunya behisht ast, hamin ast, hamin ast, hamin ast." ("If there is paradise on the face of the earth, it is this, it is this, it is this.")

The band of the Dorset Regiment had come over to play for them and now and again the pipes were to be heard in the distance.

THE MESS GARDEN

So spring passed to the pea-soup haze of the Frontier hot weather, and the ladies flitted, not to desert their husbands, who get on better alone in the heat, but to preserve their own and their children's health. There was little to be done save musketry and quiet training. At the end of August, Risaldar Karim Dad left the Cavalry on pension after long years of sterling service and was sent off with a sports meeting and a Khattak dance in his honour.

The Mess house was done up and recoloured and washed and the wood of red shisham scraped of its varnish.

There was a reunion this year at the Training Battalion at Sialkot to which many of the Guides pensioners went, for again "Once a Guide, always a Guide," and the new Pipe Band went too.

Among dress items was the abolition of the graceful Wolseley helmet for officers in favour of the hideous but extremely protective helmet known as "the Bombay Bowler." Both Corps agreed that a drab and red muslin slip should be worn showing over the top of the puggaree and the silver regimental badge in front, and permission was applied for. The old Review Order had been reintroduced in 1937 for the cavalry for guards and ceremonials—*i.e.*, blue lungis, with varying degrees of gold for I.Os. and duffadars, red kammarbands and black puttees with long boots for the I.Os., and for mufti long cream-coloured coats to wear over shirts and pyjamas. There were also to be changes in the head-dresses of the rank and file of the Paltan. It had always been the custom in the Punjab regiments for each class company or varying platoons to tie their regimental puggaries in the styles of their own races, which differed from one another considerably, and the long red kuta or skull cap around which they were tied was not very suitable, and smaller kullas and a more universal pattern of tying were introduced for the various Muslim races. The Sikh puggaree must of course remain even if a bit shorter, while the Dogra one was always manageable.

The Autumn, 1938, and Early 1939

Autumn of the last year of peace, and they knew it not, was now coming. Mardan was looking its best with some signs of chrysanthemums and the winter flowers. The only new gadget to think about was the new field drill in threes and the new snipers' course, which naturally appealed to the Pathans. As usual, on the anniversary of the storming of Delhi telegrams were exchanged between the Guides, the 60th Rifles and the 2nd Gurkhas, in memory of that long camaraderie on the Ridge. On 29 September the Colonel laid wreaths on the graves of Godfrey Meynell and Tony Randall, who died on that fierce day at the head of the Wucha Jawar Nullah.

On 11 November the usual "White Mufti" Armistice Day parade of Risala and Paltan was held under the Subadar-major, while Colonel Hammond read the service in the church. Afterwards the Pipes played in the Mess garden.

It being the twentieth anniversary, there was a special service at Kohat to which Captain M. H. H. Baily and Jemadar Faqir (Khattak) took a wreath to lay at the foot of the Frontier Force War Memorial, the little party marching past with the troops on parade.

Both Cavalry and Infantry left Mardan for brigade training, the Cavalry taking part in a training march with manœuvres against troops in the Peshawar and Kohat districts, on the way back fighting the Paltan in the Nowshera hills.

In November the Battalion went to a training camp at Manki, spoilt by the terrible tragedies of assassination in a regiment in a camp near by, it being called on to send senior officers to take command till the crimes had been assessed and new officers appointed. At Nowshera the Paltan met the new Territorial Battalion of the 12th F.F. Regiment which was numbered 11.

Christmas week was not on quite the large scale of the reunion year of 1937, but the bachelors were "at home" to the station on Christmas Eve, and kept it up till dawn. On Christmas Day the serving Indian officers and pensioners came to the Mess, among them Khan Bahadur Risaldar Moghul Baz, now Minister for the Public Services Commission in the Province. It was he who had presented his portrait to the Corps, wearing no less than seventeen decorations. MacNamara and Griffith and their ladies also turned up at mid-day. Christmas Day passed as usual, the Chaplain of Risalpur being able to get over and hold Matins and Communion.

And so the old year passed out, in peace and happiness. The doings and celebrations, even those which had been held for so many years, have been recounted, now that the two units of the Corps were together again. This account will recall the happy life and camaraderie that always obtain in good regiments, and especially perhaps in the Guides, the last of the once composite corps which in pre-Mutiny days were in existence in many of the more disturbed parts of India.

The New Year opened with the usual Proclamation Parade that perpetuates the taking over of the more direct control of India by the Crown in 1858 from the spacious hands of the Honourable East India Company, which was of course but the Crown in Commission. Ralph Griffith and the Pollards and Baileys turned up from their outside appointments for the occasion.

Colonel Hammond took the parade and the two units were commanded by Major Eales and Lieutenant-Colonel Garrett respectively, and both marched past the Corps Commander. It was a notable occasion as the last Proclamation Parade on which the Cavalry and Infantry would be together and parade as one Corps, and photographs were taken in the Mess garden.

The year saw a change in the review order of the Infantry of the Corps. It was really a reversion to the old dress depicted in the coloured plate in MacMunn and Lovat's "Armies of India." It reintroduced the red kammarband—$4\frac{1}{2}$ inches broad—worn under the belt, with the end hanging down level with the coat just in front of the bayonet.

Now, too, came a new order regrouping the companies of the Paltan. In earlier days most of the Frontier Force regiments had from time immemorial formed their companies by class, so that most of the various races served in one company. This was always adjudged the best for Frontier warfare, where each race contributed its special qualities—the Pathan élan and activity; the Sikh that stubborn fighting spirit; the Dogra fire and chivalry; and the Punjabi Muslims the backbone of the discipline and balance. But this system did not lend itself, it was held, to the heavy casualties and

[Photo: R. B. Holmes, Peshawar

BRITISH OFFICERS
Cavalry and Infantry, January 1939

Back Row (L. to R.)—Phillips, Griffith, Lord Kensington, Birnie, Pollard, Egerton, Watt, McCausland, MacMunn.
Centre Row—Reid, Pratt, Moore, Eliott-Lockhart, *R. V. Hodson, Baily, Bailey, Hamilton, Mainwaring, Hutchinson.
Front Row—Duncan, Eales, Garrett, Hammond, Cumming, Walton, Coleman.   * Note initials to distinguish him from his brother, Michael Hodson.

To face page 96

mass reinforcements of modern war. So the companies would in future be Sikh, Dogra, Pathan, etc. The Paltan regretted, but acquiesced in the necessity of the change, which took place in 1941.

The most stirring happening, however, of the early part of this year was the feat of the Cavalry in winning for the second time in succession—a very unusual feat—the Indian Cavalry Polo Tournament, with largely a new team, viz :

Captain Lord Kensington, No. 1 ; Lieutenant Roffey (Captain), No. 2 ; Captain the Hon. R. A. H. Plunkett, No. 3 ; Lieutenant Garforth Bles, Back.

It was to prove to be the last year of this Tournament too, and when in 1947 the flag came down, the Guides, sadly enough, were the final holders. The description of the play in this great final, as it appeared in the *Civil and Military Gazette*, is given in the Polo chapter.

Alas ! In May 1939 came the fatal order, long rumoured, that Mardan was to be given up and that the Corps of Guides would resolve into separated component parts. This was, of all things, one of the recommendations of the Chatfield Report. The Guides Cavalry were to move in the course of relief to Quetta, and the Infantry would go to the Khajuri plain on the Peshawar border. The bare announcement is epitaph enough. For over ninety years the Corps of Guides had held and tamed the Yuzafzai borders, even making good soldiers from the wildest ruffians, as Kipling wrote :

> "Last night ye had shot at a border thief,
> To-night 'tis a man of the Guides."

The rest of the Indian Army chuckled at this, but it described a great work of civilization grandly carried out.

The principal matter that required attention was the disposal of private buildings. The sharing of the collected treasures of the Officers' Mess and suitable arrangements for care and reverence of their church and immovable memorials had to be made.

The sharing of the Mess treasures was carried out by a committee in the greatest amity, submitted to a general Mess meeting and old officers of the Corps, and a record of the division unanimously accepted.

It was rumoured that the cantonment would become a police school, but whatever may have happened during the Second World War, at the end it became more suitably the home of the R.I.A.S.C. school, who kept the place in splendid order while the Raj lasted.

By the middle of 1939, the war clouds were gathering and what happened must wait for the next chapter.

Regimental Happenings, 1937-39

Birnie, the No. 1, well known as an explorer of mountains, had recently, with Bailey, joined the Guides from Sam Browne's on the reorganization.

Eliott-Lockhart, who had been S.S.O., Dosali, and who had joined the Paltan for the operations against the Faqir of Ipi, rejoined, being the last officer of the Cavalry to serve with the Guides Infantry on active service, as already noted. In earlier days, when Risala and Paltan were one, this had often occurred.

It was decided regimentally that the cavalry trumpeters should have silver trumpets, to be gradually given by officers, and one was presented by the Paltan, which was much appreciated.

In the Peshawar District Hockey Tournament, the Paltan were the winners against their own Risala. John Redding presented a case of six miniature Victoria Crosses, with the name of the winner below each, no mean record for a corps. This year the Government of India undertook the providing of officers' chargers, an entirely new departure in the Indian Army, and the Battalion received some fine horses from the Risala.

The Paltan was pleased to hear from "The Owl," otherwise their Canadian attaché, Crowe, that he was happily married and looked forward to being the only officer in Canada to wear the new Frontier Medal.[30]

Subadar-major Sapuran Singh passed to pension after 27 years of service, of which 17½ years had been with the Guides, and naturally received a great send-off. The Pipe Band escorted him to the Kabul Memorial and the C.O.'s car took him to the station. He had presented a handsome cup to the Battalion for the Inter-platoon Hockey Tournament and, very suitably, it was his platoon who had won it in the first year.

Subadar Rur Singh, I.O.M., was the new Subadar-major.

During the spring the Guides, on behalf of the District Soldiers' Board, arranged a most happy reunion of some 2,000 pensioners, of whom a very large proportion were old Guides. The reunion was attended by Sir George Cunningham, Governor of the Frontier Province.

The Cavalry were to lose their C.O., Lieutenant-Colonel Hammond, appointed a G.S.O.1 at the War Office.

An unfortunate incident followed the Regimental send-off to Colonel Hammond, when Risaldar-major Muhammad Tuhair was fatally injured in a car accident while returning. His elder son, Ghulam Qadir, who went to Dehra Dun from the Battalion, had just received the King's Commission and was attached for a year to the Dorset Regiment in Nowshera. His second son is a duffadar in the Risala.

"Peter" Moore was born and duly christened in the Guides' Church in April. A wireless set was now bought for the men. The Pathans of the Infantry were allowed to follow the custom in the Cavalry of wearing a blue lungi and gold kullas with their white mufti, a privilege much appreciated by the "nuts." The other classes were allowed six colours to choose from.

At the end of April, unrealized at the time, took place the last Mardan week, much as the one of 1938 just described, attended by Guides officers from far and near.

---

[30] Alas! killed whilst commanding his battalion of The Royal Canadian Regiment. He had received the D.S.O.

MARCH PAST OF THE CORPS
1 January 1939

CHAPTER VIII

THE EARLY DAYS OF THE SECOND WORLD WAR

The Second World War and the Last Days in Mardan—Regimental Happenings—The Tragedy of Major-General C. I. B. Hay—The Cavalry go to Quetta and are Mechanized—The Infantry march out to the Peshawar Border—The Early Days of the War—The Golden Square Coup and the Rebellion of the Iraqi Army—Brief Outline of the Persian Story, 1914-39—The Allies enter Persia in 1941—Services of Major Duncan.

The Second World War and the Last Days in Mardan

When the Second World War broke out the whole of the Corps of Guides was present together for the last time in Mardan. For the moment there was no urgent demand for the Armies of India in any particular field and energies were devoted to raising new units, developing training for possible modern fields of battle other than the mountains and jungles, and coping with the constant experience which was now crowding in so far as training and equipment were concerned. In Northern India the first tasks were obviously to watch and steady the Frontier in case the feeling of general unrest might result in trouble from the tribes. Fortunately, Turkey in this war was not an enemy, but in her proper historical position of our very close friend, therefore the disturbances due to the Sultan's declaration of Jehad by the Sheik Ul-Islam that accompanied Turkey's joining the Central Powers in the First World War were not apparent. British officers of the Regiment at Home, in common with all others, were of course recalled and came out in a very crowded convoy in great discomfort, which was relieved by the excellent arrangements made for their reception on arrival at Bombay. The officers who returned were "Goff" Hamilton and Michael Hodson.

In the First World War, as already related in Vol. I, extra war battalions were raised by many of the old regiments, thus the Guides had extra battalions of their own. But the later grouping of the Army meant that any extra battalions would be raised for the regiments—viz., in the Guides' case the 12th F.F. Regiment, of which they were the 5th Battalion. But they were, of course, called on to find officers as well as some trained rank and file which amounted to 2 British officers and 219 N.C.Os. and men. This was a drastic measure, and while it gave promising young soldiers a lift in promotion, to be followed later by another levy, it also meant great efforts to complete and train the new entry.

Up till July 1941, many temporary or I.A. Reserve officers joined the Battalion for training and duty, some of whom stayed with it all the war, and when at the end they were demobilized they were much missed from the Corps, in which they had become for the while deeply incorporated.

Three weeks after the outbreak of the war, the first exodus from Mardan began and the Guides Cavalry left for Quetta as part of the programme for reliefs; but everybody knew that the famous ninety-year-old station was going, and before the Cavalry marched there was a big reception which the old Sirdars and men of the Regiment attended in large numbers. The rank and file had also all been recalled from leave. A week after the Cavalry left, the Royal Deccan Horse marched into the Guides' Lines.

Regimental Happenings

It was at this time that the new Frontier medal was issued, the fourth in the series that covered ninety years—the ribbon buff, coloured with a narrow red stripe and a rather wider green on each side. The former previous Frontier medals, of which the Corps had had ample share, were :

(a) The India Medal of 1854, which had 28 clasps, of which the first was "Pegu" and the last was "Waziristan 1894"—a medal now seldom seen as the wearers have "piled their arms," and it is irreverently known as "The Old Man's Medal."

(b) The Indian Medal of 1895, first issued for the Chitral Relief expedition for the "Relief" and also the "Defence" of Chitral. Ribbon—alternate red and green stripes. This medal had many clasps.

(c) The India General Service Medal of 1908, of which the first clasp was "North-West Frontier 1908." One clasp was for the extraordinary internal happenings of the widespread rebellion in the Moplah country, largely owing to the fury of Muhammadan agitation against the treaties that broke up Turkey after the First World War. The last clasp was "North-West Frontier 1935." There were twelve in all.

(d) The Indian General Service Medal of 1936—clasp "North-West Frontier 1936-37" is the one just referred to as being issued. There was one later, "1937-39."

In October, to the great grief of everyone, there died in hospital in Peshawar a very distinguished officer of the Regiment—Major W. J. C. Duncan, D.S.O., M.C., of whose services a résumé is given at the end of this chapter. His body was brought to Mardan to be laid to rest with solemn ceremony by men of all ranks and creeds of the Guides in the presence of Major-General Dashwood Strettell, C.B., commanding the Peshawar District, and the Commander of the Risalpur Brigade.

The tragedy of Major-General C. I. B. Hay, C.B., C.M.G., C.B.E., D.S.O., must be referred to here.

This distinguished officer, then retired, was killed with his wife, the much-beloved Agatha, by a Boche bomb in the Langham Hotel (London) in 1941, in the midst of many activities. He was commissioned in 1897, joined the Guides, 28 November 1900, and served with them till 1920, when he was transferred to the 19th Punjab Infantry, holding afterwards important appointments.

The Cavalry go to Quetta and are Mechanized, 1939

The last break with Mardan took place on 25 September when the Cavalry left by train, arriving on the 28th, in relief of the Royal Deccan Horse, whose horses they were to take over, having left their own to the unit which relieved them at Mardan—a transfer that is always a grief to a mounted unit. The send-off was a great occasion : the Paltan

THE QUETTA HOUNDS

THE GUIDES CAVALRY'S FAREWELL TO ITS HORSES, QUETTA, 1940

EARLY DAYS OF THE SECOND WORLD WAR

lining the road, their band at the head, with all British officers from the Risalpur Cavalry Brigade and the Brigadier, Filose, and his wife to say farewell.

The cavalry lines at Quetta were in process of being rebuilt on most modern lines for a mechanized unit—garages in lieu of stables. To its satisfaction, the Corps found itself in the command of the well-known "Piffer," Brigadier Finnis. Four sons were born to the Regiment in the first months of 1941—to the Plunketts, Shebbeares, Eliott-Lockharts and Gradidges—"*Bara-mubarik.*" In September came the greater parting, the handing over of their horses to an I.S.F. unit (the 3rd Gwalior Lancers). The Regiment held its last mounted parade on 26 September, being inspected by Major-General Evetts, past whom it marched by squadrons, eventually forming a hollow square for an address by the General; after which Colonel Gradidge gave the pathetic order, "For the last time—make much of your horses." Then the B.Os. and V.C.Os. fell out, and the Regiment marched home under the Regimental Duffadar-major to the strains of "Auld Lang Syne"—a mournful scene, for horses and men are not easily parted. The Colonel wrote that never had he seen the Corps turn out so magnificently.

Yet officers and men were reconciled by the excitement of a new vision, of petrol over horses, of the new world of war that was coming to them, for there is one glory of the moon, and another of the stars.

With the horses gone, courses—infinite and varied—were the order of the day, with much new knowledge and much new skill to be acquired by the old bold hearts. The vehicles supplied for training were out of their sheds for all the hours of daylight.

The vast expansion of the Indian Army took many of the older V.C.Os. to training jobs, and many pensioners wrote to urge their recall! Colonel Gradidge's order to the Regiment after the parade, and General Evetts' stirring address must now be quoted:

"SPECIAL ORDER BY LIEUTENANT-COLONEL J. H. GRADIDGE, O.B.E., COMMANDING GUIDES CAVALRY

"*Farewell Parade to Horses on 26 September 1940*

"*Today I had the honour to command the last mounted parade of the Regiment on horses. As I anticipated, it was a truly memorable parade—carried out with the precision and efficiency that only a really good regiment can produce.*

"*I wish to congratulate all ranks on their magnificent performance and I look forward with confidence to the future, knowing that change of mounts can make no difference to the spirit which was born in us so many years ago and which has been handed down from father to son for nearly a century.*

"*We have a difficult time ahead of us, we have to learn new work and assimilate new ideas, but I am confident that with our past war traditions, our present spirit and comradeship will enable us to surmount all difficulties and that whatever role we may be asked to perform, either in the near or distant future, it will be performed in the spirit in which we said Goodbye to our horses today and so turned over another page of history.*"

This order also gave the General's address.

"Speech to the Guides Cavalry: Major-General J. F. Evetts, C.B., C.B.E., etc.

"Today is a most important day in your history and the history of the Indian Army. This is the last time one of the most distinguished Indian Cavalry Regiments will appear on parade mounted on horses. For nearly one hundred years the Guides Cavalry have been associated with the horse, which in addition to being a real friend, has been a most faithful servant. It is always sad to part with good friends and good servants, but at the same time we must move with the times, and I know well that the Guides Cavalry do not wish to become an obsolete arm of the service.

"In a few days' time, therefore, you will commence a new era in your wonderful history, but instead of being mounted on horses of flesh and blood you will be mounted on horses of steel.

"Do not think for one moment that because you will be mechanized you will no longer be cavalry-men. You will still ride in battle ; you will still be able to reconnoitre as cavalry soldiers and you will still be able to carry out shock action, but, as I have said before, mounted on horses of steel. So, in your new life remember always the cavalry spirit and the cavalry training which produces that spirit.

"You must be as particular in the care of the armoured and motorized vehicles as I know you are today in the care of your horses, and I would recommend that the trumpet call of 'Stables' be kept for ever as a reminder of the importance of attending to the wants and needs of your mechanical horses before attending to yourselves. . . .

"If we are to make India safe and secure her from invasion we must keep the Germans and Italians as far from India as possible. I can safely say therefore that the British and Indian troops now fighting side by side in Egypt are fighting not only for the general freedom and security of the Empire, but for India's particular security as well.

"Should you be called upon to join your comrades in arms over there, I know full well that you will not only answer, but having answered it, will add fresh honours to your already glorious record."

"(*Signed*) R. A. Shebbeare, *Captain and Adjutant,*
"*Guides Cavalry.*"

Mechanization in India was very slow at first, from want of equipment, but training on any old junk served in the initial stages, beginning with old Morris six-wheelers : and then came some light-weight Chevrolets. The whole story of the many stages through which the Regiment passed till in 1946 it became a Tank Regiment, armed with Churchills, has been supplied by the Regiment and is given in Chapter XII. The Pathans became the best drivers, and then the Dogras, while the Sikhs, who thought themselves the best, were the poorest.

The Regiment was now nominally part of the 9th Indian Division which was being got ready for the Far East ; but when this Division left in July 1941 the Regiment was not sufficiently equipped to accompany it.

By June 1941, however, enough armoured vehicles had been received to send a squadron to Iraq—where, though the rebellion had ended on 31 May, there was plenty to be done, and thus "A" Squadron under Major Gimson, with Lieutenant Estrange,

EARLY DAYS OF THE SECOND WORLD WAR

were the first armoured squadron to leave India. They left Quetta on 14 June and their adventures will be described in the next chapter.

The Regiment had now been told its role amid the varied nature of armoured units, and by 9 October 1941 was declared a "Light Armoured Reconnaissance Regiment," a role it was to hold in Iraq, Syria and North Africa till it returned to India in 1943.

The Infantry March Out to the Peshawar Border

The axe that was finally to cut the Guides from their famous home fell in March 1940 when the Infantry Battalion followed the Cavalry and marched out in relief to Bara and the new forts of the Khajuri plain, instituted after the hitherto unheard-of event of the Afridi raid on Peshawar.

Before the Cavalry left, the cutting up and dividing of the regimental treasures had taken place in perfect amity, and the whole arrangements are described in the Mess agenda dealing with the passing of Mardan. On 11 March the Battalion marched out under the command of Lieutenant-Colonel Garrett, M.C., having been inspected by Brigadier H. H. Rich,[31] commanding the Nowshera Brigade. On that day the Battalion swung into Nowshera with the Pipe Band playing heartily, and they were received by the band of the Royal Ludhiana Sikhs. Next day they started the 25-mile march to Peshawar. An hour after arrival at Bara, on the morning of 12 March, their new commander, Brigadier A. E. Hickman, paid the Battalion a short visit, and they then marched on to the Khajuri posts of Jhansi and Milward, leaving a detachment in the old Sikh fort of Bara, a name so well known to many generations of both British and Indian soldiers. During the early months of 1940 the changes in equipment, partly due to war requirements, were carried out, all leather equipment being withdrawn and web belts, etc., taking its place. British officers ceased to wear their swords, though Indian officers continued to do so, while light-reflecting badges were removed and field service dress had embroidered badges. The silver "Guides" title on the shoulder was replaced by "Guides" embroidered in drab in "training" order of dress.

At the end of April 1940, Major M. H. H. Baily and Captain Alec Moore were suddenly ordered to leave India for the United Kingdom, their destination being Norway, where mountains abound. Owing to the gradual setback there, only Baily actually joined and he was attached to the Irish Guards, gaining great distinction and being awarded the D.S.O. in the withdrawals from the mountains. This expedition to Norway, which took place before Dunkirk, was doomed to failure, for there were few fit, trained troops, no "services" and no possibility of adequate air cover. Baily's duties among units quite unready for such a trial, cover a good deal more than the facts that are given in the citation, and constitute an almost impossible episode, redounding to the credit of his force of character and judgment. The following description of his action gave great satisfaction to the Battalion while eating its heart out in the heat of the Khajuri plain :

---

[31] A brother of E. P. Rich, the Guide.

> *"This officer throughout the action at Pothus showed coolness and disregard for personal safety. He was first with the Irish Guards while they engaged the enemy at close quarters for several hours and assisted in guiding them back through the enemy during their withdrawal. The next day he climbed a mountain, collected an independent company and guided their withdrawal. While the Company withdrew, he remained with the wounded men and assisted them on the way back to Rognan, at times under fire, and never giving any regard to his safety."*

As the year rolled on in the performance of not very exciting duties but plenty of exercise to prevent the troops getting what is known as *quilaband*, *Anglicè* "tied to their defences," they were shocked by the news of an old Guide's murder. Major H. H. Barnes, C.I.E., was murdered in Fort Sandeman on 4 October 1940, shot in his office by a man of the Jagozai tribe who cherished a grievance. This part of the world has often been troubled by such outrages.[32] Major Barnes, always known as "Barney," had joined the Regiment in 1919 and was transferred to the Political department in 1926. He had been through the incredible Red Shirt troubles at Charsadda, having only just escaped with his life on several occasions.

THE EARLY DAYS OF THE WAR

In 1940 and the greater part of 1941 the World War had not put any remarkable strain on India. Indian troops, including the famous 4th Division, had distinguished themselves greatly in North Africa and Abyssinia, but speaking generally the Indian Command had time to lay the foundations of India's great share in her own salvation and in the immense support to the British Empire that she was later to give, both in military and industrial development. The collapse of France had brought Japan and her tame Chinese into the now discredited French Empire of the East, but it was many months yet till the tragedies of 1942. The first occurrence to openly bring the war within reach of India was to come from the west in the combined German and Vichy French scheme for a *coup d'état* in Iraq. Before this actually occurred, however, and before the usurping régime showed actual hostility, in accordance with our treaties with Iraq, Indian troops were moving to the Tigris to strengthen the general communications with the Levant. When the *coup d'état* which is described in the following section, "The Golden Square," took place, the Persian Gulf problem threatened to become intensive, and as it was this that so affected the share of the Guides (Cavalry and Infantry) in the war, the story of "Golden Square," of Persia from the First World War onwards, and of the situation which led up to the Allied occupation of Persia, must be briefly outlined. In the meantime the Guides Infantry, whom we have just seen moved to the Khajuri plain in March 1940, were moved to the Khaiber outposts, outposts that made training impossible.

The sojourn of the Infantry in the Khaiber posts was not to be very long (four and a half months). India was spreading itself to develop all the varieties of mechanized units and the complicated but essential system of inter-communication had to be mattered. This system to the uneducated, staunch men of the Frontier or yeomen of

---

[32] The writer of this book was there so far back as 1891, when outrages by fanatics for the glory of God were fairly common.

the Punjab was no easy matter. Yet done it was. For the purpose of a special War School, the large cantonment of Secunderabad on the plateau of the Deccan was selected, a peculiarly well-suited area with a summer climate certainly far less trying than the Khajuri plain, though without the brace of a Frontier winter.

Secunderabad, "the pleasant abode," was just outside the capital town of the great Nizam and was the cantonment of the "Subsidiary Force"—namely, the force of British and Indian troops originally maintained by treaty to protect the Nizam from his enemies.[33]

To this historic site and fine training ground the Guides went from the Khaiber in April 1941. They were not to be there long, however, for on 5 September they left for Bombay *en route* for Iraq and Persia.

The "Golden Square" Coup and the Rebellion of the Iraqi Army

Before tracing the situation that brought the Guides Cavalry and Infantry to Iraq and Persia, we must look at the *coup d'état* of the "Golden Square" military clique which drove out the Regent at Bagdad and eventually formed a short-lived Government.

On 4 April the political coup took place, the Regent escaping to Egypt and one Raschid Ali declaring himself Regent. On the 17th a British force, sent in accordance with our Treaty with Iraq, arrived at Basra, to keep open our communication with the Levant and also to watch the oilfields, especially the large British ones in South Persia. On 1 May the Revolutionary Government objected to the arrival of a second convoy of troops at Basra and surrounded the R.A.F. cantonment at Habbaniyeh on the Euphrates. On the 2nd Iraqi troops attacked the R.A.F. Cantonment near Basra; but the British troops attacked and dispersed them. The British, with many refugees from Bagdad at Habbaniyeh, were now heavily attacked and bombed, but by the 6th the Iraqi Army was attacked and driven off with 1,000 casualties, including 28 officers and 408 men captured. They were heavily pursued by the Air Force as they retreated to Bagdad.

The defence and riposte from Habbaniyeh was a most astounding story of training and obsolete machines rigged as bombers, and redounds to the Air Force's credit, the total garrison in this epic being 1,000 all ranks of R.A.F., 1,200 Assyrian Levies and 350 men of the King's Own Royal Regiment flown in from Karachi. With less than 80 semi-combat planes, these flew 1,600 sorties, dropped 100 tons of bombs and fired 250 rounds.

In the meantime, mechanized and airborne troops were coming up from Palestine, arriving on 13 May, and some of the troops of the Emir Abdullah from Transjordania. The combined forces now captured Bagdad, and on 1 June the Regent re-entered the city and Raschid Ali fled to Persia. By 3 June, Mosul was occupied by troops from the Levant. The revolt was now over, order was soon restored and Iraq properly garrisoned, the principal rebel leaders having also fled to Persia.

The immediate result of the trouble in Iraq—the arrival of German planes, but with

---

[33] This force is not to be confounded with the famous Hyderabad Contingent, a force maintained by the State but officered by British officers and now merged in the Indian Line.

the commander, Von Blomberg's son, dead—and all that now came to light of German plans and Vichy French co-operation was the necessary decision to turn Vichy out of Syria. General Dentz, the French Governor-General, had successfully exploited the anti-British atmosphere in evidence for years among the French in Syria, and a full-fledged campaign by the British and Free French, including Indian troops from the Euphrates, was unhappily necessary, and it was not till after severe fighting that General Dentz asked for an armistice. Eventually, our terms having been accepted, on 16 July General Maitland Wilson and General Catroux entered Beyrout and the Vichy French were transported home.

But the great change had now arrived. On 22 June 1941 the best of the German Army poured into Russia from the Baltic to the Black Sea, and this necessitated a considerable development in our Middle East policy, which will be outlined after a brief description of the situation in Persia between the two World Wars.

Brief Outline of the Persian Story, 1914–39

As the Allies were now about to enter Iran and both Guides Corps were to serve there, the modern story of Persia may well be outlined here. During the First World War, western Persia was badly overrun by forces of both the Central Powers and the Allies. First, Turkish troops occupied the land between the frontier of Mesopotamia and Hamadan, and these were driven out by Russian troops, who before the Bolshevist revolution were co-operating with the Allies and were marching down towards Bagdad in support of the British troops coming up-country. Neither the Turks nor the Russians were particular as to whose food they took, with the result that the country that was within reach of their forces was left devastated and starving. Eventually it was British troops who pushed up into Persia when the Russian armies had broken away from their officers. In 1917 a specially selected force of officers and N.C.Os. had been sent out to the Tigris with the idea of organizing the Armenians against the Bolsheviks. The forces of Armenia, however, had joined the Bolsheviks, and these selected cadres under Major-General L. Dunsterville were sent towards the Persian Caspian port of Enzeli, and eventually ordered to support the Tartars of Russian Azerbaijan against the Russians while a British flotilla was organized on the Caspian. All these operations were too late as far as Armenia and Azerbaijan were concerned, but the British forces firmly held the road from Mesopotamia to Enzeli, at which place a considerable force was maintained. In 1919 the forces at Kasvin were increased by cavalry and horse artillery in case the Persian Cossack force under Russian officers and commanded by Colonel Staraselski should give trouble.

During the first war a considerable party of British officers under Major-General Sir Percy Sykes had, in agreement with the Persian Government, organized a force, mostly from the Turkish tribes, known as the South Persian Rifles, its object being to put an end to various disturbances on the shores of the Persian Gulf that had been so tiresome a feature in the earlier days of the war. These troubles were largely owing to the intrigues of German agents, and part of the duties of the force was to combat these activities.

The force along the roads from Bagdad to the Caspian, among other duties, took a large share in feeding the starving North Persians, and in fact Persia owed a very large debt of gratitude to Great Britain during the First World War. During all this time, the Shah of Persia himself had been in Europe and, as the British Government after the war withdrew all its troops, we see the phenomenon of Riza Pahlevi, a true Persian as distinct from a Turk, rising from being an officer in the Persian Cossacks to a height which enabled him to seize the Persian throne. For practically two hundred years the dynasty in Persia had been a Turkish one (of the Khajar tribe), growing singularly effete at the end. Riza Shah, as he now became, produced some measure of organization, but very soon spent the country's money on an extravagant programme of hotels and western amenities without doing very much to organize what was most wanted—namely, an honest and incorruptible Civil Service. It will be remembered with what boosting the Riza Shah régime was received by philo-Persians and such admirers as the late Sir Denison Ross; but those who were behind the scenes had long feared that some catastrophe must follow.

The Allies Enter Persia in 1941

During the years before 1939, and especially after the German victories of the early war years, Riza Shah became more and more impregnated with German doctrines and propaganda, while the country was honeycombed with German agents with both political and commercial proclivities. It was highly important that the example of the "Golden Square" coup in Iraq should not be repeated in Persia.

The German threat to the Caucasus and Persia and Turkestan was now a very serious possibility. Turkey might be forced to give passage and there was no time to be lost in securing Persia and the possible routes whereby aid to Russia could be made available. The civilized world was horror-struck at Germany's turn against Russia (22 June 1941), with whom she had so recently made a treaty of alliance in fulsome terms. The "Big Three"—Churchill, Stalin and Roosevelt—though Pearl Harbour still lay months ahead, were fully determined on aid to Russia, and they met in Moscow. To counter-attack the German proclivities of Iran, British and Russian Forces marched into Iran from north and south. On 25 August Riza Shah and his Government would not accept the situation and tried to oppose the British forces which now entered Iran, or Persia as it was again to be known, and advanced on three points:

(a) A landing was made at Bandar Shapur on the Persian Gulf, where eight beached or damaged German and Italian ships with their crews were captured.

(b) Another force landed at the Anglo-Iranian Oil Company's base at Abadan on the Shatt-el-Arab, and airborne troops were sent to the oilfields in the mountains.

(c) North-east of Bagdad, troops advanced from Khanaqin, occupied the local oilfields and advanced up to the Persian plateau by the Pai-Tak.

The Russian forces also entered Azerbaijan. The British forces met with some show of resistance, especially on the northern road and in Khuzistan, but the Persian troops either surrendered or retired. Two Iranian sloops and four gun-boats were sunk in the Gulf and a floating dock and depot ship were captured. At Teheran on 28 August a new Cabinet had come into power who wisely accepted the benevolent inevitable, and sent a flag of truce to the troops advancing upon Kermanshah and Ahwaz, while the Russians occupied Urmia to the north.

The situation was now peaceful, but not satisfactory, for the German Legation was still open and German agents still about. The situation, however, was cleared by the abdication of Shah Riza Pahlevi and the accession of his son Prince Muhammad Riza Pahlevi. The ex-Shah, who was in poor health, accepted British hospitality and was removed with courtesy and consideration to Mauritius where, ere long, he passed away. Two days after the abdication, Russian and British troops reached the outskirts of Teheran, the latter occupying the Skoda machine-gun factory east of the city.

The clearing-up of the Persian situation took some time, and the question of who had diplomatic rights among the foreigners took some settling. All danger, however, was now over, and the development of the unproductive mountain railway that Riza Shah had made from the Gulf of Persia to the Caspian into an effective life-line to Russia now commenced. This was eventually undertaken by the Americans who, with immense energy, developed the ports on the Persian Gulf and enlarged the whole system, so far as the extremely difficult mountain alignment permitted, while the Russians looked after the Caspian end.

It was to join the forces in Persia that the Guides Infantry were sent from the training cantonment of Secunderabad, too late, however, to share the comparative excitements of the first entry into that land of romance. They formed part of the 6th Indian Division. "A" Squadron of the Cavalry were sent earlier to Iraq and took part in the advance up the Karun river and attendant fighting (*vide* next chapter).

Services of Major W. J. C. Duncan, D.S.O., M.C.

"Duncy" received his first commission in the Australian Forces in 1915, and served with them in France from November 1916 to November 1918, winning the Military Cross on 17 September 1917 at Messines, the D.S.O. for conspicuous bravery in the defence of Villers Bretonneux and a bar thereto in the operation south-west of Bouchavesnes in August 1918—the amazing distinction of three immediate awards which carried with them mention in Sir Douglas Haig's despatches in 1918 and again in 1919.

He joined the Guides in 1919, and from 1935-38 was administrative commandant of the Frontier Force Regiment, and in 1919, 1930, 1933 and 1935 saw service in Frontier operations. The death from heart failure, in October 1939, of this distinguished officer was a loss not only to the Guides but to the whole Army. On his tomb were written the famous lines of the Legion epitaph:

"Tranquil you lie, your knightly virtue proved,
Your memory hallowed in the land you loved."

CHAPTER IX

THE GUIDES IN IRAQ AND PERSIA

The Outline Story of PAI Force—The Guides Cavalry ("A" Squadron) in Iraq and Persia—The British Invasion of Persia on the Karun River—The Share of "A" Squadron—The Guides Infantry in Persia and North Kurdistan—The Guides Cavalry in Iraq and Syria—Brigade Training at Khanaqin and the March to Sultanabad.

OUTLINE STORY OF PAI FORCE, 1941-45

BEFORE following the days of the Guides after the Iraq rebellion took place, the set-up in Persia and Iraq must be outlined. The Japanese were not in the war, and with General Wavell in Egypt with his hands full, it was India that had to undertake the major responsibility. The 20th Indian Brigade, as related, already "strategically" embarked as a Malaya reinforcement, was hurried to Basra, but had[34] to be as far as possible tactically rearranged in the Gulf, a difficult matter. The desert column from Palestine that reached Habbaniyeh had, of course, been dispatched by Wavell. The whole situation on the Tigris and in Persia had been immensely complicated by the discovery that Vichy France and Dentz in Syria had allowed the Germans' planes to use Syrian bases and opposed the column of British and Free French, with the result already described. When to this Syrian trouble there was added our set-back in Greece, Crete and the Desert and there came the German invasion of Russia, the threat to the Caucasus was obvious and a very large military organization was gradually evolved in Iraq and Persia.

The hasty dispatch from India of the 20th Brigade was followed by the rest of the 10th Indian Division and later the 8th and 6th Indian Divisions, the latter including the Guides Infantry, and these first formed the Iraq Force, commanded by General Quinan under the Indian Command, which also occupied Persia. In February 1942 the Iraq Force was renamed the Tenth Army, and was transferred to the Middle East Command.

Later in 1942, as the threat to the Caucasus intensified, PAI Force (Persia and Iraq) came into being under General Maitland Wilson and was built up into two Infantry Corps, with many other formations attached—viz. :

3rd (British) Corps
21st (Indian) Corps } The divisions assigned to these Corps were frequently changed according to the varying calls for troops
31st Indian Armoured Division

---

[34] "Strategically" means that the stores and kits were loaded in the most compact manner, that needed rearrangement on arrival. "Tactically" embarked meant so that units could land and get on their equipment quickly and go into action. The latter method is uneconomical in shipping space.

1st Indian Armoured Brigade
43rd Indian Lorried Brigade (Gurkha)
Two Polish Divisions forming and training.

The War Cabinet and the General Staffs were looking ahead, and various oddments, including a force of "Static Troops"—viz., units equipped for defence and not movement, such as the Afridi Battalion, Indian State troops, garrison companies, etc.—were formed.

Considerable defences on a large scale to meet a threat from the Caucasus were made on the Pai-Tak and elsewhere.

This large force was of course not kept in this terrain any longer than necessary, but the above detail shows clearly the vast and interesting organization of which the Guides Cavalry and Infantry were components. To supply it all an advanced base was established at Musayib, on the right bank of the Euphrates not far from the famous Hilla barrage, a feat of British Engineers.[35] As early as possible, troops that could be spared were moved to more active theatres, the 31st Armoured Division as well as the 10th Indian Division, the latter going to Italy in 1944, also the lorried brigade of the 31st Armoured Division. General Maitland Wilson was soon needed elsewhere and General H. Pownall was appointed Commander, to be succeeded in 1944 by Sir Arthur Smith.

As the Caucasus threat passed with the defeat of the Hun in Russia, the Polish Corps and the 8th Indian Division went to Italy, and the 5th British Division also left. Their transfer left only the 6th Indian Division and 60th Infantry Brigade with most of the static units aforesaid and the work was mostly guard duties, two brigades of the 6th being then employed and one kept for training.

As the fighting formations left PAI Force a deceptive façade was erected to delude the Hun, administrative and static areas receiving divisional and brigade numbers. Late in 1944 the 6th Indian Division was broken up, first one brigade and then a second being withdrawn to India to train for the Far East. Eventually Sir Arthur Smith was relieved in command by Lieutenant-General R. A. Savory.

"A" Squadron the Guides Cavalry in Iraq and Persia

The first Guide formation to take part in the Second World War was the Guides Cavalry. The Regiment itself was preceded by "A" Squadron (Dogras) under Major W. A. Gimson, which was dispatched to join the troops in Iraq. The Squadron left Quetta on 15 June and sailed from Karachi on 27 June 1941, arriving at Basra on 2 July and Bagdad on the 14th. The rebel party, however, in Bagdad had asked for an armistice on 31 May, which was accepted, and the loyal Regent had returned, so that the Squadron was chiefly employed in rapid movements about the country to give the impression that we had more armour than was actually the case, at the outset spending some time at Khanaqin.

---

[35] Sir John Jackson & Co., from Sir William Willcocks' plans, a few years before 1914.

THE GUIDES IN IRAQ AND PERSIA

In early August the Squadron was sent down to Basra to join the 8th Indian Division for the invasion of Persia and the brief operations from 24 to 29 August, after which it came under the 6th Indian Division and was moved about Persia till we find it, as narrated in the story of the Guides Infantry, who had arrived in September, with them at Senneh in North Persia.

The Allied decision to occupy Persia for the "duration" was naturally a secret, though the Iranian Government had ample reason to expect it, and appeared likely to resist as already outlined.

THE BRITISH INVASION OF PERSIA ON THE KARUN RIVER

The operation to occupy Persia suffered from some hesitation and changes of instructions; but the British portion of the plan was now set in train, to move into Persia from the Khanaqin direction and into the province of Khuzistan from Basra. This last was almost an essential movement both to secure the all-important Anglo-Iranian Oil Company Works on Abadan Island and the actual oilfields in the mountains beyond at Haft Khana. The long pipe-line also was an anxiety. It is the latter operation with which "A" Squadron is concerned, for that unit received orders to proceed from Kirkuk on 5 August, arriving at Tanooma opposite Basra, on the left bank of the Shatt-el-Arab.

The 8th Division was assembled about Basra and Tanooma and in constant training. It may perhaps be explained here for those who do not know the rather complicated conditions, that the Shatt-el-Arab is the joint Tigris and Euphrates, and is navigable to ocean ships of close on 30-ft. draught to some miles above Basra. From the head of the Persian Gulf to a point some ten miles above Khurramshahr, at the junction of the Karun river from the north-east, a total distance of some seventy miles, the territory is part of Iran or Persia. During the last war it was ruled by the Arab chieftain Sheikh Khazal of Muhammerah, our very good friend, a subsidiary chief of the Persian Government. The town of Khurramshahr is the former Muhammerah. The 8th Division was a composite one, but was now increased by various units and formations with little time to be worked into the organization. The Commander was Major-General C. C. Harvey. The Division for this operation consisted of the following main units:

> The 13th Indian Lancers.
> The Guides, "A" Squadron.
> The 3rd Field Regiment, R.A.
> An Anti-Tank Battery.
> 7th and 9th Companies, S. & M.
> 18th, 24th and 25th Infantry Brigades.

The Guides Squadron quickly arrived at Tanooma and, till the 24th, was engaged in refitting and constant exercise with the 18th Brigade, especially in a small sub-force known as "Rapier," consisting of themselves, a troop of the 3rd Field Regiment, No. 7 Company of the S. & M. (less one section), and the 5th/5th Mahrattas.

The various plans of operation were under discussion, but eventually that known as "Countenance" was to be the one. Under this General Harvey intended to seize

Abadan Island, ten miles below Khurramshahr, to secure the oil works, Khurramshahr itself, and with the Navy to seize the port of Bandar Shapur, on the Khor Musa, an inlet a few miles east of the Shatt.

On the 24th orders came for the troops to start their operations next morning, as follows :

(a) The 24th Brigade with some artillery to Abadan before dawn.

(b) The 18th Brigade with a battery, the Guides and a battalion of the 24th Brigade to march so as to be at Khurramshahr by 0410 hours.

(c) The 25th Brigade with the 13th Lancers were to operate to Kasr Sheikh wide on the north-eastern flank of the 18th Brigade.

Everything went as to plan ; at Abadan there was some delay as the Officer Commanding the 2nd/6th Rajputana Rifles, Lieutenant-Colonel Ridley, was shot at the moment of landing. The troops at Abadan, asleep in their barracks, escaped, but the Guards in the place put up unfortunately a stout resistance, 28 dead being found in one place alone. Unfortunately, too, three British employees of the Oil works were killed and seven wounded, owing to the manager having sounded the siren, and the employees were proceeding to their alarm stations. Owing to the difficulty of clearing out the Persian resistance without damaging the all-important oil refineries, the oil station was not fully in our hands till 1700 hours.

The British losses were not trivial, as 2 B.Os., 1 V.C.O., and 1 O.R. were killed, while 1 B.O. and 11 I.O.Rs. were wounded.

The march of the 10th Infantry Brigade with column "Rapier" in advance, a distance of thirty-two miles, went well, "Rapier" reaching a point a mile from Khurramshahr wireless station. At first light there was some resistance, soon overcome by the artillery ; but during the encounter a sad occurrence took place, due to Iranian intransigency, which had commanded a futile resistance. The commander of the Persian Land and Sea force (a few gun-boats), Admiral Bey Endor, was killed. He had an English wife and was always personally friendly to the British. All that could be done was to bury him with Naval honours due to his rank. Colonel Henry now led "Rapier" (which included "A" Squadron) westwards towards Pul-i-Nao, where the main Persian defences were. The 1st/2nd Gurkha Rifles, however, were also approaching from the north, on which the Persian troops surrendered promptly. Local Arabs gave some guerrilla trouble and here too it was dusk before the whole neighbourhood was cleared. Two mountain batteries and some 500 prisoners were taken. The 18th Brigade casualties were not very heavy—viz., 2 B.Os. wounded, 1 I.O.R. killed and 9 wounded.

In a landing at the mouth of the Karun, after H.M.Ss. *Falmouth* and *Yarra* had accounted for the Persian Navy, by a company of the 3rd/10th Baluch Regiment and a naval party, Lieutenant Vokes, commanding 3rd/10th, was mortally wounded and one I.O.R. was wounded. Control of the area at the mouth was soon gained.

The 25th Brigade and the 13th Lancers moved at first daylight and secured Qasr Sheikh by mid-day. Most of the Persian garrison got away over the Karun, but a mountain battery and some 300 prisoners were taken. There were 60 killed. British casualties were 1 B.O. killed, 2 B.Os. wounded; one I.O.R. killed and 1 V.C.O. and 17 O.Rs. wounded.

Next day, the 26th, the advance on Ahwaz was made. A ferry was established opposite Marid, and the 18th Brigade group was across by Friday the 27th, while the 25th Brigade was reconnoitring towards Ahwaz. On the 27th that brigade moved to within twenty-five miles of that town, and by the 28th all was ready for the advance. Reports of large concentrations of troops, mostly false, had come in.

The force now advanced in two groups on either side of the Karun, gaining their first objective easily, when an envoy arrived to say that the Persians had laid down their arms, confirmed a little later by an envoy from the General in command. That settled the whole question of the all-important oilfield. A company of the 3rd/10th Baluchis went off in lorries to Haft Khel and Masjid-i-Suleiman in case of tribal trouble.

At Ahwaz, General Harvey with Colonel Galloway, his political adviser, met General Mahommed Shahbakhti, the commander of the Persian troops in Khuzistan. "A" Squadron, as part of Colonel Henry's "Rapier," after forming up on the F.U.P., led the advance on Khurramshahr: at 0445 hours they attacked the wireless station, which was in our hands by 0645 hours. They then moved north towards Pul-i-Nao (the New Bridge) and joined the 1st/2nd Gurkhas in their clearing operations, returning to the wireless station by 1430 hours. From here they marched up-river to reinforce a company of the 3rd Gurkha Rifles at Marid. At 1500 hours they reported that artillery and one company were in position five miles east and they themselves arrived at Marid at 1700 hours, when they took up a position to cover the sappers making a ferry.

On the 26th, after covering the advance of the 18th Brigade to Marid, they were ordered to cross the Karun, and at early dawn on the 27th to reconnoitre up the west bank towards Dorquain, and they now received orders to camp there, where a conference for the capture of Ahwaz was held.

On the 28th the forces advanced, having a slight engagement with a Persian detachment, of which 20 were captured after 7 had been killed.

The Share of "A" Squadron

So much for the general story; the share of the Guides was straightforward and important, as "A" Squadron led the advance. It was 0410 hours when the Navy opened fire, and as "A" advanced on the wireless station they were met by the gleaming light of Admiral Bey Endor's car as he tried to get away. Meeting the Guides' advanced armoured cars, he left his car, entered the wireless station, and there met his death as already related.[36] Risaldar Garkha Ram was leading and the defenders soon opened a sharp fire.

The Squadron crossed a defence ditch fairly easily, getting behind the wireless station, which was in our hands by 0645 hours, after the field artillery had opened up. They then moved north towards Pul-i-Nao, crossed over, and joined the 1st/2nd Gurkhas in their clearing operations, returning to the wireless station by 1430 hours.

---

[36] His flag became a trophy in the Mess of the Guides Cavalry.

From here they marched up-river to reinforce a company of the 3rd Gurkha Rifles at Marid. At 1500 hours they reported that artillery and one company were in position five miles east, and they themselves arrived at Marid at 1700 hours, when they took up a position to cover the sappers making a ferry. On the 26th, after covering the advance of the 18th Brigade to Marid, they were ordered to cross the Karun and at early dawn on the 27th to reconnoitre up the west bank towards Dorquain, an oil pumping station, where the Anglo-Iranian Company's families were to be rescued. The Persians, however, had removed them and the troops now received orders to camp there, where a C.O.'s conference for the capture of Ahwaz was held.

On the 28th the forces advanced, having a slight engagement with a Persian detachment as related.

Before noon came the news of the Persian surrender, and the Squadron parked that night at Kot Abdullah north of Ahwaz and for several days was engaged in refitting. On the 30th it returned to the Dorquain area and resumed maintenance—the life of a mechanized unit when not moving!

On 14 September, the Squadron and their old comrades of the Delhi Ridge, the 2nd Gurkhas, were able to keep Delhi Day in due and ancient form, a joint festival that had not occurred for many a day. A few days later the two units were sent to Shahgan some twenty miles east of Dorquain to bring in 1,000 Persian troops who had fled from Abadan and suffered terribly from thirst and heat. The road had been strewn with corpses. They surrendered eagerly but would not face the road again and were brought to Ahwaz in lorries, and that was the finish. At the end of September the 8th Division handed over to the 6th which, under General Thompson, had arrived from India to form the main portion of the British force in Persia and Iraq. The Guides Squadron was now attached to the 24th Indian Brigade (Brigadier le Fleming) and with this formation moved to Agha Jhazri, and Gach Sarran, in the hills east of Kot Abdullah where the oilfields were threatened by Bakhtiari tribesmen. However, nothing special occurred and order was restored, the force being back by 7 October with a good deal of repairs to be done after very bad hill roads.

On the 12th the Squadron moved off towards Teheran, via Khurramabad, Malayer and Kermanshah. They were long treks, and great was their pleasure and surprise to find four miles from Kermanshah their own Paltan, who had a great feast prepared.

The rest of their story together is related later, and how they spent some months in the reconnaissance of many Persian districts and provinces, before marching in September to join the Regiment, which had now arrived in Iraq.

The Khuzistan despatches mentioned Lieutenant L'Estrange and Risaldar Garkha Ram of the Squadron.

The Guides Infantry in Persia and Northern Kurdistan, 1941

The Guides Infantry ordered to join PAI Force reached Bombay at 0645 hours on 5 September and were embarked for the Persian Gulf by 1045 hours, the convoy sailing at 1100 hours—good, prompt work. In Bombay they were unexpectedly to lose Major S. B. Good, who was pulled out of the train with orders to return to Bannu to command

OFFICERS AND V.C.Os. OF THE GUIDES INFANTRY SHORTLY BEFORE EMBARKING FOR IRAQ
Secunderabad, 1941

Back Row (*L. to R.*)—Jem. Balder Singh, Jem. Sardara Singh, Lieut. M. Lord, Jem. Bawal Khan, Lieut. ———, Jem. Munsha Singh, Jem. Nar Hussain, Sub. Fatteh Khan, Lieut. I. F. Ancott, Jem. Chajju Ram, Lieut. ———, Jem. Allah Ditta.
Centre Row—Lieut. Mohd Rafi Khan, Sub. Arram Gul, I.D.S.M., Sub. Guncha Gul, Lieut. P. Phelps, Sub. Nihal Singh, Medical Officer, Sub. Mohd Hayat, Lieut. R. G. Maslen-Jones, Jem. Swab Gul, Jem. Kehar Singh, Jem. Mathra Dass.
Front Row—Capt. D. M. Brett, Sub. Sardar Khan, Capt. W. G. Watt, Sub. Chandhri Ram, Lt.-Col. E. P. Rich, Sub.-Maj. Rur Singh, O.B.I., I.O.M, Major S. B. Good, O.B.E., Sub. Sobhat Khan, O.B.I., I.O.M., Capt. A. A. Pugh, Sub. Mehal Singh.
Absent—Major M. H. H. Baily, D.S.O, Lieut. W. J. Stansfield, Lieut. B. Berdoe, Sub. Pala Singh, Jem. Warshan Singh.

a battalion of the 8th Punjab Regiment. He was succeeded as Second-in-Command by Major M. H. H. Baily. The Battalion was exceedingly fortunate in having its own M.T. on board with it in H.M.T. *Santhia* (B.I.), and reached Basra in good heart on the 12th, but a fortnight after the British had moved into Persia. The short stay at Secunderabad, and also the lack of equipment, made the Battalion anxious to complete its training, especially in M.T. work, and it was glad to find itself installed for a month in Rafidiyeh, a hot and desolate spot. They were destined to follow the force up the Pai-Tak along the road to Kermanshah and Hamadan and on 3 October moved to Khanaqin at the foot of the hills, a rail party following on the 8th. On the 11th the Battalion were embussed to Kermanshah and ran into their old friends the former 57th Wilde's Rifles. After a short stay in Kermanshah the Battalion, less two rifle companies, left for Senneh some ninety miles to the north. Senneh is the capital of Persian Kurdistan and Lieutenant-Colonel Rich (the C.O.) found himself practically a political officer and forming a fender between the Persians and their dissatisfied subjects, the Kurds. This portion of the Kurdish country has always belonged to Persia, but had never been brought under very effective control and had felt the disruption of the First World War. Under the reborn Persia of the Riza Shah, this section of the Kurdish race was gradually brought under a more effective Persian control than formerly. Some note on the Kurdish situation generally is of interest, for this ancient race have never been autonomous and have long been part of the Turkish and Persian Empires. After the First World War, when the Mesopotamian province became eventually the Kingdom of Iraq, the Kurdish hills between the plains of the Tigris and the Persian border became part of that kingdom. That disputed border had been fixed by a boundary commission shortly before the war of 1914–18. Thus the Kurds were now under three authorities instead of two, Turkish, Iraqian and Persian.

During the prolonged discussions that preceded the Treaty of Versailles, Kurdish intelligentsia revived a long-voiced demand for an independent Kurdistan. This, however, could never be a practical demand, for Kurdish and partly-Kurdish Persia ran right across to Azerbaijan.

During the post-war British control of Mesopotamia some Kurdish rebellions, notably that of Sheikh Mahmud of Sulimanieh, occurred, but the British and after them the Arabs have ruled the Kurds through their own leading men and Aghas. The Persians had not been so wise and relations between the tribesmen and the Government machinery were none too cordial and rarely wise, often cruel. Good behaviour was enforced by taking hostages and by heavy garrisoning, while the badly paid Persian officials had their own pockets to fill. There was therefore an atmosphere of deep hatred for anything Persian.

During the short Allied-Persian hostilities the Kurds had tried to get their own back.

This was the atmosphere into which the Guides were plunged and which Colonel Rich had to handle. One point was paramount and took precedence of their sympathy for an unhappy state of affairs with which they had no permanent connection, viz., order must be maintained and the communications of the Allies properly secured.

Senneh had already been occupied after a forced march over the mountains by a battalion of the 5th Royal Gurkhas, as a Russian force also was approaching. It was not desirable in the symmetry of things that Senneh should be in their zone. A force of a few hundred Kurdish rebels, with three Kurdish chiefs, threatened Senneh from the west. The first night of his arrival, indeed, Colonel Rich received a message from them asking leave to attack the Persians in Senneh. His answer to this was that they must return to their own districts. But the Persian Governor, General Amini, had gone to discuss affairs and was taken prisoner by the rebels, who now demanded a ransom of 5,000 tumans. After some parleying—a mixture of Robin Hood and sheer farce—the General was safely returned, with his ears still on his head. The Guides patrols now toured the country and were happily received by the Kurds, while relations with the Persians were also cordial. During their stay at Senneh, a partial reunion of the whole corps took place, in that the Colonel had under his command "A" Squadron (Dogras) of the Guides Cavalry under Major W. A. Gimson, M.C., with the two squadron officers, Lieutenant Humphreys and Second-Lieutenant L'Estrange. As was to be expected, the old enthusiasm of the Corps of Guides was to the fore, and the resulting work markedly efficient. The two rifle companies, however, could not be spared from Kermanshah, and later went back to Pai-Tak to take part with other units in the fortification of this important pass on the main line of communications with Iraq which was some forty miles within the Persian border.

At Senneh all was quiet enough till an unfortunate happening on 10/11 December, when a patrol sent out by Major Baily was attacked by Kurds fifty miles north of Senneh and Subadar Sardar Khan and one driver of the R.I.A.S.C. were killed. The Subadar, a Ghakkar of the Punjab, was a great loss, all the more so because the Kurds had mistaken Baily's party for Persian troops and the two stout lives were thrown away. Four transport vehicles, stuck in the snow, had to be abandoned, to be recovered later.

Senneh, though in a wide, well-watered valley on a stream edged by Lombardy poplars, stood 6,000 feet above the sea, and the winter that now ensued was severe. By the end of the year the roads to the north-west and south were blocked and patrolling at an end. The snow-falls in the valley and the mountains around made the views more than beautiful, but minds were now turning to the varified beauties of a Persian spring in this upland valley. Fate, however, was to decree otherwise.

The troops were well enough equipped with poshteens (sheepskin coats) and the high Gilgit boots, so admirable to bivouac and ride in. Motor vehicles could only be used with chains and special precautions were necessary to protect them against cracked cylinders. The rank and file had been got under roofs and a liberal supply of oil stoves issued. The officers and their mess, and Headquarters offices, were accommodated in the upper storey of the Hotel de Ville while the Persian authorities continued to use the ground floor. This arrangement helped the increasing liaison and cordial relations between British and Persians, and Persian troops were actually saluting British officers. This cordiality unfortunately was not always in evidence elsewhere in the country despite every effort on the part of the British and the Indian troops.

In Senneh one great feature was the Subadar-major of the Battalion, Honorary Lieutenant Rur Singh, whose snowy white beard and dignity of mien earned for him the local (and Muslim) title of "Hajji," and local folk credited him with command of the Battalion. So the winter passed happily away. In February, several expeditions under Captain Pugh and Second-Lieutenant Berdoe were made to retrieve the four vehicles lost in the snow by Major Baily's patrol, a task of considerable risk in bitter weather, but at last achieved.

Unfortunately the operations by the Persian troops against the Kurds continued. The Persian force under General Amini had gone some 140 miles north of Senneh, with the object of recapturing Saqqis, the headquarters of Muhammad Raschid Beg, one of the principal rebel leaders. The Persian force was practically destroyed and General Amini killed. The General was a great loss both to the British and to Persia, as well as to the people of the province, among whom he had a remarkable reputation both for honesty and tolerance.

THE GUIDES CAVALRY IN IRAQ AND SYRIA

The war was rolling on on its inevitable course, and Quetta was no place—frontier *place d'armes* though it was—for an armoured reconnaissance corps, rapidly approaching a state of efficiency despite many hindrances.

It came therefore as a great relief, a few weeks after the Paltan had gone, when orders came for the Risala to follow them and "A" Squadron to the Gulf. It was on 11 October that they sailed from Karachi in the *Medina*, arriving at Basra on the 15th, with the almost unique record of sailing without a single absentee. The armoured vehicles were old Chevrolets to begin with, and the carriers were new, made in India, but stood very little hard work and were replaced a little later. The soft vehicles arrived a few days later in the *Subadar*. They then marched out to Shaiba in a real Iraqi dust-storm, and now had to "run in" their carriers, which had only joined them at the port. The Regiment was at first ordered to march up the Tigris by the old marching road of the First World War, showing the armour to the Tigris Arabs. The road was then well equipped with marching posts and water storage, and all mounted units and vehicles went by it—a dull route that had long been out of use. On 23 October Lieutenant Monteith was sent, with a detachment of "C," to report on it as far as Kut, some 240 miles—a very different sight from 1917, when steamers were crowded with troops and stores, the long road columns of horses and guns and a railway to Amara combining to put the fear of God into the Turk. He was back by the 30th, reporting that the repair of the road was poor, but that it was passable for mechanized transport.

However, plans were changed, and on 8 November they were ordered to Ur junction hard by the famous Ur of the Chaldees. On the 9th and 10th they left by road for Bagdad and by the 11th were in camp by the Iron Bridge and joined the 10th Indian Division, then commanded by the famous General "Bill" Slim. Orders then came to march to Tekrit, some way above Bagdad, later changed to Qayara still farther north, and it was not till March 1942, that they joined the Division at Habbaniyeh for training.

Let it be understood that it was now a peaceful land. The rebellion was over, the Swastika had been well rubbed into the rebel army in saltpetre; the rebel leaders had been shot, the false Regent had flown for his life, and a British military mission was reconditioning the Army.

Neither the Guides Infantry nor Cavalry (other than "A" Squadron) had been in time for the fighting with the rebels or the brief excitement of the three-day Persian War, and the Infantry were by now away in the Kurdish hills north of the Caspian road.

But though it was peaceful now, as the German invasion pushed relentlessly across the Cossack countries towards the Caucasus the new role of PAI Force, as the troops in Persia and Iraq were now to be known, opened up—viz., the herculean task of preparing a line of resistance from near Mosul across the Kurdish and Persian hills as described hereafter.

The knowledge acquired in the First World War was not sufficient for a mechanized force and the Guides Cavalry were now detailed to carry out far-flung reconnaissances of the *Jezira*, the "island," between the Tigris and Euphrates, and of the great Kurdish hills and passes north and south of Rowanduz.

First came that of the lands between Qaiyara and Rawa opposite Anah on the Euphrates, and then that of the hills of the Jebel Sinjar, where lived the Devil worshippers, and Tel Affar near Mosul. The line of the Jebel Hamrin, the mountain range on the east bank of the Tigris, through which the river cut its way at the Fatteh Gorges, as the hills passed on to the north-west, was an admirable line of defence. Here, Sir William Marshall with Cobb's and Egerton's Corps and Cassel's Cavalry Brigade, had defeated Hakki Pasha and the Turkish Army of Mosul, and had occupied Mosul, somewhat to the chagrin of the French. West of the fag-end of the Jebel Hamrin on the west bank ran the long Wadi Tartar, from the ruins of Hatra and the hills of the Jebel Sinjar. The Guides found that, with its steep cliffs, the Wadi was for the most part a good tank obstacle.

From Tel Affur and the Jebel Sinjar, the Guides marched away from the worshippers of Malik Taous and back to Qaiyara, and thence on to Mosul itself, opposite the great ruins of Nineveh on the left bank of the Tigris, and on over the Greater Zab to Erbil at the foot of the mountains of Kurdistan, which they reached early in December. Here it was, under its name of Arbela, that Alexander of Macedon destroyed the hordes of Persian Darius, crossing to the southern bank of the Greater Zab to get at them. Coming down to Erbil from Mosul by the east bank of the Tigris the Corps traversed the route of Xenophon and his Ten Thousand. They heard the Kurdish mountaineers calling to one another across the hills, which Xenophon too recorded, speaking of the "shrill-voiced Carduchi"—for these be very old lands of history to which the motorized units of the British Empire had come.

From Erbil there was plenty to do, reconnoitring the passes through the mountains east towards Lake Urumiya and south to Sulimaniyeh, the famous valley where grows the best Turkish tobacco.

All December and the first week in January 1942 were spent in various reconnaissances to report on the possibilities for motor transport of the roads into Persia, and on defensive positions in the mountains. Among the reports to be rendered was one on the suitability of the Greater Zab in its higher waters for anti-tank defences. The most

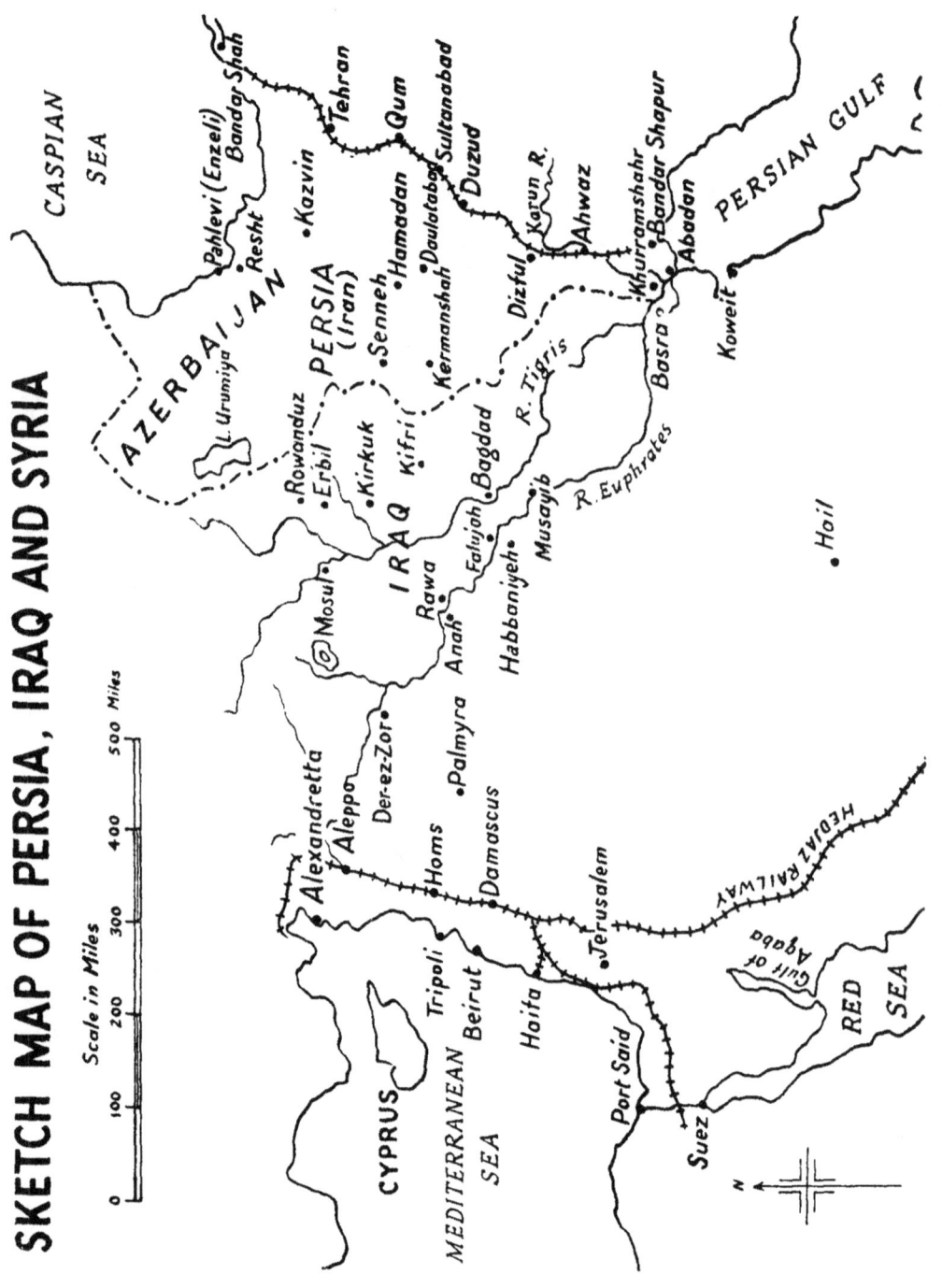

interesting and important of these reconnaissances was that, deep into the Kurdish hills, by Captain Plunkett with a selected party of "B" Squadron. This included the passes towards Sekiz, all deep in snow, and the party had to be equipped with pack ponies and even skis. At Qala Deza, seventy miles from Sulimaniyeh, the Kaimakhan and the Police Commandant welcomed them heartily, and it was soon evident that the countryside were hoping for political freedom by the help of God and Britannia. The start was made from Sulimaniyeh via Qala Deza to Gardash. Sulimaniyeh had been the centre from which Agha Sheikh Mahmud had started his rebellion against the British in 1919 and arrested several British officers of the Kurdish levies. He was finally defeated and shot through the liver on the Bazian Pass by a Kachin corps in Fraser's Force. The countryside were profuse in their help and called up large parties of Kurds to open up the passes and help generally, though they were a little puzzled as to why anyone should come in mid-winter. However, Plunkett, treated more as a political harbinger than a military commander, was able to explore all the various passes, the Aghas extending a very genuine hospitality.

These reconnaissances, in which all the squadrons took part, continued till the middle of February, when the snow was not too bad. By February the spring vegetation had turned the country round Erbil into a paradise of green downs and flowers, and on spare days, so far as cartridges permitted, black partridge, woodcock and duck were to be shot. On 14 February, the Corps marched to Mosul and eventually camped on the ground that had been occupied by 1st/2nd Gurkha Rifles. From Mosul reconnaissances were made in the direction of Nisibin and round the north side of the Jebel Sinjar, till 10 March when they marched to Habbaniyeh to train with the 10th Division, the squadrons working with the brigades.

On the 25th had come, to everyone's delight, orders to march to Egypt, and frantic steps had to be taken to get out scales and equipment necessary. Starting on the 29th and marching 460 miles, the disappointing order came to turn north and go to Damascus, showing the flag, supporting the Free French, and report again on roads, such as they were. Eleven days were spent in Damascus itself where, the first armoured units to be seen, the Corps received much attention.

Here the Regiment played its last game of polo—on horses provided by the Free French—the team including two members of the winning team of the last Indian Cavalry tournament, viz., Randall Plunkett and Gradidge, with Freddy Watson and an orderly.

On 14 April they marched north to Homs in the delightful leaf and fruit blossom of a Syrian spring, largely on reconnaissance work on routes, and thence hied back to Der ez Zor on the Euphrates, the scene of Ramzan Shallash's filibustering raid on the British outpost in 1919, which necessitated the hurried march of a British mounted column of relief.

Here the scene of 1942 was very different, for it was a station of the Free French, who received them enthusiastically—and with whom, if you please, was Madame Alys Delysia. With her they shared the highlight of the *Fête du Printemps*. From there they marched on 4 May to continue their reconnaissances of armoured vehicle routes and flag-showing, via Bab and Djerablous to Aleppo. At Aleppo the Free French commandant, as the Regiment marched past him, embraced Lieutenant-Colonel Gradidge with great affection and enthusiasm. By 21 May they were back in Damascus via the historic Palmyra-in-the-Desert (Tadmor), having received on the 20th the long-awaited orders for North Africa. With them, to everyone's disappointment, came the order for Lieutenant-Colonel Gradidge, who had mechanized and trained the Regiment, but who had reached the new age limit for regimental command in North Africa, to hand over to Walton. Gradidge, however, was appointed G.S.O.1 in Cairo and could thus help his regiment. They had need of time for a complete overhaul of vehicles and equipment, but this could not be allowed and on the 22nd they started on a non-stop 600-mile trip which finished with them distributed between Daba and Sidi Barrani by 30 May. Since they cared for their cars as much as they used to care for their horses—a point on which they were often complimented—they did get to the Desert without loss of a vehicle, a considerable feat under the circumstances. The story of their six months in the Desert and Delta during and after the retreat to El Alamein, which they helped to cover, belongs to a separate chapter.

Brigade Training at Khanaqin (Infantry) and back to Persia, 1941-42

In December 1941 had come the epoch-making news of the treacherous attack of the Japanese on Pearl Harbour and the vista of even more extended and intense war than before. The Guides Infantry therefore gladly received orders to proceed from the mountains to Khanaqin on the Iraqi frontier, for intensive training with the rest of their brigade, under its commander, Brigadier Blaxland. There the useful lesson was inculcated that officers of a brigade group must be on Christian-name terms if full co-operation were to be achieved. With them were the Field Artillery Regiment and the Field Company of Sappers attached.

On 14 April, after six weeks' training, orders unexpectedly came for the brigade group to march for Sultanabad, a town on the high plateau 150 miles south of Teheran on the trans-Persian railway. The Persian Government were proving difficult about various essential points of good relationship and effective working and the success of the communications with the Allies' Russian supply lines. The Brigade assumed that they were a factor in the game of oriental politics, and took satisfaction, without any definite warrant, that their move north had some effect in showing the Persian Government that they must play up to Allied advice. Sultanabad, on the trans-Persian railway from Teheran to the west, like Senneh, was some height above sea level and on 19 April when the Brigade reached the vicinity, the weather was cool and delightful. No further advance was needed and the group settled down to rigorous training. For the Guides, however, this was to be but short, for on 14 May 1942 the Battalion left for "temporary" duty at Bagdad, marching at three and a half hours' notice. This was no mean tribute to the efficient state of the Brigade, when a unit can start on a 400-mile march with so short a time of preparation.

The march down through the Persian spring was beautiful and the prospect of hot and dusty Bagdad and local duties was none too attractive. *Mais c'est la vie du soldat.*

CHAPTER X

THE GUIDES CAVALRY IN NORTH AFRICA

The Strange Sequence of Events in Libya and the Levant—The Guides Cavalry arrive and move up—The Withdrawal to the El Alamein Position—"B" Squadron in the Desert—War Patrols in the Desert ("Chicago Tribune")—Behind the Line—The Changed Scene—The Great Offensive and the Disappointment of the Guides Cavalry.

The Strange Sequence of Events in Libya and the Levant

The sequence of the operations from Egypt into Libya, the immense strain on General Wavell's communications—the come and go, the rise and fall until the crowning event of Field-Marshal Montgomery's great campaign—are more than confusing; but since the Guides Cavalry were now coming on the scene some epitome will be helpful.

(1) *December 1940 to February 1941.*

Wavell's destruction of almost the entire Italian Army, with the infliction of some 200,000 casualties, and the successive capture of Bardia, Tobruk, Derna, Benghazi and the advance to El Agheila, induced the policy of sending a force to help Greece.

(2) *8 March 1941.*

The great Naval victory of Cap Matapan, with the sinking of three 8-inch-gun cruisers, two 6-inch, and two destroyers.

(3) *March and April withdrawal of troops to Greece.*

But the policy that demanded aid for Greece was, in addition to its failure and the Cretan tragedy, to lose us the fruits of Wavell's astounding victory. Unknown, presumably, to the British High Command in London, Rommel had brought over heavy German reinforcements with armour to help Italy. The demands of the Grecian expedition had perforce left but one armoured brigade and one infantry division to hold Libya, which under no circumstances could they do.

(4) *2–12 April 1941.*

Rommel's armoured advance was surprising and overwhelming. Benghazi was hastily evacuated and stores destroyed. By the 12th, Bardia was lost and our front was back several hundred miles to Sollum. A garrison, however, had been left in Tobruk to carry out the famous defence, which denied the valuable port to Rommel. In the process of falling back we had had severe losses; three leading generals had been captured and 2,000 prisoners taken.

(5) *9-21 April* 1941.

The Greek venture had not been successful, for the dice was too heavily loaded. The Imperial Forces landed early in April, over 40,000 of them, and General Maitland Wilson had taken over command there. On 21 April, owing to Germany declaring war on Yugoslavia and Greece and pouring troops into Greece, the Yugoslav Army could offer little opposition to the German forces; the Greek Army could do no more, and on the 21st it was decided to withdraw our forces to Crete and Egypt, losing equipment.

(6) *May* 1941. *Crete—Rebellion in Iraq—Defence of Habbaniyeh—Defeat of Rebels— Conquest of Vichy Syria.*

In May 1941 the British were compelled to evacuate Crete. In April had come the usurper's coup in Iraq, the defence of Habbaniyeh on the Euphrates and the British victories over the rebel Iraqi army. It had become necessary to put an end to the Vichy régime in Syria, which took place with the help of the Free French in June and July.

(7) *Summer of* 1941.

In Egypt, during the summer of 1941, the recovery was remarkable. The troops from Greece and Crete had been re-formed and re-equipped, and American tanks had arrived. From Britain had come troops and equipment by the long sea route.

During all this while untoward crises in the Levant and Iraq had added to Britain's troubles and had been most sturdily faced.

The really bright spot was the victorious end to the brilliant campaign in Abyssinia when, on 20 May, the Duke of Aosta surrendered.

There was one more trouble to be put right, that of Persia and its Nazi penetration.

(8) *June* 1941.

Germany launched her fateful attack on Russia. In August Britain and Russia decided to crush the Nazi penetration and depose the despotic Shah of Persia. British and Russian forces entered Persia and, after a three-day war, the latter wisely surrendered. Early in August Generals Auchinleck and Wavell changed commands and Wavell, after his amazing responsibilities—Abyssinia, Libya, Greece, Crete and Syria—went to what seemed for the moment a less anxious sphere in India.

(9) 4 *November* 1941 *to May* 1942.

Preparations were steadily going forward in Egypt, and on 18 November Auchinleck launched his Eighth Army in the second great Libyan offensive, which drove Rommel back helter-skelter again the 500 miles to El Agheila, relieving Tobruk and retaking Derna; but alas! General Ritchie had not the transport to maintain his success and Rommel, his armour replaced, once more swept forward in the Libyan see-saw. Benghazi was again evacuated and the British line for the moment was formed on the general line southwards from Gazala, slanting back into the desert. There fierce fighting took place south of Acroma and our armour, after some successes, was almost annihilated. It was at this stage that the Guides Cavalry arrived in North Africa.

THE GUIDES CAVALRY IN NORTH AFRICA

(10) *May 1942: Back at the Frontier of Egypt.*

By 26 May the Axis forces were probing the British front, bent on attacking. Rommel, in his desire to turn the British flank, had sent his armour south and was attacking the water-point at Bir Hacheim, resolutely held by the Free French. Heavy fighting was taking place south of El Adem and at Acroma. This continued for days with varying success in a perpetual see-saw, in which British armour at one time had achieved considerable success, while Bir Hacheim repulsed several assaults, British and Indian troops coming to the aid of the French, who were eventually withdrawn on 10 June. The bitter fighting south of Acroma continued until, at last, the staunch British armour, out-weighted, was practically destroyed and the Eighth Army began to fall back towards the Egyptian frontier in a state of considerable disarray, its soft vehicles and broken tanks pouring back along the roads eastward. By 18 June the Army was back on the frontier, a force being hastily flung into Tobruk with the hope of repeating the former defence. Alas! this force had no chance to settle in before it was attacked and by 21 June overwhelmed.

(11) *21 June.*

The now broken Eighth Army was falling back far into Egypt in great confusion, and General Auchinleck himself took command on 26 June and steadily pulled it together.

All the while the help and cover from the R.A.F. had been beyond all praise and almost beyond belief. In the more desperate period of the retreat one squadron brought down fourteen Stukas out of fifteen and one fighter, a pilot complaining that he had "run out of Stukas."

(12) *June to October. Battles of El Alamein.*

After the loss of Tobruk, any idea of trying to stem the Hun on the stony hinterland of Mersa Matruh, the limit of Wavell's withdrawal in 1941, was wisely abandoned by Auchinleck. The Eighth Army was now withdrawn in good order to El Alamein, where it was firmly established by the end of June, repulsing a fierce attack by Rommel and itself attacking Rommel, who once more was coming on. At this period there were three distinct battles of El Alamein, as Auchinleck held the narrow lands between the sea and the Qattara Depression : viz., the last attack of the Axis, Auchinleck's riposte against the exhausted Rommel, 1–12 July (Alexander relieved Auchinleck, 18 July) ; the third, the defeat of Rommel's attack at Alim Halfa by Montgomery at the end of September —a fine prelude to the great battle that began in the last week of October.

THE GUIDES CAVALRY ARRIVE AND MOVE UP

The foregoing outline brings this story of the amazing and often glorious Libyan see-saws up to the time when the Guides Cavalry arrived in Egypt. It was just as Rommel was attacking Ritchie and stretching out south to Bir Hacheim that they marched in from Syria, Lieutenant-Colonel F. Walton in command.

On 24 May, before the final smash-up in "The Cauldron," they were pushed out into the Wadi Natrun, that long alleyway that leads north-west from Cairo towards the Mediterranean and thence up the coast, coming under the orders of the 10th

Indian Motor Brigade. By the 26th they were at Dabaa, a march of 145 miles, and next day "B" Squadron moved to Matruh and the Regiment itself to Baggush, leaving, however, "A" Squadron at Dabaa. "C3" Troop was pushed out to Abu Haggag on the high ground near the coast where it came under the orders of the O.C. Skinner's Horse. At Baggush were the headquarters of the 10th Brigade.

They were now well on the road to the front and much of the unhinged rear services from the Eighth Army were moving past them towards Egypt. By the 28th "B" Squadron was pushed forward to Sollum and "A" Squadron to "Charing Cross," the well-known road junction some seven miles south-west of Matruh. Next day "B" Squadron was ordered to the oasis of Jarabub (Giarabub).

Early in June, Headquarters and "C" Squadron carried out extensive patrolling in the areas south of Baggush to the Qattara Depression, chiefly to check maps. On the 9th Jemadar Ali Shah captured five Germans from a crashed plane. Several untoward accidents took place, Sowar Nauroz Khan being killed and two men being injured by a sea mine on the coast near Ras Hawala, and a couple of days later (11 June) a land mine killed Sowar Dharam Singh and Cook Babu Ram.

The Regiment now received Bren guns in exchange for their V.-Bs., and a tommy-gun per armoured vehicle. The fighting in the "Witch's Cauldron," south of Acroma, was now at its height and more debris and rear services of the Eighth Army were coming through, the seriousness of the situation being apparent to all. By 18 June the British line was hastily formed on the old Italian frontier, or had withdrawn north to Tobruk, the latter force, however, without the organized system of the year before. The Guides Cavalry were now ordered to turn westward, a fresh and unshaken armoured unit, though for fighting purposes only a reconnaissance one. But of all things, what was now essential was the combating of Axis penetrations and reconnaissances. Thus on 18 June, the Regiment (less "B" Squadron) was ordered from its position to kilometre 91, some half-way between Matruh and Sidi Barrani, a point some fifty miles nearer the enemy. Arriving there next day, they came under the orders of the 1st Armoured Division, the C.O. reporting to the headquarters of this division on the morning of the 20th at Aba el Hallah (6736), and dug in, being visited next day by the Divisional Commander.

The situation, however, was growing worse and worse, and on that very day the force that had hurriedly occupied Tobruk and had not had time to organize their defence, were smothered. The only possible course was to withdraw farther rather than attempt to hold the line that Wavell was able to hold in 1941, and on the 23rd the Regiment was ordered to pull out and get back as fast as it could to the vicinity of Fuka, less "B" Squadron, which had been at Jarabub since the beginning of June. Its services there with the Free French Dencol were of a distinguished nature and must presently be described.

By now General Auchinleck had taken over the actual command from General Ritchie, and had been compelled by the state of the troops and armour to give up any idea of holding a line at Matruh, which line indeed Rommel was endeavouring to encircle. The troops retiring were fighting fiercely, counter-attacking or breaking out.

THE WITHDRAWAL TO THE EL ALAMEIN POSITION

In marching to Fuka on the 23rd the Regiment itself was heavily bombed and machine-gunned west of Charing Cross, Sowar Bije Singh being mortally wounded.

Next day the Regiment was ordered to go west again, and join the 22nd Armoured Brigade (British) as their reconnaissance regiment, and arrived at Bir Qaim some twenty-five miles south of Mersa Matruh at 1830 hours, where it spent three days, "A" and "C" Squadrons covering a front of seventy miles. On the 25th the excitement began, to the joy of the unit, who had come so far and hitherto seen so little. The Hun was pressing on and that night "A," in touch with the 12th Lancers, spent the night in the box at Mersa Matruh. On the 26th and 27th the Regiment was practically covering the rear of the Eighth Army on the edge of an escarpment facing west, while the Axis troops were pushing on down the coast, a movement which had caused the Brigade some anxiety. On the 27th there was "the father and mother" of a tank battle on their front between the Huns and the 22nd Armoured Brigade, and the Regiment was also being engaged with patrols. When this fight was over, it was ordered back some ten miles, still on the escarpment, while the enemy had got as far as Baggush on the coast. During this movement "C" covered the rear, and three vehicles had to be destroyed to save them from the enemy. Next day orders came from the Brigade to move fifteen miles south and 100 miles east, taking with them a mixed force of gunners who had become detached from the 50th Division. Halting for the night in the desert, the road, or rather terrain, being atrocious for vehicles, they arrived at what was practically the Ruweisat ridge at 1330 hours, having been bombed and machine-gunned without loss. Vehicles were lost for want of spare parts. Here were many staff officers arranging to get the troops into position on the El Alamein position, from which Rommel was soon to be beaten back, and orders from the 30th Corps now directed them to cover the front and work in with the 18th Infantry Brigade (Indian). Alec Moore, of the Paltan, was D.A.A. and Q.M.G. of the Brigade and got in touch with them.

The Headquarters and "A" Squadron harboured for the night at 883.278, nine miles south of El Alamein and a mile or so south of Ruweisat Ridge. Next day, the 30th, "C" Squadron, still covering the movement, joined Headquarters.

The first of July was spent at Deir Es Sheim (875.280), a strong point (less "B," who were under direct orders of the Eighth Army), patrols of "C" being in constant touch with the enemy's armour. Jemadar Babu Ram's carrier was hit by tank fire and captured. Jemadar Zarin Khan's carrier was also hit and Lance-Duffadar Sinjab Singh killed, but carrier and crew escaped. At 1530 hours the Regiment withdrew twenty miles eastwards to 445.895[87] on the ridge two and a half miles south of El Imayid railway station, fifteen miles east of El Alamein, and harboured there for the night of 2 July. The C.O. reported to 30th Corps and was ordered to come under 50th Division, to whom it reported that five patrols could be furnished from the two squadrons at present with Headquarters.

From 3 to 7 July, "A" and "C" Squadrons were detached to various artillery

---

[87] The Grids are now numbered as on the Egyptian maps.

columns, who put up a vast, unending barrage to their front for several days. On the 3rd John Reid, with the Pathan Squadron ("C"), made short work of a German party they ran into, killing 5, capturing 35, making their bag of prisoners 42. During all this harassing time of important service the actual dead loss to the Risala was 2 killed and 4 missing (believed prisoners of war). Then came the good news that "B" Squadron was at Amirya[38] workshops and would rejoin on the 9th. The Regiment now came under 1st Armoured Division again.

"B" Squadron in the Desert

It has been related how "B" Squadron, commanded by Randall Plunkett, was pushed on in advance of the Regiment on 27 May to Matruh where, under the orders of the O.C. Matruh, it was concerned in various coast reconnaissances working, curiously enough, with the Royal Yugoslav Guards, who could not be used at the front as the Axis shot any prisoners. They were pleasant comrades, though none had any English. At Matruh the reconnaissance position was not improved by the fact that the Sapper officer who laid the minefield had gone and left no map, which dereliction later cost the lives of two men of "A" Squadron. On the 28th "B" Squadron was moved up to Sollum, though the fighting was a mile west at the moment. On the way a refugee officer from the front gave them ghastly but quite untrue stories of disaster evolved by his shaken brain. Arriving at the Bay of Sollum and filling up with petrol, they received orders to move straight on up the Halfaya (Hell-fire) Pass to Capuzzo, where they found the 4th Indian Division deployed along trenches and standing-to. At Area Headquarters there was some sign of "flap" (a word of dismay, later forbidden by Montgomery, though originally in the Army it merely meant "something on"). Here, to quote "B" Squadron's diarist, "Frantic staff officers in desert boots and armed with fly-whiskers paced the dugout. Desert boots and fly-whisks were then essential equipment for the desert warrior." At Capuzzo orders were received a little indicative of the "flap," in that if attacked they were to move to the sound of the guns—whatever that might mean. In view of the bright moonlight, Plunkett ordered semi-harbour for the night—viz., in a triangle at fifty yards interval. This was fortunate, as Capuzzo was heavily bombed that night, one bomb falling harmlessly in the triangle. Next morning came orders, not for the "Cauldron," but to march south-west to join an Anglo-French detachment at Jarabub to relieve a squadron of a South African regiment moving off to rejoin at the front. The going was good, along the wire of the Italian frontier, which ran the whole way to the oasis and through the debris of knocked-out tanks and vehicles of earlier battles. The first stage of this march into the desert was the long one of 150 miles.

At 1000 hours tanks were heard on the listener, and they moved quietly six miles on. Two or three German bombers passed over their open harbour, but without molesting them. Next day they came within the French area, for they passed posts of bearded French, but earlier they were met at Fort Maddelena and during the afternoon moved down the escarpment into Jarabub. This oasis is a large one and the principal centre

---

[38] On the railway six miles south east of Alexandria.

DAVID MONTEITH

DESERT RECONNAISSANCE, "B" SQUADRON

[Photo: War Office Official

[Photo: War Office Official

THE GUIDES CAVALRY IN THE DESERT

of the Sennusi tribes. A badly bombed Italian fort in the centre was now the Allied Headquarters. The garrison, originally known as Dencol, after Colonel Dennis of the Punjabis, was also referred to as the "Lion Brigade" in an attempt to bluff the enemy, but more often the "Long Range Desert Force."

There was a French Commandant (le Bavière) with a British Town-major. The actual force was an interesting mixture :

- 1 company of British Commandos.
- 1 company of French Senegalese.
- 1 company of French Moroccan regiment.
- 1 armoured squadron (now Indian).
- 1 company of French North African regiment.
- 1 mixed French battery (75 and 25 mm. anti-tank), with various small special detachments.

Most of the water was brackish and there was only one sweet-water well. Just south of the oasis was the great sand sea of Kalansho, a terrifying area of white sand dunes, shifting constantly in the wind and stretching as far as the eye could see. To the north was sand, mixed with pebbly areas, and to the west the ground was very broken. The names on the map, of which there were many, usually referred to broken cairns and mined, deserted buildings. The oasis was of course occupied as an observation post and denial area and far-ranging patrols by the Squadron were the main duty.

The diarist recalls an interesting incident as they took over from the South African unit. The Guides officers, accompanied by the South African Second-in-command, encountered a South African patrol who established identity by firing a round from a gun. This was a trick from the Boer War when, in the guerrilla stage, British mounted columns pom-pommed a distant force, to be sure, since the Boers had none. When the troops met, the South African officer with the Guides introduced them thus :

South African officer : "Sergeant Bourke, have you read 'The Story of the Guides'? "

Sergeant Bourke : "Of course, sir, I read it at school."

South African officer : "Well, here is Mr. Penly and five Indian troop commanders of these very Guides come to relieve us."

And such was the British Empire, before half was poured down the drain.

Two days later the desert work began, very difficult for a unit whose knowledge was but hearsay, and who had come to a more than usually "deserty" corner, while German armoured cars were known to be far superior in armament and speed.

However, the patrols were always bravely out on their far-flung rounds. The heavy shifting sand was the chief enemy, but the tricks of tackling this with their none-too-suitable equipment were steadily evolving. The diarist gives this instance to show what it all meant during the expedition to Jalo :

First Message : "Hullo Colo, Sano calling, Hamara left walla armoured car-ke half-shaft tut gya." ("My left armoured car's half-shaft is broken.")

Second Message: "Hullo Colo, etc., hamara right walla armoured car ke short propeller shaft tut gya." ("My right armoured car's short propeller shaft is broken.")

Third Message: "Hullo Colo, etc., hamara apna armoured car rhet men fass gya." ("My own car is stuck in the sand.")

By "cannibalizing" broken cars it was possible to repair the major portion and for the force to push on towards Jalo. But the sands of Libya were running out for the time being, and consequent on the defeat of the Eighth Army and the loss of Tobruk on 21 June, a motorized Indian brigade, fighting fiercely farther north, and the Jalo column, were the only Allied troops left in Libya. The day of the disasters in the north brought the order to withdraw to Jarabub, which was done without incident. Orders to hold Jarabub at all costs were in force for a week, and then came instructions to fall back to the oasis of Siwa, the famous site of the temple of Jupiter Ammon. The people of Siwa were dismayed, however, when two days later came the final order to retire on El Alamein as best they could, a move for which there was not enough petrol. There were three courses before them:

(1) Withdraw to the Bahariya oasis and there wait for petrol to be sent them.

(2) Attempt to march by Qara, which might be held by the Axis, over the little-known and quicksandy Qattara depression. They had petrol to get within 100 miles of Cairo.

(3) The third course was one that somewhat appealed to the French, who had felt great chagrin at the withdrawals, and was to march north and surrender.

The second course was obviously the most promising despite the story of bog which sagged ominously under the motor vehicles, and after Penly had ascertained that Qara was clear the column made their adventurous march through morass-edged and rock-strewn roads—from Jalo to Mena was 750 difficult miles.

The Squadron eventually pulled up at a staff tent, whence they were sent to Amirya workshops for such repairs as might be possible and, after a week, marched up the Cairo road and met the Regiment at Burg-el-Arab.

That is the end, in brief, of this very remarkable desert trek with our allies, among the very distant oases in important reconnaissances, under considerable difficulty and much endurance by all ranks and the "*Operation 'Phantom' vers Jalo.*"

One member of the Squadron is worthy of mention: he was with them for the whole trek—viz., the mascot, Dumba Singh, adopted Dogra and fat-tailed sheep. Dumba Singh was born of a ration sheep in Kurdistan when the Squadron was there; he eventually returned with it to India, and as he was getting too busy with his horns, was sent home to a Sikh village.

The Squadron was to see the desert once more as related below, when Wal-Col turned to Baharia. The desert record of the Squadron caused it to be selected for a film "E Boats of the Desert." Thus . . .

THE GUIDES CAVALRY IN NORTH AFRICA

How Watchdogs of War Patrol African Desert
BY SAM BREWER
(*Chicago Tribune* Press Service)

With an Armoured Car Patrol in the Western Desert, 13 August.—While the main British and Axis forces spar for an opening along the front near the coast, the immense reaches of the desert, stretching more than a thousand miles into Central Africa, are the province of light forces. They are always busy, no matter what "lull" the main coastal forces may have.

I have just been out on an "offensive patrol" with an armoured car squadron, seeing the work they do—one of the few dashing, glamorous jobs in the grim business of modern war.

The main forces of the Allies and Axis have been fighting all the battles you've read about in the last couple of months within a few miles of the Mediterranean coast. Beyond them to the south, lightweights—armoured car and motor patrols—carry on their work.

BEST AT SCOUTING

Armoured cars sound formidable, but they are really intended less for fighting than for scouting. "They're my eyes and ears; I would be lost without them," one general remarked in the last campaign.

We moved off on patrol with our unit at the first light of day. We had camped in a hollow far out in the desert the previous night, with sentries watching through the night atop surrounding knolls. There was no breakfast lest the enemy see the fires.

The commander led the way in his car, a dim shape bobbing up and down ahead with its wireless mast waving crazily against the sky. British correspondent, Edward Howe, and I were passengers.

We travelled by compass and dead reckoning. Most parts of the desert have no reliable landmarks, and patrols treat it like the sea.

LIKE CRUISERS AT SEA

Moving fast in close formation, to take advantage of the short time before sunrise, the cars followed low ground so they wouldn't be visible against the skyline. Once the sun rose, they turned on another course and cut around behind the area where enemy patrols were believed to be snooping.

Armoured patrols work like cruisers at sea. Cars cruised on both sides and ahead of the commander, nosing into all suspected depressions and reporting constantly by radio.

Suddenly, as we approached a rise, the commander halted the patrol, swung his car at right-angles and rolled up to a hull-down position near the crest of the rise so that only his head showed above it. The cars in the rear swept up and around to deploy across the front, while the leaders spread out fanwise, then raced out of sight over the skyline.

The commander pointed to two black objects in the distance. Already the desert had switched from the biting chill of the dawn to the heat of the day, and everything near the ground shimmered in the rising heat waves.

ENEMY OR OIL BARRELS

The objects could have been enemy tanks or trucks, or they could have been oil barrels. The mirage sometimes magnifies and sometimes shrinks distant objects.

This time it was two squat bushes, desert rarities.

"It's usually bushes or petrol tins," the commander remarked, "but the time the desert really catches you is when you say 'they're probably only bushes.' That's always the time when they turn out to be the enemy."

All day the hunt continued according to careful plan, back and forth, in and out of wadis (dry channel beds). Sometimes one group was detached to prowl through a large wadi while the commander took the rest of the force around behind in case they scared up anything.

In the desert it is astonishing how easily a large group of vehicles can hide in depressions. One enemy patrol often passes within half a mile of another without seeing the hidden group, and in the great expanses of the desert half a mile is only a drop in the bucket.

OFF TO THE ATTACK

Suddenly, as we continued our search, the commander roared "Halt!" into his radiophone and followed with crisply spoken orders. The scouts raced across a flat stretch, then converged on distant objects which we all agreed were vehicles moving slowly from left to right near the horizon.

The rest of the force rolled after them in fighting formation, strung out across the plain.

As the first cars grew nearer "the enemy," we saw them swell in the mirage until they seemed gigantic and it was only then we realized we were charging a row of grassy hummocks, magnified and distorted by the mirage, which also gave the impression of movement.

In these wide reaches, without points of comparison, it is most difficult to judge the size or distance away of things you see or even to tell whether they are moving, particularly if you are moving yourself. Puffs of dust behind a vehicle are usually the only reliable indication of movement, but the mirage causes a glare which distorts the base of anything standing on the ground in the distance and makes it look much like dust around a moving car.—*Finis*.

BEHIND THE LINE

The Eighth Army was now behind the El Alamein line and in fighting trim despite its need for re-equipping, and it was resisting firmly all German attacks. The Guides Cavalry was also behind the line after its strenuous rear-guard work.

It was now proposed to make one serviceable squadron of five patrols. "C" was thus made up and "A" marched on 10 July to the workshop area at Amirya.

Next day, however, "C" was ordered to hand over sixteen carriers and seven wireless sets to the 9th Australian Division at El Alamein, and the Regimental Headquarters and "C" Squadron to Khataba on the Cairo–Alexandria road to refit, taking a party of German prisoners to Alexandria. On 11 July, Headquarters and "C" marched to Amirya, the whole Regiment coming under the 10th Indian Division, that Division being responsible for protecting the left flank of the Eighth Army—viz., from the Qattara Depression and specially the aerodromes and repair shops of all kinds in the Wadi Natrun. A battle group was now pushed forward along the "Barrel Road," commanded by O.C. Guides Cavalry (Lieutenant-Colonel Walton), consisting of :

Regimental H.Q. and "B" Squadron, Guides ;
1st Battery, 28th Field Regiment ;
2nd/11th Sikhs, less two companies ;

the group to assemble on the Cairo–Alexandria road, where it remained for some days, "B" Squadron being ordered to Black Paps[39] area on the 13th to carry out reconnaissances.

---

[39] Hillocks on the western edge of the wadi.

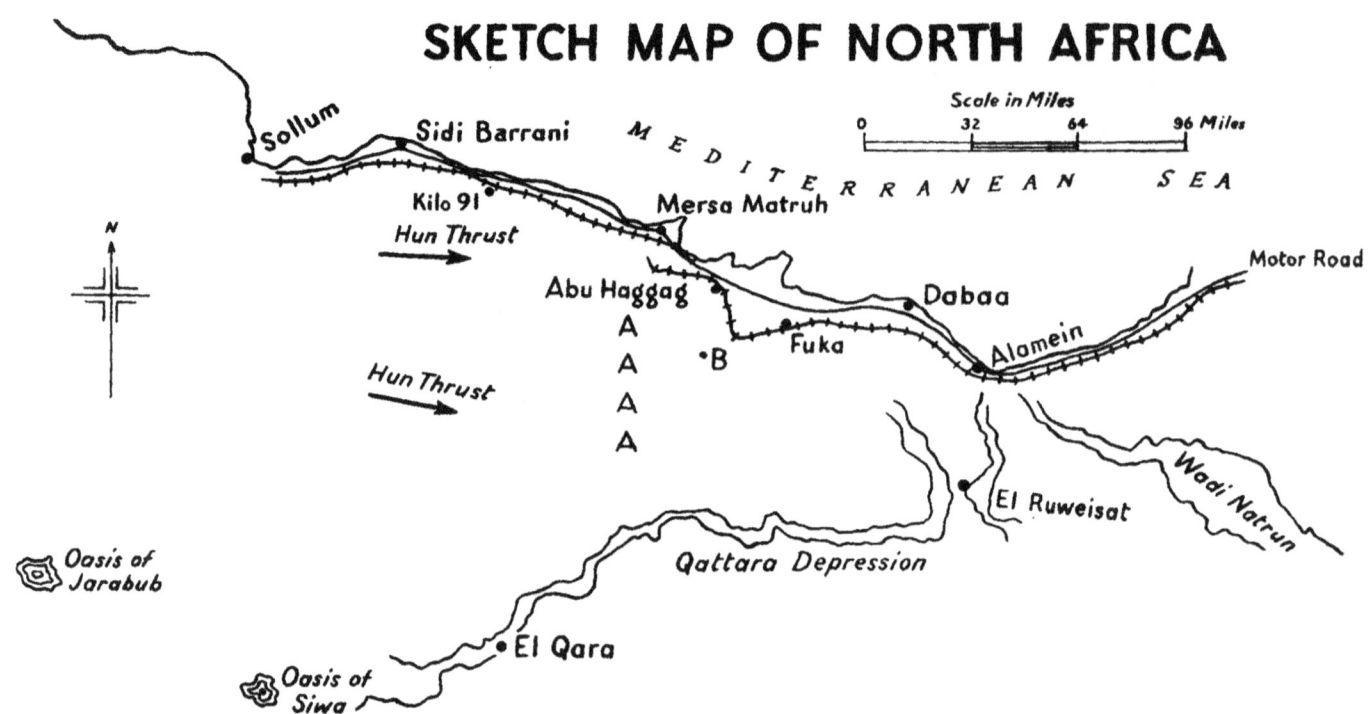

The Battery, just arrived from home, had no experience of desert-driving, so that the column made very slow progress. The road was very bad, many vehicles breaking down, and the Squadron was recalled. On the 20th the battle group was practically broken up, "B" Squadron returning to Black Paps area. "C" Squadron was now ordered to Abbassia till it could be refitted, and "A" Squadron rejoined the Regiment and on the 28th was ordered to relieve "B" Squadron. From 1 to 5 August the Headquarters were at K.106 on the Cairo–Alexandria road, and on the 5th they marched to Mena and on that day the unit (less "C" Squadron, still refitting) was concentrated. All responsibility for the flank and aerodrome defence of the Eighth Army was now transferred to B.T.E., under whose orders the Guides now came. On the 8th "B" Squadron was sent to the Bahariya oasis, 200 miles south-west of Cairo, an important sounding point, with 1st Company, 4th Motor Battalion (12th Division), to be known as "Barforce," under command of Captain R. Plunkett (Guides) till relieved by Colonel Kellett of 4th Motor Battalion, arriving there on the 10th.

On the 10th orders came for the Guides Cavalry, at present organized as a divisional reconnaissance unit, to be arranged and equipped as an armoured car regiment. This and the various adjustments in war establishment already experienced made administrative work very heavy.

THE CHANGED SCENE

But by now the British line at El Alamein–Ruweisat was strongly established, and Rommel had shot his bolt, and no more of the "Alexandria in three days" announcements were made to the expectant Axis public.

But great changes had come over the scene. In the last week of July, General Auchinleck had staged the second Alamein. The fighting swayed for several days along the thirty-five miles of front, and especially on the dusty shoulder of Ruweisat, backed heavily by Tedder's Air Force. It ended pretty much where it had begun, but showed how the Eighth Army had recovered its verve. The Prime Minister had come, and General Smuts also; the Commander-in-Chief, with a few trenchant explanatory remarks, prepared to hand over to General Alexander, and the much-admired General "Strafer" Gott took over the Eighth Army, only to be killed next day in an air accident, which brought General Montgomery into his place.

During August, reinforcements to Army and Air Force were pouring in and General Montgomery was busy rearranging his army to his satisfaction.

The new organization found the Guides very short of vehicles, of which the establishment was much increased, and at the middle of the month there seemed very little prospect of their being completed.

On the 24th "A" Squadron was detailed for "Delta Force" under the 10th Indian Motor Brigade and "B" Squadron was to return from Bahariya, while the Regimental Headquarters and that Squadron were to remain at Mena.

On 1 September the actual disposition was:

Headquarters at Mena;
"A" with Delta Force at Jebel Ruzza;

"B" was returning from the Bahariya oasis;
"C" at Abbassia, re-equipping.

On 5 September "C" Squadron joined Headquarters. The day before, the Regiment received operation orders to come into effect in the event of a break-through of the enemy at El Alamein. On 7 September the 10th Indian Motor Brigade, with which was "A" Squadron, came under orders of B.T.E., and next day the Guides Cavalry (less "A" Squadron) left the command of the 12th Division and also came directly under B.T.E. On the 11th "Walforce" was brought into being, consisting of Guides Cavalry and 1st L.A.F. (Libyan Arab Force), with the definite role of protecting the southern end of the Wadi Natrun, and access to the Mena–Alexandria road, Lieutenant-Colonel Walton being in command.[40] The instructions to Walton indicated that the most likely form of enemy action, so far as his force was concerned, was likely to be long-distance raids, parachutists and sabotage.

On the 23rd L.G. 237, in the Guides Area, was bombed by three M.E.104's without casualties.

During October actually life with "Walforce" was quiet, but subdued excitement simmered throughout the force as it was obvious that the hour of Generals Alexander and Montgomery was approaching. On 20 October the following six "British" officers joined the regiment: Lieutenants D. R. Poynton, J. H. Chibber, E. S. Corner, A. J. Peacock, P. P. Howes, Mohamad Farukh Khan.

During the month various exercises to test the new organization and equipment of the Regiment were carried out.

The Great Offensive and the Disappointment of the Guides Cavalry

October had almost run out and the great hour had arrived. Just before 2200 hours on the 23rd of the month the artillery opened the ever-memorable Fourth Battle of Alamein that was to put Egypt out of Axis thoughts for ever.

For the Guides Cavalry the only excitement was the capture of two escaped German prisoners by Risaldar Zarin Khan ("C1" Troop).

November opened with "Walforce" still carrying out its special role in the Wadi Natrun. On the 3rd, however, this force was dissolved and the Guides received orders to draw vehicles deficient to the war establishment and exchange defectives. On the 5th came the long-hoped-for orders to join the Eighth Army, now pushing after Rommel's defeated troops, and to be at Amirya by the 10th.

Rommel had returned from his leave a few days before Montgomery opened, in time to see a heavily protected convoy making for port devastated from the air—a grim omen! At Mena on the 8th came the actual orders to march to the Eighth Army, on the 10th came the route to be followed from Mareopolis, via El Alamein and Sidi Abd-el-Rahman, and on the 11th they had marched accordingly.

---

[40] Colonel Walton was in hospital on sick leave from the 10th to the 23rd and could not take command till that date.

COLONEL GRADIDGE WITH GENERAL ALEXANDER IN SYRIA

But alas and alack! as Colonel Walton went to contact the rear of the Eighth Army a despatch rider arrived with orders for the unit to return to Amirya. It was on loan from PAI Force to help the Eighth Army when its armoured force was broken. The German approach to the Caucasus was ominous, the hour of PAI Force might soon come, and back to PAI Force it must go.

So the Regiment sorrowfully turned its vehicles round, and its face, from the all-victorious vista in front and wended its way to the East once more. From 11 November to the 20th it remained at Mareopolis, its actual orders to march to Bagdad coming on the 17th, and on the 21st it marched for Ismailia and the canal. By the 29th it joined the 5th Indian Division at Quetta camp and next day marched to Latafiyeh,[41] where the whole of January 1943 was spent. Courses of all kinds were now the order of the day for operations in terrain often very like the Libyan desert. On 21 January the Regiment was inspected by Lieutenant-General Martel.

The 5th Indian Division, to which the Cavalry returned, was commanded by Major-General Sir Harold Briggs, who writes very appreciatively of the Corps and describes the situation of the Division before they were all moved to Ranchi (India) *en route* for Burma. The Cavalry were taken away from the Division, which was sent to Burma:

"At the time they joined us we had just been relieved by 4th Indian Division in the desert and sent to Iraq as G.H.Q. reserve to PAI Force against a possible German advance through the Caucasus into Persia. We were formed into a special Armoured Division comprising:

Divisional Cavalry—Guides

7th Armoured Brigade of 3rd Armoured Rifles, motorized battalion R.H.A. Regiment

9th Indian Infantry Brigade

161st Indian Infantry Brigade

Divisional Artillery

2nd Anti-Tank Regiment, R.A.

"We had some most interesting and intensive training and recces and felt capable of taking on anyone and anything. The Guides took a prominent part in this and were excellent. They were equipped with Humber 'Q' cars. All brigades had by then much war experience. Unfortunately the threat passed and our movements were (for Guides and the bulk of the Division) to move to India whilst 7th Armoured Brigade were to move to the Desert. On arrival in India we were ordered to Burma, less the Guides, in whose place we had to take an infantry recce unit. We were all most disappointed to lose the Guides, who went to the North-West Frontier."

---

[41] The large camp twenty miles south of Bagdad on the road to Babylon, twenty miles south of Bagdad on the Latafiyeh estates farmed by Mr. Garbutt, whose son was later an officer in the Guides Cavalry.

THE GUIDES

Regimental Affairs

Officers with the Regiment at Bagdad:

Lieutenant-Colonel F. Walton.
Major Hon. R. A. H. Plunkett.
Major J. B. Reid.
Major D. G. Egerton.
Major D. J. Monteith (A.).
Captain W. G. O. Butler (T.).
Captain D. R. Poynton (A.).
Captain P. Graham (T.).
Captain J. Eliott-Lockhart.
Lieutenant J. George.
Lieutenant Har-Prasad.
Second-Lieutenant J. M. Penty.
Second-Lieutenant T. R. Conway.
Second-Lieutenant E. S. Corner.
Second-Lieutenant C. M. O'Rorke.
Second-Lieutenant P. J. Horner.
Second-Lieutenant N. A. G. Brooks.
Second-Lieutenant Sultan Khan Malik.
Second-Lieutenant Muhd. Faruk Khan.
Second-Lieutenant E. A. L. Reid.
Second-Lieutenant A. J. Peacock.

February 1943 was also spent at Latafiyeh, where the "B" vehicles were inspected, the report giving high praise for their condition and high standard of maintenance. On 24 May, W. Eliott-Lockhart rejoined from Staff duty, being posted to the command of H.Q. wing.

CHAPTER XI

THE LONG YEARS WITH PAI FORCE (INFANTRY)

BAGDAD AND MUSAYIB (1942)—BACK TO PERSIA AND THE 27TH BRIGADE, 1942—COLONEL RICH LEAVES THE BATTALION—THE LENGTH AND BREADTH OF IRAQ—THE STORY OF THE POLES IN IRAQ—THE DISAPPOINTMENT OF THE LEBANON—ON THE TRANS-PERSIAN RAILWAY—SOME REGIMENTAL HAPPENINGS (INFANTRY)—THE INFANTRY RETURN TO IRAQ AND THENCE HOME.

BAGDAD AND MUSAYIB, 1942

THE march to Bagdad was not the old tramp of the foot-soldier, for in buses the Guides rolled into the Tigris capital on 17 May to relieve a Gurkha battalion and take over Headquarters and advanced base guards of all kinds. Training was impossible and the shoddy semi-western amusements of Bagdad appealed to no one. Hotels and cinemas, third rate at that, were exorbitant and now came a hint of duty in Bahrein on the Persian Gulf in the worst season of the year; but this did not mature, though to its chagrin the Battalion was definitely removed from the 27th Brigade and posted as "Army troops," the pleasant term for maids-of-all-work, and all were naturally disappointed for the moment.

In July came orders to proceed to Musayib on the Euphrates and on the rail from Basra, not far from Bagdad, an important point on the communications especially now that news of the Japanese successes was reverberating through the coffee-shops that are such a feature of Arab life. Musayib in the First World War had been our advanced railhead from Bagdad for that portion of our operations on the Upper Euphrates against the Turks. But the Lower Euphrates was then neither navigable nor protectable, nor had the through rail to Bagdad been made, and the Euphrates force was supplied from the advanced base at Hinaidi just below Bagdad.

A few small motor boats for work on the river had been brought across the desert on which the line was eventually laid. Musayib had the added advantage of being near the great Hindiah Barrage, made by a British firm for the Turkish Government in "pre-fourteen" days to restore irrigation in the Hilla region. The remains of the old base were still extant, but in a miserable state. It was now to be developed as the main base for the forces in Iraq and Persia on the rail from Basra to Bagdad, which was, of course, non-existent in 1914–18. The desert on the bank included a salt pan and in July was as hot, dirty and dreary a spot as troops from the Persian upland could well ask for. After the Iraqi rebellion, the place had been revived and was still a huge dump of army stores of all kinds, base hospitals and the like. There was an immense amount of valuable stores, very attractive to that prince of thieves, the local Arab, who was quite reckless of life in the attempt to get rich quick. It should be realized that motor tyres alone were fetching about £100 apiece in the Bagdad bazaar.

When the Guides marched in, this enormous area was guarded by some untrustworthy Arab *chowkidars* and 200 inexperienced "first reinforcements" mounted from a nearby camp. A few weeks before the Battalion had arrived, a well-planned and well-executed raid had taken place and some 30 or 40 camel loads of loot were carried away including nearly half a million rounds of S.A.A. Gossip said that the raiders had even brought a party complete with dancing girls for the delectation of some of the sentries. It was not the guard's fault and it transpired at the Court of Enquiry that some of the unfortunate sentries had only one night a month off duty. This raid had naturally enough stirred the harassed Headquarters to take the situation seriously, and hence the dispatch of the Guides who spent 4½ months there from July to December 1942. The first night they took over they killed four Arab thieves and, in all, slew twelve of them. It must be realized that Musayib had now become the happy hunting ground of professional thieves for many miles round and they were hindering our war effort to a considerable extent. Iraq was not yet at war and local officials were more than lenient, so that the rifle and the bayonet had, perforce, to see justice done. This fact was soon found to be a considerable deterrent, while the gradual erection of proper wire fencing was putting the whole of the base on a better footing. Nevertheless, the Arab thief was persistent, subtle and resolute. Subadar Chowdhri and "D" Company fought with apparently the same gang for three nights running, eventually finishing them off. The experience of the troops of the Tigris in the First World War was exactly similar, and the Tigris Arabs were very clever at knifing sentries.

It was a thankless task and very arduous for the men who, during August 1942, were having two nights on guard and one off, though every possible hand was pressed on to the roster. The officers slept out in the various depots along the perimeter. Conditions gradually improved but in July and August the heat was intense and in October, when the rain came, the salt pan in the centre of the area became a sea of glutinous mud. After, apparently, the manner of an inefficient staff, the Battalion was camped in the salt pan where they had the delightful experience of living in a dust-storm while wading about in a sea of mud. It is not too much to say that never since the winter on the heights before Sebastopol had troops been worse encamped. The only thing in favour of Musayib was that there was grand black-partridge and duck shooting and both officers and men took part so far as the obtainable cartridges (few and sixpence a round) permitted.

Now occurred an example of one of the many pieces of amateurism inseparable from India. A "War-Dog Unit" arrived—just the very thing to tackle the Arab marauders! The "War Dogs"—six in all—were the private pets of enthusiastic folk and had been trained at a so-called training unit. They were in charge of "handlers" and the book of regulations prescribed that these dogs were not to be fondled or even spoken to, save by the "handlers"—Indian soldiers who had been on leave and who had done a course at the training centre. These men were delightful people and the dogs no more than pets—viz., three Alsatian puppies, one Labrador, a skittish golden retriever bitch and one plain, unpretending dog named "George." The dogs had no idea of their duties, slept on guard, but enjoyed a gallop after a hare. When sent on a message, they would return smiling, the message undelivered.

The joy of the Guides Infantry was great when the Cavalry, recently returned from the Middle East, came to camp twenty miles away. A grand party was obviously needed and soon twenty-five of the Corps including some from the Staff in Bagdad dined together at Musayib while the Infantry N.C.Os. were entertaining the Cavalry ones at the same time. It was recalled how, a quarter of a century earlier, in the first World War, at Hinaidi near by, at almost the same date, the Cavalry, joining what was then the Mesopotamian Expeditionary Force (M.E.F.), had met the Infantry going down the Tigris to Palestine by the long sea road.

On 5 December 1942 the Battalion, in the pleasant Mesopotamian autumn, was relieved by the 4th/8th Punjab Regiment, and shook off the dust of the evil Euphrates base, en route for Bagdad and Khanaqin once more. Their old place in the 27th Brigade was re-made for them.

Back to Persia and the 27th Brigade

From Musayib of evil memory to Khanaqin was done by rail and by the end of the first week in December 1942 the Battalion rejoined the 27th Brigade, which had moved up on to the plateau at Kasr-i-Shirin (The Castle of Sweetness), twenty miles over the Persian frontier with a romantic story attached to it. Here, the Division to which the 27th Brigade, now commanded by Brigadier Barker, belonged was encamped, and brigade and divisional training was the order of the day. But it was a cold, snowy and wet winter and tents and huts were blown away in repeated gales. Exercises away from camp always seemed to coincide with a new storm but, despite this, the troops were healthy and cheery, especially the Guides to whom anything was paradise after Musayib. It is interesting to note that even "paradise" is of Persian origin, for the word is but a Greek rendering of "fardous," a "hunting park," the heaven of a Persian king.

On 23 January to everyone's regret the benign Subadar-major, Honorary Lieutenant Rur Singh, Sirdar Bahadur, the "Hajji" of the Senneh story, left on transfer to the machine-gun battalion of the Frontier Force Regiment.

To a man so honoured and respected the Battalion farewell was a hearty and perhaps pathetic ceremony. At fifty the old soldier who had had 22 years with the "paltan" was unusually hale and hearty, for all his white beard, which he did not, as most Sikhs did at his age, dye jet black. In 1946 the old soldier was in great form in his own village some twenty-four miles from Jagraon in the Ludhiana District, and George MacMunn was present at the marriage of his son in November that year. The sister, a tot in Mardan in earlier days and now a charming girl, took him especially under her wing and his reception was one of those delightful and enthusiastic welcomes that make life in the Indian Army so peculiarly fascinating to those who probe goodwill and camaraderie to their depths.

Rur Singh was succeeded by Subadar-major Chowdri, Sirdar Bahadur, O.B.I., a Dogra, and the first of that martial folk to hold that position in the Guides Infantry.

Colonel Rich leaves the Battalion

The time had now come for the Battalion to lose the commander who had brought it through the long years of important but disappointing work in Persia and Iraq. Colonel Rich left in June 1943 to take up the important appointment of Inspector Quartermaster-General to the British Military Mission to the Iraq Army, an appointment for which he had many qualifications, notably that of having served with the same mission in its earlier days from 1925-28. Colonel Rich was the only officer left with the Guides Infantry who had served in the 1914-18 War, having joined it in Mardan in 1915, serving with it in Mesopotamia, Palestine, Syria, in Egypt from 1917-20, during the War and its aftermath. From 1929-31, on his return from the Iraqi Mission, he commanded a company in the Training Battalion. After three years with the Battalion he went, in 1934, to the advisory staff with the Indian State Forces, returning to the Training Battalion in 1938 as Second-in-Command, and back to the Guides Infantry itself in 1939. Next year, September 1940, he was appointed to the Command. Once a Guide always a Guide, and in his 27 years in the Corps, now in regimental duty, now away on important work, his touch was always of the closest, and his three years of command had more than ever endeared him to all ranks. The Command now passed to Major M. H. H. Baily, D.S.O.

The Length and Breadth of Iraq, 1943-44

The stay at Kasr-i-Shirin was succeeded for the Battalion by a year of moves up and down the whole length of Persia and Iraq commencing with a pleasant two months training in Persia near the famous rocks at Bisitun. It was here that a century ago Major Rawlinson had copied the giant cuneiform carved inscriptions, in the different languages from which the script was deciphered. During this period, the Guides Infantry took part in an interesting flag march through the district of Bujurid in the heart of Persia. Eventually the 27th Brigade were to go across to Tripoli for a course of mountain training in the Lebanon. Before the Lebanon, the Battalion found itself once more detached for army duty, and by the summer of 1943 was back with 27th Brigade, but this time north of Bagdad, at Kifri on the edge of the Kurdish hills, for as hot and dusty a spell as anywhere in the land. The general disturbance due to the Iraq Army folly had not settled down, and this part of Iraq and the railway which ran along the line of hills on its way towards Mosul, were important enough. By August, the next move was a short distance north to take over the care of the Kirkuk oilfields from the Poles. Here they were followed by the rest of the Brigade, which, without artillery, had ceased to be, for the time, a field army formation. The story of the Poles in Iraq needs some telling and it should always be remembered in the extraordinary *bouleversement* of races and armies that were such a unique and, for the Allies' share therein, so amazing a feature of the war. In short, it had been arranged by the Big Three that Polish prisoners of war in Russia should be brought from Russia to Persia, and there organized and equipped by the Allies, to be employed as might be. When the time came to take over there were difficulties, for neither side could speak each other's lingo and to quote the Battalion diary *"The Liaison Officer has seen fit to remove himself from the area."* The taking over was not without its amusing side for it is related that one hot night a junior staff officer at Headquarters in Bagdad was rung up with the news that the Poles had refused to hand over one of their picquets and that a bloody battle was about to ensue. This, however, apparently boiled down to a message that a Polish general would attend the ceremony and bring a band. That, however, the Guides were fain to decline as they could produce neither of these military show-pieces to balance the compliment.

Many months were to be spent in Kirkuk and thereabouts, an undesirable place in summer and at the time of the First World War a curious remnant of an old-world settlement of Seljuq Turks who wore the head-dress and clothes that we associate with Bluebeard and the Pashas of the Arabian Nights. There was too, then, a Jewish or possibly Israelite settlement where Hebrew was the breakfast-table language. In the rest of the world Hebrew was a dead language, till it was revived in the so-called "Jewish National Home" in Palestine.

The Story of the Poles

Mention has just been made of the taking over of posts from the Poles by the Guides in Iraq and a brief outline of the Poles' story, after the decision of the Big Three, will be of interest. These Polish prisoners of war, in very poor condition, were brought to Teheran and there received British uniforms. The fit men were then brought down in bitter cold to Khanaqin, there to be organized and trained, eventually to become part of General Anders' Corps in Italy. Those very sick were taken direct from Teheran to hospital in Basra. Orders were given that they were to have double British rations, though this soon proved to be too much for them, but ere long they recovered condition. Fortunately there were among the released officers several who spoke English and were quite at home in a British Mess or any society and these made admirable liaison officers. The re-formed Polish units had of course to be entirely fitted out by Britain—for Pa always pays—guns for the artillery, and gradually all the equipment that made General Anders' Corps so efficient in Italy. The training was to be on British lines and British officers were with them to help. A very good job they made of it.

The language difficulty prevented much fraternization, save with the liaison officer, and perhaps, as allies of Russia, against whom they seemed to have much more resentment than against the Germans, the Poles at first looked on us with some suspicion despite the fact that it was in their cause that we had gone to war.

This little story of the Poles in Iraq may be ended with the story of happiness of a very sick Polish soldier who was being evacuated to Basra. At a little station, Durud, was the daily up-train in the siding. In it he saw, in a carriage nearly opposite his, his lost fiancée whom he had not heard of since 1939. She had escaped and was now nursing and was being sent to a Polish hospital. She jumped excitedly out of her train, and insisted on going down to nurse the long-lost lover. Let us hope that they lived happily ever after.

The Disappointment of the Lebanon

In December 1943 the Battalion moved down from the Kurdish border to Bagdad where two companies were left, and once more to Musayib—the accursed—to find it a very different place with proper hutting and roads and with a defensible wire fence electrically fitted and booby trapped. Even then the Arab thief was persistent and on leaving again in February the Divisional Commander congratulated the Battalion on being the only one to defeat all attempts.

In February 1944 the Battalion once more rejoined its brigade, and in March, to their great excitement, the whole formation went to the Lebanon, there to go through a strenuous mountain-warfare course, a prelude, it was expected, to a move to join the Army in Italy. The fact that Lieutenant-Colonel Baily and other C.Os. were flown to Italy—first for a course at the tactical school and then on a liaison visit to the front, lent colour to this pleasing belief. So with MacMunn in command of the Guides Infantry, the Brigade cavalcades set forth.

The story of the six weeks' trip to the Lebanon, however, is of such great interest and was such a delightful change from the years in Iraq and Persia that it is worth telling in some detail. It had been rumoured for some time that the 6th Division was to go to Italy. On 23 March the whole Brigade Group under Brigadier Attfield marched (embussed) for Syria from Khanaqin in three separate lorry convoys of some 200–300 lorries each on three successive days. The trip took seven days at an average of 110–130 miles a day. The troops were in excellent spirits and when a board was passed saying "PAI FORCE ENDS" a young Sikh asked if they were in Italy now. The route ran through Damascus and Homs to Tripoli, the last stage in appalling rain. The long journey had met with little mechanical mishap; but a sad tragedy occurred, two R.I.A.S.C. officers of the convoy unit drove over the side of a bridge on the way up to the hills from Tripoli into a raging torrent, their bodies being carried several miles down stream. The training school in the Lebanon was most efficient and the course stringent, hardening and interesting, while the men much appreciated the mountain air and the green hillside. The Lebanese were agreeable and hospitable and eager to show their predilection for the British. Those who remember the history of the middle of the last century, also the bitter persecution and war between these Christian Maronites and the Druses, will recall how the Lebanon became, under the protection of Europe, "Partant pour la Syrie," the French quickstep dating from these times, but the latter never succeeded in endearing themselves to the Lebanon under their mandate.

The Lebanese roads were very narrow and damaged by heavy rains and some of the Guides' drivers displayed great gallantry in staying on carriers half-over a drop to keep the brakes on—one N.C.O. was crushed to death under his vehicle which went over.

Here is a happy little incident. In Tripoli an excited little man accosted Captain Bailes and asked if he was in the Guides: looked on with suspicion, he carried Bailes off to his office and showed him pictures of Guides officers, Christmas cards from them, etc., saying, "The Guides are my dearest friends." It transpired that, an orphan boy in 1917, he had been taken on by the 1st Guides in Palestine as a Mess servant. Eventually he went to the railways, became station-master at Tripoli and was now a prospering travel agent. So Jacques Bandali now made himself very helpful. One rather sad and unpleasant incident in which the Brigade had to take part was the disarming of a Greek armoured car regiment. It was a repercussion of the trouble that had occurred

GUIDES INFANTRY ATHLETIC TEAM
Winners of the Northern Iraq Area Championship and the King Faisal Cup, Bagdad, 1945

To face page 140

in Egypt over dissatisfaction with the Greek Government in exile, the grievance being that members of the Resistance Movement had not been incorporated in the Greek Government. Perhaps what we now know of E.L.A.M. may have been the cause of this decision. At any rate there were political agitators in the ranks, and it was decided to take the ticklish step of disarming the unit (near Tripoli) and arresting the trouble merchants. In great secrecy the 27th Brigade surrounded the unit, who wisely accepted the situation when they found themselves enveloped and exits blocked.

The six weeks' strenuous training terminated, and the Brigade, to their consternation, were ordered back to Iraq and the Persian railways instead of Italy.

The situation in Burma apparently had brought about a decision to earmark all surplus troops for India if required. The Brigade then re-embussed, going via the Lebanon and Anti-Lebanon to Durud, where they arrived on 23 May (with MacMunn still in command of the Guides Infantry) and took over from the 24th Infantry Brigade, who now moved over to the Lebanon.

On the Trans-Persian Railway

The disappointment that was felt when the Lebanon training did not bring the expected move to Italy was not lightened by this move to the trying but important task of guarding a sector of the trans-Persian railway that climbed from the Persian Gulf across Persia to the Caspian. The importance lies in the fact that it was one of the routes by which the vital war supplies were brought to Russia. The line had been built at vast expense by Riza Shah, more because it was the thing to have a railway than for its economic possibilities. These and the expenses of running had no relation to the hard matter of costs. As an engineering feat it had much to be admired, as it travelled from sea-level at Bandar Shapur on the Khor Musa at the head of the Persian Gulf to Bandar Shah on the Caspian, by gorge and rift to a height of 7,000 feet and had a length of 872 miles. The line, a single one, was of standard gauge, with, however, a scanty rolling stock and comparatively few crossing places, on which the capacity of a single line largely depends. A lorry-road in the same direction went up from the Gulf to Hamadan and Pahlevi, or to Teheran which, improved by the Americans, carried the lorry convoys to be described. To make this line and road an effective feeder for Russia was a considerable enterprise and beyond the power of Britain to do much for at the moment. So on 1 January 1943 the United States took over the expansion and management of the line from the British and Persians, the latter controlling the civilian passenger service. The protection of the line was a British responsibility carried out by static troops reinforced by a brigade from the 6th Division. The American personnel, though nominally soldiers, were all technical civilians and the American set-up was known as the "Persian Gulf" Command. The American organization also included large motor convoys and was a matter of first-class organization and excellent canteens, and once a fortnight a train of Persian "artistes" was brought down the line. American canteens were officially dry, but the usual "subterfuge" allowed of sufficient drink appearing when necessary and liquor in Persia is always obtainable, indeed it is Muslim India alone that obeys the precepts of *El Qoran* regarding liquor.

The tunnels on the line were winding and very narrow and sometimes as long as three miles. This made patrolling by troops a dangerous duty only overcome by an efficient system of warning and a well-practised drill for taking cover. The fact that goods wagons often had doors swinging open was an added chance of misadventure.

However, the rail was protected adequately and, by rail and road convoys, stores for Russia poured up, so that the duty was more than worth while.

The variety of allied nationals on the line was noticeable, for the Russians formed the guards on the train, the Americans the operating staff, the British Indians guarded the line, Poles, coming to be re-formed, travelled down it, and the Persians controlled the passenger traffic, under the Americans. The duty of guarding the line was an unpleasant one, for though in the upper section below Sultanabad the climate was better and orchards and fields abounded, malaria was very prevalent and of the malignant type, so that every day men had to take a tablet of mepacrine, the anti-malarial drug, and endure the somewhat depressing effect and the enyellowment of the skin. The lower reaches of the line were extremely hot and trying, though streams with fish, to be caught by line, a net, or even dynamited, gave some diversion to the men.

The line held by the Brigade ran from Teheran to Telezang. The 4th/5th Royal Sussex from Teheran down to Sultanabad, next the Guides Infantry, the 1st/10th Baluchis and on the extreme left a machine-gun battalion of the Dogra Regiment. Beyond the Guides' left was a war-time unit—an Afridi battalion, later to become the revived Khyber Rifles—chiefly concerned with protecting telephone lines from the copper-robbers, a delightful illustration of the poacher-turned-gamekeeper.

The actual sector held by the Guides Infantry ran from below Sultanabad to Bishe, 12 miles in all, the Battalion Headquarters with one reserve rifle company being at Durud. The modern Indian soldier, like the modern Atkins, fraternized readily and the Guides and the American railwaymen got on well, especially where one of the men knew some English and the amenities of life were readily shared and exchanged. But when their three months of malaria, mepacrine, and heat came to an end it was gladly exchanged for duty in Iraq.

Some Regimental Happenings

Besides the movement of officers shown in the lists, various items of regimental interest occurred.

George MacMunn departed for Italy to take command of the 3rd/5th Mahratta Light Infantry, recruited from that race of the western India hills, who had been famous in the old Bombay Army, and who had come to great fame in both the world wars.

Griffith took over command till Baily who, from Italy, went home on two months' leave, came back and then commanded an F.F.R. battalion in Indo-China.

Subadar-major Chowdri Ram, O.B.I., the Dogra, left for the Regimental Centre[42] after 30 years' service, the last man who wore the medals of the First World War, and was succeeded by Subadar Sadhu Singh, I.D.S.M. Subadars Hayat Muhammad and Azram also went to pension.

---

[42] From the centre he became A.D.C. to the C.-in-C., India, joining in Persia later.

Ralph Griffith was in India (about to take command of a battalion). Pat Macnamara was a brigade commander and Gordon Watt went to Italy as second-in-command of an I.S.F. battalion. Bob Maslen Jones was with the 4th Sikhs and Archie Pugh had been demobilized. George Sawdey, with the Regimental Centre in India, had gone to the Judge-Advocate-General's department and Wyon Stansfeld left for India to take his place. Alec Moore went to the Tochi Scouts as second-in-command, after his repatriation leave as an ex-prisoner of war.

BACK TO IRAQ IN 1944 AND HOME IN 1945

The Guides left the Persian railway in September 1944, and took over duties from the 60th Infantry Brigade, normally under the 2nd Indian Division (an inflated term for the Bagdad area to conceal the fact that many troops had gone from PAI Force). They were, however, to remain under the 6th Division for training and to watch the Kurdish situation which had again become disturbed and, in preparation for a move to Burma, carried out preliminary training in jungle warfare at a site near Kirkuk. A change of policy, however, led to the 6th Indian Division being broken up at the end of 1945 and the Guides once more moved to Khanaqin to join a new brigade formed, with two Indian State Forces battalions, for security in Persia. In the early spring of 1945 the Brigade carried out an interesting flag march through the middle Euphrates to show some sign of strength in an area apt to listen to propagandists. They went into the highly irrigated area below the Hindiah Barrage. This magnificent feat of British engineering (pre-1914) amazed the men, who were equally impressed with the industry and ability with which the *Felahin*, viz., settled Arab, as against the *Bedouin* (the nomad desert Arab) had made use of the water with which they were now endowed. On one occasion the Battalion marched into a district where the Arabs were classed as "bad," viz., unruly, and, owing to the absence of marching roads, thought themselves inaccessible. However, the Guides gave them the unwelcome surprise of their presence and had arranged to soften the incursion by taking flour and sugar for distribution and sweets for the children. But the Arab is selfishly unmanageable on such occasions, and it is recorded that the distribution was, in every case, an occasion for a free fight among the recipients. There were, however, no hostile occurrences and the tribe, save for the breaking of their own heads in the worry-worry, learnt the lesson of their non-immunity simply enough. In the metaphor of the Indian Frontier their "purdah had been lifted."

The second tour in the spring of 1945 was up to Northern Iraq beyond Kirkuk, in all the glory of the Mesopotamian spring, where the desert for a while is a carpet of flowers almost of hot-house lusciousness, and when a white terrier running among them will reappear stained all the colours of the rainbow. They also visited the magnificent Rowanduz Gorge, through which a well-engineered motor road now winds to Rowanduz and up on to the Persian plateau and Lake Urumiya, a feat that has been described as "Kurds and way." The Brigade was to train with the reformed Iraqi Army which after the *coup d'état* was being helped by a military mission.

In June the Commander-in-Chief, Sir Claude Auchinleck, flying back to India via

Bagdad, promised that the Guides Infantry should be the next unit to be called back. In fact orders came to return to India by the end of July after the battalion had moved into camp in Persia to train for jungle warfare. But here came the news that Japan had followed Germany down the drain, and that the Second World War was over. That was the end of ambition for the "Bubble reputation" as the old saw wrongly has it—four years of very hard work, and only the sense of duty more than well done to show for it.

In September the Battalion marched down to Basra and arrived in India in October, when, after a certain amount of wandering, they found rest awhile at Kohat, the men going on leave and the unit not reappearing "in being" till December 1945.

CHAPTER XII

THE LAST YEARS OF THE RAJ

THE CAVALRY IN INDIA AGAIN (1943-46)—THE VICTORY CELEBRATIONS AT DELHI (1946)—THE INFANTRY RETURN TO INDIA (1945)—THE CENTENARY OF THE CORPS OF GUIDES (1946) IN AHMEDNAGAR AND WAZIRISTAN—GARDAI TO RAZMAK (INFANTRY), 1947—REGIMENTAL HAPPENINGS: CAVALRY, 1944-46—A NOTE ON THE ORGANIZATION AND EQUIPMENT OF THE GUIDES CAVALRY, 1922-46—THE RINGING TO EVENSONG—FAREWELL, THE RAJ—THE SPECIAL SERVICE IN THE GARRISON CHURCH AT RAZMAK—THE FAREWELL ORDER OF THE DAY FROM THE COLONEL—OFFICERS WITH THE GUIDES CAVALRY ON 15 AUGUST 1947—OFFICERS SERVING WITH THE BATTALION WITH APPOINTMENTS IN WAZIRISTAN, 1946

THE CAVALRY IN INDIA, 1943-46

NOT long after their return to PAI Force the Cavalry were ordered back to India as part of the 5th Division, with great hopes of going to Burma. This, however, was not to be, and they were sent back to the Frontier to Kohat as a Frontier defence unit, with two squadrons on detachment at various places in Waziristan.

The Commander-in-Chief himself, knowing the Regiment's bitter disappointment at leaving the Eighth Army before El Alamein, wrote to Colonel Walton saying he knew how great their fresh disappointment about Burma was; but the Frontier need was urgent. Their new role was that of an armoured car regiment. From Kohat the Corps went to Dera Ismail Khan, where they spent another year, also with squadrons in the hills of Waziristan. In this year, 1945, Sir Claude Auchinleck again wrote to Colonel Walton, now with the 2nd Gwalior Lancers, saying that he still hoped to get the Guides Cavalry to Burma, adding: "I was up the Frontier the other day and met a Guides squadron between Bannu and Kohat. They looked as good as ever, and that is saying a good deal as you know." So the Guides tried to possess their souls in patience once more.

During these years on the Frontier, parties were sent into their recruiting areas to explain to the old men how the cavalry were now armoured regiments, and also to attract recruits. They had a loudspeaker with them on which Risaldar Ram Singh gave most effective commentaries on the display shown.

The area first visited covered the Sikh, Dogra and P.M. districts, and later the Pathan Squadron was equally successful in the Frontier Provinces.

At Dera Ismail Khan orders came for Orchha in Central India. The first order said to join the 8th Division forthwith, which looked like Burma, and the orders for Orchha were changed to Talbahat, thirty miles from Jhansi. They were to be a recce regiment in the 8th Division, but found that the Division was a reserve one held in India and they had to be re-equipped, as they had been ordered to leave their stuff with the 6th Lancers at Kohat.

The Regiment left Kohat after handing over their equipment in November 1945, and trained to Talbahat, a pleasant enough camp in the cold season. There they came under the orders of Major-General D. Russel, an old friend of the Corps, known in the Army as "The Pasha." New vehicles appeared like magic, Daimler armoured cars with a troop of Stuart tanks in each squadron. There was a tank school at Babina, fifteen miles away, and for the first time they were really well equipped. Talbahat and Bambina, new names to old hands, of war-time creation, serve as an illustration of the vast war creation of camps and schools that had opened in India.

The Victory Celebrations at Delhi, 1946

In early February, half the Regiment—viz., R.H.Q. and two composite squadrons, including all classes—moved to Delhi, camping there with the 45th Cavalry and many details. As the Victory Parade was not till March there was time to repaint and reletter and polish all that was polishable, enough to gladden the heart of a Horse Artillery commander of the old days.

The celebrations began with the Remembrance Ceremony on 5 March, at which detachments of all units in Delhi were present. Captain Jahanzeb Khan and twenty men represented the Regiment, and Risaldar-major Shanker Singh of the Guides, as the senior V.C.O. in the Indian Armoured Corps, had the honour of laying the wreath from that Corps on the memorial arch.

Next day was the rehearsal for the Victory March, and the ancestral pride of the Guides had a shock. It was ordered that the red-and-white lance pennons should be flown from the aerials, and from time immemorial the Guides had flown theirs with the white on top; the rest of the army flew red on top, and the Commander-in-Chief ruthlessly ordered the Guides to conform!

Then came that remarkable Victory Parade, in which East and West African troops, "marching like guardsmen," and American troops in rubber-soled boots took part, Indian W.A.C. and Wrens marching too, and even Nagas dressed in feathers and nothing else—the whole a most moving, stirring and glorious spectacle.

The only marring incident was a change of route in the return to camp, lest folk with a bitter bug in their heads should roll down boulders on the troops from the railway bridge!

But peace had now come and economy was the inevitable order. So in March 1946 the 8th Division was dispersed on reduction, and the Regiment was moved to the delightful old-world cantonment at Fyzabad in Oudh and settled down to do their share in a "grow more food" campaign. The starting of flourishing gardens, however, was obviously the signal for another move. By July they had orders to hand over their reconnaissance corps equipment and proceed to Ahmednagar in the Deccan—a fair example of the "soldier's phrase"! They were to become a tank regiment (Churchills).

The Infantry Return to India, 1945

In 1945 the Guides Infantry returned to India after their long and faithful but neventful sojourn in Persia and Iraq. By some mistaken order they handed in the bulk of their equipment other than rifles, and therefore on arriving at their destination—Kohat—found themselves seriously deficient, with little prospect of early reissue.

THE VICTORY PARADE AT DELHI—CAVALRY—I

To face page 146

THE VICTORY PARADE AT DELHI—CAVALRY—II

To face page 147

As they could not go to their Mardan home they could have had no pleasanter station than the comfortable little cantonment of Kohat—thirty miles across the Indus, on the broad-gauge line—and here too they found the Risala. So they proceeded to settle down, to bring their regimental accessories and their share of the mess treasures and to inaugurate the modern amenities for the rank and file. But, alas! *l'homme propose* —hardly had they unpacked, when the "exigencies of the Service" suddenly required their presence in Waziristan once more, and they moved, not without an inward curse, to Gardai, the high-pitched L. of C. post not far from Razmak.

Waziristan was in a quiet and quiescent state since Sir John Coleridge's stringent campaign, but the *haramzadas*, "the sons of shame," were still on the snipe at the camp picquets, and on 4 December, Subadar Raghbir Singh, who had only lately joined the Guides from the Kumaon Rifles, was mortally wounded without rhyme or reason. By bad luck the sniper escaped a day or two later through the jamming of a light automatic, not, however, it was currently reported, before his ardour had been cooled by a couple of bullets through his pants. The Subadar had already made great friends and was much respected. A day or two later Havildar Mardan Ali was also hit, but not seriously.

The khaki drill of the Indian Army, which had been of a greenish shade for twenty-four years, had now been changed to olive green, and the men were pretty shabby till the much appreciated new stuff arrived. Olive green was a useful cross between the claims of the Frontier hills and the Burma jungles.

The Centenary of the Corps of Guides in Ahmednagar and Waziristan

The centenary of the raising of the Corps was due to be celebrated with as much rejoicing and ceremony as possible on 14 December—the Risala at Ahmednagar, the Paltan at Gardai. Failing a supreme occasion at Mardan, Kohat would have been a very suitable spot to which many could have come. The sudden move to the outposts of the Infantry, however, immediately limited the whole celebration, for few old members of the Corps could be present and no ladies, so that the scope of rejoicing was sadly confined.

The story had best open with the original order as given in Vol. I of the Saga of the Corps. It is pithy enough.

"*Governor-General's orders. Foreign Department, dated camp Bhyrawah Ghat 14. December 1846. . . .*

The Governor-General is pleased to direct that a Corps of Guides shall be raised for general service of the following strength and organization, with the specified rates of pay. [Here follows pay details.]

Lieutenant H. B. Lumsden of the 59th Regiment of Native Infantry is appointed Commandant of the Guides."

That was all on which the Corps of Guides was built, from Henry Lawrence's vision of the Guide Corps of Napoleon's *Grande Armée*. The Cavalry, as related, were in the pleasant old-world cantonment of Ahmednagar, redolent of memories of Arthur Wellesley and the storming of the Pettah so far ago as 1803, but now the home of modern army establishments, notably the A.C. School, of which Colonel Gimson of the Corps was commandant. Here, far away from their twins who were celebrating in Gardai, the unique occasion of the centenary was enthusiastically enacted. The distances were so great that but a small contingent from each Guide unit could visit the other ; but from Gardai had come Captain Penty, Subadar Mehal Singh, Jemadar Azam Khan and several N.C.Os., while up to Gardai had gone Jemadar Mala Singh and a party of two warrant officers and duffadars.

Joyful telegrams were, of course, exchanged. But the distance of Ahmednagar from their homes and the inaccessibility of Gardai prevented the large gathering of veterans, to whom such occasions were normally sheer delight.[43]

However, the Risala was able to get two railway coaches of "old tykes" down from the Frontier and Punjab, though one got disconnected and arrived a day late. The first coach arrived on 12 December, and when the derelict arrived on the 15th there were 120 of them.

The eventful 14th opened with a ceremonial parade. Field-Marshal Sir Claude Auchinleck—the Commander-in-Chief—had visited the place a few days earlier and inspected the Regiment, but could not fit in his times to be present on the day ; and as no general could be obtained, the Regiment was lucky enough to have Colonel Gimson, M.C., to take the parade, the same Major Gimson who led "A" Squadron in the occupation of Khuzistan. He was the senior officer of the Corps available in that part of India. After inspecting the Regiment, he gave a stirring address, and the Risala then marched past on foot, which was but a faint shadow of the glory of a mounted ceremonial. The rest of the morning passed in meeting and chatting with the pensioners—"The grizzled drafts of years gone by," in Rudyard Kipling's effective phrase.[44] The afternoon followed with regimental sports and competitions, in which "B" Squadron came out on top. In the evening there was a concert party for the V.C.Os. and I.O.Rs. and a guest night at the Mess for all Guides officers and their ladies, among whom were Lieutenant-Colonel and Mrs. Jilani. Colonel Jilani was now commanding the station hospital but was formerly medical officer with the Corps (Mardan, 1929-30) ; for three and a half years he had been a prisoner with the Japs, and but lately returned, happily (apparently) none the worse.

Next day the missing railway coach with more veterans turned up, to everyone's satisfaction, and the photograph of the occasion could now be taken. In the afternoon the visitors were driven to see the exhibition which had been arranged for the local War Services Week, which ended with a tank battle and flame-thrower demonstration, to the great delight and marvel of all the old "Draw swords and holla" folk, though to the younger pensioner some modern equipment was not unknown. The evening ended with a "blow out," *i.e.*, a *bara khana*, in the lines for all ranks. The festivities continued over the week-end, the veterans being given rides in tanks in the morning of the 16th and a cinema show in the afternoon. In the evening there was a Khattak dance, at which

---

[43] The author well remembers the old men of the Guides and " Cokis" who came to the Darbar of King Emperor George V at Delhi and their tears of joy if they met any old Sahib of the Army, who had *Bailey Guard gya* or even anyone who could speak of it. The Bailey Guard was the name by which the Residency Area at Lucknow was known to the Army, after some very early Resident.

[44] "The Galley Slave."

the officers were "At Home" to the officers of the Station. Great preparations had been made for this; *mirasis* (Frontier musicians) had been brought down from the Frontier, while Hon. Captain Khoran Khan—a Cavalry sirdar—and Jemadar Azam Khan from the Paltan, both of course Khattaks, supervised the arrangements. Swords were a difficulty as the Cavalry swords had gone to be cut up for surgical instruments owing to the difficulty of getting good steel!

And that finished this remarkable occasion, as the Raj was about to fade away.

Up on the Frontier somewhat similar scenes and fervour were being enacted at the rough camp on the Razmak road. Gardai, a small plateau surrounded by small hills on which the Guides had their picquets, was not much of a place for celebration save that its atmosphere was an emblem of their hundred years on the Frontier—*Roulez tambours pour couvrir la Frontière*.

It was decided to relieve the picquets on the morning of the 14th, and there was a cinema display that night for the battalion and their guests. Next day at 1 p.m. all sat down to another *bara khana*—at which the Brigade Commander was present, and the Corps was filled with good food and good temper.

At 3 p.m. Khattak dances and *tamashas* followed, including a lively sketch showing how a recruit joined in the olden days—and how his musketry instruction began with "*Khub zor se kaincho*" on the carbine trigger.

At 5.30 p.m. the Pipes and Drums played a ceremonial "Retreat." At 6.30 p.m. the Viceroy's commissioned officers were "At Home" to British officers and K.C.Os., the Brigadier being present. The officers went to supper, but whether they went to bed or "danced upon the Master of the Ceremonies' head" is not recorded; and while this junketing was in progress the men had been given *carte blanche* with the buniya. Next day was Sunday, the 15th, and at mid-day the British Officers were "At Home" to all B.Os. and V.C.Os. in the station. After lunch the Commanding Officer, with the Subadar-major and the other B.Os., visited the hospital with sweets. The afternoon was spent in *pagal* sports and merriment, and the evening with the cinema for half the battalion and the visitors. Arora, the Razmak photographer, attended, and the two-day celebrations ended with a formal guest night in the Mess.

Guests from outside were perforce few. Brigadier Johnson, commanding the Brigade, was with them, and Benjy Bromhead, the Political Agent in northern Waziristan, was able to look in. Pat Phelps from Dosali and Robin Hodson with a party of Tochi Scouts also. Lieutenant Chaudri Ram and Subadar Rangin with eight rank and file from the training centre completed the party. Jemadar Mala Singh brought a "namoinda" party from the cavalry at Ahmednagar far away.

Thus in deed and heart were the two distant Corps united, and so the great event passed, with many a sad heart at the likelihood of a century of endeavour and sacrifice passing to a new dispensation.

A special centenary calendar, designed and painted by Lieut.-Colonel Olaf McLeod[46] for both cavalry and infantry, was published. A copy of this was sent to the King

---

[46] Of Coke's Rifles.

and Queen by the O.C. the Guides Infantry and, having received a gracious reply, he issued the following Battalion Order:

SPECIAL ORDER OF THE DAY
LIEUTENANT-COLONEL A. R. E. POLLARD, O.B.E.
COMMANDANT 5TH BN. (Q.V.O. CORPS OF GUIDES) THE F.F. REGIMENT

RAZMAK,
13 *April*, 1947.

The Commandant is pleased to announce that having sent a Corps of Guides Centenary calendar to His Majesty the King Emperor and to Her Majesty The Queen and to Their Royal Highnesses Princess Elizabeth and Princess Margaret, the following reply has been received:

BUCKINGHAM PALACE,
10 *February*, 1947.

"My dear Colonel,

"I am commanded by Their Majesties, The King and Queen, to thank you for the Guides calendar which you have sent to Their Majesties and Their Royal Highnesses Princess Elizabeth and Princess Margaret.

"Their Majesties much appreciate your kind thought and send their best wishes to the Regiment during the coming year.
"Yours sincerely,
"EDWARD LORD, *Captain*."

THE OFFICER COMMANDING,
QUEEN VICTORIA'S OWN CORPS OF GUIDES,
GARDAI CAMP,
WAZIRISTAN,
INDIA.

GARDAI TO RAZMAK (INFANTRY), 1947

The sniper was extremely persistent around Gardai. But as the country round was uninhabited, both the 2-inch mortars and the 25-pdr. post gun could fire ranging shots on all the points round and every officer fired rounds from the latter. There was a Punjabi Muslim deserter, one Faqira, and Zamira, a deserter from the Tochi Scouts, who seemed to head the local bad-hats. Sepoy Resham Singh, of the Guides, was mortally wounded in No. 11 Picquet at Gardai, two days, poor lad, before his release from the Army, from a shot five yards from the picquet in a split-second exposure. Two snipers got away though seen and fired on. The demobilization—*i.e.*, release—had given infinite trouble and the centre at Sialkot had been sending men from the machine-gun battalion to make up strength. All release had to be finished by 15 April, and 64 Kumaonis went to the Kumaoni Battalion, 16 electing to stay till due for discharge. Their departure was much regretted, for they reminded the Corps of the days when they had Gurkhas.

The Gardai Brigade championship games came on in April and the Guides lost the football final to the 1st/4th Gurkhas 1–2 after playing two periods of extra time. The Guides won the rifle shooting and lost the 100 yards flat, as their man who was leading ran out, thinking the cheering meant that he had won. The tug-of-war was lost to the

OFFICERS AND V.C.Os. OF THE GUIDES INFANTRY SHORTLY BEFORE THE PARTITION OF INDIA

Razmak, August 1947

Back Row (L. to R.)—Jem. Udham Singh, Jem. Nanak Chand, Jem. Baghel Singh, Sub. Allah Ditta, Capt. Saddiqe, Jem. Gul Hassan, Capt. Mohd Sarwar, Jem. Azam Khan, Jem. —, Sub. Shandi Gul, Sub. Bhuri Singh.
Centre Row—Capt. Mohd Iqbal Malik, Jem. Nurkhan, M.C., Lieut. K. M. Butt, Jem. Amir Hamza, Lieut. Kukde, Jem. Abdul Rehman, Capt. A. M. Vohra, Sub. Mohd Afsar, Capt. Shahzada Khan.
Front Row—Capt. B. D. Malhotra, Sub. Pala Singh, Major G. A. MacMunn, Sub.-Maj. Mehal Singh, Lt.-Col. A. R. E. Pollard, O.B.E., Sub. Narain Singh, Major A. M. W. B. McDermott, Sub. Matti Ullah, I.O.M., Capt. Aziz-ur-Rehman.
Absent—Major R. G. Hutchinson, Major D. D. Slattery, M.C., Capt. Sarbang Singh, Sub. Swab Gul, Sub. Ibrahim, Jem. Shankar Singh, Jem. Pritham Singh.

To face page 151

THE LAST YEARS OF THE RAJ

Mountain Gunners, but the khud race was won, with the first three places, 17 men in the first 19, and also the 22nd and 23rd places—a great record, 4 seconds better than the record time of 16 minutes 20 seconds. So the Guides Infantry won the Brigade shield for the second time running.

Many of the Battalion were on leave during the Punjab riots, but all got back on time, by great endeavour. One of these, a Pathan, was beaten up by Sikh rioters near Amritsar, who robbed him of everything; all other Muslims they butchered. This trouble delayed the coming of the "Cokis" to relieve them at Gardai.

On 25 March the Battalion took a reluctant farewell of their Subadar-major, Sadhu Singh, I.D.S.M., to pension after twenty-four years' service, Subadar Mahel Singh succeeding him. On 29 March the Battalion marched, on their flat feet, to Razmak, took farewell of their own Brigadier—Johnston—and climbed up to Razmak Narai in hail and snow, where the 2nd Baluch Regiment greeted them. Coming into Razmak, to the surprise and pride of the men, all the garrison was out to meet them, and their own Pipe Band and that of the 3rd/14th Pubjabis, as the sun broke through the snow clouds. The new Brigadier—Marinden—remarked to Colonel Pollard as they marched up, "Splendid! the Guides march in. The first unit to come on their feet, or wanted to for many a day."

The Battalion soon settled down in the Razmak Brigade, where it had been during the Waziristan Campaigns of 1936-37 and where the duties, especially camp picquet, were much lighter than at Gardai.

Regimental Happenings: Cavalry, 1944–46

During 1944, Major-General Hammond, whom we last saw handing over command before the war to go to the War Office as a G.S.O.1, and now a District Commander, received both the D.S.O. and the C.B.

This year a very promising young officer—Jim Peacock, who had been with the Cavalry two years—lost his life, to everyone's great regret, by the overturning of a jeep; the men with him being injured.

Captain and Risaldar-major Rattan Singh was rewarded with the Membership of the Order of the British Empire, and the following were Mentioned in Despatches: Major G. M. Strover, Captain J. W. Humphries, Risaldar Garaki Rani, Risaldar Ram Singh, and Jemadar Alif Shah.

In March 1945 news came of the passing at the age of eighty of Brigadier-General G. M. Baldwin, D.S.O., Colonel of the Corps of Guides, 1930-35, a famous old Guide.

George Strover won the M.C. in Italy, where he was Brigade-major of the 21st Indian Brigade, and George Butler the M.C. and Bar for service with the Chindits in Burma.

David Monteith had lost his life in Burma under very gallant circumstances and, there being no posthumous rewards other than the V.C., his memory can only be officially enshrined in a Mention in Despatches, the story of which is recorded later.

Two pensioned sirdars, who had rejoined, received recognition. Risaldar Ganda Singh, O.B.I., I.D.S.M., being made an Honorary Lieutenant, and Risaldar Makhan

Singh, a marvel in the drill line, received the 2nd class of the O.B.I. A third sirdar, Risaldar-major Karim Dad, also rejoined and became Risaldar-major at the armoured school.

During 1946, while the Regiment was at Kohat, Robert Bailey was married to Jean Leadbitter in the Guides Chapel at Mardan; a large party of B.Os. and V.C.Os. went over, and the R.I.A.S.C., who were occupying the Guides' Mess, lent the garden for the reception. The R.I.A.S.C. school, who had kept up everything magnificently, were, however, leaving.

While at Kohat, to everyone's delight, the Paltan arrived there too, but only to be whisked off to North Waziristan after a very short reunion, the first since Musayib on the Euphrates—the "good river Frat"—in 1942. At Ahmednagar came the news of another old Guide passing to his rest—Lieutenant-Colonel Buist—the last active commandant of the Corps before its resolution into two units in 1921. He was, before World War I, one of the best polo players in India and had excelled at all games.

The Risala was now to settle down and to release many of its officers.

In the King's Birthday Honours of 1946:

Lieutenant-Colonel Charles Thomas, O.B.E., and Risaldar-major Shankar Singh, O.B.I.—2nd Class.

Risaldar-major Karim Dad—who had returned from pension—was made an Honorary Captain on his second retirement. His son, Tor Khan, a jemadar in the Regiment, became a Captain, and is engaged in teaching Afghan officers.

Risaldar-Major Ratan Khand was advanced to First Class of the O.B.I. and made an Honorary Captain on retirement.

Lieutenant-Colonel Gradidge was Mentioned in Despatches (1945) and was made a Brigadier.

A Note on the Organization and Equipment of the Guides Cavalry, 1922-46

The constant changes in mechanized equipment have been freely mentioned in this history and an outline of what happened is now given.

On reorganization after the war of 1914-18, the Regiment was organized on a basis of three sabre squadrons and H.Q. Wing. Each sabre squadron consisted of Squadron H.Q. and four troops, each of three sections. H.Q. Wing contained the Regimental staff, the Signal Troop of 26 signallers and the Machine Gun Troop of two sections, each of two Vickers machine guns. In 1932 four motor cycles were added for inter-communication, and a year or two later three Austin 7 cars.

This organization remained until the horses were got rid of in 1940. Remounts were trained regimentally under the Adjutant. Recruits were trained regimentally up till 1937, when three recruit training centres were started to train recruits for all Indian Cavalry. The Regiment was dependent on the centre at Ferozepore, which was Sam Browne's Cavalry, F.F., converted to a training centre. From then on, recruits were all trained centrally at Ferozepore, which became the Armoured Car School till 1946, and from October, 1946, at Babina, the old Tank School with which the Armoured Car School was combined. The first six months of a recruit's training was carried out at Recruit Training Centre at Lucknow.

In October 1939, just after the outbreak of war, the Regiment moved to Quetta and started to mechanize. Horses were, however, retained until September 1941 when they were all handed over to 3rd Gwalior Lancers. The future role of the Regiment was in doubt for some time and was changed several times before it was finally decided. This did not affect training much as mechanization was still in the early stages of learning to drive and maintain motor cars. For this purpose a very mixed collection of old military and civil vehicles was held for training drivers.

There were three possible future roles: the Frontier Armoured Regiment, organized with two armoured car squadrons and one squadron of Mk. VI Light tanks; the Tank Regiment, composed entirely of tanks; and the Infantry Divisional Reconnaissance Regiment, composed of a mixture of vehicles. After being ordered to adopt all these establishments in turn, the final decision was that the Regiment should be Divisional Reconnaissance to 9th Indian Division which was forming in Quetta. The organization of a Divisional Reconnaissance Regiment was as follows: H.Q. Squadron, consisting of regimental staff. Three squadrons, each consisting of one Armoured Car Troop of 3 cars. Two wheeled Carrier Troops of 8 carriers. One Lorried Infantry Troop of 4 trucks.

The armoured cars were old Chevrolets, armed with two Vickers machine guns and a Boys anti-tank rifle. The carriers were new vehicles, the Indian pattern wheeled carrier Mk. I which was most unsatisfactory and did not last long. The Mk. I carriers were replaced in 1941 by Mk. II carriers, a much better vehicle, and the Chevrolet armoured cars were gradually replaced by Fords and Marmon-Harringtons made in South Africa. By the spring of 1942 this change-over was complete.

The original organization was kept till May 1942, when the Regiment moved to the Western Desert. It was then found to be far too unwieldy for reconnaissance and squadrons were reorganized with five troops of three vehicles each, the vehicles being a mixture of carriers and armoured cars. This was the standard organization for an armoured car or reconnaissance regiment in the Middle East.

On return to India in 1943, the Regiment moved to Kohat. In January 1944 the organization was again changed, two rifle troops being substituted for two armoured car troops in each squadron. Humber armoured cars Mks. II and III were taken over from the 47th Cavalry; but the vehicles for the rifle troops were not received till November 1944. These were Ford armoured trucks and again unsatisfactory, lacking power on hills and being difficult to drive safely. During 1944-45 frequent changes of armoured cars were made between Humber Mks. II, III and IV. Mks. II and III were much alike. Mk. IV was equipped with a 37 mm. gun instead of a 15 mm. Besa.

In October 1945 all vehicles were handed over to 6th Lancers and the Regiment was re-equipped on joining 8th Indian Division near Jhansi. Daimler armoured cars were received in place of Humbers. One Armoured Car Troop in each squadron was replaced by a Light Tank Troop, consisting of three Stuart light tanks Mk. V. Rifle Troops were carried in Dodge 4 × 4 15-cwt. trucks.

In July 1946 the Regiment moved to Ahmednagar and joined 2nd Indian Armoured

Brigade. This entailed a complete change of equipment on conversion from a reconnaissance regiment to an armoured regiment. The Regiment was now organized as three squadrons, each of four troops with three Churchill tanks. All Churchills were Mk. VI armed with a 75 mm. gun except for two Mk. VIII's in each squadron, H.Q. being equipped with 95 mm. guns. All Stuart light tanks in the Regiment were transferred to H.Q. Squadron to form the Reconnaissance Troop.

This was the existing organization in 1947.

The Ringing to Evensong

The Centenary of the famous Corps had been but the precursor of the sad end under the British régime. The kaleidoscopic state of affairs in India, with the terrible massacres in Calcutta and Behar, had obviously sobered the Indian politicians. Earl Wavell's resignation and the coming of Viscount Mountbatten and the hurried decision to modify the "Quit India" programme to the formation of two Dominions, meant the scrapping of the plans for the all-India Army that had been worked out, and entailed the division of famous forces into two armies. This called for the pathetic break in the old camaraderie of the northern armies and the transfer of the Hindu or Sikh portions of the regiments to "Hindustan," and the men were asked to accept the new condition, cancelling their oath of allegiance to the King Emperor. This produced intense scenes of mass-hysteria, for the Corps had a deeper "pull" than the religions, which were so soon allowed to fall on each other, to the meaningless cruel massacre of thousands.

To the Guides Infantry, however, as well as in the northern regiments, it went off with many farewells of deep and genuine sorrow—under British rule, Hindu and Muslim lived with each other, as comrades in the regiments. How deep this brotherhood was, the following story will show, which happened when the author was G.O.C.-in-C. in Mesopotamia in 1919. There had been trouble in North Kurdistan and a column of a Frontier Force battalion and a couple of mountain guns marched into difficult hills. They were surprised in an inadequately picqueted pass—and lost heavily, including one of the guns. A biggish clump of Sikh and P.M. prisoners were taken, including a young P.M. naik, and they were brought before the Kurdish Agha. He said, "I see you and several others are Muslims, and your lives will be spared ; but who are these long-haired brutes with black uncut beards ? They are not Muslims." And then that young naik up and he spoke, "Yes they are ; they are an ugly crowd, I admit, but they are just as good Muslims as the rest of us—and if you don't believe me, *strip them* and see." Comment is unnecessary. The bluff was not called, and the Sikhs were spared. The author had the great satisfaction of giving the immediate reward of the I.D.S.M. to this courageous naik and comrade. It may be added with satisfaction that a few days later General Cassels took tea with that Agha and his merry men, and recovered all prisoners and the gun.

Lieutenant-Colonel Pollard had been working hard preparing the Battalion first for the transfer to the all-India Army, and next for the quick-change division between Pakistan and Hindustan (a more convenient name than the later "India").

It was on Tuesday 5 August that the Paltan gave a right royal farewell to the Dogra company. In the words of George MacMunn, who was taking over in a few days, "It was a shockingly moving business with scarcely a dry eye from the C.O. downwards."

The Dogra company was to pick up the Dogra company of the 2nd Sikhs and go with them to join the 3rd Grenadiers at Thal in the Kurram. But on arrival there, while hospitably received, they learned that the bewildered Army Headquarters had sent a wrong order and the Grenadiers had already been made up. Colonel Pollard, due to retire on the 14th, felt that he might well tell higher authority what he thought about it—a satisfaction not usually available to the officer !

The Sikh Company was to await orders, and the story of their secret departure foiling tribal threats to destroy them, is told in Chapter XV (Pakistan Postscript).

Farewell, the Raj

The evening of 14 August a select party at Razmak drank the King's health as the Union Jack was lowered at sundown for the last time at the Residency. On 15 August all the sahibs in Razmak played up as the sahibs always will, as the old flag was pulled down on the Residency for ever and that of Pakistan was hoisted amid Muslim cheers, *after* a service in the English church, at which "George" read the lesson.

In the cool of the evening there were regimental *pagal* sports. The Farewell Order of the Day, just arrived from the Colonel of the Corps of Guides, Brigadier Hector Campbell, was read out by the new Commandant.

This was followed by a guest night in the Mess of Muslim and British officers, and the health of the King (of Pakistan) and the health of Pakistan itself were drunk. That of Pakistan was proposed by the senior "Union"—viz., Union of India—officer, and that of "The Union" by the senior Pakistan officer. In a speech the Commandant said all British officers looked and prayed for a successful Pakistan and a successful "Union," and also for the prosperity of the Guides Infantry in their new future.

And while all this was in progress the tribesmen joined in with a little more sniping.

The Special Service in the Garrison Church at Razmak

Allusion has just been made to a service at Razmak and, as it is so illustrative of the spirit in which the British were helping the Indian Dominions, some account of it is desirable. The object of the service was two-fold : to thank God for the life and work of those who have served India in the past, and to pray for His Blessing on all who are to be responsible for guiding the destiny of the two dominions of India and Pakistan. For these objects the service was specially drawn up, hymns and bidding prayers and lessons being specially selected. They were :

Hymns.
"All people that on earth do dwell."
"God moves in a mysterious way."
"Thy kingdom come, O God."
"Through the night of doubt and sorrow."

Bidding Prayers.
>I bid you give thanks for . . .
>Praise ye the Lord.
>The Lord's name be praised.
>I bid you pray for . . .
>O Lord, hear our prayer,
>And let our cry come unto Thee.

Lessons.
>1st   Ecclesiasticus, 44, 1-15.
>2nd   St. Matthew, 5, 1-16.

A choir of British officers and other ranks was specially formed, and the first lesson was read by Lieutenant-Colonel A. B. M. Way, R.I.A.S.C., and the second lesson by Major G. A. MacMunn of the Guides. A special address was given by Lieutenant-Colonel D. L. O. Woods, O.B.E., and the main service was conducted by the Chaplain and Major H. G. Ayres.

A large congregation attended, and it was altogether a remarkable occasion.

And so ended in confidence and amity[46] the last days of the Great British Raj, before the terrible tragedies had occurred in the Eastern Punjab which have so blotted the record of all who shared in pouring the *Pax Britannica* down the drain.

SPECIAL ORDER OF THE DAY
by
BRIGADIER HECTOR CAMPBELL, C.B., D.S.O., M.V.O.
COLONEL, Q.V.O. CORPS OF GUIDES

OFFICERS AND MEN OF THE GUIDES.

It is with deep feelings that I comply with the request of the Commandant to address you on this historic occasion when the two new Dominions, Pakistan and India, come into being.

For exactly a hundred years the Guides have had British Officers under the British Crown.

Now a great change has come about and the Government of Pakistan and India is handed over to Rulers and Ministers of your own Country and you will form part of their new Armed Forces.

Your old Officers and Comrades who have been bound to you with ties of affection and comradeship for so many years feel this wrench very greatly, but as Colonel of the Regiment, and I speak on their behalf, I can emphasize that our hearts and thoughts will be with you in the new era that now commences.

Knowing the spirit that has always existed in the Corps we are confident that you Officers and Men of the Guides will show that same loyalty and devotion to duty to the new Government as you have done in the past and that you will let no unworthy act on

---

[46] The story of the march-out from Razmak and the opening days of the Guides in the Dominion of Pakistan are given in Chapter XV, "Pakistan Postscript."

THE LAST DAYS OF THE RAJ

your part tarnish the fair name of the Regiment you have the honour to belong to and that our great name will be worthily upheld by you.

May I be permitted to say that I, personally, feel this great change most particularly for I was born in Hoti Mardan. My father commanded the Cavalry, the Infantry, and the Corps, and my uncle the Infantry, and I wore the Guides Badge for over twenty-seven years.

No unit in the Army has higher traditions than that borne by the Corps of Guides and your old Officers and Comrades trust that the "Camaraderie" and "Esprit de Corps" that has been so characteristic of the Guides and the Punjab Frontier Force will ever endure.

Though so many of us will be far distant we will be with you in spirit.

God be with you.

(*Signed*) HECTOR CAMPBELL, Brigadier.

LIST OF OFFICERS SERVING WITH THE GUIDES CAVALRY ON 15 AUGUST 1947 WHEN THEY BECAME A UNIT OF THE PAKISTAN ARMY

PRESENT WITH THE REGIMENT

Lieutenant-Colonel W. Eliott-Lockhart	Commandant. On long leave, United Kingdom.
A./Lieut.-Colonel R. A. Bailey	Offg. Commandant.
Major J. B. Reid	Offg. Second-in-Command.
Major Mohd Abbas Khan Durrani	Squadron Commander.
Captain Aman Ullah Khan	Squadron Commander.
Captain A. D. Raza	Squadron Commander.
Captain Jahan Zeb Khan	Adjutant.
Captain Mohan Singh	Technical Officer.
Captain K. Parkash Chand	Squadron Second-in-Command.
Captain K. Bhupindera Singh Uberoi	On Course at A.C.S.
Captain Tara Singh	Quartermaster.
Captain Bhagwan Singh	On Course at Tact. School, Dehra Dun.
Lieutenant Shilendra Chandra Raghubir	Squadron Second-in-Command.
Captain D. Morgan, R.E.M.E.	O.C. L.A.D.

SECONDED

Lieutenant-Colonel F. Walton	C.L.O., Punjab States.
Lieutenant-Colonel E. St. J. Birnie	Staff Appointment, G.H.Q. (I).
Colonel W. A. Gimson, M.C.	Commandant, A.C.S.
Lieutenant-Colonel D. G. Egerton	Commandant, Probyn's Horse.
Major L. A. J. Roffey	Mily. Secy. to H.E. Governor of Punjab.
Lieutenant-Colonel G. M. Strover, M.C.	A./Q. 1st Armoured Division.
Major J. R. C. Phillips	On leave in United Kingdom.
Major W. G. O. Butler, M.C.	G.H.Q. (I).
Major Har Prasad	Staff College, Quetta.
Major J. H. Chibber	Staff College, Quetta.
Major J. M. Penly	Khyber Rifles.
Captain Mohinder Singh Randhawa	Staff College, Quetta.
Captain Mohd Faruq Khan	55th Services Selection Board.
Captain Sultan Khan Malik	A.C.S.
Captain G. L. Fonceca	A.C.S.
Captain Mohd Mohiyyud Din	T.T. Wing, Babina.

THE GUIDES

LIST OF OFFICERS SERVING WITH THE BATTALION WITH APPOINTMENTS IN WAZIRISTAN, 1946

Lieutenant-Colonel G. A. MacMunn	Offg. Commandant.
Major R. R. Griffith	Offg. Second-in-Command.
Major R. G. Hutchinson	Administration Officer—O.C. Administration Coy.
Major A. M. W. B. McDermott	On leave.
Captain A. M. Vohra	O.C. "B" Coy.
Captain Z. M. Penty	Adjutant (on leave).
Captain Mohd Azan	O.C. "C" Coy.
Captain I. W. Stiven	Mortar Officer and O.C. H.Q. Coy.
Captain Sarbang Singh	O.C. "A" Coy. and Education Officer.
Lieutenant Shahzada Khan	O.C. "D" Coy.
Lieutenant Mohd Shaffi	Intelligence Officer.
Lieutenant W. W. S. Breem	Signals Officer and Offg. Adjutant.
Lieutenant D. R. M. Glasse	Transport Officer.
Lieutenant P. Ashcroft	Quartermaster.
Second-Lieutenant R. T. M. Gray	Assistant Transport Officer.
Second-Lieutenant Mohd Iqbal Malik	Offg. Quartermaster.

SECONDED

Colonel G. V. L. Coleman	Director of Man Power (G.H.Q.)
Lieutenant-Colonel M. H. H. Baily, D.S.O.	Commanding Zhob Militia, Fort Sandeman.
Brigadier P. R. Macnamara	Commanding 5th Indian Infantry Brigade, Poona (Comdt.-elect).
Lieutenant-Colonel A. R. E. Pollard	Commanding 17th Mahratta L.I., Belgaum.
Lieutenant-Colonel A. C. S. Moore	Tochi Scouts (on leave in England).
Lieutenant-Colonel G. J. Hamilton, D.S.O.	Commanding 7th/16th Punjab Regiment, Thal.
Captain R. V. E. Hodson	A.P.A. South Waziristan Agency, Wana.
Major W. G. Watt	Staff Captain A., Quetta Sub-Area.
T./Lieutenant-Colonel J. W. Hodges, M.C.	4th F.F.R., Tavory, Burma.
Major W. M. Chisholm	Mily. Secy. Branch, G.H.Q. (I).
Major Mohd Rafi Khan	Zhob Militia, Fort Sandeman.
Captain P. J. L. Phelps	Tochi Scouts, Dosalli.

OFFICERS, GUIDES CAVALRY, 1941
"C" Squadron away at Loralai

Back Row (L. to R.)—Reid, Jem. Garka Ram, L'Estrange, Lack, Humphries, Monteith, Graham.
Centre Row—Jem. Chuni Lal, George, Ris. Shankar Singh, Bailey, Van Renan, Jem. Balwant Singh, Butler, Jenkins, McCausland, Roffey.
Front Row—Plunkett, Ris. Gurdial Singh, Prioleau, Ris.-Maj. Sardara Singh, Gradidge, Ris. Indar Singh, Walton, Ris. Nawaz Jang, Shebbeare.

WINNERS, INDIAN CAVALRY POLO TOURNAMENT, 1938

Birnie.   Gradidge.   Roffey.   Plunkett.

CHAPTER XIII

THE GUIDES POLO CHAPTER

THE GUIDES POLO, 1922-39; ACCOUNT OF THE SEMI-FINALS AND FINAL OF THE LAST INDIAN CAVALRY POLO TOURNAMENT, 1939; THE RECORD OF MATCHES PLAYED, 1929-39.

THE GUIDES POLO, 1922-39[47]

POLO had long been the amusement of British and Indian units in India, and the Guides, both Cavalry and Infantry, had been among the foremost. The First World War had of course broken up the continuity for many corps, but on the termination of World War I and the post-war overseas garrisons, the rebuilding of the sport and game was taken up in leisure hours, and no one ever dreamt that the victors of that war would allow another war to be prepared.

After World War I it took a long time to build up a polo team with any pretensions at class. The acquisition of the necessary type of pony and in requisite numbers was also a stumbling-block. The Corps lacked that priceless asset, a good buyer, and the methods adopted were haphazard. The playing of hired troop horses gave the Cavalry a great advantage over the Infantry, and a Corps team became but a memory. The Infantry struggled on well into the thirties, but moves to such places as Aden and the Khaiber did not help their polo, and their efforts were generally confined to somewhat spasmodic appearances in local tournaments.

The Cavalry, with a team consisting of No. 1, Lieutenant Abdul Rahim Khan; No. 2, Captain E. K. Wood; No. 3, Captain C. P. J. Prioleau; and Back, Captain C. H. H. Eales (on one occasion Captain A. V. Hammond), made a promising start in 1923, being actually unbeaten in that year and winning tournaments in Nowshera, Rawalpindi (Tradesmen's), Mardan, Abbottabad and Peshawar (Christmas). But they were all handicap tournaments and the side was lightly penalized in this respect. Entry in 1924 into the Indian Cavalry Tournament at Lahore exposed the nakedness of the land. For the next ten years the struggle continued and improvement took place, but no major success. They could not put a first-class regimental side into the field adequately mounted for an open six-chukker tournament. (In 1928 Prioleau went to Australia with an Army-in-India team.)

In 1935 and 1936 the efforts began to be rewarded in that we reached the final of the Indian Cavalry tournament only to be defeated on both occasions by Probyn's Horse. We won this tournament in 1938 and 1939, and so became the last holders of the trophy though it must be admitted that teams such as the C.I.H. and P.A.V.O. were absent on both occasions. Representatives of the Regiment on these four occasions

---

[47] Compiled from a note by Brigadier Prioleau in the first person.

included Gimson, Wood, Plunkett, Garforth-Bles, Gradidge, Roffey, Prioleau, Birnie and Edwardes. The team entered for the Indian Polo Association Championship in Calcutta in 1938, but were defeated in their only game by the all-conquering Jaipur side. A regimental Polo note would be incomplete without reference to the perfect Mardan grounds which, in 1939, were as good as they had ever been.

The final success that came was due most of all to the effort that Prioleau and Gradidge had made through the long years to achieve it. The total of tournaments played in by Risala and Paltan must be studied to show the long road upward in the game which finally brought the Cavalry to the proud position of winning the Indian Cavalry tournament in 1938 and 1939, the last years of peace and of horsed regiments. It shows also the lesser record of the Infantry, whose years since 1922 were largely spent trans-Frontier. This record opens with the historic match on the occasion of H.R.H. The Prince of Wales's visit to India that year, when, on coming to Mardan, he and three members of his Staff played the Guides.

Before coming to the Record, those who served at the time, and indeed all those older Guides who loved the game, will read with some excitement the story of the last win, recorded in the *Civil and Military Gazette* of Lahore—the paper on which Kipling worked and which published some of his earlier "turnovers"—as follows:

Letter from the late Major-General Sir George Younghusband, at one time Colonel of the Corps of Guides, to Lieutenant-Colonel Hammond on the occasion of their winning the Tournament in 1938.

St. Thomas's Tower,
Tower of London.

"My Dear Hammond,

"Heartiest congratulations to you all on winning the Tournament. Hector Campbell has just telephoned down to me. It is a long and steep ascent to victory but once on top it is not so hard to keep there. I think it took us thirteen years to make the first ascent and then we had many good years. Our first team was at Kabul, on grass-cutters' ponies mostly, and consisted of your father, Hughes, Daly and Adams as far as I can remember.

"Continued success and the very best luck to you all.

"Yours very sincerely,

(*Signed*) "George Younghusband."

"Civil and Military Gazette," Thursday 2 February 1939.

Indian Cavalry Polo Tournament: Semi-Finals

The 13th D.C.O. Lancers will on Friday meet the holders, the Guides Cavalry, in the final of the Indian Cavalry Polo Tournament. The Guides Cavalry on Wednesday beat Skinner's Horse by nine goals to three after scoring five goals without reply in the first of the six chukkers. They were the better mounted, and they played much better together as a team, save in the second chukker, with the result that Lieutenant-Colonel Broadfoot, Skinner's "star," was playing a lone hand.

In the other semi-final the 13th D.C.O. Lancers were somewhat lucky to win, although they should have made victory certain in the sixth chukker when they were pressing nearly all the time and managed to score only one goal—and that an equalizer. Then, after the goals had been widened, the 8th K.G.V's.O. Light Cavalry gave their opponents a tremendous fight and nearly snatched the victory, but after two minutes' anxiety the 13th got away and settled the issue.

The indications point to a very keen final with really hard galloping and much keen marking. It is to be hoped that it will not be spoiled by too much "whistle."

GUIDES CAVALRY v. SKINNER'S HORSE

First Chukker.—Immediately after the start a good backhander by Roffey sent Plunkett through to score a goal for the Guides. Changing over, the Guides scored another goal from a mêlée (2-0). Plunkett hit up well to Kensington, who scored the third goal for the Guides. A little later Plunkett went through and scored with a good hard drive (4-0). A long backhander by Plunkett sent Kensington away but the latter missed the flags. Plunkett took the ball on the far side of the ground and centred well. He followed through to score himself. Near the end of the chukker Skinner's Horse were unlucky not to score. Later the Guides also failed to score. Guides 5, Skinner's Horse 0.

Second Chukker.—Skinner's Horse pressed for some time and scored with a great cut shot by Broadfoot. Coaker hit up towards the goal and Cullinan scored with a good shot (5-2). Broadfoot was prominent for Skinner's Horse in this chukker. Guides 5, Skinner's Horse 2.

Third Chukker.—The Guides enjoyed a territorial advantage for a short spell, but later Skinner's also attacked and just missed scoring. Returning to the attack, the Guides made a good rally, but were unable to add to their score. A 60-yard hit was awarded against Skinner's Horse. Plunkett took the hit and missed the flags narrowly. Immediately after this Kensington scored a goal for the Guides. On changing ends Plunkett scored another goal for the Guides. Skinner's Horse were attacking when the bugle sounded. Guides 7, Skinner's Horse 2.

Fourth Chukker.—Early in this chukker Roffey scored for the Guides. Play was then confined to midfield for some time. A good long shot by Plunkett gave Roffey an opportunity to score, but he sent the ball wide. Broadfoot then made a fine run down the ground but was unable to score. Guides 8, Skinner's Horse 2.

Fifth Chukker.—From the throw-in Skinner's Horse attacked, but shortly afterwards Roffey scored for the Guides. Skinner's Horse failed to reduce the lead from a good attempt. Up-and-down play followed for a short period. Towards the close of the chukker Broadfoot just failed to score after a clever shot from underneath his pony. Throughout the chukker Plunkett was hitting well but most of the attacks were thwarted by Broadfoot, who was playing a great defensive game. Guides 9, Skinner's Horse 2.

Sixth Chukker.—From a 30-yard hit Skinner's Horse scored a goal through Broadfoot soon after the start (9-3). A 60-yard hit was awarded Skinner's Horse for a cross; a good save by Plunkett prevented them from scoring. The Guides now made a concerted raid and just failed to score. Then followed a short period of mid-field play. Plunkett and Roffey played well for winners, while Broadfoot was outstanding for the losers. Coaker also did a lot of useful work. Guides 9, Skinner's Horse 3.

Guides Cavalry: Captain Lord Kensington, Mr. L. A. J. Roffey, Captain the Hon. R. A. H. Plunkett, Mr. G. D. G. Garforth-Bles.

Skinner's Horse: Mr. C. R. D. Gray, Mr. W. E. Cullinan, Lieutenant-Colonel W. A. Broadfoot, Mr. R. E. Coaker.

Umpires: Brigadier R. Dening and Major-General G. de la P. Beresford.

THE GUIDES

"Civil and Military Gazette," Saturday February 4 1939.

INDIAN CAVALRY POLO TOURNAMENT: FINAL
HOLDERS RETAIN TROPHY—13TH D.C.O. LANCERS BEATEN BY GUIDES

Brilliant weather favoured the final of the Indian Cavalry Polo Tournament, which was played in the presence of a large crowd on the Lahore racecourse on Friday.

The Guides Cavalry, Mardan, the holders, defeated 13th D.C.O. Lancers, Sialkot, by eight goals to four. The Challenge Cup and the prizes were given away by His Excellency, the Governor.

GUIDES CAVALRY *v.* 13TH D.C.O. LANCERS

First Chukker.—The Lancers attacked from the throw-in but the Guides soon retaliated. Following another attack, the Lancers took the lead, Hughes being the scorer. Changing over, the Guides made a determined raid. A 60-yard hit was awarded against them for crossing. Messervy took the hit but sent wide. Once Roffey made a good clearance. Play was then confined to the side line for some time. Just as the bugle sounded Kensington equalized. Guides 1, Lancers 1.

Second Chukker.—Immediately after the start Messervy put the Lancers in front, scoring from close range. Just after the change-over Plunkett secured the equalizer (2–2). The Guides attacked again, but the ball was well cleared by Messervy from near the goal mouth. Plunkett led another attack for the Guides, but sent wide. A little later a 60-yard hit against the Guides was unproductive. Another 60-yard hit was awarded against the Guides without result. The Lancers made a concerted gallop and Garforth-Bles, the opposing back, saved well with an excellent clearance. Guides 2, 13th Lancers 2.

Third Chukker.—This opened at a fast pace. Soon after Messervy pulled a leg muscle and the game was suspended for a few minutes. He returned to the field and the Guides scored a goal through Roffey. Messervy, however, was unable to continue and the game was again suspended. He eventually retired and his place was taken by Captain Farran. The Guides attacked but sent behind. A little later the Guides scored through an excellent effort by Roffey. Guides 4, 13th Lancers 2.

Fourth Chukker.—Two goals in arrears, the Lancers attacked from the throw-in. The Guides soon retaliated and Kensington failed to score from under his pony. Garforth-Bles then increased the Guides' lead (5–2). On changing ends the Guides missed the flags narrowly. Fast end-to-end galloping was witnessed at this stage. Just after the bugle sounded the Guides further increased their lead. Guides 6, 13th Lancers 2.

Fifth Chukker.—Following a concerted run, the Lancers scored through Farran, who sent in an excellent shot. The Guides were now hovering near the Lancers' goal. Eventually they met with success, Roffey scoring from a mêlée. The Lancers made a good attack and were unfortunate in not scoring. It was a good hard galloping chukker, in which the exchanges were fairly even. Guides 7, 13th Lancers 3.

Sixth Chukker.—The final chukker opened with a throw-in. There was little interest left in the game, as the Guides had made practically certain of victory. The 13th Lancers attacked for some time and then, following a raid by the Guides, the Lancers returned to the attack. They kept play in the Guides' area and at last scored (7–4). Then followed a short period of midfield play. The Guides then increased their lead through Plunkett. Guides 8, 13th Lancers 4.

13th D.C.O. Lancers: Mr. G. C. Garlick, Captain T. L. Hughes, Lieutenant-Colonel F. W. Messervy, Lieutenant-Colonel F. R. R. Bucher (Captain C. C. Farran replaced Colonel Messervy).

The Guides Cavalry: Captain Lord Kensington, Mr. L. A. J. Roffey, Captain the Hon. R. A. H. Plunkett, Mr. G. D. G. Garforth-Bles.

Umpires: Lieutenant-Colonel W. A. Broadfoot and Captain J. M. W. Martin.

THE GUIDES POLO CHAPTER

GUIDES CAVALRY AND INFANTRY

SEASON

1921/1922 *Abbottabad.* April. Won.

Mardan. Visit of H.R.H. The Prince of Wales.

Teams

H.R.H. The Prince of Wales.	Mr. H. N. Weber.
Captain E. D. Metcalve.	Captain F. A. Davies.
Colonel R. Worgan.	Major N. A. Prendergast.
Colonel C. O. Harvey.	Captain J. H. G. Gradidge.

1922/1923 *Lahore.*
Corps team sent at Christmas. Lost to Probyn's Horse first round and Subsidiary Tournament to 8th Cavalry in final round.

Nowshera.
Cavalry Team. Won v. Royal Scots Greys.

Rawalpindi, Tradesmen's Cup.
Cavalry Team. Won v. 24th Brigade, R.A.

Mardan. April.
Cavalry Team. Won v. 8th Cavalry.

Abbottabad. April.
Corps Team. Won.

1923/1924 *Peshawar Christmas Tournament.*
Cavalry Team. Won v. 8th Cavalry.

Rawalpindi, Frontier Force Tournament.
Cavalry Team. Lost to P.A.V.O. in final after extra time.

[48]*Native Cavalry Tournament, Lahore.* February.
Guides Cavalry. Lost to 6th Lancers in first round.

Mardan Tournament. April.
Guides Cavalry. Lost to 8th Cavalry in semi-final round.

Abbottabad Tournament. April.
Corps Team. Lost to P.A.V.O. in final round.

1924/1925 *Peshawar Christmas Tournament.*
Guides Cavalry. Lost to Probyn's Horse in semi-final round.

Mardan Tournament. April.
Guides Cavalry. Won v. C.I.H.

1925/1926 *Peshawar, Frontier Cup.* Christmas.
Guides Cavalry. Lost to 8th Cavalry in third round.

Nowshera Tournament. January.
Guides Cavalry. Lost to 5th/6th Dragoons in final round.

Peshawar Vale Novices, Gai Cup. March.
Guides Cavalry. Won v. "Dragonflies."

Rawalpindi, Tradesmen's Cup. March.
Guides Cavalry. Lost to Sam Browne's Cavalry in second round.

Mardan Tournament. April.
Guides "A." Lost to Poona Horse in second round.
Guides "B." Lost to 5th/6th Dragoons "A" in first round.

---

[48] The old name.

THE GUIDES

SEASON
1926/1927 *Peshawar. Christmas.*
　　Cavalry Corps Teams. Six-Chukker Tournament. Lost first round to Poona Horse.
　　Cavalry Corps Teams. Four-Chukker Tournament. Lost second round to C.I.H.
Punjab Frontier Force Tournament.
　　Cavalry team. Won v. P.A.V.O.
Risalpur Tournament.
　　Guides "A." (?)
　　Guides "B." Lost to "E" Battery in first round.
Rawalpindi, Tradesmen's Cup.
　　Cavalry. Lost to Sam Browne's "B" in second round.
Lahore, Indian Cavalry Cup.
　　Guides Cavalry. Lost to C.I.H. in second round.
Peshawar, Gai Cup.
　　Guides "A." Lost to "E" Battery in second round.
　　Guides "B." Lost to "Dodos" in second round.
Mardan Tournament.
　　Guides "A." Lost to Poona Horse in second round.
　　Guides "B." Lost to "E" Battery in second round.
Indian Infantry Tournament.
　　Guides Infantry Team. Lost to 4th/14th Punjabis in final round.

1927/1928 *Lahore, Indian Cavalry Tournament.*

1928/1929 *No Polo.* Regiment in quarantine for glanders and could not move horses.

1929/1930 *Peshawar Christmas Tournament.*
　　Six-Chukker. Won v. 20th Lancers.
　　Four-Chukker. Won v. Poona Horse.
Infantry Tournament.
　　Guides Infantry Team. Lost to Seaforth Highlanders.
Risalpur Tournament.
　　Guides Cavalry. Lost first round. Won Subsidiary Tournament.
Punjab Frontier Force Cup.
　　Guides Cavalry. Won v. P.A.V.O.
Rawalpindi, Tradesmen's Cup.
　　Guides Cavalry. Lost to P.A.V.O. in first round. Won Subsidiary.
Mardan American Tournament.
　　Guides Cavalry. Second to 15th/19th Hussars.

1930/1931 *Peshawar Christmas Tournament.*
　　Guides Cavalry. Lost to Hodson's Horse in semi-final round of four-chukker tournament.
Sialkot, 12th Lancers Cup.
　　Guides Cavalry. Lost to Kashmir in final.
Risalpur Tournament.
　　Guides Cavalry. Lost to Hodson's Horse in final round.
Indian Cavalry.
　　Guides Cavalry. Lost to Scinde Horse in first round.
Mardan Tournament.
　　Guides Cavalry. Lost to Poona Horse in final round.

SEASON	
1931/1932	*Frontier Challenge Cup.*

SEASON
1931/1932   *Frontier Challenge Cup.*
      Guides Cavalry. Won v. 25th Field Battery.
  Sialkot, 12th Lancers Cup.
      Guides Cavalry. Won v. "Hittites."
  Lahore, Hodson's Horse Cup.
      Guides Cavalry. Lost to 13th/18th Hussars.

1932/1933   *Indian Cavalry Tournament.*
      Guides Cavalry. Lost to Probyn's Horse in semi-final.
  Peshawar Club Cup.
      Guides Cavalry. Won v. 25th Field Battery.
  Peshawar, Frontier Challenge Cup.
      Cavalry "A." Lost to "Fascisti" in second round.
      Cavalry "B." Lost to 20th Lancers in third round.

1933/1934   *Indian Cavalry Tournament.*
      Guides Cavalry. Lost to Probyn's Horse in first round.
  Inter-Regimental Tournament.
      Guides Cavalry. Lost to C.I.H. in first round.

1934/1935   *Risalpur, 8th Cavalry Cup.* (Also a Guides Infantry Team.)
      Cavalry "A." Lost to Skinner's Horse in first round.
      Cavalry "B." Lost to Skinner's Horse in third round.
  Peshawar Club Cup.
      Guides Cavalry. Lost to Skinner's Horse in first round.
  Frontier Challenge Cup. (Also a Guides Infantry Team.)
      Cavalry Team and "Cavalry Subalterns" result not recorded.
  Meerut, Subalterns' Cup.
      Guides Cavalry. Lost to 19th Hussars.
  Rawalpindi, Tradesmen's Cup.
      Guides Cavalry. Won v. Probyn's Horse.
  Lahore, Indian Cavalry Tournament.
      Guides Cavalry. Lost to Probyn's Horse in final round.

1935/1936   *Risalpur, 8th Cavalry Cup.*
      Guides Cavalry. Lost to "Covenanters" in first round.
      Won the Subsidiary Tournament.
  Peshawar Club Challenge Cup.
      Guides Cavalry. Lost to Skinner's Horse in first round.
  Peshawar, Frontier Challenge Cup.
      Cavalry "A." Lost to 18th K.E.O. Cavalry "B" in semi-final.
      Cavalry "B." Lost to Probyn's Horse in first round.
  Nowshera Low Handicap Tournament.
      Guides Cavalry. Lost to "Chokras" in second round.
  Rawalpindi, Tradesmen's Cup.
      Guides Cavalry. Lost to Scinde Horse in semi-final round.
  Risalpur, 15th/19th Hussars Cup.
      Cavalry "A." Lost to "Blue Birds" in second round.
      Cavalry "B." Lost to "Swans" in semi-final round.
  Mardan Polo Tournament.
      Cavalry "A." Lost to 18th Cavalry in final round.
      Cavalry "B." Lost to "Ocean and Accident" in first round.
  Lahore, Indian Cavalry Tournament.
      Guides Cavalry. Lost to Probyn's Horse in final.

THE GUIDES

SEASON

1936/1937 *Peshawar Christmas Tournament.*
    Guides Cavalry Team in six-chukker tournament scratched in final owing to injuries to players.
    Guides Cavalry Team in four-chukker lost to 4th Field Brigade, first round.

Lahore, Indian Cavalry Tournament.
    Guides Cavalry. Lost to Scinde Horse in second round.

Delhi, Baria Cup.
    Guides Cavalry. Won v. 17th/21st Lancers.

Meerut, Subalterns' Cup.
    Guides Cavalry. Lost to 17th/21st Lancers in first round.

1937/1938 *Risalpur, 8th Cavalry Cup.*
    Cavalry "A." Lost to 16th Cavalry in second round.
    Cavalry "B." Lost to 13th/18th Hussars in first round.
    Cavalry "C." Lost to 13th/18th Hussars in semi-final.

Risalpur, 13th/18th Hussars Cup.
    Cavalry "A." Lost to Skinner's in final round.
    Cavalry "B." Lost to "Dodos" in third round.
    Cavalry "C." Lost to Skinner's "A" in semi-final.

Risalpur and Mardan Tournament (at Mardan).
    Guides Cavalry. Lost to Probyn's Horse in first round.

Delhi, High Handicap Tournament.
    Lost to 19th Lancers in semi-final round.

Delhi, Prince of Wales' Tournament.
    Lost to "Red Shirts" in first round.

Delhi, Baria Cup.
    Lost to 2nd Lancers in semi-final round.

Risalpur, 15th/19th Tournament.
    Cavalry "A." Lost to Skinner's Horse in semi-final round.
    Cavalry "B." Won v. Skinner's Horse.

Mardan Spring Tournament.
    Cavalry "A." Lost to "Pessimists" in semi-final round
    Cavalry "B." Lost to 16th Cavalry in semi-final round.

Lahore, Indian Cavalry Tournament.
    Cavalry. Won v. Skinner's Horse.

Team
Back Major J. H. Gradidge.
3 Captain R. Plunkett.
2 Lieutenant L. A. S. Roffey.
1 Major E. St. J. Birnie.

1938/1939 *Lahore, Indian Cavalry Tournament.*
    Cavalry. Won v. 13th D.C.O. Lancers.

Team
Back Mr. G. D. G. Garforth-Bles.
3 Captain R. Plunkett.
2 Mr. L. A. J. Roffey.
1 Captain Lord Kensington.

CHAPTER XIV

SACRIFICES AND SERVICES

I. THE STORY OF GLORY :
   THE GLORIOUS STORY OF FLIGHT COMMANDER H. DANE, D.S.O. (LATE THE GUIDES)—THE STORY OF LIEUTENANT DAVID MONTEITH, THE GUIDES CAVALRY—LIEUTENANT-COLONEL A. K. MURCOTT, THE GUIDES INFANTRY—MAJOR M. H. HODSON, THE GUIDES INFANTRY—LIEUTENANT-COLONEL C. H. H. EALES, M.C., THE GUIDES CAVALRY.

II. SERVICES OF DISTINGUISHED OFFICERS :
   BRIGADIER HECTOR CAMPBELL, C.B., D.S.O., M.V.O.—LIEUTENANT-GENERAL SIR KENNETH McLEOD, K.C.I.E., C.B., D.S.O.—MAJOR-GENERAL A. V. HAMMOND, C.B., D.S.O.—BRIGADIER J. H. GRADIDGE, C.B.E.—BRIGADIER R. MACNAMARA, D.S.O.—BRIGADIER K. A. GARRETT, M.C.—BRIGADIER C. P. J. PRIOLEAU—BRIGADIER G. V. L. COLEMAN—TEMPY.-BRIGADIER M. H. H. BAILY, D.S.O.—BRIGADIER W. H. BLOOD, M.V.O.

I. THE STORY OF GLORY

THE Services of those officers of the Guides who gave their lives during the Second World War are recorded here—viz., Squadron Leader R. Dane, Lieutenant David Monteith, Lieutenant-Colonel A. K. Murcott, Lieutenant-Colonel C. H. H. Eales, M.C., and Major M. H. Hodson—and those who have served with special distinction attaining the ranks of general and brigadier.

The attainment of high rank does not come to every good soldier for many reasons, and those who reach it, in addition to their own attainments, have usually had the luck of opportunity to further their own qualities. But it is right that some record should be given here of those who have so attained.

The details given in the short biographies below show how varied have been the services rendered, and how versatile the personal equipment of the officers themselves. Before coming to them, let us glory in and mourn for those whose deaths are now recorded, and let us say with old Malachi—the Messenger of God—"They shall be mine, said the Lord of Hosts, in that day when I make up my jewels."

THE GLORIOUS STORY OF
FLIGHT COMMANDER HENRY DANE, R.A.F.V.R., D.S.O. (LATE GUIDES)

This story only came fully to light at the end of the war with Japan. Dane was first commissioned 24 August 1912, joined the Guides 18 November 1913, resigned as a captain on 4 August 1923, and became general manager of the Perak River Hydro-Electric Power Company in Malaya. Dane was greatly interested in flying, always saying he would fight the next war in the air, and became captain of the Flying Club at Ipok. He was, for a while, their flying instructor, having undergone a course of special training, becoming chief instructor at the outbreak of war, as the Club pilot instructor (on leave) was retained at home. In 1936 Captain Dane had to go home himself on business. He was given an R.A.F. commission while at home and gained his wings at Yatesbury, specially training in low flying and low bombing. Returning to Malaya in January 1941, he found he had been appointed to the command of the Peak Flight ("C") of the Malaya Volunteer Air Force. Despite his own business, he was intensely busy in training his own and other men. He was sent to Singapore to start the training of an embryo Observer Corps—started, alas ! too late to develop effectively.

On Sunday night, 7/8 December 1941, the "balloon went up." The Japs had landed in Malaya. The Peak Flight was embodied and flown to the Rabang Airfield in Johore, then under construction, and able to take only light craft. Dane was now promoted to Flight Lieutenant and was allowed to pick his own men and aircraft and collected a magnificent crowd. There was nothing on the half-made airfield and "C" Flight had to improvise everything, which they did in a marvellous way. Their machines were Avro Cadets, Gypsy Moths and a Miles Majestic. These they fitted with bomb racks, but their only weapons were revolvers, and they had no parachutes, and no Mae-Wests, but the hearts of lions. The R.A.F. dubbed them the Suicide Club, and a daring suicide club they were. They had to dodge the Jap fighters (though one pilot, with no armament, kept up a fight with two for twenty minutes), their work being chiefly reconnaissance for the 1st Division. Finally they were strafed out of Rabang and moved into Johore Bam, but soon had to leave as the Japs advanced. But it was from this strip that Dane's exploit won him the D.S.O. (posthumous). His wife, who had also learnt to fly, was in Singapore and saw him next day and found him extremely reticent, merely remarking that he had managed to save a few lives. A little later he came on a large body of Japs, who had spotted him. He dived at them at full throttle and they scattered, and he, though maimed, got away.

On 30 January the unit came in to Singapore, as all troops were leaving the mainland, and the causeway was blown up. The R.A.F. had gone to Java, but Dane's flight remained for a few days doing reconnaissance, and then the V.A.F. was also summoned to Java, flying by Palembang in Sumatra, refuelling there just before it was captured. In Batavia the Volunteer Air Force was to be disbanded, but as Dane's Flight had planes it was retained under Air Vice-Marshal Maltby, an old friend.

Mrs. Dane and her children were brought away from Singapore in the last ship, leaving her car derelict on the quay.

Henry Dane was, for the moment, safe in Java, but very soon the forces there had to surrender. The prison camps in Java were reasonable, but after a few months they were shipped in a "Hell ship," driven below at the point of the bayonet and taken in winter, in the bitter climate of Japan, to Mitanshim camp near Tokio; there they received treatment that several Hiroshimas can scarcely blot out—many ill with dysentery and pneumonia, arriving only to die, and among the dying, gallant ex-Guide and airman Henry Dane. It truly was of such as he that old Malachi's text just quoted speaks.

Many letters eventually came to Mrs. Dane from Sir Thomas Shenton, the Governor, from Air Vice-Marshal Sir Philip Maltby, from General Sir Trevor Heath also, who had commanded the 3rd Corps in Malaya—the latter specially eulogizing Dane in his little Moth, defying the Japanese naval planes, and finding the whereabouts of his 6th/15th Brigade and giving them a message which resulted in their rescue by the Navy from a point on the coast. The Vice-Admiral writes: "No man could have done more, more loyally with so little and inadequate resources, than he and those with him in the M.V.A.F. in Malaya and Java. In my report I am going to spread myself about them, and your husband in particular." Captain Dane received a posthumous Distinguished Service Order, a fitting tribute to the murdered hero, and a story only matched by the improvised Air Force at Habbaniyeh that strafed the rebel Arab Army.

SACRIFICES AND SERVICES

THE STORY OF DAVID MONTEITH

Though the story of both Corps of the Guides in the Second World War, with one or two brief exceptions, was an uneventful sentry-go, watching against dread events that never happened, the same does not apply to individual officers. The Indian Army was so enormously expanded that trained officers had to be switched to many points, their places taken by emergency commissioned officers, who in their turn, when trained and experienced, were urgently wafted elsewhere.

Many Guides officers from both Corps earned honours and rewards elsewhere, many served staunchly in many theatres. Here should be told another Cavalry story, that of young David Monteith, the serving officer of the Risala who was killed in action on or about 9 June 1944 outside Mogaung—a town on the Mogaung Chaung, which flows into the Irrawaddi just about Sinbo above the Third Defile. The story is told by Lieutenant-Colonel H. Christie, commanding the 1st Lancashire Fusiliers. Monteith was serving with the Lancashire Fusiliers, who were part of the Chindits. He had been awarded the M.B.E. in 1943, for rescuing the crew of a bomber that had crashed with a full load of bombs. Colonel Christie writes: "He had an independent platoon, with a Vickers and a wireless set, and was given the task of dominating the Irrawaddi between Khatha—Bhamo—Sinbo. So successful was he that though all the towns were in Japanese hands, local boats on the river flew the Union Jack. In May the battalion columns were amalgamated and Monteith commanded one of the rifle companies. There were two engagements: in the first Mogaung was taken, Monteith's company, after marching ten hours with their packs, being brought up to carry the last position. Then followed the attack on the Pirimhi Bridge—thirty yards long—held by a Jap platoon on the far side. After bombardment by a 3-inch mortar, a platoon tried to get across. Half-way over the bridge the commander was hit and lay helpless in the middle of the bridge, and his platoon could not help. Monteith went and brought him in and then got the platoon away, and all their wounded brought in. But the wounded platoon commander had crawled away from where he had been put, and had fainted. Monteith found him again and brought him in. It was next day the former was killed. The bridge was again being attacked, a company from another battalion having got over the river by a ford, and in placing a mortar for a frontal attack on the bridge, he was shot by a sniper in the spine and killed instantly."

Christie also wrote of the services of George Butler of the Guides Cavalry, who had had a hell of a time in the "White City," his position being attacked on thirteen consecutive nights by the Japs. He was in command of Lancashires, South Staffordshires, West Africans and Gurkhas, who between them killed—beyond dispute—several hundreds of Japs. He was wounded, but not seriously.

LIEUTENANT-COLONEL A. K. MURCOTT

This distinguished officer of the Guides Infantry lost his life in an air accident in Burma.

In 1943/44 he was commanding the 8th/12th F.F.R. in the Burma Campaign (a war unit), and then became A.Q.M.G. of the 505th District, S.E.A.C., with its headquarters at Meiktila, south of Mandalay.

Just as the war with Japan was drawing to its close, and they had suffered the defeat which finished them in Burma, a month before the preliminary surrender arrangements were signed with the Japanese envoy in Rangoon, Andrew Murcott and three other officers of the District Headquarters left Meiktila for Imphal by air about 0800 hours on 24 July.

That evening it was reported that the plane had not reached Imphal. All planes on the route and the R.A.F. Rescue Service searched in the hundreds of square miles of jungle and mountains of 10,000 feet. The plane was found, crashed, near Kani on the Chindwin between Monywa and Kalewar, and all the occupants killed. They were reverently buried on the site. Writing to Mrs. Murcott, Major-General S. H. G. Snelling, the District Commander, said: "There is no need for me to tell you how Andrew had endeared himself to us all. Always cheerful in spite of difficulties, so quiet, thorough and reliable." Murcott had two Mentions in Despatches for this campaign. The loss was deeply felt in the Guides.

Major M. H. Hodson

Michael Harry Hodson, younger brother of Robin, great-nephew of G. B. Hodson and a more distant connection of W. S. R. Hodson (second Commandant of the Guides), joined the Guides Infantry in April 1939. In September 1941 he proceeded to Iraq as a liaison officer with H.Q., 6th Indian Division, with whom he served later as G.S.O.3 (O) in PAI Force. After passing out of the Staff College, Quetta, in 1944, he was flown into Imphal to be Brigade Major of 49th Indian Infantry Brigade and saw several months of active service in the jungle until the Brigade was withdrawn for rest and later returned to India. For his distinguished services in Burma, Hodson was mentioned in despatches.

During the winter of 1944-45, 49th Indian Infantry Brigade underwent intense training in combined operations near Bombay, and in August 1945, Major Hodson embarked with his Brigade Commander, Brigadier Mallaby, a day or two before the Japanese surrender, to take part in the invasion of Malaya, known as Operation "Zipper."

After a few weeks of pleasant conditions in Port Dickson, 49th Indian Infantry Brigade was ordered to Soerabaja in Java, there to become involved in one of the saddest postscripts to World War II. The tragic story of misunderstanding and treachery, of British patience and Indian gallantry, has been vividly told by a senior officer present with the Brigade H.Q. in the October 1948 issue of the *Royal Artillery Journal*. Describing the events of the day (30 October 1945) on which both Brigadier Mallaby and Brigade-major Hodson gave their lives in the hopeless attempt to make propaganda-maddened Indonesian extremists see reason, the writer says:

"Another truce was announced. As on former occasions, the Indonesians made no attempt to observe it. Brigadier Mallaby sent his Brigade-major with Major Harte to deliver a note of protest to Indonesian Headquarters some three hundred yards away. The two officers were stopped within two hundred yards of Brigade Headquarters and taken out of their jeep. Soejono, the chief of Police, rescued them from the mob and hid them for safety in a building. Later they were taken by the Pamoedas to the Hotel Brunet to be interrogated. On the way they were seized from their captors by the mob and shot in cold blood."

Another account states that, finding their place of hiding surrounded by a howling mob, Mike Hodson and his companion decided to try and shoot their way out, but the

SACRIFICES AND SERVICES

evidence is unreliable. For some time it was hoped that the bodies of Hodson and Harte had been buried in the garden of the Hotel Brunet, but subsequent search proved fruitless. The body of Brigadier Mallaby, who had been similarly murdered a few hours later, was returned by the Indonesians. At all events, another gallant young officer of high promise and endearing qualities had gone the way of so many earlier Guides.

LIEUTENANT-COLONEL C. H. H. EALES, M.C.

There is yet another Guide who lost his life in the service of his country in the Second World War. Lieutenant C. H. H. Eales joined the Guides from the I.U.L. in August 1914. Gaining the Military Cross in the First World War, he served with the Guides Cavalry till 1939, and when Second-in-Command went to extra-regimental employ.

In August 1940 he was appointed Officer Commanding the Seychelles, where he was responsible for organizing the defence of the islands.

In March 1941 the cruiser *Dorsetshire* visited the islands, and on 5 March Eales asked to be taken on a reconnaissance flight in the seaplane from the cruiser, to inspect his defence arrangements. When the plane was coming down after the reconnaissance an explosion occurred in it, followed by a burst of flame. The plane crashed on the battery, resulting in the death of Eales and three officers of the Fleet Air Arm. After a solemn Requiem Mass in Mahé Cathedral, Eales was buried at sea with full military honours.

II. THE SERVICES OF DISTINGUISHED OFFICERS

BRIGADIER HECTOR CAMPBELL, C.B., D.S.O., M.V.O., *The Last Colonel of the Guides*

Brigadier Campbell was the last Colonel of the Corps of Guides—that is to say, the Colonel of the two Corps, which remained as one as far as the Honorary Colonelcy was concerned—having become the Colonel in August 1935 and being so till the end of the Raj. His family connections with the Corps were very great. Born in Mardan, he was the son of Major-General R. B. Campbell, C.B., the seventh Commandant of the Corps, while his maternal uncle was General Sir Frederick Campbell, K.C.B., D.S.O., who commanded the Infantry from 1895 to 1899. Joining the Gordon Highlanders in 1897 from Sandhurst, he served with them through the Tirah campaign, including the struggle for the Chagru Kotal and the storming of Dargai, and the withdrawal down the Bara. He was posted to the Guides in 1898. He served in the China War (Boxer) of 1900 with the 1st Sikhs (P.F.F.), and in 1904 became Adjutant of the Guides Infantry till 1908, during which period (1906) he was in charge of the King's orderly officers, being created an M.V.O. for the service. In 1914 he commanded the Infantry in the attack on the Malandri Pass in Buner (D.S.O.). In the First World War, he was in the defence of the Suez Canal (1914-15) and the fighting at Anzac (Gallipoli) with the 1st (K.G.O.) Sikhs, commanded columns in Sinai and the 20th Brigade before and at the third Battle of Gaza, and took part in various operations in Palestine with the Anzacs, including the advance on Amman. Back to the Guides, he was commandant of the 2nd Battalion from 1921 to 1926, and from 1926 to 1930 was Recruiting Officer in the Delhi–Lucknow area. In 1931 he became Military Adviser-in-Chief to the Indian States Forces till 1935. Next year he received the gratifying appointment of Colonel of Q.V.O. Corps of Guides, Cavalry and Infantry, for which he was so eminently qualified.

Lieutenant-General Sir Kenneth McLeod, K.C.I.E., C.B., D.S.O., p.s.c.

The services of Lieutenant-General Sir Kenneth McLeod were distinguished both in India and Europe. Typical of the story of those who redeemed the fallen India, he was the fourth in the generations of the McLeods of Ulinish in Skye to have served in the Army, the third to have served in the armies of India, and the third to have attained to General's rank. His record is a striking instance of the variety and versatility that Army service affords and demands. His first commission was in 1903, and he joined the Guides in 1905 and was Adjutant of the Cavalry from 1910–14. When the First World War broke out he went to France with the Lahore Division, was with the Lucknow Cavalry Brigade, also G.S.O.3 of the X Army Corps and Brigade-Major of the 95th Infantry Brigade of the 5th (British) Division. He was wounded on the Somme, and subsequently served as G.S.O.2 with both the XIII and XI Army Corps.

In 1917 McLeod returned to India at Army Headquarters, and he rejoined the Guides Cavalry in Mesopotamia, being acting Commandant. He later officiated as commander of the 11th Cavalry Brigade till ordered in 1920 to the Staff College, Camberley, after which he served awhile as G.S.O.3 at the War Office (1921–22) till he returned to Camberley as G.S.O.2 of the Directing Staff (1923–25), rejoining the Guides Cavalry in 1926, becoming their Commandant in 1928 till 1932. From that appointment he went to the command of the Secunderabad Cavalry Brigade in 1933 and commanded the Risalpur Cavalry Brigade, 1934–36, when he was promoted Major-General. In 1937 he became D.A. and Q.M.G. of Northern Command, and from 1938 to 1941 commanded the Force in Burma. Was at the Imperial Defence College, 1932.

During his tenure at the War Office he attended Mr. Lloyd George at the Supreme Council in Paris, on the Turko-Greek question, and the War Council (Marshal Foch) as representative of the Turco-Greek section at the War Office. He also attended the Turkish Peace Conference at Lausanne, at the revision of the Turkish Peace Treaty, as part of the British delegation under Lord Curzon in 1922.

After his retirement, he served in the Mediterranean theatre as Commissioner of the Joint War Organization of British Red Cross and Order of St. John (1945–46). This may well be summed up as an astounding record for any army officer, let alone an officer of the Indian Army and the Punjab Frontier Force.

Major-General A. V. Hammond, C.B., D.S.O., p.s.c.

The services of General Hammond again illustrate the succession of generations to serve in India, he being the fourth, and like Brigadier Campbell intimately connected with the Guides. His father was the famous Colonel Sir Arthur Hammond, V.C., K.C.B., D.S.O., eighth Commandant of the Corps, who earned the V.C. at Kabul in 1881.

General Hammond was first appointed to the I.U.L. in 1911 and attached to the 2nd Royal West Kent Regiment for the usual year, joining the Guides in 1912. After war service on the North-West Frontier in 1915, he was attached to the 32nd Lancers in Mesopotamia as squadron commander and was Adjutant of the Guides Cavalry, 1918–21. He was at the Staff College, Quetta, 1925–26; Staff Officer to the Major-General, Cavalry, 1927–28; Brigade-major, Bareilly Brigade, 1928–32, and after being Commandant of the Guides Cavalry for 1936–39, was G.S.O.1 at the War Office, 1939–40, covering the outbreak of the War. He was G.S.O.1 at Army Headquarters, India (1940–41), when he was posted to command the 123rd Indian Infantry Brigade (1941–43) and during 1943–46 was President of the Selection Board, G.H.Q., India, having himself been promoted Major-General in 1943 (with seniority 1942), and for 1944–45 commanded the Lucknow District, retiring in 1947. He earned a Brevet Majority and Lieutenant-Colonelcy, and in 1943 was appointed A.D.C. to the King. For his services in the Second World War he received the D.S.O. and, in 1944, the C.B.

His war tally of active service included the North-West Frontier (1915), the First World War, Mesopotamia, 1917–20 (Despatches), North-West Persia, 1920–21, and in the Second World War against the Japs in Assam and Aracan, 1942–43 (D.S.O.).

We now come to the services of the Brigadiers, most of whom have had their military prospects, which their endeavours had earned them, cut short by the extraordinary policy of the "Quit India" and the way it was handled.

The Services of Brigadier J. H. Gradidge, C.B.E.

Brigadier Gradidge began at the beginning, in that he joined the North Somerset Yeomanry in 1914, becoming a Second-Lieutenant the same year, and in 1916 was transferred to the 5th Dorsets in France as a Captain, going to the Indian Army in 1917. Here he joined the 14th Lancers' depot in India, and that regiment in Mesopotamia in 1918, whence next year he was appointed to the Guides Cavalry. He went to the Cavalry School at Saugor in 1922 and was appointed Cavalry Instructor to the Iraq Army in 1924, and Chief Instructor of the Iraq Cavalry, with the local rank of Colonel, in 1927, rejoining the Guides Cavalry in 1929, and in 1936 became Military Adviser, Southern Indian States Forces, with the rank of Lieutenant-Colonel. From 1939–42 he was Commandant of the Guides Cavalry, and in 1942 was promoted to Colonel and took command of the Indian reinforcements at G.H.Q., Middle East Forces. In 1942 he took over the Reinforcement Command of the Fourteenth Army in Burma, with the rank of Brigadier, and in 1945 went to similar duty at Singapore. He received the O.B.E. for services with the Iraq Army against the Kurds, and the C.B.E. for service in Burma, being mentioned in General Slim's despatches. His campaigns were the First World War, with the 5th Dorsets in France and the 14th Lancers in Mesopotamia; while in the Second World War they were in Iraq, North Africa and Burma.

Brigadier Gradidge was permitted to retire on compassionate grounds in 1946.

The Services of Brigadier "Pat" Macnamara, D.S.O., p.s.c.

Brigadier Pat Macnamara joined the Guides with a sad and glorious connection, for he was the son of Second-Lieutenant C. R. Macnamara, Guides Infantry, killed in action, and was commissioned in the I.U.L., joining the Guides Infantry in August 1923. After many years of regimental service he entered the Staff College, Quetta, and then became G.S.O.3 (Intelligence) at the Northern Command in India in 1939, and Brigade-major, Peshawar Brigade. In 1940 he was appointed Instructor at the Quetta Staff College and in 1942 G.S.O.1 at Headquarters, 10th Army (PAI Force), after a course at Cairo. In 1943 he took over command of the 3rd/5th Punjab Regiment in the 27th (and later 21st) Brigade (8th Indian Division) and then to train in Syria.

The Division embarked for Italy in September 1943, and were in action at the River Trigno. In 1944 they were at the final action of Cassino and the advance to the Plains of Lombardy. In January 1945 he was appointed to command the 17th Infantry Brigade of the 8th Indian Division, and took part in all the final operations in North Italy up to Padua, when the Division was ordered back to India. In 1946, when the Division was broken up, he took over the Brigade command at Poona and finally at Amritsar, whence he retired. In September 1944 he was awarded the D.S.O. for the attack on the Gothic Line, when he was wounded by a shell splinter. Twice mentioned in despatches.

The Services of Brigadier K. A. Garrett, M.C., p.s.c.

Brigadier K. A. Garrett served but for a short while with the Guides, having been appointed Commandant of the Infantry on the death of Lieutenant-Colonel Pat Grant in Waziristan. He had had a long and distinguished career with the 51st Sikhs, which he joined from the I.U.L. in 1914, having been commissioned from Sandhurst and attached for a few months to the Royal Sussex Regiment. He served with the 51st Sikhs in Mesopotamia, being wounded and receiving an immediate M.C. He went to Palestine and Syria with the Regiment and was decorated with the Order of the Nile (4th Class).

Again, in 1923, he served with the 51st in Waziristan, and in 1930 went to the Staff College at Quetta, whence he was posted to the 53rd Sikhs, but never joined them. As Brigade-major, Rawalpindi Brigade (1934–36), he served in the Mohmand operations (Despatches) and in Waziristan, and became Commandant of the Guides Infantry on 5 October 1937. In September 1940 he left the Corps to command the 15th Infantry Brigade. In 1941 he served in Malaya, where he was wounded, and in 1942–43 was A.A.G. in the Central Area in India and commanded the Allahabad Area from September, 1943–46 (Brigadier).

The Services of Brigadier C. P. J. Prioleau.

Lieutenant Prioleau received his first commission in 1917—on the auspicious date of 18 June, and a few days later was posted to the Guides Cavalry with whom he served in Mesopotamia and Persia (1917–20), being wounded and mentioned in despatches. From 1922–26 he was Adjutant of the Guides Cavalry and in 1927 was A.D.C. to General Sir Robert Cassels when G.O.C. Peshawar and G.O.C.-in-Chief, Northern Command. From 1928–30 he was staff officer to the Major-General of Cavalry and Instructor of Equitation to the Cavalry School.

In 1936 he was appointed Military Adviser to the Southern Indian States Forces and from 1936 to 1940 was A. and Q.M.G. of the Hyderabad State Forces. In 1941 he left the Guides to raise the 45th Cavalry, and in 1944 he was appointed Commandant (Brigadier) of the Fighting Vehicles School and Officers' Training School at Ahmednagar, and in 1946 Director of Armoured Corps, India, retiring in 1948. Brigadier Prioleau was thus the leading spirit in the important war training and organization of the mechanized fighting units of the Army in India.

The Services of Brigadier G. V. L. Coleman, p.s.c.

Brigadier Coleman joined the Indian Army in October 1918, during the First World War, and was almost immediately posted to the Guides. He was Adjutant of the

Infantry, 1926-29, and went to the Staff College, Quetta in 1931, returning to the Corps till appointed G.S.O.3 in 1934, and Brigade-major in 1939, and in 1941 was again appointed to the General Staff as G.S.O.2, becoming a G.S.O.1 in 1942 and Assistant Major-General of the Ordnance in 1943 with rank of Colonel. He was A.G. (Co-ordination) in 1944, and in 1946 Director-General of Manpower (Brigadier).

In 1947 he closed his long years of war administration in India as Adjutant-General's member of the Armed Forces Reconstruction Committee (1947).

THE SERVICES OF LIEUTENANT-COLONEL M. H. H. BAILY, D.S.O. (TEMPORARY BRIGADIER).

Lieutenant-Colonel M. H. H. Baily was first commissioned in the Indian Army in July 1921, attached to the 2nd Gloucester Regiment and joined the 129th D.C.O. Baluchis, whence, in September 1923, he was appointed to the Guides Infantry.

From 1932-35 he served with the Southern Waziristan Scouts, being their Adjutant from 1933 on. He was promoted Major in August 1938, and was sent to the Force in Norway in 1940 as an officer experienced in mountain warfare, as described in Chapter VIII, where he served with great distinction, receiving the D.S.O. From 1943-46 he was Commandant of the Guides Infantry and in 1946 Commandant of the Zhob Militia. In 1947 he became Inspector-General and Secretary, Frontier Corps, N.W.F., with rank of Brigadier, till the curtain of the Raj fell.

THE SERVICES OF BRIGADIER W. H. BLOOD, M.V.O.

Brigadier Blood was first commissioned in 1905. After a year with the 18th Royal Irish Regiment at Rawalpindi, he joined the Guides in 1906. He was an Instructor at the Cavalry School, Saugor, 1913-14.

From August 1914 to October 1918 he was Adjutant, Guides Cavalry. During that period he was Staff Captain, 3rd Infantry Brigade, in August 1915, for operations on the Buner border. He went with the Regiment to Mesopotamia in 1917 and took part in the operations of the 15th Division and 11th Cavalry Brigade at Khan Bagdadi, Slus Band and Ana, and was mentioned in despatches. Brigadier Blood then returned to India and was appointed I.A.Q.M.G., 1st (Peshawar) Division, taking part in the Afghan operations, 1919, and receiving a brevet majority. He was Brigade Major, Sialkote Cavalry Brigade, from March till December, 1920.

During the visit of H.R.H. The Prince of Wales in 1921-22 he was A.Q.M.G. on special duty at G.H.Q. and was awarded the M.V.O. After three years with the Regiment he became Staff Officer to the Military Adviser-in-Chief, I.S.F., from 1925 to 1928.

From March till November 1930, Brigadier Blood officiated in command of the Guides Cavalry and was made brevet lieutenant-colonel after operations against the Red Shirts in the Peshawar District.

He commanded the Guides Cavalry from 1931 to 1936, when he retired and became secretary of the National Horse Breeding and Show Society of India until 1944.

Rejoining the Army in 1940, he was Administrative Commandant, Delhi Area, until May, 1942, when he was transferred to G.H.Q. (India) as Chief Administrative Officer, with the rank of brigadier. He retired for the second time in March, 1944, and became Civil Passage Controller and Deputy Secretary, Defence Department, Governor of India, until September, 1945, when he returned to England.

CHAPTER XV

PAKISTAN POSTSCRIPT

THE DIVISION OF THE KING EMPEROR'S EMPIRE AND ARMY—THE ARMY OF PAKISTAN—THE FRONTIER FORCE REGIMENTAL CENTRES—THE GUIDES INFANTRY AT RAZMAK—THE MARCH OUT FROM RAZMAK—THE TWO GUIDE CORPS, CAVALRY AND INFANTRY, AT KOHAT.

THIS Volume—Part II of the History of the Guides—was intended to close when the British Raj handed over to India—an undivided India, which not very wise politicians thought possible. But in view of the pitiful sequel, and the constitution of Pakistan as a dominion with its own army and the fact that George MacMunn stayed awhile to rebuild the Guides Infantry, this Pakistan postscript has been added, carrying on the story till May 1948. The fact that a British General commands the Pakistan Army for a time makes this brief outline the more interesting to the Officers of the late Indian Army and especially to those of the Punjab Frontier Force.

General Sir Frank Messervy, who was commanding the Northern Army, had undertaken to command the Pakistan Army in the first instance, and was faced with the vexing problem of cutting every regiment in two with all the inefficiency involved. Before this took place he contributed complete units to Headquarters for a "Boundary"[49] force of sorts under Major-General Rees, in case there was to be trouble owing to the wicked haste with which politicians had decided to divide India, showing an ignorance of the problem abnormal even among politicians of that type. The sequel showed this force, though not yet upset by the separation of Muslims and Hindus, to be sadly inadequate for the task. It operated under the orders of the Supreme Commander. The storm of hatred between Muslim and Hindu, long quiescent and assuaged under the British Raj, broke with an unexpected and incredible fury and bloodshed, destroying hundreds of thousands of people of all ages and sexes, and also, for the time being, magnificent revenue-producing canal land which British capital had constructed and which made the Punjab a garden. This terrible tragedy, not even paralleled by the mass massacres of Ghengis Khan, will throw for many a generation a sad pall over the knowledge or wisdom of the British Cabinet, the Government of India and its politicians, and the disregard of the advice of those experienced Britons who had at any rate an inkling of what might happen. The outcome was one which no one could have believed possible.

Naturally the effect of the massacres meant the uprooting of millions of refugees in their hurry to escape—Hindus and Muslims—among them the people who have so magnificently served the King Emperor all over the world. The hurry and sense of powerlessness under which General Messervy had to work can well be imagined, while all the time the

---

[49] Mr. Churchill has declared that there should have been an element of British troops therein.

few remaining British officers leaving the units under the arrangements previously made were coming through to Europe with their tales of bloodshed. The letters of some of the officers of the Guides Infantry are pitiful beyond belief.

Then, on the top of all this, came two more separate, ill-winded pirns which most undoubtedly should have been foreseen and provided against. The tribal frontier runs very close to Kashmir and, obviously not at the instance of the Pakistan Government, the frontier tribes, stirred by fierce Muslim propagandists and by reports of massacres of Muslims in Jammu, swarmed into northern Kashmir to slay and loot.

To make things worse, another Muslim movement began in Jammu and Poonch. Just to make it quite plain, it may be stated that the realm of Jammu and Kashmir, whose ruler, a General in the British Army, had been prominent in London during the War Councils of the last war, consists of Kashmir on the far and northern side of the mountainous snow range of the Pir Punjal and of Jammu and Poonch amid the doons and lower hills on the Punjab side. Here there is considerable mingling of Muslim and Hindu, and from here so many of the best Dogras of the Imperial Army came. Dogras themselves are entirely charming and admirable people and actually count kin with many of the Muslims who intermingle with them. West of Jammu we have the tributary state of Poonch, a Dogra state, but with a considerable Muslim population, largely of a clan known as Sudans, who of late years have given most valuable military service. Stirred by the urge of Islam, they too broke into rebellion against the Maharajah who had joined the Indian Union rather than Pakistan. It was obviously the most difficult case in the whole of the break-up of India and should have been fully decided, militarily as well as politically, before the division. The story of the little kingdoms and khanates on the hitherside of the Pamirs, whose control and protection were carried out by the Agency at Gilgit, and the swamping of the Kashmir border by tribesmen, has not been told to the public. The arrangements for the transfer of power to a united India legislated for continuance. In the division the work of forty years for Indian safety has been poured down the drain. The irony of it was that, speaking generally, access by any sort of road to Kashmir or Jammu from "India," except by ill-constructed tracks, was non-existent, and the result is still the one running sore which has yet to be healed (1949).

Incidentally, as already mentioned, in all these troubles, though Government have refrained from telling the public what has really happened, a good many English people lost their lives—a matter which some years ago would have stirred John Bull to the depths. Lieutenant-Colonel and Mrs. Dykes were killed at Baramullah by the tribesmen and their child thrown down a well; two R.E. officers were killed near Amritsar; and, so far as the Guides were concerned, there was a terrible tragedy. The Guides Cavalry were, as just related, at Ahmednagar in the Deccan and were allotted to the Pakistan Army and ordered to move to the Frontier. In the ordinary course of routine, Major Reid of the Corps with two Muslim non-commissioned officers was dispatched ahead to take over lines, etc., at Dera Ismail Khan on the Indus. They were *never heard of again*. It is presumed that they were killed somewhere in the Jat country below Delhi, and it may be assumed that they lost their lives in protecting some other unfortunates.

There has appeared in the *Journal of the Royal United Service Institution* an account of the Punjab tragedy by Lieutenant-Colonel M. C. A. Henniker, R.E.,[50] who, having taken part in the inauguration of Pakistan at Karachi by the Viceroy and having practically passed through the whole of Pakistan at this time, including a visit to Kashmir, describes the immense difficulties with which General Rees's Boundary Force contended. He also describes the death of the two R.E. officers referred to when a Hindu and Muslim Army formation fell out. It was never known what happened to them; presumably they lost their lives in trying to prevent this fracas. Nothing could be more pathetic or indeed more agonizing than this story.

This book, however, is not the place to record the details and cataclysms of the hasty division; but one cannot envisage the forming of the Army of Pakistan, which should have run on so peaceably, without recognizing these cataclysms which have never been paralleled in the world before. As, however, the last screams died away, and cholera and malaria among the refugees supervened, the machinery of the Pakistan Army, thus interrupted, began to work to reorganize the forces that were to defend India from the north-west and restore order on the borders. How arduous that work was is only intelligible if we realize that every unit was cut in two and awaited transferred Muslim squadrons, companies, etc., or odd drafts; while the transfer of their Hindu components to Hindustan, from the Frontier, in the face of excited tribesmen, as already described, presented unforeseen difficulties and tragic incidents.

The Army of Pakistan

The elaborate arrangements for handing over an all-India, a demobilized but adequate army, that Field-Marshal Sir Claude Auchinleck and his staff had so long worked at, as stated, had naturally been destroyed by the decision to form two Dominions.

The cutting of all mixed units into two meant that in Pakistan there were practically few cavalry regiments or battalions fit to go into the field, which made it difficult to carry out the Dominion's policy when the tribesmen from the Frontier marched on Kashmir.

In 1948 the Pakistan Command was taken over by General Sir Douglas G. Gracey, K.C.I.E., C.B., C.B.E., M.C., in pursuance of the Qaid-i-Azam's (Mr. Jinnah's) policy of obtaining all the help possible from British officers. By this time the necessary moves and readjustments had taken place and unit commanders were engaged in rebuilding their units, brigade and regimental commanders being largely Muslim. The units of the Indian Army allotted to Pakistan on partition are given in detail so that they may be recognized.

It will be seen that six battalions of the F.F. Regiment (one Paratroop) and six of the F.F. Rifles are included, as also, of course, the Guides Cavalry.

---

[50] "Early Days of Pakistan," by Lieutenant-Colonel M. C. A. Henniker, D.S.O., O.B.E., M.C., R.E., *Royal United Service Institution Journal*, February 1948.

PAKISTAN POSTSCRIPT

Major units allotted to Pakistan on partition

Armoured Corps
- 5th Horse (Armoured Regiment)
- 6th Lancers (Light Armoured Reconnaissance Regiment)
- 10th Guides Cavalry (Light Armoured Reconnaissance Regiment)
- 11th Cavalry (Light Armoured Reconnaissance Regiment)
- 13th Lancers (Armoured Regiment)
- 19th Lancers (Armoured Regiment)

Artillery:
- 21st Mountain Regiment (four batteries)
- 2nd Survey Battery
- 38th Medium Regiment (two batteries)
- 3rd Field Regiment (three batteries)
- 4th Field Regiment (three batteries)
- 5th Field Regiment (three batteries)
- 33rd Anti-Tank Regiment (three batteries)
- 25th L.A.A. Regiment (three batteries)
- 18th H.A.A. Regiment (three batteries)

Infantry:
- 1st/1st Punjab Regiment
- 2nd/1st Punjab Regiment
- 3rd/1st Punjab Regiment (Para.)
- 5th/1st Punjab Regiment
- 15th/1st Punjab Regiment
- 1st F.F. Regiment (Para.)
- 2nd F.F. Regiment
- 3rd F.F. Regiment
- 4th F.F. Regiment
- 5th F.F. Regiment
- 8th F.F. Regiment
- 1st F.F. Rifles
- 2nd F.F. Rifles
- 4th F.F. Rifles
- 5th F.F. Rifles
- 6th F.F. Rifles
- 9th F.F. Rifles
- 1st/14th Punjab Regiment
- 2nd/14th Punjab Regiment
- 3rd/14th Punjab Regiment
- 4th/14th Punjab Regiment
- 1st/15th Punjab Regiment (M.G.)
- 2nd/15th Punjab Regiment (M.G.)
- 3rd/15th Punjab Regiment (M.G.)
- 4th/15th Punjab Regiment
- 6th/15th Punjab Regiment (M.G.)
- 1st/8th Punjab Regiment
- 2nd/8th Punjab Regiment
- 3rd/8th Punjab Regiment
- 4th/8th Punjab Regiment

5th/8th Punjab Regiment
6th/8th Punjab Regiment
8th/8th Punjab Regiment
1st Baluch Regiment
2nd Baluch Regiment
3rd Baluch Regiment (Para.)
4th Baluch Regiment
5th Baluch Regiment
7th Baluch Regiment
17th Baluch Regiment
1st/16th Punjab Regiment
2nd/16th Punjab Regiment
3rd/16th Punjab Regiment (Para.)
4th/16th Punjab Regiment
7th/16th Punjab Regiment

The two F.F. Regiments are those that belong to this story and a brief account of their organization follows, and then the dramatic event of the withdrawal from Razmak and the true story of the inception of that Fortress.

The Frontier Force Regimental Centres

Under the arrangements for the Pakistan Army the Centre of the Frontier Force Regiment and the Frontier Force Rifles was established at the pleasant cantonment of Abbottabad, where the Frontier Force Rifles' centre had always been, and the battalions were commanded and stationed as follows:

Unit	C.O.	Station
Centre	Lieutenant-Colonel E. B. Blackburn	Abbottabad
1st F.F. Regiment	Lieutenant-Colonel Khalid Jan	Lahore Cantonment
2nd F.F. Regiment	Lieutenant-Colonel D. B. Sedgwick	Mir Ali
3rd F.F. Regiment	Lieutenant-Colonel Aziz-ud-Din (F.F. Rifles)	Lahore Cantonment
4th F.F. Regiment	Lieutenant-Colonel P. C. Gupta, M.C.	Punjab various
5th F.F. Regiment	Lieutenant-Colonel G. A. MacMunn	Razmak
8th F.F. Regiment	Lieutenant-Colonel C. W. Pearson, M.C.	Dacca

It is interesting to note that Lieutenant-Colonel Khalid Jan is the nephew of Sir Hissam-ud-Din, who used to be in the second battalion. Lieutenant-Colonel Aziz-ud-Din joined as a sepoy in 1933 and worked his way up to his present rank, an entirely desirable career which, it is hoped, may continue in many others.

All old Guides will remember the trophy that was carried down from Mundah in 1895 on the shoulders of *jawans*, and known as the Mundah Gun, that stood in front of the Kabul Memorial at Mardan. When the Guides left in 1940 the gun was transferred to the Regimental Centre at Sialkot, and when the Centre went to Abbottabad in 1948 the gun went with them. It has lately been presented by the Corps to the Pakistan Military Academy at Kakul.

The Guides Infantry at Razmak

With the Guides Infantry, like the Cavalry, broken in two, the reconstruction of the battalion was vigorously taken in hand, in measures that could only be tentative. But the urgent matter was the getting of the Sikhs away in safety. The destruction of the *Pax Britannica* and this unbelievable folly of the hasty division of the Punjab had produced the vast massacres—to make a politicians' holiday—and it had re-raised the Sikh and Muslim enmity that had lain low in the centuries of British rule. The Frontier had sworn to have the lives of the Sikhs.

It has been related in Chapter XII how the Dogra company from the Guides had been sent by mistake to the 3rd Grenadiers at Thal in the Kurram, and remained with them till the battalion was withdrawn, early in September 1947, to Hindustan. This unit arrived safely by train as far as Kohat, but as it proceeded towards Kushalgarh on the Indus, which runs below the hills occupied by the Adam Khel Afridis and other Pathans, the train was attacked near Gumbat by a large Muslim mob. The Dogra company was in the thick of it and put up a fine fight, the Muslims being beaten off with heavy loss; but, alas, it had six killed and twelve wounded. "Bob" Shebbeare, formerly of the Guides and grand-nephew of the Delhi V.C., was in command of the Grenadiers and was wounded in the foot.

The Muslim companies at Razmak were terribly shocked at this occurrence following on the heel of massacres in the Punjab, and the question of safe evacuation of the Sikh companies was now a serious matter. For three weeks they were held in readiness to move at a couple of hours' notice. Fortunately a farewell *bara-khana* to the men and a mess party to the V.C.Os. had been given early in the proceedings.

On 9 October the Regiment went out on road opening, on the most dangerous section, that from Razmak Narai to Razani and no one but their Colonel knew that when they returned the Sikhs would be gone. In hooded lorries they were rushed through. George MacMunn dare not even wring the hand of his old friend the Subadar-major as he went out with the Battalion, and dared not wave to them as the convoy passed below him along the road. When the Battalion got back to camp he was very thankful to hear they had arrived safely at Miranshah, whence they were flown to Chaklala near Rawalpindi, eventually to be sent, to begin with, to Jubbulpore and attached to the 7th/11th Sikhs.

During this long wait at Razmak the Sikhs had been very steady, and stood the strain admirably, though with no news of their families amid the holocausts in the Western Punjab. However, the Commandant had been able to get a goodwill Muslim party through, who had brought back reports of their safety. Mehal Singh, the Subadar-major now commanding the company, as the officers Vehra and Malhautra had gone to the Gurkhas, had written that all was well.

In most of the corps the elimination of the Sikh and Hindu squadrons and companies had been followed by the transfer of Muslim companies from Hindustan units, and this had occurred in the case of the squadrons of the Cavalry. In the Infantry, however, this was not possible, and they were made up of recruits from the Centre, drafts from the Rajput Regiment, hurried up to Razmak after a very few weeks' training. The efforts to make them into two companies, naturally mingled with some of the older hands, was not unsuccessful, for their behaviour during the somewhat trying march out of Razmak was very creditable. Many of the worst "hats" among the tribes, however, were busy in Kashmir or resting content with their loot.

The March Out from Razmak

The time had now come to abandon the magnificent upland Cantonment of Razmak, concerning which many ignorant statements have occurred, and it has been referred to as "The Indian Frontier Folly."

Nothing could be farther from the truth, and an outline of the story is worth recording and we must go back to the post-Mutiny period to understand it. During the Mutiny, with many of the Frontier regiments at Delhi and Lucknow, the tribal raids into British territory had been considerable, and in the early sixties a punitive expedition, with severe fighting, took place. Ever since then the tribesmen, especially the Mahsuds, have been most aggressive, and in 1894 staged a quite unnecessary attack on the Commission delimitating the boundary between Afghanistan and India. Again, in 1897, the great Frontier revolt, much stirred by the Islamic excitement of the Graeco-Turkish War, opened with a surprise attack by one of the Wazir tribes on a British force.

During the First World War, Mahsud raids on the settled border tracts had developed into invasion, the repression of which had resulted in very heavy fighting with the raw Indian units available to meet them. When the war was over, a severe campaign was necessary to bring them to their senses. It is to be remembered that through the years, better and better hand-arms had found their way into tribal hands, so that every other man had a breech-loading rifle.

So the Government of India put its thinking cap on, the General Staff drawing up a memorandum showing the number of raids, the number of punitive expeditions, their cost and the toll of army lives. They pointed out that the Frontier cantonments of Bannu, Dera Ismail Khan and, to a lesser degree, Kohat, on the Indus level, were appallingly hot and malarious in summer, and no place to keep troops fit, while there were plateaux in Waziristan running up to 7,000 ft. where troops could live and train in the best conditions.

The Civil Government were anxious to protect the territories within their border, stating moreover that the tribal outrages were to some extent due to over-population. If profitable developments were undertaken, with the entirely wanting hospital arrangements introduced, a great amelioration might be expected. It was also suggested that something in the way of medical treatment was our duty. Mission hospitals at Bannu tried to help and were adept at grafting noses on women whose husbands had cut them off in jealousy.

The Frontier experts said that the only way to peace was to get behind the tribes— as Sandeman had been able to do in the days of the pacification of British Baluchistan.

And so the Government of India, with the approval of His Majesty's Government, decided to make a brigade cantonment on the pleasant Razmak plateau. It was well done with good huts for a British battalion and the Indian troops. An English Church was built, with canteen and cinema, mosque and Gurdwara and *mandr* for the Hindus.

In that very church, the British officers held the special service described in Chapter XII to pray for the success and happiness of Pakistan, realizing, perhaps, that Islam is in some respects a desert derivative of Judaism and Christianity.

And that is the story of Razmak which it pleased newspaper men to call the "greatest monastery in the world," ignorant that leave to their homes for all and sundry was a regular occurrence.

There were two objections—one that troops were locked up in a position from which they could not be withdrawn if need be, the other the considerable expense, but the Government preferred to face this in return for a peaceful border. In those days, none dreamed that mishandled politics would destroy their great work, or that our Punjabi soldier classes would be allowed to massacre each other, with their women and children, to make a politicians' holiday.

For fourteen years all went well; the tribesmen waxed prosperous, the chiefs grew wealthy, when Government's failure to deal promptly with the Red-Shirt mischief was followed by the prolonged Waziristan trouble of 1936–37. During the Second World War the country remained very quiet.

It was not possible for Pakistan, with its small army and embarrassed finances to continue the occupation, and it was decided to hand over this magnificent cantonment to the care of the tribal militia and the political officers.

The end, therefore, was the "March out." How the fortress (for such it really was) was handed over to Pakistan has already been described.

The actual "March out" of the Pakistan Army was colourfully described in the British Press. It was a remarkable scene, and one accompanied by some anxiety, lest the occasion should prove too exciting for the Wazir tribes. The Divisional Commander, Major-General Le Fleming, had come up to command and, with the Brigadier, carefully rehearsed the military precautions necessary to secure points and passes from which an ambush could be laid or a concerted attack made. Before the day came there had been weeks of evacuation of the military stores of the cantonment, and especially the large quantities of ammunition, by carefully picqueted convoys, and mouths of the tribesmen watching on the hills watered! Rifle ammunition at two rupees a round was sheer border treasure.

At last the day came (15 December) on which the Infantry Brigade, and its attendant artillery, set out, with its impedimenta reduced to a minimum, over the seventy-two miles of mountain pass to reach the old cantonment of Bannu in the open plains. The Guides Infantry took their full share of picqueting, and the recruits behaved excellently.

So good were the arrangements that a few parting shots alone had greeted them and the troops in Bannu had little to do save to safeguard the passes of debouchment. Razmak, for good or evil, was evacuated and the Frontier back where the Sikh Raj had made it a century earlier.

The Two Guides Corps, Cavalry and Infantry, at Kohat

The Guides Infantry then marched on by the old Frontier road to the pleasant and famous Frontier station of Kohat, where in the spring of 1948, to their great joy, came the Guides Cavalry from their Indus cantonment of Dera Ismail Khan.

Life now passed in much the normal way. There were plenty of amenities for the rank and file, and the games of other days went on as usual. A combined Guides Mess was formed in the old Piffer Club. The order of dress for supper was to be uniform, dinner jacket or black *achkan*. At dinner, on guest nights, the King's health and that of Qaid-i-Azam were drunk. Cantonment life was naturally very different. A few British officers of various arms remained in the cantonment.

The Kashmir disturbances had of course much upset law and order in the trans-Indus cantonments, much to the concern of the Pakistan Government and that of the Frontier Province. Tribesmen returning to Waziristan or Tirah, laden with loot, would "loose off" their rifles in light-heartedness at any time of day or night. In January 1948 MacMunn went to Mardan in connection with the disposal of Guides memorials and records, meeting uniformed armed parties from the Trans-Swat Khanates marching as formed bodies for their share of Kashmir spoil. *Sic transit Pax Britannica.*

The Infantry at Kohat had their first job of any consequence—the pathetic one of going up to Kurram to bring away the survivors from a Hindu refugee camp of traders, clerks, etc., who had been waiting transfer, under the care of the efficient Kurram Militia (largely a Shiah corps). Unfortunately, this camp was attacked by Mongols from over the Afghan border, and despite a very stout resistance from the Militia, who punished the raiders severely, 130 of the Hindus were killed, 59 wounded and 69 women carried off. The Battalion with all its lorries got up to Thal and brought them all safely away. The older women had been recovered by the political officers, but not the younger ones!

In March, the Cavalry under Lieutenant-Colonel Raza arrived, and under the new Dominion the two corps found themselves united once again.

The Brigade was taken over by Brigadier Akbar Khan, whose lady came up from Pindi for the day and all the Muslim ladies in the station, who were out of *purdah*, were invited to a party at the Club to meet her, and announced their intentions of keeping the old social life of the club going.

In May 1948, George MacMunn handed over the Infantry to Lieutenant-Colonel Karim Dad, not hitherto known to the Guides, and himself took over G.S.O.1 of the 9th (Frontier) Division (Peshawar), now extending from Nowshera to Dera Ismail Khan. At Peshawar the Province was settling down; several English ladies were there in May 1948, and could go to the "Gallies" for summer residence.

The Pakistan border was now established, with the Frontier hills homogeneous in religion, though what hope that can give of peace only the future can show.

Now the story of the two units of Lumsden's and Henry Lawrence's Guides comes to an end with this outline of the Dominion's set-up; but we can see the old Guides spirit fain to remain, the officers the British have brought on grasping their responsibilities heartily; while Brigadier Hector Campbell's farewell message (Chapter XII) and the service in the Razmak Chapel are evidences which evince the good wishes given to Pakistan, as well as to the Sikhs and Dogras who have left them.

The Guides are dead! Long live the Guides!

In December 1949, the Director of Artillery with the Pakistan Army writes: "Mardan is now occupied by the Royal Pakistan Artillery, who are taking great care of the cantonment and mess."

APPENDIX I

The Victoria Cross

Award of the Victoria Cross to Captain Shebbeare, Delhi, 1857

In the original History the name of Captain R. H. Shebbeare was omitted from the Roll of those who had won the Cross, because the information was not available. It has now come to hand, and this officer's name heads the Roll in the new History.

"While the three assaulting columns were busily engaged inside the city with more or less success, the fortune of war went against us on the right. The Fourth Column, whose duty it was to clear the suburb of Kissengunj and enter the city by the Lahore Gate, met with a definite reverse. An advance through the tortuous suburbs was made without the support of artillery fire, which had been promised but failed to materialize. The consequence was that upon assaulting the foremost breastworks, the enemy, untouched by artillery fire, withheld their musketry fire until our troops were within fifty yards. They then poured a heavy and well-directed volley of fire into the Sirmoor Battalion of Gurkhas and the Guides, who suffered severely. An endeavour was made by the Guides, led by Captain Shebbeare, to storm a large loopholed courtyard in the suburb of Kissengunj. Twice Captain Shebbeare charged up to the wall, twice were the stormers driven back. He tried to organize a third attack, but one-third of the Europeans and many of the native soldiers had fallen. He then collected some men and covered the retreat of the column. He came out of the action with a bullet through his cheek and a bad scalp wound from another. For this act of gallantry Captain Shebbeare was awarded the Victoria Cross of which the second Regiment was to be so proud, when he commenced to raise them a month later.

"Shortly after the capture of Delhi, Captain Shebbeare wrote to his mother as follows :

" 'I had little time and less convenience for writing, but I wrote each time to tell you I was happy and well. You will also have seen my name twice in the list of wounded, which would rather alarm you as you did not receive my letters.

" 'I was wounded by three bullets on the 18th July, and again by one on the 14th September, but I am glad to say that I was not seriously hurt by any of them. In addition to these wounds, two musket balls went through my hat ; one while in the trenches at Hindu Rao's House and the other in Kissengunj on the 14th September. The first slightly grazed my scalp, giving me severe headache and making me very sick. The second cut through a very thick turban and knocked me down on my face, but without doing me any injury. I was hit oftener in the campaign than any other officer, I think, but was always so little hurt than my friends used to laugh and say I was made of india rubber !' "

The above account of the storming of Delhi and a letter from him to his mother are from the "History of the Sikh Pioneers," to the command of the 2nd Regiment of which he was soon after appointed.

THE GUIDES

AWARD OF THE VICTORIA CROSS TO THE LATE CAPTAIN G. MEYNELL.[51]

"The King has been graciously pleased to approve of the award of the Victoria Cross to the undermentioned officer:

"The late Captain Godfrey Meynell, M.C., 5th Battalion (Queen Victoria's Own Corps of Guides), 12th Frontier Force Regiment, Indian Army, for most conspicuous gallantry and extreme devotion to duty.

"On 29th September, 1935, while operating against the Mohmand tribesmen in the attack on Point 4080, Captain Meynell was Adjutant of the Battalion. In the final phase of the attack the Battalion Commander was unable to get information from his most forward troops. Captain Meynell went forward to ascertain the situation and found the forward troops on the objective, but involved in a struggle against an enemy vastly superior in numbers. Seeing the situation, he at once took over command of the men in this area. The enemy by this time was closing in on the position from three sides.

"Captain Meynell had at his disposal two Lewis guns and about 30 men. Although this party was maintaining heavy and accurate fire on the advancing enemy, the overwhelming numbers of the latter succeeded in reaching the position. Both the Lewis guns were damaged beyond repair and a fierce hand-to-hand struggle commenced. During the struggle Captain Meynell was mortally wounded and all his men were either killed or wounded.

"Throughout the action Captain Meynell endeavoured by all means to communicate the situation to Headquarters, but determined to hold on at all costs and encouraged his men to fight with him to the last. By so doing he inflicted on the enemy very heavy casualties which prevented them from exploiting their success.

"The fine example Captain Meynell set to his men, coupled with his determination to hold the position to the last, maintain the traditions of the Army and reflect the highest credit on the fallen officer and his comrades."

Captain Godfrey Meynell, M.C., was the eldest son of Brigadier-General Godfrey Meynell, of Meynell Langley, near Derby. Born on 20 May 1904, he was educated at a private school at Norris Hill, was elected to college at Eton, and passed out of Sandhurst thirteenth in his year. A gifted linguist, he specialized in the languages of North India and joined the Guides in 1926. He was wounded while serving with the Tochi Scouts in Waziristan in 1930. He rejoined the Guides and subsequently won the M.C. in operations on the Frontier. He had been adjutant of the Guides for three years. Captain Meynell left a widow and one son, who are both in India.

Extract from "The Times," Friday 27 December 1935.

---

[51] Captain Meynell's name was included in the supplementary lists in Volume I of the Guides History, but is included here in the period to which it belongs.

APPENDIX II

A.—Colonels of The Guides.

B.—Commandants and Risaldar-Majors (Cavalry).

C.—Commandants and Subadar-Majors (Infantry).

A.—COLONELS (HONORARY) OF THE GUIDES (VACATED AT 70 YEARS OF AGE)

	From	To
Major-General C. Stewart, C.B.	13/5/04	12/1/28
Major-General Sir George Younghusband, K.C.M.G., K.C.I.E.	31/1/28	8/7/39
Lieut.-General Sir Raleigh Egerton, K.C.B., K.C.I.E.	9/7/29	24/9/30
Brigadier-General G. M. Baldwin, D.S.O.	25/9/30	23/3/35
Brigadier Hector Campbell	30/8/35	—/8/47

B.—COMMANDANTS AND RISALDAR-MAJORS, CAVALRY.

CAVALRY COMMANDANTS FROM 1922

Rank and Name	From	To	Remarks
Lieut.-Colonel C. W. Carey	10/10/20	10/9/24	—
Lieut.-Colonel H. Dening	11/9/24	10/9/28	—
Lieut.-Colonel D. K. McLeod, D.S.O.	11/9/28	10/9/32	Eventually Lieutenant-General, K.C.I.E., C.B., D.S.O.
Lieut.-Colonel W. H. Blood, M.V.O.	11/9/32	10/9/36	Eventually Brigadier.
Lieut.-Colonel A. V. Hammond	16/10/36	16/3/39	Eventually Major-General, C.B., D.S.O.
Lieut.-Colonel J. H. Gradidge, O.B.E.	17/7/39	25/5/42	Eventually Brigadier.
Lieut.-Colonel F. Walton	26/5/42	5/10/44	—
Lieut.-Colonel W. Eliott-Lockhart	6/10/44	Till end of Raj.	—

OFFICIATING COMMANDANTS

Major J. H. Gradidge, O.B.E.	11/9/36	15/10/36	—
Major F. Walton	17/3/39	16/7/39	—

RISALDAR-MAJORS

Nur Khan, Sardar Bahadur, O.B.I.	1/11/21	31/10/27	Punjabi Musalman.
Zardad Khan, Sardar Bahadur, O.B.I., I.D.S.M.	1/11/27	14/9/32	Yuzafzai Pathan.
Rattan Chand, Sardar Bahadur, O.B.I.	15/9/32	14/9/37	Katoch, Dogra Rajput, later M.B.E.
Mohammad Tuhair Khan	15/9/37	12/3/39	Killed in a motor accident on 12/3/39. Pathan, Akora Khattak.
Sardara Singh Bahadur, O.B.I.	13/3/39	7/2/42	Jat Sikh, Malwa. Granted English Commission and later released as T./Major.
Shankar Singh, Sardar Bahadur, O.B.I.	8/2/42	9/1/47	Dogra Rajput, Jammu.
Faqir Mohammad	10/1/47	Serving.	Yuzafzai Pathan.

C.—COMMANDANTS AND SUBADAR-MAJORS, INFANTRY

INFANTRY COMMANDANTS

Rank and Name	From	To
Brigadier-General I. V. Battye, C.B., D.S.O.	5/1/22	31/10/25
Lieut.-Colonel F. K. Hensley	1/11/25	27/4/28
Colonel D. G. Sandeman, C.I.E.	28/4/28	15/8/31
Lieut.-Colonel N. H. Prendergast, D.S.O., M.V.O.	16/8/31	16/8/35
Lieut.-Colonel P. Grant (killed in action at head of Battalion)	10/11/35	23/6/37
Lieut.-Colonel K. A. Garrett, M.C.	5/10/37	6/9/40
Lieut.-Colonel E. P. Rich	7/9/40	15/5/43
Lieut.-Colonel M. H. H. Baily, D.S.O.	16/5/43	14/1/46
Lieut.-Colonel G. A. MacMunn	15/7/46	7/2/47
Lieut.-Colonel A. R. E. Pollard, O.B.E.	8/2/47	17/5/47
Lieut.-Colonel G. A. MacMunn	18/8/47	18/5/48

SUBADAR-MAJORS

Rank and Name	From	To	Remarks
Sapuran Singh	6/5/36	2/12/38	Jat Sikh.
Rur Singh, Hon. Lieut., Sirdar Bahadur, C.B.I., M.B.E., I.O.M. (Hony. Captain)	1/11/38	31/1/43	Jat Sikh.
Chowdri, Sirdar Bahadur (Hony. Lieut.)	23/1/43	27/2/45	Dogra.
Sadhu Singh, Bahadur, I.D.S.M.	23/2/45	25/3/47	Jat Sikh.
Mehal Singh, till end of Raj	26/3/47	3/10/47	Jat Sikh.
Feroze Khan (from 11th Sikhs)	15/12/47	Serving	P.M.
Alam Khan, Bahadur, I.D.S.M.	30/12/20	30/9/23	Sagkri Khattak.
Wazir	1/10/22	31/1/24	Khattak.
Mohd Khan, Khan Sahib	7/2/24	30/11/26	P.M., Satti.
Ahmad Khan, Bahadur, I.D.S.M.	1/12/26	5/5/36	P.M., Janaoli.
Jarlok Singh	6/5/30	5/5/31	Jat Sikh.
Shade Khan, Sirdar Bahadur (Hony. Lieut).	1/11/38	22/1/43	Khattak.

APPENDIX III

Various Lists (Cavalry)

A.—OFFICERS SERVING WITH CAVALRY ON 1 JANUARY 1922

Name and Rank on Joining.	Date of Commission.	Date of Joining.	Became Non-Effective.	Cause and last Rank held with Corps.	Remarks.
1. Lieut.-Colonel C. W. Carey	10/10/94	10/6/99	10/9/24	Retired. Lieutenant-Colonel.	Adjutant, Cavalry. Commandant, Cavalry. 10/10/20 to 10/9/24.
2. Major G. G. E. Wylly, V.C., D.S.O.	5/12/00	12/2/04	27/3/25	To command 6th D.C.O. Lancers. Major.	Later Colonel, C.B, D.S.O., A.D.C., *p.s.c.*
3. Major D. K. McLeod	19/8/03	1/1/06	10/9/32	Lieutenant-Colonel.	Adjutant, Cavalry. Commandant, Cavalry. 11/9/28 to 10/9/32. Later Lieut.-General, K.C.I.E., C.B., D.S.O., *p.s.c.*
4. Major J. F. W. Ogilvie, M.C.	18/1/05	19/3/06	23/1/25	Retired. Major.	Died in England, 1928.
5. Major W. H. Blood	5/8/05	20/5/07	11/9/36	Retired. Lieutenant-Colonel.	Adjutant, Cavalry. Commandant, Cavalry. 11/9/32 to 11/9/36. Later Brigadier, M.V.O.
6. Captain H. M. Hankin	23/7/07	14/10/11	1932	To 16th Light Cavalry. Major.	Lieut.-Colonel on General List.
7. Captain A. V. Hammond	6/9/11	2/12/12	16/3/39	To Staff Appointment. Lieutenant-Colonel.	Adjutant, Cavalry. Commandant, Cavalry. 15/10/36 to 16/3/39. Son of Colonel Sir Arthur Hammond. Later Major-General, C.B., D.S.O., *p.s.c.*
8. Captain H. Dane	24/8/12	18/11/13	4/8/23	Resigned. Captain.	Died as prisoner of war in Japanese hands after Malaya, 1942.
9. Captain C. H. H. Eales, M.C.	15/8/14	10/2/16			Killed in a flying accident in the Seychelles Islands.
10. Captain J. H. Gradidge	12/10/14	18/2/18	25/5/42	To Staff appointment. Lieutenant-Colonel.	Commandant, 17/7/39 to 25/5/42. Later Brigadier, O.B.E.
11. Captain M. L. Barrett	15/11/15	19/11/15	1929	Invalided. Captain.	Died in Europe.
12. Captain D. A. A. de Freitas	23/11/15	18/11/18	19/7/22	Transferred to I.A.S.C. Captain.	Since died.

Name and Rank on Joining.	Date of Commission.	Date of Joining.	Became Non-Effective.	Cause and last Rank held with Corps.	Remarks.
13. Captain F. A. Davies	26/1/16	19/3/16	17/20/29	Resigned. Captain.	
14. Captain H. Pigot	14/11/16	18/2/18	9/10/28	To I.A.S.C. Captain.	
15. Captain C. P. J. Prioleau	18/6/17	25/6/17	1/3/41	To raise 45th Cavalry. Major.	Adjutant, Cavalry. Later Brigadier.
16. Lieut. M. D. W. Bird	21/1/18	17/3/19	13/8/22	Transferred to 2/16th Punjab Regt. Lieutenant.	Subsequently killed in a motor accident.
17. Lieut. E. K. Wood	29/1/20	12/2/30	1/11/35	To S.U.L. Captain.	Returned to duty in 1939. Later Colonel, O.B.E.
18. Lieut. I. W. Beatty	20/12/18	6/1/20	1/10/31	Retired. Captain.	Returned to duty in 1939.
19. Lieut. Abdul Rahim Khan	17/7/20	1/12/20	1/6/25	To Political Department. Lieutenant.	
20. Captain C. W. Free, M.C.	5/8/14	10/12/17	1/7/37	To S.U.L. Major.	Transferred from Infantry. Returned to duty in 1939 and died in South Africa in 1944.

ATTACHED

Rank and Name.		Date of Joining.
Captain S. S. A. Shippard	...	25/6/17
Captain H. L. Bucknall	...	25/6/17
Lieut. H. N. Weber	...	17/12/20

B.—OFFICERS PERMANENTLY POSTED BETWEEN 1923 AND 1939.

(*i.e.*, after division of Cavalry and Infantry)

Name and Rank on Joining.	Date of Commission.	Date of Joining.	Became Non-Effective	Cause and last Rank held with Corps	Remarks.
1. 2/Lieut. R. R. T. Burn, U.L.	24/4/20	31/3/22	4/9/29	To 3rd Cavalry. Lieutenant.	
Major H. Dening, 25th Cavalry F.F.	1/9/97	22/4/22	10/9/28	Lieutenant-Colonel.	Commandant, Cavalry, 11/9/24 to 10/9/28. Died 1933.
1. 2/Lieut. A. J. Dring U.L.	1/2/23	20/3/24	10/6/27	To Political Department. Lieutenant.	Later C.I.E.
2. Major F. A. Hamilton 3rd Cavalry	8/1/01	6/5/25	20/1/27	To 3rd Cavalry. Major.	Second-in-Command. Father of G. J. Hamilton.
3. Captain F. Walton, 4/6th Rajput Rifles	16/12/18	22/7/25	5/10/44	To Gwalior Lancers. Lieutenant-Colonel.	Adjutant. Commandant, Cavalry, 26/5/42 to 5/10/44.
4. 2/Lieut. D. G. Egerton, U.L.	27/8/24	5/10/25	31/8/43		Son of Lieut.-General Sir R. G. Egerton.
5. 2/Lieut. W Eliott-Lockhart, U.L.	4/2/26	28/3/27	1948		Son of P. C. Eliott-Lockhart. Adjutant-Commandant, 6/10/44.
6. 2/Lieut. The Hon. R. A. H. Plunkett	3/2/28	21/3/29	18/8/46	One year pending retirement leave.	
7. Lieut. W. A. Gimson, R.A.	20/9/18	8/3/30			M.C. Adjutant.
8. 2/Lieut. R. A. Shebbeare, U.L.	28/8/29	25/10/30		To 2nd Bombay Grenadiers, later Indian Grenadiers.	
9. 2/Lieut. L. A. J. Roffey U.L.	28/8/30	20/10/31			Adjutant.
10. 2/Lieut. G. D. G. Garforth-Bles, U.L.	30/1/30	18/10/32	30/11/43	To 3rd Madras Regt. Major.	
11. 2/Lieut. M. L. Tweedie, U.L.	27/8/31	26/10/33	31/3/34	Died at Bannu. Result of riding accident.	
12. 2/Lieut. G. M. Strover, U.L.	31/8/33	6/11/34			M.C.

Name and Rank on Joining.	Date of Commission.	Date of Joining.	Became Non-Effective.	Cause and last Rank held with Corps.	Remarks.
13. 2/Lieut. M. La T. McCausland, U.L.	31/8/33	10/3/35	13/6/44	To 14th Punjab Regt. Major.	
14. Captain The Hon. W. Edwardes, (later The Lord Kensington), 15th/19th Hussars	30/8/24	17/11/35	1/4/41	To 45th Cavalry. Captain.	
15. Captain R. Q. C. Mainwaring, Gordon Highlanders	31/8/22	7/2/36		To 13th F.F. Rifles.	
16. 2/Lieut. J. B. Reid, U.L.	31/1/35	19/3/36			Adjutant. Grandson of Sir Arthur Hammond, V.C. Murdered in train, 1948.
17. Major E. St. J. Birnie, Sam Browne's Cavalry F.F.	15/4/19	31/8/37	31/8/43	To command 2nd Hyderabad Lancers.	
18. Lieut. R. A. Bailey, Sam Browne's Cavalry F.F.	29/1/31	31/8/37			
19. 2/Lieut. N. H. D. Pratt, U.L.	28/1/37	5/4/38	10/5/40	Transferred to British Army at own request.	
20. 2/Lieut. J. R. C. Phillips, U.L.	26/8/37	26/10/38			
21. 2/Lieut. D. J. Monteith, U.L.	27/1/39	10/4/39	9/6/44	Killed in action in Burma while serving with 1st Bn. The Lancashire Fusiliers in Special Force (The Chindits).	Adjutant. M.B.E.
22. 2/Lieut. W. G. O. Butler, U.L.	27/1/38	14/9/39			M.C.
23. Lieut. J. C. D. Vanrenan, A.I.R.O.	3/9/38	28/9/40		To Army Remount Department.	
24. 2/Lieut. R. H. Waller, U.L.	26/7/39	31/1/40		To R.A.F.	

APPENDICES

C.—OFFICERS ATTACHED FOR DUTY BETWEEN 1922 AND 1946

Rank and Name.	Date of Joining.	Remarks.
2/Lieut. B. J. Crossley	27/12/40	R.A.C.
Lieut. H. C. Adcock	7/3/41	To 42nd Cavalry on 1/4/42.
Lieut. D. R. Poynton	20/10/42	R.A.C.
W.S./Lieut. Anoop Singh	13/9/42	—
W.S./Lieut. Nirmal Chandra	1/10/42	—
W.S./Lieut. P. V. Oates	4/10/43	—
2/Lieut. M. T. Charlton	19/10/44	—
2/Lieut. D. C. Richardson	16/8/44	—
2/Lieut. C. J. Lossock	3/3/43	—
T./Capt. J. M. D. Tomlinson	8/2/45	R.A.C.
W.S./Lieut. G. R. Ottey	10/9/45	R.A.C.
2/Lieut. A. A. Bertram	25/10/46	R.A.C.
2/Lieut. G. B. Butterworth	31/1/47	R.A.C.

D.—E.C.Os. POSTED FOR DUTY FROM 3 SEPTEMBER 1939 TO 31 DECEMBER 1946

Rank and Name.	Date of Joining.	Remarks.
2/Lieut. J. W. Humphries	6/3/40	—
2/Lieut. P. Graham	26/7/40	—
Lieut. O. T. Jenkins	9/9/40	To 45th Cavalry on 1/4/41.
2/Lieut. R. R. Lack	10/11/40	—
2/Lieut. F. O. L'Estrange	28/12/40	Transferred to R.A.C.
2/Lieut. C. H. Thomas	21/11/40	O.B.E.
2/Lieut. J. Eliott-Lockhart	2/1/41	—
2/Lieut. Inder Singh	11/1/41	Commissioned from ranks of Cavalry (Risaldar).
2/Lieut. J. George	27/2/41	—
2/Lieut. V. H. Norman	22/9/41	—
2/Lieut. J. M. Penly	12/4/42	—
2/Lieut. Sardara Singh, O.B.I.	8/2/42	Commission granted from ranks (Risaldar-Major) of Cavalry.
2/Lieut. C. M. O'Rorke	10/6/42	—
Captain F. W. Brett	7/5/42	(Posted, but not joined.)
2/Lieut. T. R. Conway	6/8/42	—
2/Lieut. N. A. G. Brooks	22/8/42	—
2/Lieut. E. S. Corner	20/10/42	To R.I.A.S.C. on 7/12/43.
2/Lieut. A. J. Peacock	20/10/42	Killed in an accident near Kohat on 11/9/44.
2/Lieut. P. J. Howes	20/10/42	To Malaya Police.
2/Lieut. Sultan Khan Malik	20/11/42	—
2/Lieut. F. A. L. Reid	16/1/43	To R.A.C.
Lieut. A. P. Pearson	3/3/43	—
2/Lieut. F. J. Harvey	3/3/43	—
2/Lieut. K. G. F. B. Howe	14/3/43	—
2/Lieut. J. L. Webb	27/7/43	—
2/Lieut. A. V. Wylie	6/8/43	—
W.S./Lieut G. Mc. K. Davidson	19/9/43	To Jodhpur Lancers, 23/9/44.
W.S./Lieut. Gajraj Singh	15/12/43	To R.I.A.S.C. on 8/3/46.
W.S./Lieut. H. G. Reading	15/12/43	—
W.S./Lieut. C. L. Fonceca	13/3/44	—
W.S./Lieut. K. Parkash Chand	9/4/44	—
W.S./Lieut. S. Beaumont	27/4/44	—
W.S./Lieut. Mohd Mohiyyuddin	20/5/44	—
Captain F. J. Bloomfield	5/6/44	To Remounts on 27/7/44.
W.S./Lieut. G. M. Harrington	17/7/44	—
W.S./Lieut. G. R. Rees	19/7/44	—

Rank and Name.	Date of Joining.	Remarks.
W.S./Lieut. G. D. C. M. Lewis	19/7/44	To R.A.C. and granted Regular Commission.
2/Lieut. W. D. Garbutt	19/7/44	To R.A.C. and granted Regular Commission.
2/Lieut. R. E. Stead	16/8/44	—
W.S./Lieut. M. W. Pitts-Tucker	6/10/44	—
2/Lieut. R. W. Goldsworthy	10/10/44	—
W.S./Lieut. C. J. Allman	29/11/44	—
2/Lieut. D. Morgan	20/3/45	—
2/Lieut. J. P. Hardy	5/2/46	—
T./Capt. Mohan Singh	29/9/46	—

E.—REGULAR INDIAN OFFICERS AND E.C.Os. GRANTED REGULAR COMMISSIONS, 1939–46

Rank and Name.	Date of Joining.	Date of Demobilization.	Remarks.
Lieut. Har Prasad	29/1/39	12/12/42	Regular Commission.
Lieut. J. H. Chibber	4/9/40	20/10/42	A.I.R.O.
W.S./Lieut. Mohd Abbas Khan Durrani	1/10/41	13/9/43	
W.S./Lieut. Mohindar Singh Randhawa	12/8/42	3/8/43	Granted commission from ranks of Cavalry.
2/Lieut. Mohd Faruq Khan	23/8/42	20/10/42	—
W.S./Lieut. Aman Ullah Khan	1/1/43	15/8/43	—
W.S./Lieut. Agha Daud Raza	1/4/43	6/10/44	—
2/Lieut. Jahan Zeb Khan	22/5/44	3/3/43	Adjutant.
W.S./Lieut. Bhupindera Singh Uberoi	25/11/44	19/6/46	—
W.S./Lieut. Bhagwan Singh	5/9/44	14/12/46	—

F.—MEDICAL OFFICERS ATTACHED DURING THE SECOND WORLD WAR, 1939

Captain E. Edwards	26/4/41	22/7/42	"A" Squadron.
Captain N. Chatterjee	7/10/41	4/1/42	—
Lieut. D. J. Burnett, M.C.	23/7/42	23/1/43	—
Captain S. Zacharias	22/1/43	31/3/45	—
Captain A. D. Arora	24/6/45	6/4/46	—
Captain B. B. Gandhe	3/4/46	30/9/46	—

G.—E.M.Es. ATTACHED DURING THE SECOND WORLD WAR, 1939 (INFANTRY)

Lieut. H. Hicks, I.E.M.E.	28/8/42	20/5/43	—
Lieut. E. M. Moore, I.E.M.E.	17/7/43	7/3/45	—
Lieut. R. V. Bluer, R.E.M.E.	4/3/45	3/4/45	—
Captain R. C. Bedington, R.E.M.E.	3/4/45	26/3/47	—
Captain F. J. Morgan, R.E.M.E.	26/3/47	Serving	—

APPENDIX IV
VARIOUS LISTS (INFANTRY)

A.—OFFICERS SERVING WITH THE BATTALION ON 1 JANUARY 1923

Note.—Owing to the confusion at the breaking up of the Infantry at Razmak, and the evacuation of that station, it has not been possible to make the lists for the Infantry so complete as those for the Cavalry.

Name and Rank on Joining.	Date of Commission.	Date of Joining.	Became Non-Effective.	Cause and last Rank held with Corps.	Remarks.
68. 2/Lieut. H. Campbell, U.L.	20/1/97	27/7/98	31/1/26	Colonel.	Adjutant, Infantry. Commanding 2nd Battalion, 1/2/21 to 31/1/36. Son of Major-General R. B. P. Campbell, C.B., nephew of General Sir F. Campbell, Brigadier, C.B., D.S.O., M.V.O.
69. 2/Lieut. D. L. R. Lorimer	5/8/96	20/9/98	1903	To Political Department. Retired. Lieutenant-Colonel.	
71. Lieut. A. N. Buist, Royal Scots Fusiliers	9/9/91	31/8/99	4/1/21	Retired. Lieutenant-Colonel.	Commanded Infantry, 28/1/15 to 13/11/16, Feronenth, and last Commandant, 14/11/16 to 4/1/26. M.V.O.
74. Lieut. J. Clementi, Hampshire Regiment	8/9/87	25/6/00	2/8/21	Transferred to 10/5th Mahrattas. Lieutenant-Colonel.	Raised and commanded 3rd Guides Infantry, 22/10/17 to 2/8/21. O.B.E.
75. 2/Lieut. A. S. B. Roberts, U.L.	20/7/98	14/11/00	1904	To Civil, Burma.	
76. Lieut. C. J. B. Hay, U.L.	4/8/97	28/11/00	1920	To 19th Punjabis	Major-General. C.B., C.M.G., C.B.E., D.S.O. Killed by bombs, London, 1940 (also his wife).
77. 2/Lieut. C. Kirkpatrick, U.L.	27/7/98	5/12/00	1920	Transferred to 53rd Sikhs. Lieutenant-Colonel.	Major-General. C.B., C.B.E., *p.s.c.*
81. Lieut. F. K. Hensley ...	8/1/01	23/2/04	27/4/28	Retired. Lieutenant-Colonel.	Commandant, Infantry, 1/11/25 to 27/4/28.
82. Lieut. C. E. Morris ...	4/12/01	26/4/04	1921	Burma Rifles.	D.S.O.
83. 2/Lieut. C. H. Campbell, U.L.	27/8/02	2/5/04	1919	Retired. Major.	Adjutant, Infantry. Nephew of F. Campbell.
84. 2/Lieut. D. G. Sandeman	21/1/03	9/12/04	15/8/31	To Kitchener College	Adjutant, Infantry. Commandant, Infantry, 28/4/28 to 15/8/31. C.I.E.
85. Lieut. P. d'A. Banks, Wiltshire Regiment	10/10/03	18/6/05	26/4/15	Killed in action. Captain.	With 57th Rifles in France.
88. 2/Lieut. J. F. W. Ogilvie, U.L.	18/1/05	19/3/06	23/1/25	Retired. Major.	Died in England, 1928.
90. 2/Lieut. L. S. Wells, U.L.	5/8/05	3/4/07	25/5/08	Died of cholera.	Mohmand Expedition, 1908.
91. 2/Lieut. N. H. Prendergast	29/1/06	4/9/07	10/8/35	Lieutenant-Colonel.	Commandant, Infantry, 16/8/31 to 16/8/35. D.S.O., M.V.O. Recruiting Officer, Lahore.

#	Name and Rank on Joining	Date of Commission	Date of Joining	Became Non-Effective	Cause and last Rank held with Corps	Remarks
92.	2/Lieut. C. E. T. Erskine	29/8/06	9/11/07	10/6/21	To command 10/12th F.F. Regt., T.B. Lieutenant-Colonel.	Adjutant, Infantry. Colonel, Inspecting Officer Frontier Corps. C.I.E., D.S.O., M.C.
93.	Lieut. J. V. C. Anderson, Dorset Regiment	4/5/07	24/7/09	8/6/18	Killed in action. Captain.	Palestine.
94.	Lieut. E. M. Murray, Black Watch	29/8/06	25/7/09	1/4/20	To R.A.F., Captain.	D.S.O., M.C.
95.	Lieut. L. V. S. Blacker, U.L.	19/1/07	27/3/10	1933	Major.	Lieutenant-Colonel, O.B.E.
99.	2/Lieut. P. Grant, U.L.	20/1/12	18/2/13	23/6/37	Killed in action, Waziristan. Lieutenant-Colonel.	Commandant, Infantry, 10/11/35 to 23/6/37. Brevet Lieutenant-Colonel.
102.	2/Lieut. A. W. L. Neave, U.L.	14/1/14	18/11/15	19/9/18	Killed in action. Lieutenant.	With 2nd Guides in Palestine. Adjutant.
103.	2/Lieut. E. P. Rich	15/11/15	19/11/15	1941	To Iraq Army.	Commandant, Infantry, Persia, 1941.
105.	2/Lieut. H. D. K. Money	15/8/14	10/12/15	1/11/23	Transferred to Royal Scots. Captain.	
109.	2/Lieut. I. A. Thew	27/10/17	5/11/17	1930	Transferred to I.A.S.C. Captain.	
111.	Lieut. L. V. Dart, M.C., Welch Regiment	22/4/15	16/2/18	19/9/35	Retired. Major.	
114.	Lieut. L. R. Knight, The King's Regiment	19/9/14	2/3/18	1/4/36	Retired. Major.	M.C.
115.	Lieut. J. E. Redding, The King's Regiment	22/5/15	17/8/18	—		Adjutant, Infantry.
116.	Lieut. M. V. Smelt	27/8/15	1/9/18	6/10/26	Transferred to Royal Signals.	Adjutant, Infantry.
117.	Lieut. G. F. Taylor, London Yeomanry	22/8/17	11/11/18	—		
118.	Lieut. S. B. Good, C.I.H.	14/11/16	12/11/18	—		Adjutant, Training Battalion.
120.	2/Lieut. G. V. L. Coleman, U.L.	1/10/18	15/12/18	—		Adjutant, Infantry. p.s.c.
121.	Lieut. W. J. C. Duncan, D.S.O., M.C., Australian Forces.	1/1/16	18/1/19	—		D.S.O. (with Bar). M.C.
123.	A/Lieut. L. M. Barlow, U.L.	15/4/19	23/4/19	—		Adjutant, Infantry. M.C. and Bar.
124.	2/Lieut. H. A. Barnes, U.L.	15/4/19	23/4/19	23/6/26	Transferred to Political Department. Retired.	Murdered in Baluchistan.
125.	2/Lieut. Taj Muhammad Khan, I.A.	7/10/19	7/10/19	23/4/25	Lieutenant.	M.B.E. Promoted from Subadar-Major, 3rd Guides. Son of Subadar-Major Sarfaraz Khan.

B.—OFFICERS PERMANENTLY POSTED BETWEEN 1923 AND 1939.

	Name and Rank on Joining.	Date of Commission.	Date of Joining.	Became Non-Effective.	Cause and last Rank held with Corps.	Remarks.
1.	I. Lieut. M. H. H. Baily, 3/10th Baluch Regiment	14/7/21	9/10/23	—		
2.	I. 2/Lieut. P. R. Macnamara, U.L.	31/8/22	11/12/23	—		Son of 2/Lieut. C. R. Macnamara (see Appendix D, Vol. I), *p.s.c.*
3.	I. Capt. W. J. Cumming, S.W. Militia	29/6/16	10/8/24	—		
4.	I. Major R. G. Abbott, M.C., C.I.H.	4/6/04	15/5/24	27/1/30	Transferred to 10/12th F.F. Regt.	Brevet Lieutenant-Colonel, Brigadier.
5.	I. 2/Lieut. A. K. Murcott	31/1/24	15/4/26	1944	Killed in air accident on service in Burma.	
6.	I. 2/Lieut. G. Meynell	31/6/24	6/10/26	29/9/35	Killed in action at Nahakki.	M.C., V.C. (post.).
7.	I. 2/Lieut. G. B. Still, U.L.	1/9/27	25/10/28	14/4/34	Transferred to 19th Lancers.	
8.	I. 2/Lieut. A. C. S. Moore, U.L.	28/8/29	21/10/30	—		
9.	I. 2/Lieut. A. P. S. Rendall, U.L.	28/8/30	24/10/31	29/9/35	Killed in action at Nahakki.	M.C.
10.	I. 2/Lieut. C. G. Campbell, U.L.	28/1/32	8/3/33	—		
11.	I. 2/Lieut. C. J. Hamilton, U.L.	1/9/32	3/11/32	—		D.S.O. Son of F. A. Hamilton, 2nd Guides.
12.	I. 2/Lieut. R. R. Griffith, Devon Regiment	28/1/32	11/11/35	—		
13.	I. Capt. A. R. E. Pollard, Royal Scots Fusiliers	4/2/26	3/3/36	Till 1947		Commandant, Infantry.
14.	I. Capt. G. A. MacMunn, Royal Signals	2/2/28	1/4/36	—		Adjutant, Infantry. Commandant, Infantry. Commanding with Pakistan till March 1948.
15.	I. 2/Lieut. W. G. Watt, U.L.	30/8/35	1/11/36	—		
16.	I. 2/Lieut. R. V. E. Hodson	19/2/37	—			
17.	I. Lt.-Col. K. A. Garrett, M.C., 1st Sikhs F.F.	14/1/14	5/10/37	1941	To Brigade.	Commandant, Infantry, 5/10/37. *p.s.c.* Brigadier.
18.	I. 2/Lieut. R. G. Hutchinson, U.L.	—	31/10/38			

C.—EMERGENCY COMMISSIONED OFFICERS JOINING THE BATTALION SINCE 1939

Name and Rank on Joining.	Date of Commission.	Date of Joining.	Became Non-Effective.	Cause and last Rank held with Corps.	Remarks.
2/Lieut. W. G. Sturrock	23/6/40	–/7/40	1/5/41	Acting Captain to 25th December	Garrison Company.
2/Lieut. Baird	—	—	21/2/41	Lieutenant to 3rd December. F.F. Rifles Lieutenant	Killed in action in North Africa.
2/Lieut. M. J. Moynihan	20/4/40	—	3/3/41	Major	Adjutant, Reinforcement Camp, Lahore. M.C.
2/Lieut. A. M. W. B. McDermott	21/6/40	–/7/40	27/8/47	Major	To F.F.R.C. for release in Australia.
2/Lieut. D. M. Brett	15/2/41	26/2/41	—	Captain	Released.
2/Lieut. W. J. Stansfield	15/2/41	27/2/41	—	Captain	Released.
2/Lieut. A. A. Pugh	5/5/41	—	16/3/45	Major	Released.
2/Lieut. R. G. Maslen Jones	21/12/40	13/4/41	15/12/44	Captain	To British Service, K.S.L.I.
2/Lieut. Mohd Rafi Khan	15/5/41	25/5/41	–/1/46	Major	To F.F.R.C. and then to Zhob Militia.
2/Lieut. B. W. M. Berdoe	—	16/7/41	17/1/43	Lieutenant	Resigned.
2/Lieut. P. J. L. Phelps	10/7/41	21/7/41	30/5/46	Captain	To Tochi Scouts.
2/Lieut. G. L. Sawday	19/7/41	29/7/41	24/1/44	Captain	To F.F.R.C.
2/Lieut. I. F. Aucott	15/2/41	2/9/41	2/3/42	Lieutenant	To Brigade Sub-Area.
2/Lieut. J. R. Noyce	15/2/41	4/7/42	—		Released.
2/Lieut. P. Daykin	—	25/4/42	21/7/44		
2/Lieut. M. Wray	10/9/41	25/4/42	1946	Captain	To British Service. Killed in accident in Germany when Staff Captain of Infantry Brigade. Nephew of Hector Campbell.
2/Lieut. D. P. Stovold	15/11/41	4/7/42	1946	Captain	Released.
2/Lieut. J. P. C. Burbrook	1/8/41	9/11/42	—		
Lieut. M. P. Keyes	10/9/41	16/11/42	—	Captain	A.D.C. to Governor of N.W.F.P. Grandson of Sir C. Keyes.
Lieut. A. J. Stead	10/9/41	30/11/42	—	Captain	Transferred to British Service.
Lieut. J. A. Bailes (British Service)	30/11/40	25/1/43	1946	Major	Released.
2/Lieut. T. E. C. Thompson (1st Baluch Regt.)	31/10/42	24/9/43	19/7/44	Major	Released.
Lieut. J. S. MacLachlan	26/10/40	12/4/41	1942	Lieutenant	To Headquarters, 6th Division.

Name and Rank on Joining.	Date of Commission.	Date of Joining.	Became Non-Effective.	Cause and last Rank held with Corps.	Remarks.
T./Capt. J. B. Thompson (British Service)	26/10/40	10/3/45	1946	Major	Released.
Lieut. J. H. W. Haddon	19/3/44	29/3/45	—		Released.
Lieut. I. W. Stiven	16/1/44	30/3/45	21/1/47	Captain	To 1st Para. Bn. F.F.R.
Major Z. M. Penty	3/5/42	22/9/45	28/6/47	Captain	To Northern Command.
2/Lieut. Mohd Safdar Iqbal	16/12/45	—	2/8/47	Captain	Released.
2/Lieut. D. R. M. Glasse	2/12/45	—	21/1/47	Lieutenant	To 2nd F.F.R.
Lieut. Azizur-Rehman	9/4/42	7/1/46	4/10/48	Captain	Serving.
Lieut. Shahzada Khan	19/5/45	14/3/46			To R.P.A.
Capt. Mohd Azan	14/3/43	1946	9/6/47	Major	To Embassy H.Q., Bombay.
2/Lieut. P. Ashcraft	13/1/46	1946	5/9/47	Captain	To 609 F.S. Section.
Lieut. Mohd Shafi	4/7/45	1947	28/6/47	Lieutenant	To 1st Para. Bn. F.F.R.
Lieut. G. W. Dickinson	2/12/45	1946	2/10/46	Lieutenant	To F.F.R.C. Son of Hon. Captain Rur Singh.
Lieut. Sarbang Singh	16/1/44	1946	7/8/47	Captain	Released. Son of Subadar Darwesh Mohd.
Lieut. W. W. S. Breem	23/9/45	6/10/46	17/4/47	Lieutenant	Serving.
2/Lieut. Mohd Iqbal Malik	14/7/46	10/9/46	—		Posted to M.E.L.F.
2/Lieut. R. T. M. Gray	—	16/9/46	11/1/47	Lieutenant	Serving.
Lieut. Mohd Sarwar Khan	11/2/45	6/2/47	—		Transferred to 9th Gurkhas.
Lieut. B. D. Malhautra	13/9/42	20/6/47	9/10/47	Major	To 312 Garrison Company.
T./Capt. Abdul Majid Khan (I.P.C.)	8/11/42	28/10/47	7/9/48	Captain	Serving.
Capt. A. Khaleeli	4/8/41	22/11/47	—		Serving.
Lieut. M. Rafic Tanwar	28/4/46	22/11/47	—		Serving.
Capt. A. A. Shaikh	8/10/41	10/12/47	12/10/48	Major	To 14/12th F.F.R.
Capt. Mohd Ali	30/5/43	16/1/48	—		Serving.

APPENDIX V

Honours and Rewards

A.—CAVALRY

Awarded between 1922 and 1939.

Officers.

Companion of the Bath.
Major-General D. K. McLeod, D.S.O.

Member of Royal Victorian Order.
Major W. H. Blood.

Military Cross.
Captain W. A. Gimson.

Other Ranks.

MacGregor Memorial Medal.
1929 Daffadar Ghulam Ali (specially awarded a Silver Medal).

Order of British India.
Risaldar-major Abnashi Ram (2nd Class).
Risaldar-major Nur Khan (1st Class).
Risaldar-major and Hon. Lieut. Zardad Khan (1st Class).
Risaldar Firdos Khan (2nd Class).
Risaldar-major Rattan Chand (1st Class).

Meritorious Service Medal.
1728½ Daffadar Nanak Singh.
1889 S.D.M. Shah Pasand.
1884 S.D.M. Ahmed Shah.
1410 Daffadar Ghamboo Ram.
1984 R.Q.M.D. Sant Singh.
2086 S.D.M. Kehar Singh.
2142 R.D.M. Bawa Singh.
2245 R.Q.M.D. Sham Singh.
2273 S.D.M. Tarlok Singh.
2455 R.Q.M.D. Daud Khan.
2418 S.D.M. Teja Singh.
2161 Daffadar Allah Ditta.
  31 Tr. Major Kartar Singh.
  61 R.Q.M.D. Murad Khan.

Awarded between 1939 and 1947.

Officers.

Knight Commander of Indian Empire.
Lieut.-General D. K. McLeod.

Companion of the Bath.
Major-General A. V. Hammond.

APPENDICES

Distinguished Service Order.
Major-General A. V. Hammond.

Officer of Order of British Empire.
Lieut.-Colonel C. H. Thomas.
Colonel E. K. Wood.

Member of Order of British Empire.
Captain D. J. Monteith.
Hon. Captain Rattan Chand.

Order of British India.
Risaldar-major Sardara Singh (2nd Class).
Risaldar-major Karim Dad (1st Class).
Risaldar-major Shankar Singh (1st Class).
Risaldar Genda Singh (1st Class).
Risaldar Makhan Singh (1st Class).
Risaldar Kanshi Singh (1st Class).
Risaldar Ram Singh (1st Class).
Risaldar Garka Ram (1st Class).
Risaldar Ram Singh.

Military Cross.
Major G. M. Strover.
Major W. G. O. Butler.

Mention in Despatches.
Major E. St. J. Birnie.
Risaldar Garka Ram.
Risaldar Ram Singh.
Jemadar Alif Shah.
Captain J. W. Humphries.
Major G. M. Strover.
Colonel G. H. Gradidge, O.B.E.
Major J. B. Reid.
Captain F. O. L'Estrange.
Major D. J. Monteith.
Major R. R. Lack (?).

OTHER RANKS.

Indian Distinguished Service Medal.
3860 Sowar Mohmad Afzal.

Meritorious Service Medal.
726 Daffadar Clerk Siri Ram.
1184 S.Q.M.D. Gulam Chand.
A12925 Daffadar Clerk Hans Raj.

B.—INFANTRY

(*Note.*—Owing to an error in Pakistan records, Infantry recipients of the M.S.M. have not been included.)

AWARDED BETWEEN 1922 AND 1939.

Rank and Name.	When Awarded.	Campaign.
Victoria Cross.		
Captain G. Meynell	29/9/35	Mohmand Operations, 1935 (posthumous).
Distinguished Service Order.		
Lieut. G. J. Hamilton	29/9/35	Mohmand Operations, 1935.
Captain F. J. Doherty, I.M.S.	29/9/35	,, ,, ,,
Lieut.-Colonel M. H. H. Baily		Norway, N.W.E.F., 1940.
Officer of Order of British Empire.		
Major A. R. E. Pollard	1/1/43	Eastern Army, Burma Border.
Member of Order of British Empire.		
Hon. Lieut. Rur Singh, I.O.M.		Persia and Iraq, 1942.
Military Cross.		
Captain L. M. Barlow, M.C.	16/9/32	Mohmand Operations, 1932.
Lieut. G. Meynell	,,	,, ,, ,,
Jemadar Nur Khan		Italy, Second World War, 1939-45, with I.F.F.R.
Lieut. A. P. S. Rendall		Mohmand Operations, 1932. (?)
Military Medal.		
Sepoy Zarmat Khan		Italy, Second World War, 1939-45, with I.F.F.R.
Naik Tor Baz		,, ,, ,, ,,
Indian Order of Merit.		
Subadar Rur Singh	23/8/35	Mohmand Operations, 1935.
Sepoy Dheru	,,	,, ,, ,,
Jemadar Bhari Ram	29/9/35	,, ,, ,, (posthumous).
Havildar Yusaf	,,	Mohmand Operations, 1935.
Indian Distinguished Service Medal.		
Havildar-major Lal Mast	23/8/35	Mohmand Operations, 1935.
Havildar Daya Ram	,,	,, ,, ,,
Havildar Fateh Khan	29/9/35	,, ,, ,,
Havildar Sadhu Singh	,,	,, ,, ,,
Lance-naik Munshi Ram	,,	,, ,, ,,
Lance-naik Sarban Singh	,,	,, ,, ,,
Sepoy Gurdial Singh	,,	,, ,, ,,
Sepoy Ghuncha Gul	,,	,, ,, ,,
Subadar Dost Mohd	25/11/36	Khaisora Operations, 1936.

Rank and Name.		Campaign.

Mentioned in Despatches.

Rank and Name	Award	Campaign
Major L. R. Knight, M.C.	C.-in-C's. Certificate	Mohmand Operations, 1935.
Lieut. G. J. Hamilton, D.S.O.	,, ,,	,, ,, ,,
Subadar Rur Singh, I.O.M.	,, ,,	,, ,, ,,
Subadar Khial Din	,, ,,	,, ,, ,,
Jemadar Bhari Ram, I.O.M.	,, ,,	,, ,, ,,
Jemadar Mohd Khan	,, ,,	,, ,, ,,
Havildar Yusaf, I.O.M.	,, ,,	,, ,, ,,
Havildar Sawal Khan	,, ,,	,, ,, ,,
Sepoy Dheru	,, ,,	,, ,, ,,
Sepoy Asparla	,, ,,	,, ,, ,,
Sepoy Bagh Ali	,, ,,	,, ,, ,,
Sepoy Gian Singh	,, ,,	,, ,, ,,
Sepoy Khazana	Army Commander's Certificate	,, ,, ,,
Subadar Jagat Singh	,, ,,	,, ,, ,,
Jemadar Arian Singh	,, ,,	,, ,, ,,
Jemadar Chaudhri	,, ,,	,, ,, ,,
Havildar Guajar Singh	,, ,,	,, ,, ,,
Havildar Sardar Khan	,, ,,	,, ,, ,,
Havildar Said Ali	,, ,,	,, ,, ,,
Naik Ghuncha Gul	,, ,,	,, ,, ,,
Naik Arshullah	,, ,,	,, ,, ,,
Naik Sapuram Singh	,, ,,	,, ,, ,,
Lance-naik Santa Singh	,, ,,	,, ,, ,,
Lance-naik Arab Gul	,, ,,	,, ,, ,,
Clerk Mohd Younas	,, ,,	,, ,, ,,
Subadar Khial Din	,, ,,	Khaisora Operations, 1936.
Jemadar Arjan Singh	,, ,,	,, ,, ,,
Jemadar Misri Khan	,, ,,	,, ,, ,,
Jemadar Sardar Khan	,, ,,	,, ,, ,,
Havildar-Major Sukh Ram	,, ,,	,, ,, ,,
Havildar Sohan Singh	,, ,,	,, ,, ,,
Havildar Sadhu Singh	,, ,,	,, ,, ,,
Havildar Mohd Khan	,, ,,	,, ,, ,,
Lance-naik Sardara Singh	,, ,,	,, ,, ,,
Sepoy Rais Khan	,, ,,	,, ,, ,,
Major G. F. Taylor	C.-in-C.'s Certificate	Khaisora Operations, 1936-37.
Lieut. R. M. Crowe (Royal Canadian Regt., attd.)	,, ,,	,, ,, ,,
Havildar Walayat Khan	,, ,,	,, ,, ,,
Lance-naik Murid Khan	,, ,,	,, ,, ,,
Major J. E. Redding	,, ,,	Waziristan Operations, 1936-37.
Major W. J. Cumming	,, ,,	,, ,, ,,
Lieut. A. C. S. Moore	,, ,,	,, ,, ,,
Jemadar Arjan Singh	,, ,,	,, ,, ,,
Sepoy Kartar Singh	,, ,,	,, ,, ,,
Jemadar Dad Mohd	,, ,,	,, ,, ,,
C.H.M. Sadhu Singh	Army Commander's Certificate	,, ,, ,,
Lance-naik Bishan Singh	,, ,,	,, ,, ,,
Havildar Amir Hamza	,, ,,	,, ,, ,,
Havildar Tara Chand	,, ,,	,, ,, ,,
Naik Amir Zada	C.-in-C.'s Certificate	,, ,, ,,
Lieut.-Colonel M. H. H. Baily, D.S.O.	,, ,,	Norway, N.W.E.F., 1940
Lieut.-Colonel G. V. L. Coleman	In recognition of gallant and distinguished service	Burma and N.E. India, 1942-43.

Rank and Name.			Campaign.	
Havildar Ram Ditta	...	...	In recognition of gallant and distinguished service	Persia and Iraq, 1943.
Havildar Nanak Singh	...	...	,, ,,	Italy, 1939-45.
Major M. H. Hodson	...	...	C.-in-C.'s Certificate	Burma, 1949-45.
Lieut.-Colonel A. R. E. Pollard, O.B.E.			,, ,,	,, ,,
Sepoy Amir Gul	...	...	,, ,,	,, ,,
Captain W. M. Chisholm	...	...	G.O.C.-in-C.'s Certificate	P.A.I.C., 1945.
Sweeper Gopi	...	...	,, ,,	,, ,,
Jemadar Sawab Gul	...	...	,, ,,	,, ,,
Havildar Mohd Jan	...	...	,, ,,	,, ,,
Lance-naik Ram Singh	...	...	,, ,,	,, ,,
Lance-naik Nanak Chand	...	...	,, ,,	,, ,,
Sepoy Chhail Singh	...	...	,, ,,	,, ,,
Sepoy Piara Singh	...	...	,, ,,	,, ,,
Sepoy Dholi Ram	...	...	,, ,,	,, ,,
Sepoy Hukaat Khan			,, ,,	,, ,,
Sepoy Gulal Khan	...		,, ,,	,,
Sepoy Gul Khan	...		,, ,,	,, ,,
Mohd Akbar	...	...	,, ,,	,, ,,
Sepoy Chinar Gul			,, ,,	,, ,,
Sepoy Lachi Dan	...		,, ,,	,, ,,
Sepoy Ahmad Khan	...		,, ,,	,, ,,
Sepoy Mohd Sadic	...		,, ,,	,, ,,
Sweeper Krishna			,, ,,	,, ,,
Naik Kaka	...		,, ,,	,, ,,
Havildar Barrar Singh	...		,, ,,	,, ,,
Subadar Walayat Khan	...	...	Outstanding good service. Certified by G.O.C.-in-C.	Persia and Iraq, 1945.
Havildar Baghel Singh	...	...	,, ,,	,, ,,
Havildar Mehraban Khan	...		,, ,,	,, ,,
Havildar Karam Singh	...		,, ,,	,, ,,
Lance-naik Kehar Singh	...		,, ,,	,, ,,
Sepoy Allah Dad	...	...	,, ,,	,, ,,
Sepoy Abdul Azizi	...	...	,, ,,	,, ,,
Sepoy Nanda Bullabh			,, ,,	,, ,,
Sepoy Lall Khan	...		,, ,,	,, ,,
Sweeper Kanki	...		,, ,,	,, ,,
Havildar Gurdial Singh			,, ,,	,, ,,
Naik Liban Shah	...		,, ,,	,, ,,
Captain M. P. Keyes	...		,, ,,	,, ,,

Order of British India (1st Class).

Rank and Name.						When Awarded.
Subadar Sohbat, I.O.M.	...	...	...	...	...	2/6/43
Subadar Dost Mohd, I.D.S.M.	...	...	...	...	...	,,
Subadar-major Chaudhri	...	...	...	...	...	1/1/45

Order of British India (2nd Class).

Subadar-major Chaudhri	...	...	...	...	...	11/6/42
Subadar-major Sapuran Singh II	...	...	...	...	...	,,
Subadar Daya Ram, I.D.S.M.	...	...	...	...	...	14/6/45
Subadar Habib Khan	...	...	...	...	...	1/1/46
Subadar-major Dad Mohd	...	...	...	...	...	1946
Subadar-major Sadhu Singh	...	...	...	...	...	1/1/47
Subadar Fateh Khan	...	...	...	...	...	12/6/47

INDEX

Abadan occupied, 112
Abdul Ghaffar in Yuzafzai, 1931, 33
Abdul Ghaffar, Mischief-Maker, 20
Abdur-rahman Khan, Amir, 6
Adams gains V.C., 8
Aden, Life at, 12
Afghan Boundary Commission, 19
— Lashkars in Waziristan, 71
— Pretender and Bajour, 42
— War, First, 1
— —, Second, 5
Afridi invasion of Peshawar (first), 26
Afridis and Congress, 28
—, inroad (second), 31
—, story of, 26
Akbar Khan, Bde. commander at Kohat, 184
Alamein, El, three Battles of, 131
Alexander, Brigadier-General, Hon. H. R. L. G., 43
Alexander the Great, 3
Alingar, Faqir of, firebrand, 43
Amanullah, Amir, treacherous attack, 6
Aornos, storming of, 3
Argyll and Sutherland Highlanders, 73
Arsalkot, Ipi's stronghold, 72
Auchinleck, General, assumes command of Eighth Army, 123
—, —, in Mohmand Spring Operations, 41, 42
—, —, in Mohmand Operations, 1935, 48
Ayub Khan defeated by Roberts, 7
Azram, Havildar, gallantry of, 84

Bacha Saqao, The, 36
Badshah Gul, Instigator, 45
Badshah Gul, I, II, and III, 46
Baily, Major, in Norway, 103
—, Brigadier, services, 175
Bajour Operations, 1933, 42
Baldwin, Brigadier-General, appointed Colonel, 24
Bannu, Cavalry at, 35
Barket Shah, Subadar, mission into Yuzafzai, 24
Baroghil Pass, 7
Barlow, Lieut., at Perim, 14
Barnes, Major, murdered, 104
Battye, Fred, mortally wounded, 7
Battye, Quentin, death of, 4
Battye, Wigram, killed, 6
Beatty, Lieut., killed, 66
Best, Mr., in Loe Agra, 44
—, —, killed, 46
Bhittanis raid Pezu, 73
Bir Hacheim, 123
Blood, Major, appointed M.V.O., 18
—, —, Second-in-Command, Cavalry, 17
—, Brigadier, services of, 175

"Brindian," slang, 5
British Cabinet, folly of, 80
Browne, General Sir Sam, story of, 9
Buffer states, 18
Buist, Lieut.-Colonel, dies, 152

Campbell, Brigadier H., Farewell Order, 156
—, —, services of, 171
Cavagnari, Sir Louis, murder of, 6
Chamberlain, Sir Neville, and Afghanistan Mission, 5
Charsadda, plague spot, 25
Charlie Muir, story of, 89
Chimnai, Mohmand outlaw, 47
Chitral Reliefs, 1932, 38
— — Expedition, 7
Coleman, Brigadier, services, 174
Coleman, Lieut., at Kamaran, 14
Coleridge, General Sir John, to command in Waziristan, 64
—, in command again after Shahur Tangi, 71
Crag, affair at, 76
Curzon, Lord, and the Militia system, 58

Dane, Captain, glorious story of, 167
Dashwood Strettel, General, inspection of Infantry, 85
Dhulip Singh, 2
Dilawar Khan, 91
Din Faqir, Bhittani firebrand, 69
Doherty, Captain, at "Nipple," 53
Donlatabad, Pathans at, 57
Dorah Pass, 7
Duke of Wellington's and Guides in Mohmand campaign, 1935, 48
— — — in Loe Agra, 45
Duncan, Major, death of, 100
—, —, services of, 108
Duranni Dynasty, 1
Duranni, Capt., I.M.S., killed, 70
Dykes, Colonel and Mrs., murdered at Baramullah, 177

Eales, Lieutenant-Colonel C. H. H., death of, 171
Egerton, Sir Raleigh, Colonel, 17
Election in Yuzafzai, 38
Eliott-Lockhart, Major, last Cavalry officer to serve with Infantry on service, 97
Eliott-Lockhart, Mrs., presentation by, 83
Ellis, Miss, kidnapped, 5
Evetts, General, and Guides Cavalry, 102

Feroze Khan, Farrier-major, captures raiders, 37
Free, Captain, at Bara, 29
—, —, in Katlang area, 33
Frontier Medals, list of, 100

"Galley Slave" quoted, 148
Gandamuk, Treaty of, 6
Gandhi's evil influence, 20
Garka Ram, Risaldar, in Persia, 113
Garrett, Brigadier, services of, 174
Gatacre on Lowarai, 8
Gilgit, 7
Gimson, Major, commanding "A," 110
Golden Square Rebellion, 105
Good, Major, 4080, 52
—, —, wounded, 53
—, —, orders withdrawal, 53
Gracey, General, commanding Pakistan Army, 178
Gradidge, Brigadier, services of, 173
Grant, Field-Marshal Sir Patrick, 93
Grant, Lieut.-Colonel, 72
—, —, killed, 75
—, —, appreciation, 80
Guides Infantry at Ridgeway, 77
— attack on 3rd Grenadiers, 181
— bodies recovered, 56
Guides Cavalry and Infantry at Kohat, 152
— — and Red Shirt troubles, 24
— — arrive in Wadi Natrun, 123
— — "A" Sqdn. in Iraq and Persia, 110
— — at Dabaa, 124
— — at Shekh Muhammadi, 29
— — at Sollum and Matruh, 124
— — at Ruweisat, 125
— — "B" Squadron to Jarabub, 126
— —, class composition of, 87
— — cover front, 125
— — go to Iraq, 117
— — go to Quetta and are mechanized, 100
— — in Bannu, 1933, 35
— — in First Afridi inroad, 28
— — in Mardan Area, 1931, 30
— — in North Africa, 123
— — in Second Afridi inroad, 31
— — in Syria, 48
— — in Yuzafzai, March, 1931, 33
— — march to North Africa, 120
— — move to Orcha, 145
— — ordered back to PAI Force, 133
— — refitting, 130
— — return to Frontier, 145
— — return to India, 145
— —, story of "B" Squadron, 126; join French, 127; desert stories, 127; withdrawal to El Alamein, 128; watch dogs in desert, 129
— — united behind El Alamein, 131
— — in Victory Celebration at Delhi, 146
— — withdrawal to El Alamein, 125
— — 1944-45 Honours and Rewards, 152
—, Centenary of Corps in Ahmednagar and Waziristan, 147
— Corps, Farewell Order by Brigadier H. Campbell, 157
— — formed in 1846, 2
Guides Infantry at Perim, 14; return to Mardan, 16; Infantry win Polo Tournament, 17
—, detail of fight for 4080, 52
—, formation of, 2
—, gallantry of last stand on 4080, 52
— march to Delhi, 3

Guides Infantry at Khanaqin, 120
— — at Kohat and Gardai, 147
— — at Musayib, 135; Colonel Rich leaves, 138; to Lebanon, 140; on Trans-Persian Railway, 141; back to Iraq, 143; on to India, September, 1945, 143
— — at Secunderabad, 105
— — go to Razmak, 150
— — at Razmak, 181
— —, famous fight at 4080, 50
— —, Farewell to Dogras, 154
— — go to Iraq, 116; in Persia and Kurdistan, 116
— —, C. in Chief's Eulogy, 54
— — in Chitral Relief, 38
— — in Khaiber, 103
— —, Redding takes command, 75
Guides in Mesopotamia in 1917, 8; in Palestine, 8; delocalized, 11; return to Mardan, 19, 21; renumbered, 11, 12; Infantry at Aden, 12
— in the Khaiber, 23
— return to India, 143
— return to Mardan, 1932, 37; 1937, 83
— with PAI Force, 135
— immediate rewards, 56
— losses at 4080, 55
— march out from Razmak, 182
— Memorials disposed of, 186
— note on organization and equipment, 152
— Plan of Operation, 50
— return to Mardan, 1934, 37
—, scandalous story contradicted by *The Times*, 54; letter from Governor, 55
— Sikhs spirited away, 181
Gwalior Campaign, 1

Habbanniyeh, defence of, 105
Habibullah Khan, Amir, 6
— —, —, friendliness of, 58
Hamilton, Lieut. W. R., gains V.C., 6
Hamilton, Lieut., at "Teeth," 52
Hammond, Captain A. G., gains V.C., 6
Hammond, Lieut.-Colonel, to command Cavalry, 84
Hammond, Major-General, services of, 172
Harding, Sir Henry, Governor-General, 2
Harvey, General, in Khuzistan, 111
Hawk, Lieut., murdered, 23
Hay, Bruce, General, killed by bomb, 100
Hazara Mountain Battery, Presentation, 84
Henniker, Colonel, account of Punjab tragedy, 1947, 178
Hindustani Fanatics, 4
Hodson, Major M. H., death of, 170
Hukm, decay of, 22
Hunza-Nagar Expedition, 7

Indian Cavalry reorganization, 86
Infantry, Guides' Pipe Band, 88
Infantry organization, new, 90
Ipi, Faqir of, 60
Ipi, Mizza Ali, 60
Iraq, rebellion in, 105
Islam Bibi case, 61

INDEX

Jallabad, Guides in Second Afghan War, 6
Jammu and Kashmir, 177
Jamrud, Guides Infantry at, 24
Jandola, attack at, 58
Jenkins, Secretary to Cavagnari, 6
Jhindai Khwar in Loe Agra, 44
John Company, famous rule of, 1

Karun landing, 112
Kashmir trouble, 177
Kelat-i-Ghilzai, defence of, 2
Kelly's march to Chitral, 8
Kensington School and Quentin Battye, 4
Keogh, Capt., killed, 66
Khaki and Lumsden, 9
Khajuri Plain, story of, 34
Khajuri to be held by line of posts, 34
Khaisora Operations, November, 1931, 61
—, renewed operations in 1937, 71; honours for, 85
Khan Bagdadi, Cavalry at, 8
Khassadars, 59
Khattaks, question of, 86; transfer of, 90; tribes of, 91
Khazal, Sheikh, 111
Khilafat Movement, 19
Khonia Khel Shahur Tangi, 70
Khurramshahr, 111
Kohat Church burnt, 93
Kurdish Agha and Sikhs, 154
Kurds, story of, 115

Lahej, Arab state, 13
Lawanadi, Faqir of, in Khost, 36
Lawrence, Sir Henry, raises Corps, 1
le Fleming, General, march out of Razmak, 79
Loe Agra trouble, 1st Phase, 43; 2nd Phase, 44; 3rd Phase, 45
Lowarai Pass, 8
Lumsden, H., first commander, 1
Lyall, Sir Alfred, quoted, 61

MacLean and V.C., 83
MacMunn, George, stays with Pakistan, 176
—, —, in command, 140; to Italy, 142
MacNamara, Brigadier, services of, 173
Macpherson, Mrs., presents window, 83
Mahsuds join Ipi, 64
Maiwand defeat, 6
Malakand, 7
Malka and fanatics, 4
Mardan area, quieting of, 30
— —, last days of peace, 95
— —, last years in, 92
— —, to be given up, tragedy of, 97
— Week, 1938, 94
Marks, Lieut., killed, 68
Marshall, General, letter to Guides, 77
Marshall, Sir William, defeats Turks, 118
Massacres in Punjab, 176
McCrea, Mr., in danger, 33
McLeod, Lieut.-Colonel, to command Cavalry, 17
McLeod, Lieut.-General Sir K., services of, 172
Mesopotamia and Guides, 8
Messervy, General, 176
Mess Treasures shared, 97

Meynell joins, 16
—, successful defence by, 39; killed at 4080, 52
Militia System, 58
Moberly, General B. R., 23
Moghul Baz, K. B., Risaldar, 96
Mohammed Tuhair killed in accident, 98
Mohmand, story of, 40; operations, 1933, 41; operations, 1935, 46; immediate rewards, 49; two more brigades, 50; Guides on 4080, 50
Monteith, David, death of, 169
Moplah rebellion, 19
Moore, Capt., in Norway, 103
Mountbatten massacres, 176
Mullah-Powinda, 60
Murcott, Lieut.-Colonel A. K., death of, 169
Murder of Bank officials in the Khaiber, 23
Murphy, Captain, murder of, 23
Muslim troubles, 1930, 19
Muspratt, General, assumes command, 51
Musayib Base, 135
Mutiny of Bengal Army, 3

Nagar Khanate, 7
Nipple (4080), 52
North Africa, sequence of events, 1940-42, 121
North-West Frontier, story of, from 1930, 18

Officers' Mess, Mardan, 10
Officers of Cavalry in second Afridi invasion, 31
Officers of Infantry at Aden, 13
Olai, Scout post, 77
"Owl," The, (Crowe), letter from, 98
Oxus, Mogul boundary, 57

PAI Force, story of, 109; commanders, 110
Pakistan Army, 178
Pakistan ceremony of transfer at Razmak, 155
—, special Church Services, 155
Palozin Ziarat, action at, 58
Panjdeh incident, 5
Panjkora, Guides on, 7
Pathans in Deccan, 57
Pathan Revolt, 1847, 8
Persia, invasion of, 111; Admiral killed, 112; surrender of, 114
Persian story, outline of, 106
Peshawar trouble, 1930, 21; civil folly, 21
Peshawar Brigade, operations of (4080), 54
Pipe Band, 88; dress of, 89
Plunkett, R., at Jarabub, 126
Pollard, Colonel, and transfer of Guides Infantry, 154
Poles, story of, 139
Polo, 159
— victories, 96, 162
—, last game of, at Damascus, 120
Pope, General G. R., 35
Prendergast, Major, receives M.V.O., 15
Prioleau, Brigadier, services of, 174
Punjab Irregular Force, 2

Qila Hari picquet, 45
Quaid-i-Azam, 178
Quetta, Guides Cavalry at, 100; Guides Cavalry mechanized, 102
— in Second Afghan War, 5
"Quit India," tragedy of, 154

Ragbir Singh killed in Waziristan, 147
Ranjhit Singh, 2
Razmak, true story of, 181
Red Shirt Movement, 19
Rees, General, Boundary Force, 176
Reed, Major, disappearance of, 177
Rendall, Lieut., 4080, 52; killed, 52
Review Order, old, reintroduced, 96
Rich, Colonel, in Persian Kurdistan, 115
Ridgeway Hill, affair of, 78
Ridley, Colonel, shot at Abadan, 112
Ringing to Evensong of the Raj, 154
Riza Shah, 107; deposed, 108
Roberts, General, in Sherpur, 6; March to Kandahar, 6
Rommel's last bolt, 131
Royal Stuart Tartan, 88
Rur Singh, Subadar-major, at Senneh, 116
—— leaves, 137
Russians on Pamirs, 7
— enter Persia with British, 116

Sandeman, Lieut.-Colonel, sent into Yuzafzai, 24
Scandalous newspaper yarn *re* 4080, 52, 54
Scott, Lieut.-General Sir Tommy, 13
Senneh, Guides Infantry at, 116
Shadi Khan, Hon. Lieut., at Nipple, 52
Shahur Tangi, Tragedy of, 69
Shebbeare, Lieut. R. H., at Delhi, 4
Shebbeare, Major, wounded, 181
Shekh Muhammadi, Guides at, 29
Sherpur, General Roberts in, 6
Sikh Armies, 2
— Wars, 2
Sikhs, a small race, 2
—, Rebellion of 1848, 3
Sind, conquest of, 1
Sinjab Singh, killed in North Africa, 125
Sirda Act misrepresented, 20
Stewart, Sir Donald, at Kandahar, 5
Sutlej Campaign, 2
Swat, Guides in, 8

Tekrit captured, 9
Trans-Persian Railway, story of, 140
Troops, not Civil, must be responsible, 33

Turangzai, Haji of, firebrand, 41
Turbaz Risaldar, story of, 5
Tweedie, Lieut. (Cavalry), killed in riding accident, 37
Tyler, Lieut., R.A. (4080), 53

Umbeyla Campaign, 4
Utmanzai, gathering in, 32
Utman Khel, the, 43

Vichy French in Syria, 106
Victoria Cross: MacLean, 8; Meynell, 52, 53, 55, 56, 186; Shebbeare, 185
Von Blomberg's son, killed in Iraq, 106

Walforce, 132
War Dog Unit, 136
Waters, Major, at Shahur Tangi, 70
Wavel, F.M.'s campaign in N. Africa, 122
Waziristan, story of, 57
—, Tribal economics, 59
—, operations against Tori Khel, 64
—, '36 attack on Razmak convoy, 67
—, seizure of Sham Plan, 72
—, honours for '37, 89
Wetheral, Lieut., at Shahur Tangi, 70
Wilcox, Sir James, in Khaiber, 8
Williams, Major, killed, 65
Wuchar Jawa Nullah, Mohmand campaign, 50

Xenophon and the Kurds, 118

Yacub Khan, Amir, 6
Yemen Battn., 12, 13
— disturbed, 14
Yorkshire lady, married to brother of Abdul Ghaffar, 20
Younghusband, Sir George, vacates Colonelcy, 17
Yusaf Khel (in Mohmand), 49
Yuzafzai Border in 1931, 32
Yuzafzai disturbance, 1931, 31
Yuzafzais, retention of, 91

Zakhmi Dil, 88
Zanawarchina, 51
Zerperzai, column at, 61
—, Guides Infantry at, 62

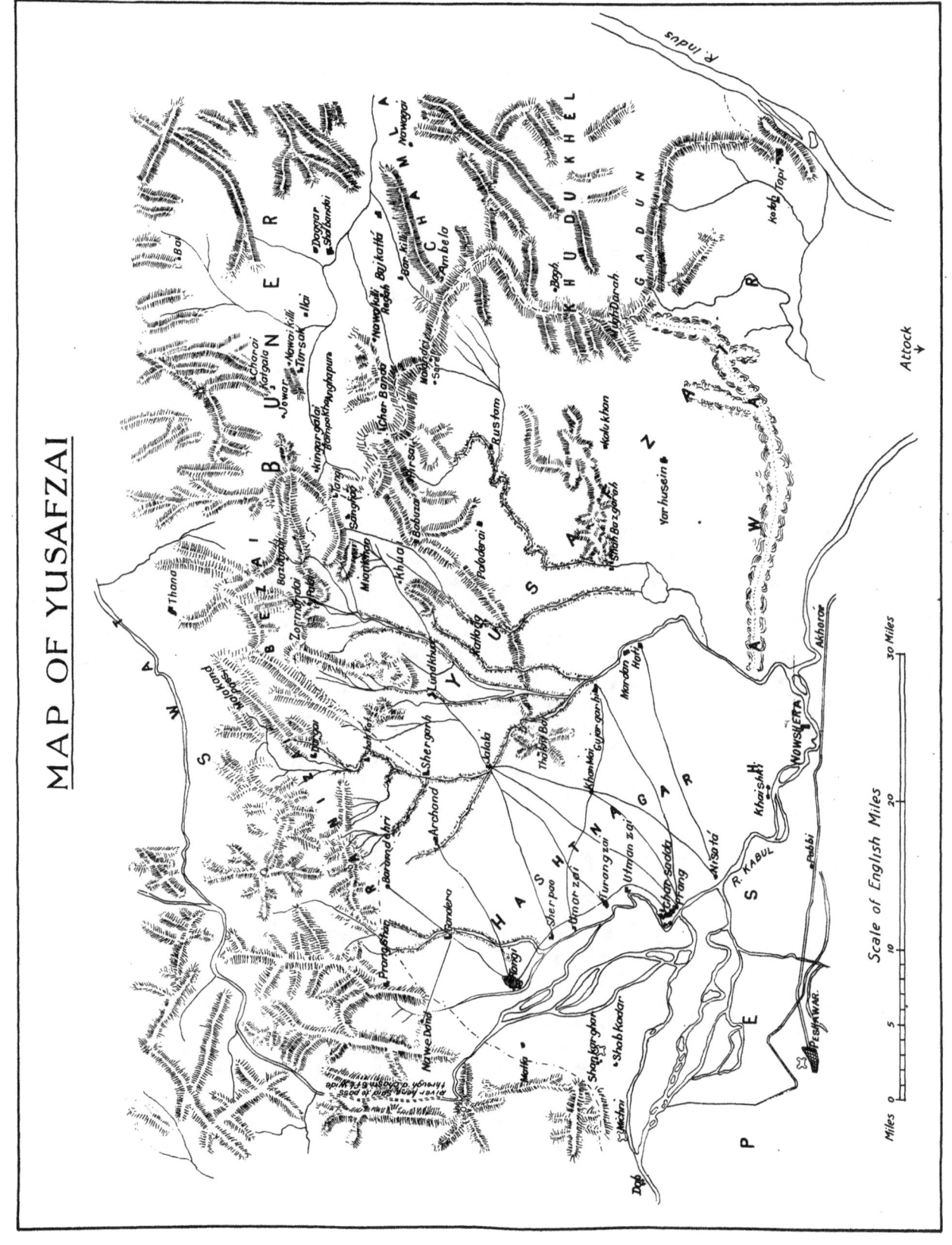

WAZIRISTAN

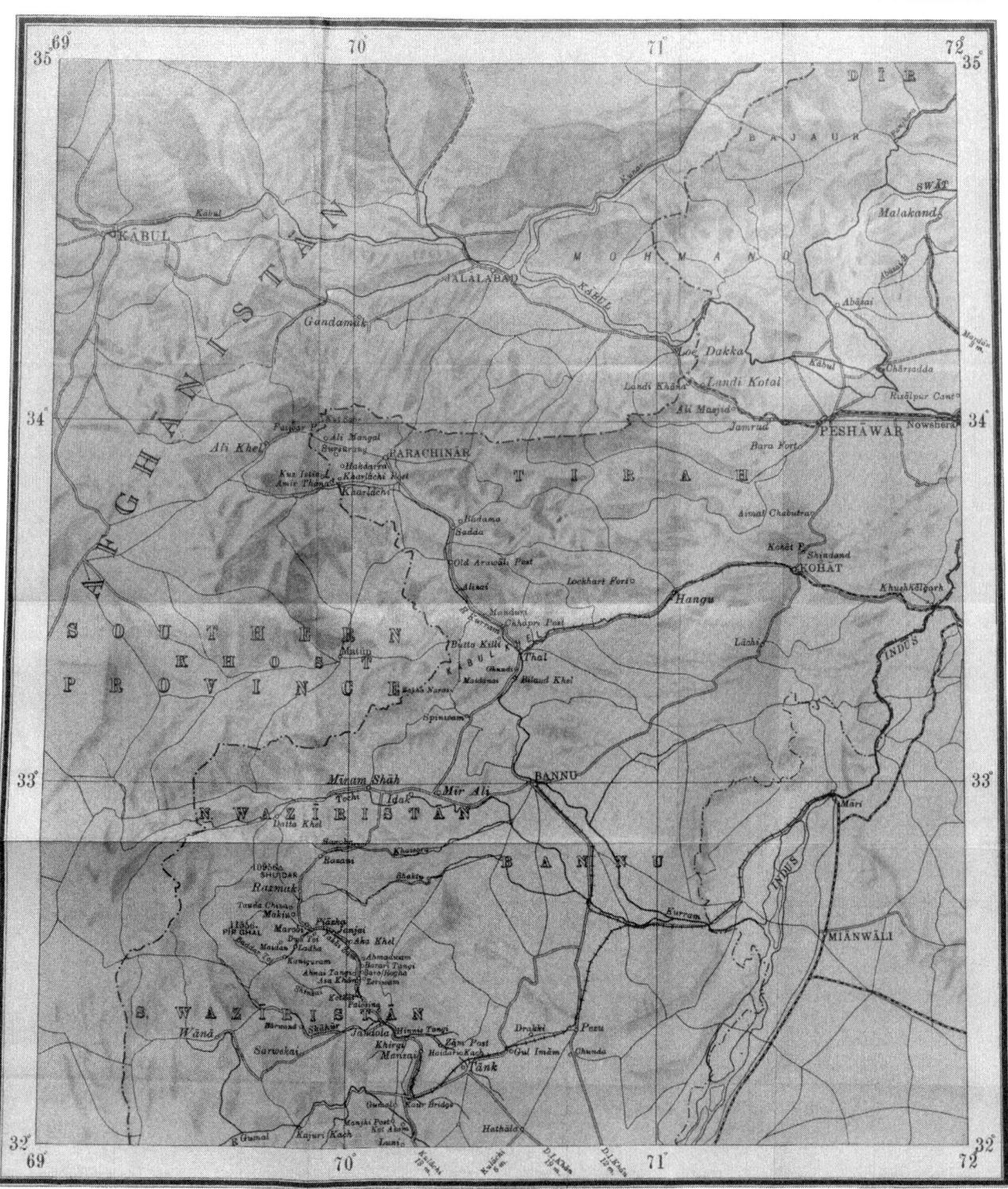

Scale 1/1,000,000 or 1.014 Inches to 16 Miles.

Reproduced from Survey of India Map, with the permission of the Surveyor General.